GOLD

The Once and Future Money

NATHAN LEWIS

BICENTENNIAL
BICENTENNIAL
1807
WILEY
2007
BICENTENNIAL
BICENTENNIAL

John Wiley & Sons, Inc.

Published by John Wiley & Sons, Inc., Hoboken, New Jersey.
Published simultaneously in Canada.

Wiley Bicentennial Logo: Richard J. Pacifico.

For general information on our other products and services or for technical support, please contact
our Customer Care Department within the United States at (800) 762–2974, outside the United
States at (317) 572–3993 or fax (317) 572–4002.

Wiley also publishes its books in a variety of electronic formats. Some content that appears in print
may not be available in electronic books. For more information about Wiley products, visit our web
site at www.wiley.com.

Library of Congress Cataloging-in-Publication Data:

Lewis, Nathan K., 1971–
  Gold : the once and future money / Nathan Lewis.
      p. cm.
  Includes bibliographical references.
  ISBN 978-0-470-04766-8 (cloth)
  1. Monetary policy.   2. Business cycles.   3. Gold standard.   I. Title.
  HG230.3.L48 2007
  332.4'042—dc22   2007005000

Printed in the United States of America.

10 9 8 7 6 5 4 3 2 1

CONTENTS

Contents

PART THREE: CURRENCY CRISES AROUND THE WORLD

FOREWORD

Not long ago, on a plane from Paris to Boston, we had the fortuitous occasion to sit next to one of the faithful: an economics professor from Harvard, whose office sat across the hall from Greg Mankiw, then chairman of the president's Council of Economic Advisers, and who is a neighbor of former IMF chief economist Ken Rogoff. He claimed to have been recruited, at one point, by the Federal Reserve chairman Ben Bernanke to teach at Princeton.

A diminutive man of French descent, the professor almost immediately set upon "chatting up" the woman sitting on his left. She, it turned out, was an executive with Genzyme, the biotech firm.

Having discovered he was an economics professor—a fact he was only too happy to reveal—she wanted to know if "offshoring" was going to pose a serious threat to wages in the biotech business. "Ah, to some extent," he replied, "but I wouldn't worry about it . . . the recovery is under way, and the jobs picture will improve dramatically very soon."

As an editor and the publisher of the *Daily Reckoning* (www .dailyreckoning.com) we could not resist. "I couldn't help overhearing your comment," we blurted out, despite our best efforts not to. "Do you really think jobs are going to reappear? Seriously? Even with public and personal debt loads going through the roof?"

What ensued wasn't pretty (especially since we were taking liberal advantage of Air France's free wine policy on the flight).

"The currency markets don't like the federal deficit, so the dollar is falling, correct?" we began our circular argument. "That is right," came the reply.

"A falling dollar cancels out gains by foreign investors, true?"

v

"Right again . . ."

"And foreign investment is needed to finance the trade deficit. So if the dollar continues to fall . . . interest rates will have to rise in order to keep foreign investors interested?"

"Yes . . ."

"If interest rates rise, won't that impede job growth?"

"Indeed . . ."

"Likewise," we continued, gloriously entertaining visions of Socrates in our head, "if an increasing money supply starts showing up as 'inflation' in the CPI, wouldn't that cause the Fed to raise interest rates?"

"*Oui, bien sûr*. But inflation is still low. And the Fed must stimulate job growth. They have a *théorie*: It is called the Helicopter Theory . . ."

"Bernanke's suggestion to throw money out of helicopters?"

"Yes, that is it . . ." He looked at us quizzically. "You know him? Because I know him . . ."

"No. I don't know him," we replied.

"He is very smart. The Japanese could have used the Helicopter Théorie . . . we don't need it . . . we only need the jobs . . ." We could tell he was getting impatient . . . clearly, he thought we just didn't "get it."

"We are all agreed," he continued (meaning his colleagues in the economics profession, we assumed), "on how the economy works. Now we only debate how much the government should intervene and 'goose' the economy."

"But once you goose the economy in the United States, aren't jobs actually showing up in India and China at lower wages? Won't any new jobs in the United States have to be competitive with those wages, effectively mutating the 'jobless recovery' into the 'wageless recovery'?" The Genzyme exec squirmed in her seat a little.

"Besides," we tried again, "at some point, won't the government, regardless of the party, have to raise taxes—or, better yet, cut spending—in order to deal with the deficit, both of which could effectively put an end to the stimulus package? And with no stimulus, where will the jobs come from? And what about the effects of a declining dollar on wages?"

"Mister Wiggin, my work is mostly on the theoretical end of things . . ."

"Well then, theoretically, where will the jobs come from?"

"Mister Wiggin, I leave the implementation to other people. And now, if you forgive me, I have a lecture to prepare for . . ."

We tried to put on a movie, but our personalized monitor was broken. As we left the plane . . . after several hours of silence and polite nudges on the arm rest . . . we scribbled an e-mail on the inside of the French copy of one of my books and pressed it into his hand.

Curiously, he never responded.

Since the publication of my book, *The Demise of the Dollar . . . and Why It's Good for Your Investments,* in 2005, I've wanted to write a follow-up book on the demise of the gold standard—and the curious, often disastrous, impact it has had on the economies of many nations. I began *The Demise of the Dollar* with an account of (then) President Nixon's devastating decision in 1971 to dismantle the Bretton Woods exchange rate system and usher in the age of the Great Dollar Standard era in which the dollar is backed by the "full faith and credit" of the U.S. government, a system that conveniently allows the government to print more money whenever it needs it—and gives control of the economy over to the capriciousness and arrogance of those whose work is merely theoretical.

Gold: The Once and Future Money is the book I wanted to write. In this delectable tome, Nathan Lewis describes the booms, the busts, the bubbles, and the crises in the economies of dozens of countries, from centuries ago to the present day. It is a romp through history, illuminating along the way money in all its forms—from wampum and shells to silver and gold—and details the catastrophic effects of inflation, deflation, floating currencies, and every kind of tax a government functionary could dream to impose on an economy. It highlights the folly of human beings throughout history who think "the economy" is but a machine to be tinkered with and fine-tuned like a Bentley, or worse, a rusty Yugo. Above all, *Gold: The Once and Future Money* reveals truth. As the late Ferdinand Lipps wrote, "The modern gold standard [of the nineteenth century] evolved naturally and was not the result of any conference, but rather the product of many centuries of experience and practice. It grew step by step, almost by accident, through its own force and because of the logic and experience gained with debasement of currencies in the past." The United States dollar circa 2007 and beyond is not likely to escape the inevitable march of history. The story of humanity suggests we will see a new and improved gold standard once again. Nathan Lewis helps us understand how.

Much of the beginning of this book focuses on the history of the U.S. economy—its parallels with the Bank of England's panic of 1797, Rome in ancient times and in the 1400s, post–World War II Germany (East and West), Mexico and various Latin American crises during the 1970s, and German reunification in the 1980s. Lewis adroitly explores money in the time of the American colonies, after the Revolutionary War, through the Great Depression, following President Nixon's final nail in the coffin of the old gold standard in 1971 (that defining moment again), and on up to the present day.

But *Gold: The Once and Future Money* doesn't stop there; in fact, this tome offers a history of money (hard versus soft) around the world: Japan from 1600 to its post–World War II economic growth; the Asian crisis, which affected Indonesia, Malaysia, Japan, Korea, and China; the breakup of the Soviet Union and the former Yugoslavia; and the Mexican and Latin American monetary crises.

"Good Money Is Stable Money," provides a quick but bizarre history of barter—where everything from farm tools to coins, shells, beaded belts, even cigarettes and chocolate was traded—around the world, from ancient China to ancient Rome, from the British empire to post–World War II Germany. Barter is not a very stable system of money, however, because prices are expressed in terms of each of the goods available in trade. After all, who cares what corn is worth if you don't want corn? In contrast, in a money economy, everything has only one price, which leads to the main idea here: Throughout history, and in every country, people want the most stable money attainable, because that allows greater productivity and prosperity. And what's the most stable money? That's a no-brainer: It's a currency pegged to the gold standard.

"Hard Money and Soft Money," takes us on a tour of money (and banking) around the world, from prehistory up to today. Metal has been used as money since the seventh century BC, when coins that were a mixture of gold and silver were used in Lydia (at the time, a Roman province, located in present-day Turkey). Ancient Greece used coins; ancient Rome had a stock exchange; the first paper money was used in China in the ninth century; the king of Persia printed money in 1294; and Holland standardized gold coins in the seventeenth century. From the 1870s to the early twentieth century, many national money systems were extremely unstable, however, and many countries suffered alarmingly from increasingly high trade tariffs (in Germany, France, the United States, Switzerland, Italy, and Russia, to name just a few).

Britain was the first country to establish a gold standard of money, and by 1900, every major economy in the world (except China) had adopted it; this hard-money system facilitated "the first great age of globalization." But World War I and then World War II threw economies into disarray, and for much of the twentieth century, many countries were ruined by war debts, deflation, high taxes, recession, devaluations, and/or hyperinflation, until the gold standard was killed by President Nixon in 1971. The world has been on the great dollar standard ever since.

In "Supply, Demand, and the Value of Currency," you'll see how an international monetary system *really* works by comparing it to a simple exchange of dollar bills for quarters: Trading U.S. dollar bills for coins is just like trading U.S. dollars for Japanese yen.

You'll get into the nitty-gritty of "Inflation, Deflation, and Floating Currencies" and you'll read an intriguing range of commentators on the subject of inflation: from Ernest Hemingway (who called inflation a "panacea for a mismanaged nation") to Copernicus (who wrote—in 1517, no less!—that inflation was one of the "scourges [that] debilitate kingdoms") to Adam Smith, who in 1776 blamed inflation for causing a "most pernicious subversion of the fortunes of private people." Inflation causes prices to rise, of course—Lewis calls this "laughably simplistic," and he's right, but are you curious about what else inflation ruins? Well, here's a brief list: It not only destroys foreign exchange markets, wages, the tax system, debt, and the stock market, but also causes "a conspicuous decline of morality and civility," illustrated by the decline of Rome, Weimar Germany in the 1920s, the United States in the 1970s, and even the breakup of the Soviet Union and the former Yugoslavia, where ethnic hatred was fanned by the flames of devalued currency. Deflation also creates artificial winners and losers, and floating currencies aren't so great, either, because they're produced by government manipulation rather than by the market itself.

What's the bottom line? It's simply that "an economy will naturally function best when the currency's value is near the center of gravity, and held there."

Even people who are worlds apart in some ways can still agree in others. What did Karl Marx and Andrew Carnegie agree on? That gold is the only worthwhile money, and "The Gold Standard," offers lots of reasons why. Throughout history, many types of currency that were rejected in favor of gold: cowrie shells, cows, wheat, giant stone disks, strings of beads, cauldrons and iron tripods, metal rings, copper, bronze, silver, and even cocoa beans and whales' teeth! The use of a gold standard by multiple countries essentially creates a world currency, and (even though gold is a commodity) the gold market is extraordinarily similar to a foreign exchange market.

"Money in America," traces various forms of money used in the American colonies (where beaver pelts and other commodities were traded) through the Revolutionary War, the tariffs of the nineteenth century and the problems of Northern versus Southern banking during the Civil War, and several financial breakdowns: in 1839, 1873, and, of course, 1929. And check it out: In between those financial disasters, the first income tax was instituted in 1861.

In "A History of Central Banking," you'll learn about an ancient Egyptian banking system based on wheat; the creation of the U.S. Federal Reserve in 1913 by President Woodrow Wilson; "the curse of usury" in ancient Rome; the creation of the Bank of England (which eventually became a central reserve bank); and the wildly free banking system in the United States during the mid-1800s—a system that supported almost 10,000 different notes issued by almost 1,500 different banks, all of which were accepted as money! Remember, the purpose of creating the Federal Reserve System was to provide a lender of last resort during liquidity-shortage crises—in other words, during economic emergencies. The Fed has done that, but it has also overstepped its original boundaries by venturing into currency manipulations, and is therefore more often part of the problem rather than the solution.

"The 1930s," describes the Great Depression in the United States after the stock market crash of 1929. Look at the government's misguided efforts to boost the economy by spending on public works, and then check out the parallels between these efforts and the mercantilists from 1600 to 1750, as well as with the economic ideas of John Stuart Mill, ancient Chinese philosophers, Richard Nixon, and the liberal capitalist economies of Hong Kong, Korea, and Taiwan during the past 50 years. Finally, you'll see what President Hoover and then President Roosevelt tried to do in the United States; and you'll observe the retrenched economies of Japan, Germany, Britain, France, and Austria during this period's dismal breakdown of monetary order.

In "The Bretton Woods Gold Standard," you'll see the effects of the economic accord that was established in 1944 at a meeting of world leaders in Bretton Woods, New Hampshire. This meeting, of course, was no small potatoes: A version of the gold standard was reestablished, and three new governing organizations were created: the IMF, the World Bank, and the International Trade Organization, all in the hopes of avoiding another economic disaster like the one that occurred in 1930s, which, of course, led to World War II. You'll review the worldwide economic struggles during the post–World War II years, and you'll get an update on tax hikes and tax cuts during the 1950s and 1960s under Presidents Truman, Eisenhower, Kennedy, and Johnson, culminating in Nixon's knocking the dollar off the gold standard in 1971 (there it is again!)—which caused worldwide monetary devaluations, massive inflation, and floating currencies that exist to this day, not to mention a long decline in the U.S. stock market.

Under the Great Dollar Standard era, the world monetary system is in complete disarray. It is subject to the whimsy of those in power and to the arrogance of academics. "The present monetary system is a slap in the face of law and order, civilization and civility," suggested Herr Lipps, "but most importantly it is a threat to our freedom." Nathan Lewis devotes much of the latter part of this book to documenting the monetary mayhem our current system has wrought.

"Reagan and Volcker," covers not only the U.S. economy during the late 1970s and 1980s but also the savings and loan crisis; the suffering of agriculture and blue-collar industries like steel, even while other sectors had wild growth; what Margaret Thatcher did to England; and the "debt blowouts" that were happening in Mexico and Latin America during this time period. That's a lot of ground, but the focus is on the U.S. recession of the late 1970s that occurred because of Fed head Paul Volcker's "monetarist experiment," which failed miserably, followed by a blessed bounceback during the 1980s in the Reagan era—a soaring economic expansion that lasted until 1990.

"The Greenspan Years," discusses the dramatic events following Greenspan's taking over the Federal Reserve in August 1987. After giving a few press interviews that revealed his nonchalance about the falling dollar and then watching (causing?) the stock market crash on October 19, 1987, he never gave another media interview. Nathan Lewis reviews the serious recession that followed, which was dramatically worsened by President Bush's forgetting (or ignoring) his promise to "read my lips: no new taxes" and hiking taxes instead. Ironically, it was Clinton who resurrected the Republican Reagan's economic boom, this time lasting from 1991 to 2001.

The chapter, "Japan's Success and Failure," takes us through the unification of Japan in 1600 and the system (if you can call it that) of coins, paper bills, and barter that needed to be sorted out: By one account, there were almost 1,700 types of paper money in circulation, in addition to gold notes, silver notes, copper notes, rice notes, even potter's wheel notes! We'll also look at the reform of taxes— from more than 1,600 official taxes down to a reasonable 74 in 1875—and the transformation of an isolationist nation to one of the most trade-friendly countries in the world, beginning in the mid-1850s. In 1897, Japan adopted a gold standard, and its economy grew, then struggled somewhat after World War I and again after World War II, but surged again in the 1950s and 1960s and yet again in the 1980s. In the 1990s, things were not so good: tax increases, deflation, a bear market, and the crisis in Asia overall. The chapter concludes by considering some recommendations for what Japan should do to recover and grow again.

"The Asia Crisis of the Late 1990s," covers not only the economic disasters in the late 1990s experienced by Thailand, Indonesia, East Timor, the Philippines, Malaysia, Korea, China, and Hong Kong, but also problems in Brazil, Russia, and Argentina. Wow. All of these countries suffered miserably because of a rising dollar and broken currency pegs. George Soros thought the Russia situation wasn't so bad, so he made a huge investment in a Russian telephone holding company, and he argued for major tax reform. His recommendation was great, but no one listened, and Soros lost more than $1 billion and admitted this was the worst investment of his professional career. Was there any good news in any of these countries? Sort of. The disasters cleared the way for major policy changes. One idea was to create a "pan-Asian currency" (like the euro, which could be called the "asian"), that would be pegged to gold. Unfortunately, the lesson that was learned from the Asian crisis seems to have been that the current system can sustain shocks, and the dollar standard continues unabated.

"Russia, China, Mexico, and Yugoslavia," reviews the history of the Russian economy from 1897 through the perestroika reforms 100 years later. You'll see how Russia first pegged the ruble to gold at the end of the nineteenth century; how the ruble collapsed in 1914 with the beginning of World War I; how Lenin linked the ruble to gold again in 1921; how Khrushchev in 1950 pegged the ruble to the dollar (which was pegged to gold); and how the Russian economy eventually became "a vast mafia." This disintegration led to the breakup of the Soviet Union itself, which created 15 new countries and 15 new currencies. China, too, converted its 1930 silver standard to paper money and immediately suffered devaluation, followed by hyperinflation in the 1940s and inflation in the 1970s, before its current experiment with market capitalism beginning in the 1980s. You'll learn how the Mexican peso suffered three devaluations beginning in 1941 and how the Mexican economy never recovered from the recession of 1982. Finally, you'll see how the former Yugoslavia broke apart not only because of ethnic hatred among its various regions but also because the dinar had become a confetti currency.

"The Return to Hard Currencies," sums up this world tour: Soft money doesn't work; hard money is the only way to go; and the best system is one that ties currency to a gold standard. "Gold and economic freedom are inseparable," wrote the former Federal Reserve chairman Alan Greenspan in 1966. "In the absence of the gold standard, there is no way to protect savings from confiscation through inflation. Gold stands as the protector of property rights. If one grasps this, one has no difficulty understanding the statists' antagonism toward the gold standard." Bring this up in a cocktail party full of Wall Street economists, hedge fund managers, or Beltway public policy wonks today and you'll be roundly laughed out of the punch bowl line. All they lack, we humbly submit, is a little imagination.

ADDISON WIGGIN, AUTHOR *DEMISE OF THE DOLLAR*
PUBLISHER, AGORA FINANCIAL, LLC

PREFACE

Low taxes, stable money. Could it really be so simple? The idea that lower taxes could lead to a healthier, more vibrant economy—and healthier, more vibrant government finances—is timeless and arguably self-evident. It was rediscovered in the 1970s and put into action in the 1980s, as governments around the world experimented with lower tax rates. The economic boom that was set off helped put an end to the tax-hike/inflation disaster of the 1970s. The "supply-side revolution" lost political momentum in the United States by the early 1990s, but it continues to this day with the new team of flat-taxers in Eastern Europe, who seem to be enjoying exactly the results promised.

Stable money was also part of the plan, and it probably seemed, in the late 1970s, that little needed to be said about it. The world was on a gold standard only a few years previous. Leaving it in 1971 had caused an inflationary convulsion unprecedented in U.S. (and world) history. Wasn't it obvious? Ronald Reagan had always envisioned a return to the gold standard—the system in which he lived almost his whole life up to that point—as part of his economic recovery strategy.

This book focuses on the "stable money" part of the formula, the more technically difficult aspect and one that has, until now, never been properly laid out in print. Finally, the policymaker should have virtually everything today's classical economists can offer to help create economic abundance now, tomorrow, or a hundred years from now.

Oddly enough, just as the "low taxes" aspect hardly received discussion in two centuries of economic texts, it is difficult to find any useful description of the mechanics of a gold standard and managing currencies, either. But then, I have never seen a correct and complete description of how today's central banks work, nor have I seen a lot of evidence that others understand their workings, even central bankers themselves.

No wonder people find these problems so difficult! A rocket scientist with an interest in economics once mentioned that monetary theory is more difficult than rocket science. At least there are books from which one can learn rocket science. Actually, monetary theory could be grasped by a dedicated student in less than a year, which is about nine years less than the time required for rocket science— unless, of course, that student already has an advanced degree in economics, in which case it may take a lifetime, if he or she is lucky. Everyone uses money, and everyone has an instinctual understanding of how it works.

Gold: The Once and Future Money is intended to stand alone. It could be picked up by an auto mechanic, a homemaker, a high school student, a real estate agent, or even a politician, journalist, or central banker, who would find everything they need to solve the major economic problems of the day and create a functioning world monetary system from scratch. It is my expectation that enough auto mechanics, homemakers, high school students, and real estate agents will read it that politicians and central bankers will have to clean up their act out of sheer embarrassment.

NATHAN LEWIS

Part One

Money in All
Its Forms

CHAPTER 1

GOOD MONEY IS STABLE MONEY

How People Make a Living through Monetary Cooperation

Coinage is imprinted gold or silver, by which the prices of things bought and sold are reckoned. . . . It is therefore a measure of values. A measure, however, must always preserve a fixed and constant standard. Otherwise, public order is necessarily disturbed, with buyers and sellers being cheated in many ways, just as if the yard, bushel, or pound did not maintain an invariable magnitude.

—Nicholas Copernicus, "Treatise on Debasement," 1517[1]

The Individualistic Capitalism of to-day, precisely because it entrusts saving to the individual investor and production to the individual employer, presumes a stable measuring-rod of value, and cannot be efficient—perhaps cannot survive—without one.

—John Maynard Keynes, "Social Consequences of Changes in the Value of Money," 1923[2]

Humans have a problem, and the problem is this: Food does not fall into their mouths. Even if it did, they would soon foul the place where they are lying. They could be burned by the sun, soaked by the rain, frozen by the wind. They could fall ill from disease, be plagued by insects, or be attacked by predators. They must find mates and reproduce. Their children must be cared for, or the children will also perish. And if even all this were done for humans, they would quickly succumb to boredom. To survive, they must take action.

A man or woman, alone and naked, is all but helpless. Their

actions are ineffectual. They lack the natural protection of fur or shell or hide. They lack the biological tools—claws, teeth, beaks, poison— with which to feed themselves. Even walking on a natural surface, without footwear, can be difficult. But the human has hands and a brain. With these two assets the human can create tools, discover techniques, and form organizations. In this way the human, born one of the weakest of all the creatures on Earth, has become the most powerful.

Human beings are, from biological imperative, capitalists— meaning only that they invest time and effort to create tools, tech- niques, and organizations to become more productive. Catching fish with the bare hands is possible, but not very efficient. To catch one fish, it may well be more efficient to use one's hands. To make a hook and line, a spear, or a net from naturally available materials takes time, effort, and technique, but humans calculate that the investment of time and effort will pay off in greater productivity in the future. They calculate, in other words, that there will be a positive return on such a capital investment, that they will make a profit from their invest- ment of effort, that their time is better spent making a hook and line than grasping at fish with their bare hands. By making a capital invest- ment, humans expand their personal economy and productivity.

But there is no guarantee. In deciding to invest time in making a hook and line or spear, humans take a risk. They may search for days and find that the materials to make a hook and line are not available, or that the hook does not catch fish, in which case their capital investment will be wasted. Every time a tool is created and used, it is a capital investment. This is true of picking up a rock to break open a nut, and it is also true of building a semiconductor factory, which is merely a tool to make semiconductors.

Humans have a natural tendency to seek greater productivity, meaning only that they wish to act with greater effectiveness while using less time and effort. Hunters polish their tracking skills; artisans strive for beauty. Laborers adjust their loads so that they are less painful. Monks simplify their lives to allow more time for contempla- tion. Homemakers store the pots and pans where they are easy to

4

reach. The term *productivity*, as used here, may have little relationship with official statistics. It does not matter what is wished for, whether more material goods, more services, more knowledge, more leisure, better interpersonal relationships, or even a more pristine natural environment, only that humans increase their ability to attain their wishes. The ends and means of production are limitless, but the urge to increase the ability to achieve those ends is inherent.

The productivity of a single human alone in nature is tiny. Such humans may simply starve to death, especially if they do not enjoy the intellectual capital of their forebears, knowledge of tools, plants, animals, and the seasons. Also, from a Darwinian standpoint, a solitary human may as well be dead, since he or she will not reproduce. The human must find a mate and produce a child, thus engaging in cooperation with other humans.

Unlike many species whose reproductive responsibilities are completed when they deposit their eggs or scatter their seeds, humans naturally form long-lasting families. The woman in late pregnancy may have difficulty feeding herself, and the child must be nurtured for years before it is capable of surviving alone. In the basic family unit, humans not only invest their capital to make tools, but cooperate through the division of labor, specialization, and trade to improve their productivity still further. The wife is, by biological fact, responsible for the child's gestation, and is almost universally responsible for the child's care as an infant. The husband typically specializes in the production of food and shelter for the family. Although one rarely thinks of transactions at such an intimate level as "trade," functionally it is no different than the trade that takes place between people living on different continents. This is more efficient than having each parent gather, hunt, cook, and care for the child in equal proportion, although of course the contemporary world offers all manner of alternative arrangements.

The husband and wife can also pool their efforts to produce and share the fruits of their efforts. The husband and wife can, together, create a cooking pot, which will aid in their production of foodstuffs. Each contributes capital (i.e., labor and time) and shares the fruits of their capital investment: the use of the pot and the cooked food. They are shareholders. Though there is no legal agreement between them, there is a mutual understanding, probably unspoken, that the ownership of the new capital good, the pot, is shared by the people who helped create it. If the husband suddenly claimed sole possession of the pot, barring his wife from its use, the wife would quite reasonably become angry. Today, the division of the family corporation is handled in divorce courts.

The husband and wife also expend a large amount of capital in the care and upbringing of their child, which even in a primitive context can be expected to last at least 10 years and likely closer to 15. In turn, the child is typically expected to care for the parents if needed, particularly in old age when parents are no longer able to easily support themselves. Young children "run up a debt" with their parents, and when the parents are elderly the children "repay the debt" by caring for their parents and also by raising their own children. This debt, or promise, is a bond. It is an obligation to offer goods and services in the future in trade for goods and services today. The child, which cannot support itself at first, must indebt itself to survive. The adult, seeking to create a "savings" that it can rely on in old age or times of need, must accumulate credits.

Thus, even in their most simple state, humans can hardly exist without creating tools and building knowledge (capital investments), engaging in specialization and trade, jointly entering into productive endeavors (equity investment), and forming contracts, or promises, with others (bonds). The primary features of the modern capitalist market economy are apparent in the primitive family unit. The primary features of socialism, such as caring for the sick, wounded, or otherwise unfortunate, are also apparent. All societies will have some form of "taxation" to fund communal efforts, even if this takes the form of an informal expectation that the person will help build the central gathering hall or provide some food to the hunter who has twisted an ankle. All human societies are a varied mixture of the capitalist impulse to produce and the socialist impulse to ameliorate misfortune.

Families are rarely found living in solitary isolation. The smallest human societies typically consist of groups of 20 to 60 people. In such a group, the activities of capital creation, trade, specialization, organization, shared equity, and obligation can become much more complex. The circle of exchange broadens beyond the family unit. The group shares a campfire. The men hunt in teams and share the fruits of their labor. Women trade off child-care duties. The spear-maker specializes in toolmaking, trading his tools for food provided by others specializing in hunting. A successful hunter shares his catch with others who came back empty-handed, with the understanding that when the others are successful and he is not, they will in turn share their food with him. Trade takes place with other bands, leading eventually to intermarriage.

Already, at this simple stage, the human has entered into hundreds or thousands of arrangements with other humans (i.e., "equity" and "debt" investments), and the records are kept informally in the memory. If one woman constantly watches another's children, but no attempt at retribution is made, the woman confronts the other about her "debts." If a man's contribution to the hunt is lazy or inept, thus contributing little capital, the others may agree to reduce his share of the proceeds of the hunt, acknowledging his small "shareholding" in the "enterprise." The spearmaker may not ask for his "payment" immediately, but remembers exactly how much is due to him from each of his customers, and if they do not pay up he regards them as deadbeats and refuses to make any more spears for them. People may even form "derivatives," such as wagering on tomorrow's weather. This has been institutionalized in today's markets for financial weather derivatives.

As humans deal with other humans to whom they are less closely related, their transactions become more abstract and formal. With a member of another group, the buyer may have to pay up on the spot, engaging in barter—say, five bags of nuts for one beaver pelt. Otherwise, the two may have to establish some kind of formalized contract, since they cannot rely on a relationship formed and enforced through

7

daily association. When transactions become anonymous and numerous enough they begin to acquire the flavor of "the market," though there is a continuum from the most intimate interactions to the most abstract. In this way, humans are able to extend the scope of their specialization and trade beyond the limits of their immediate or extended family, or band, thus increasing their productivity still further. Because each trade is voluntary, it would not be undertaken unless it provides a benefit for both parties.

Historically, simple human societies of the tribal size have functioned quite successfully without strictly delineated private property, an arrangement with notable advantages. It should be recognized that this is a thought exercise, illustrating the fundamental nature of today's market economies, not a study in anthropology.

Money is created, slowly and organically, when one commodity becomes used, in barter, as a medium of exchange. One commodity is accepted in trade, not because the acquirer plans to use it, but because he or she expects to be able to trade it again in the future. In ancient China, farm tools became a medium of exchange. As the tools were used more and more for exchange and less and less for farming, they became abstracted and miniaturized. By the second millennium BC, the Chinese had developed a type of coinage that consisted of tiny metallic replicas of farming tools. Virtually the same process happened in Britain, where the Romans found the original British using miniaturized, abstracted swords as money. Hoards of bronze double ax heads, too small for practical use and likely a form of money, have been found in burial mounds across continental Europe.

Using a miniaturized scythe or a sword was an extremely vague symbol for money, subject to natural "currency debasement" as swordmakers sought to discharge their obligations with ever simpler and cheaper swords. The ultimate conclusion of these efforts was the creation of coinage where the "sword" was finally simplified to a round disk, its value defined primarily by its metallic content.

Money, or indirect exchange, allows humans to make a quantum leap in their ability to generate capital, engage in specialization and trade, and form contracts of joint ownership (stocks) or obligation (bonds), particularly with strangers. No longer is it necessary to make direct barter trades with others. People can use money to trade indirectly with the world at large. Nobody invented money. It is as natural as clothing or shelter and has emerged independently all over the world. Certainly governments are not necessary for its creation. All manner of goods have been pressed into service as money: cowry shells, slabs of salt, elaborate beaded belts (wampum), giant stone wheels, tobacco, and so forth. Even in modern times, if no better medium is available, people will adopt as money whatever available commodity is most suited for the task. After World War II, when the reichsmark was rendered useless, German citizens used cigarettes as money. During the inflation in Italy in the 1970s, candies traded as small change.

Monetary exchange vastly expands the ability to specialize and engage in trade through the creation of a unit of account, a measure of value. In a money economy everything has one price, expressed in terms of the monetary standard. In a barter economy, prices are expressed in terms of each of the goods available in trade. In very simple economies, with just a few traded items, barter may easily suffice. For example, among four goods in a barter system, there are six market prices. But for 1,000 goods, 499,500 barter exchange rates would be needed. In a money economy, 1,000 goods have 1,000 prices, all denominated in the monetary standard, or *numeraire*.

It is possible to imagine a time in the not-too-distant future when paper money and coinage would all but disappear, replaced by some sort of credit or debit card that can be used for all transactions. But even then, money's function as a measure of value would remain. In the past it was common to make barter trades in a monetary framework without actually using money—$10 worth of wheat in trade for $10 worth of blankets, for example. This practice lives on today in computerized barter markets, where companies trade goods with one another within a framework of quasi-imaginary "barter dollars."

Money allows more than just trade. It allows, for instance, the creation of credits and debts measured in monetary units rather than in specific obligations. No longer do adults need to rely on their obligations accumulated with their children for their old age. Those adults can loan money—to anyone—and thus expand the scope of their credits throughout society. This is "savings." Very little in the economy is actually saved in a warehouse, for example. Virtually everything is consumed or put to use within no more than a year of its creation. To save for the future through debt obligations (bonds), humans don't stockpile goods, or even money for that matter, but they accumulate promises, which are massless and, ideally, don't deteriorate over time. Banks were the main means to stockpile monetary debt obligations, with direct bond finance pioneered first by governments and followed later by corporations.

The creation of the joint stock company allowed humans to pool their capital in endeavors much larger and more complex than could be attempted without the organizing principle of money. A hundred investors pooling their money to fund a shipping expedition to China are not inherently different than five humans building their own boat and setting sail on a trading expedition with a mutual understanding that they will split the winnings of their voyage. The main differences are the scale and the ability to divide ownership and its spoils through written contracts and numerical values rather than through an unstructured partnership based on direct association.

The monetary market economy, though it has elements of competition, is primarily a system of cooperation. Until the past two centuries, the majority of humans directly produced their own food. They were hunters and gatherers, and later farmers. Most productive activity took place outside the monetary economy, within the circle of the agrarian family. The land provided food, clothing, shelter, and entertainment. Money and exchange were only intermittently necessary. People's cooperative interaction with others was, by today's standards, rather limited.

Over time, people have become more and more specialized in their actions and more involved in trade and the money economy. The circle of cooperation has expanded. Winemakers can build their own houses, as the pioneer farmer did, but their house-building abilities are poor. They lack tools, knowledge, experience. Carpenters can make their own wine, but their winemaking abilities are poor. The carpenter calculates that the most efficient way to obtain wine is to build houses and trade them for wine with the winemaker. The winemaker calculates that the most efficient way to acquire a house is to make wine and trade it with the carpenter. By engaging in specialization and trade in this way, both the winemaker and carpenter enjoy more wine and better houses.

Consider a modern citizen, perhaps an advertising account executive. She does not grow her own food. She does not make her own clothes, build her own house, construct or even repair her own car, generate her own electricity, or drill her own oil. She may even have someone else clean her house, have a different person take care of the garden, and eat most of her meals in restaurants. Instead, she specializes in certain services related to advertising, which themselves are not very useful alone but only as part of a complex organization, the advertising agency. She consumes basically none of her primary production of advertising services, all of which she trades, indirectly through the money economy, for the goods and services provided by other people. She feels independent, maybe even isolated compared to the tight-knit farming communities of the past, but she, like everyone else, is embedded in a system of interdependency far more absorbing than those of long ago. The ever-increasing productivity of the advanced economies has been accomplished through ever-increasing specialization and trade. However, there is a danger inherent in such complexity, namely that a breakdown of the system would collapse the productive advantages with potentially disastrous results. It is not possible to go back to hunting and gathering, or even to the situation of a century ago in which most people were farmers. The concept of unemployment is a relatively recent phenomenon, which did not occur in traditional farming societies where you could always fall back on the fundamental economy of eating what you grew. People today are more dependent on the smooth functioning of the money economy than they have ever been.

11

Our day-to-day lives are so familiar to us that it is worth a moment to consider the awesome complexity of the cooperative order that we participate in. We buy a cup of coffee on our way to work. Someone has just provided a service for us. Perhaps that service was provided by a large corporation, built with the bits and pieces of capital of literally tens of thousands of investors. The employees have struck their own contracts and agreements with the corporation. The coffee itself comes from Colombia, brought to the United States by a series of independent transport companies and wholesalers who buy their transport equipment from another set of companies. The Styrofoam cup was produced by yet another corporation, which acquired its raw materials from petroleum products suppliers, using equipment built in Japan and Germany by corporations that have their own tens of thousands of investors. If enough cups of coffee are sold, the coffee seller makes a handsome profit. Its stock rises on the exchange. It undertakes a debt-fueled expansion, borrowing the capital of further tens of thousands of savers, while other companies compete for the same limited supply of capital. It employs construction companies, equipment makers, investment bankers, consultants, advertisers. In the end very nearly the entire world, in some way, was cooperatively involved in producing this cup of coffee.

The extended order encompasses virtually all of human activity and includes politics and government as well (which can be seen as another kind of cooperation, a necessary component of the extended order). Economics can't be separated from politics, both of which might be considered a form of anthropology, because the political system is the means by which the citizenry adjusts the operating conditions of the extended order. In the nineteenth century, the two weren't separate, but combined in the study of the political economy.

Because money is so vital to the extended order that has made the high productivity and indeed large populations of today possible, it is worth taking a close look at exactly what it is. Modern money very nearly doesn't exist at all. For small transactions, coins and paper bills are used. The paper's material value is almost nil, and the coins are mere tokens that no longer contain precious metals. For larger transactions, bank checks are common—nothing but a scrap of paper and a scrawl. Transactions on an institutional scale are almost completely electronic and ephemeral. Money today is mostly just the arrangement of bits in computers. Money, in other words, is information.

Not a single person knows how the cup of coffee was produced. The system is not planned. The extended order is organized through the use of money. It is far too complex to be arranged by rational thinking—the classic argument against the feasibility of the Stalinist Soviet model. Even the Soviets depended on money to help organize their economy. Through the system of markets and prices, exact real-time information is conveyed about how much coffee to grow, how many Styrofoam cups to produce, the most efficient arrangement of trucks and ships to move the materials around, coordinating the efforts of millions of people in vast networks of exchange to produce a cup of morning coffee—at a paltry price, a sign of the system's extraordinary efficiency and productiveness.

There is no alternative to the money economy. The only choice is to make it work poorly or to make it work well. Though there have been enduring regimes in the past that were centrally managed with little monetary organization (e.g., ancient Egypt and the empire of the Incas), organizing a complex industrial economy by such means would be impossible.

Because money is information, and the messages sent by the monetary economy dictate in hard, clear terms the actions of billions of people, naturally humans have taken great pains to develop means to keep this information as pure and uncorrupted as possible. If an engineer orders a mechanical shaft of "500 millimeters," and the machine shop produces one of 500 millimeters, but due to fluctuation in the meaning of *millimeter* it is 10 percent shorter than the engineer desired, both the engineer and the machine shop have become unable to cooperate productively. The information contained in the phrase "500 millimeters" has become corrupted, meaning different things at different times. The engineer may decide to machine the parts himself, the machinist to take up engineering. The circle of exchange is broken, and the productivity of both decline.

Throughout history, humans have sought the most stable money attainable, because stable money, or uncorrupted information, allows greater productivity and prosperity, while unstable money, or corrupted information, cripples productivity and prosperity. It is impossible to improve the system's productivity by corrupting the information that enables it to function. Such a corruption may result in more production—a greater volume of goods and services, a greater number of hours worked or employees hired, a blip in statisticians' charts—but much of the increased production will be wasted, or the greater effort will produce less results, and thus true productivity declines.

There have always been those who have sought to twist and manipulate the monetary system, because any change, though it hobbles the smooth operation of the overall extended order, provides a benefit for one group or another. War enriches weapons makers. Crime provides a livelihood for police officers, lawyers, and prison keepers, and disease is the bread and butter of doctors and undertakers, and there are those who can benefit from monetary instability and devaluation. Debtors benefit at the expense of creditors. Exporters benefit at the expense of importers. The unemployed benefit at the expense of the employed.

Historically, governments are the prime offenders, the institution with both the motive and the ability to carry out the deed, and many industrial or social groups are always ready to entice the government into manipulating the currency for their benefit. But governments rest on the approval of the entire citizenry, not just one part, and no government can act at the citizenry's expense indefinitely and remain in power. Democratic governments can be cleansed by the vote, and the members of less flexible political systems will eventually resort to assassination, civil war, emigration, military coup, or secession.

Today the forces for a sound currency are again ascendant. Governments and central bankers around the world today agree unanimously on the desirability of stable money, ever more so after some monetary disaster has reduced yet another economy to smoking ruins: Mexico in 1994, Thailand, Korea, Indonesia, and the Philippines in 1997, Russia and Brazil in 1998, Japan throughout the 1990s, Turkey in 2001, Argentina in 2002, Germany in the 1920s, Latin America in the 1980s, and virtually everyone in the 1970s, to name just a very few of the more well-known cases. The governments and citizens cry out together for good money, stable money, boring money, forever the same, supremely reliable, the bedrock upon which the extended order can flourish, not this stuff that wiggles and waggles unpredictably every second of every day, a never-ending chaos that saps the vitality of all countries' economies. On the political side there is near total unanimity. The problem, first, is that nobody apparently knows what exactly this stable money consists of. Second, nobody knows how to accomplish the task of creating and maintaining it.

But even the briefest study of history shows that today's condition of floating currencies is a very new phenomenon. It began August 15, 1971, the day Richard Nixon severed the dollar's link with gold and destroyed the world monetary system, which at the time went under the name of the Bretton Woods system. In the three centuries before 1971, the world for the most part had stable money. After 1971, or more properly after a series of steps in the late 1960s and the early 1970s, it did not. The capitalist economy since the Industrial Revolution, and a long time earlier as well, was based on stable money. The advocates of laissez-faire never ceased to support stable currencies. Their critics, the early socialists and communists, agreed with them on little other than the necessity of a sound unit of account. Floating currencies are not a phenomenon of the free market but the market's inevitable reaction to unceasing currency manipulations by world governments. Since the system today is the exception rather than the rule, it should be easy to find a solution to the monetary problems that plague humanity on a daily basis.

Government money manipulation and floating currencies have appeared since before the birth of Christ; and also since before the birth of Christ, the discontented citizenry has brought to the fore political leaders to return their country's currency to stability. Alexander of Macedonia unified the Mediterranean world under a hard silver coinage; 25 centuries later, he remains known as "the Great." Julius Caesar returned Rome's currency to a gold standard, and he remains an icon of Rome's greatness. Alexander Hamilton helped launch the United States with a gold dollar, and his face today graces the $10 bill. The person who hired him, George Washington, is on the $1 bill. Napoleon returned France's currency to a gold standard, and the French accepted him as their emperor. Lenin returned hyperinflationary Russia to the gold standard, and statues of him were erected throughout the land. Mao Tse-tung returned China to a gold standard, and the country rallied around him. The U.S. occupation government in Japan returned the hyperinflationary yen to the gold standard in 1949, and the Japanese allied themselves with the country that attacked them with nuclear weapons only three years earlier. Richard Nixon plunged the world into monetary chaos, and he remains the only U.S. president ever torn from office.

Ronald Reagan, the "Teflon president," whose popularity endured through crisis and scandal, came close to returning the dollar to the gold standard in the 1980s, but settled instead for an end to the devaluation policies that dominated the 1970s. Bill Clinton may have learned his lesson: An economic boom based on his administration's strong dollar policy—abandoning a century-long tradition of cheap-dollar Democrats—put voters in a forgiving mood regarding his other dubious escapades. The voters know that it is by no means certain that future presidents will be so wise.

Chaotic currencies have been stabilized countless times. It has already happened three times in United States history alone—or five, depending on how you count. The situation today is not unique in that sense, though the challenge facing governments, politicians, and the citizenry today is as great as it has ever been. Until 1971, in all of history the world had never faced a situation where the entire monetary system of the globe had been separated from its traditional metallic anchors. There had always been floating currencies, but never had all currencies floated simultaneously. More than ever, it will take a leader with deep understanding, vision, and backbone to guide a return to monetary stability. That leader would best be an American, since the U.S. dollar remains the world's leading currency, but might turn out to be European, Chinese, English, Japanese, Russian, or Argentinean. If so, after a number of years the world might drop the floating dollar and adopt the euro, renminbi, pound, yen, or yes, even the ruble. The first U.S. currency was confetti issued by a government that soon collapsed. For two centuries afterward, "not worth a Continental" was a casual term for worthlessness. It wasn't until the introduction of the gold-linked dollar that the U.S. currency grew to be accepted throughout the world. The British pound had been the world's premier currency for two centuries, but after Britain broke with gold in 1914 and again in 1931, the world abandoned the venerable pound and the dollar rose to world supremacy.

Fortunately, monetary systems are better understood today than at any time in the past. The theory and history in this book is from a classical standpoint, which is fundamentally different than the conventional wisdom of today, often called *neo-Keynesian* but perhaps rightly labeled "neo-mercantilist." Classical economics is the original economics of the Industrial Revolution and the original economics of capitalism. It is a counterpoint to constitutional democracy, just as the mercantilist system was a reflection of absolute monarchy and despotism.

The classical viewpoint is as old as civilization and is echoed in the writing of Confucius, Mencius, and Lao-tzu. In the days of Adam Smith, David Ricardo, and John Stuart Mill, all economists were classical economists. Even Karl Marx was a classical economist at the core. The thread of study was taken up in the later nineteenth century by thinkers such as William Stanley Jevons, Carl Menger, and Léon Walras. In the first half of the twentieth century, classical monetary theory was developed further by the Austrian school under the guidance of Ludwig von Mises and Friedrich von Hayek. Murray Rothbard, Henry Hazlitt, and other writers carried many of the Austrians' discoveries into the latter half of the twentieth century. Beginning in the 1960s, major new advances were made in the understanding of taxes, tariffs, and regulation by such people as Robert

Mundell and Arthur Laffer, which in turn helped clarify monetary issues still further. The classical framework is the product of an unbroken line of investigations stretching centuries.

Although the economic theory presented here may seem unorthodox, that's because its roots are so old that much of the knowledge has been forgotten by today's academics and monetary authorities. A hundred years ago, much of it was conventional wisdom, so self-evident that it hardly needed repeating. The proof of the pudding is in the eating: This theoretical structure produced decades and even centuries of stable money and economic abundance. It has been thoroughly tested, and it works. Those who are confused by today's conventional wisdom are more likely to throw up their hands and swear it cannot be done. Nonsense. It can be done; it has been done; and if history is a guide, it will be done again.

CHAPTER 2

HARD MONEY AND SOFT MONEY

Currencies and Economies around the World—from the Seventh Century BC to the Twenty-First Century AD

> After experience had shown that pieces of paper, of no intrinsic value, by merely bearing upon them the written profession of being equivalent to a certain number of francs, dollars or pounds, could be made to circulate as such, and to produce all the benefit to the issuers which could have been produced by the coins which they purported to represent; governments began to think that it would be a happy device if they could appropriate to themselves this benefit, free from the condition to which individuals issuing such paper substitutes for money were subject, of giving, when required for the sign, the thing signified. They determined to try whether they could not emancipate themselves from this unpleasant obligation, and make a piece of paper issued by them pass for a pound, by merely calling it a pound, and consenting to receive it in payment of the taxes. And such is the influence of almost all established governments, that they have generally succeeded in attaining this object; I believe I might say they have always succeeded for a time, and the power has only been lost to them after they had compromised it by the most flagrant abuse.
>
> —**John Stuart Mill**, *Principles of Political Economy*, 1848[1]

Hard money is intended to be as stable and reliable as possible. It is represented as a definite, inviolable, mutually agreed-upon contract, such as the definition of the currency as a specified amount of gold. It is thus said that hard money is based on the rule of law, although any naturally occurring commodity money, such as cowrie shells, are also hard monies.

Soft money is usually intended to be adaptable to short-term policy goals, and because it is subject to the changing whims of its managers, soft money is said to be based on the rule of man. Soft money has no definition. Soft money is really only possible when the monetary system has been monopolized, since, if given the choice, citizens will naturally conduct their business in terms that are definite, inviolable, and mutually agreed upon. The only entities that have been able to monopolize the monetary system are governments and private entities in collusion with governments. (Most central banks today are privately owned.) Soft money is, literally, monopoly money. History has produced a natural cycle between hard and soft money, which has also typically been a cycle between government and private market control over the monetary system. The world is now in a soft money cycle; there are no hard currencies today.

The citizenry prefers the most stable money possible as a foundation for contracts and trade. However, certain interest groups may influence the government, or the government may be seeking an advantage of its own, or the government may simply be grasping for solutions in a time of crisis as it turns once again to the monopolization and manipulation of the monetary system. Even if devaluation isn't the explicit goal of this *monetary policy* (the modern term for this manipulation), because deflation is so starkly recessionary, the trend has always been toward inflation.

As the adverse effects of monetary policy become more severe, the citizenry's desire to return to a stable currency intensifies, and it begins searching for a way to do so. The citizenry will eventually abandon the increasingly useless currency or even abandon the offending government itself as it seeks a return to a stable monetary system. Just as with taxes, the rise and fall in currency quality is mirrored in the rise and fall of states and empires.

The first known example of coinage in the Western world was actually an early example of soft money. Although textbooks typically assert that coinage was developed to standardize the weights of monetary metals, which had traded as money for centuries, the first coins were minted to get metals to pass for more than their commodity value. The electrum coins of Lydia, in the seventh century BC, were a mixture of gold and silver, a natural combination found in the beds of the Patroclus River near Sardis. It is pointless to verify the weight of an electrum coin, since the proportion of gold to silver is unknown. The Lydian coins were not made of natural electrum but of a manufactured alloy, which allowed the kings to lower the gold content and increase the silver content compared to natural electrum. The stamp on the coins signified that the coins passed *ad talum*, by their face value, as though they were made of natural electrum, although their commodity value was perhaps one-third of this. To maintain the coins' artificial scarcity, a variety of laws were enacted to create an effective government monopoly on the production of electrum, gold, and silver.

The failures of soft-money experiments in the ancient Greek states no doubt inspired Solon of Athens, who, soon after he assumed power in 594 BC, struck a new coin and announced that anyone who debased the coin—including himself—would have his hands chopped off. In 508 BC, democracy was established in Athens, and the city-state enjoyed a long period of economic and social advancement. The Athenian "owl" was used throughout the Mediterranean, as the Athenians scrupulously maintained the coin's integrity and refused to devalue it even when the Treasury was depleted in times of war. It was a widely accepted currency for six centuries.

However, despite this success, the temptation to fiddle with currencies remained. The philosopher Plato, an infamous soft-money man, held in *The Laws* that domestic money should be nonexportable, restricted in its supply, and exchangeable with other monies only through a government authority—in short, that money should be managed by philosopher kings. In 388 or 387 BC, Plato made the first of two trips to the island country of Syracuse. Soon after, perhaps because of Plato's arguments, the ruler Dionysius issued tin coins at a face value about four times above their commodity value.

21

This was apparently successful, for Dionysius later issued silver coins overvalued by a factor of 2 and demanded that they be accepted at face value under penalty of death. The death penalty didn't work; the coins' market value soon fell to their commodity value. This failure apparently cut short Plato's career as a monetary adviser. Plutarch reports that Dionysius sent Plato to be sold at the slave market at Corinth, where, luckily for him, a group of fellow philosophers happened to be standing by to purchase his freedom.[2]

Plato's student, Aristotle, rejected his teacher's soft-money philosophies and advocated a hard currency consisting of full-weight coins. Aristotle in turn taught this to his student, Alexander of Macedonia, who came to power at age 21 and in the following 12 years unified the ancient world under a reliable silver standard. With lower barriers to trade, an expanding circle of commerce, and a sound monetary system, the citizenry under Alexander's rule could go about happily making themselves wealthy. The citizenry had found their champion, and throughout the Mediterranean world the pendulum swung back toward a unified hard currency.

After Alexander's death in 323 BC, the quality of currencies around the Mediterranean deteriorated and the monetary system again fractured. Hard currencies were revived by the Roman Republic, which began on a sound bronze standard that soon included silver. In the second century BC, large companies were formed that could accept contracts from the government for tax collection, road construction, and public buildings. Shares in such companies were bought and sold daily at a market in the Forum, the first Roman stock exchange.

After many years of success the Roman coinage eventually fell into disarray and debasement, paralleling the decline of the Republic itself. Roman coinage was made a hard currency once again by Julius Caesar. His silver-and-gold-based system was spread throughout the ancient world alongside the expansion of the Roman Empire. After peace in 54 BC, typical interest rates on gold-denominated commercial loans fell to 4 to 6 percent annually, the lowest in Roman history.

After Caesar's assassination in 44 BC, Rome again fell into civil war and currency debasement, but a hard currency was reestablished by Caesar's adopted son Octavian in 31 BC. It formed the foundation for Rome's economic strength and the consolidation of the empire. Octavian took the name Augustus and ruled until AD 14 on the principles of sound money, moderate taxes, free trade, free enterprise, and private property. The circle of commerce again encompassed the ancient Mediterranean world. Augustus's rule was the high tide of Roman monetary quality and finance. From 25 BC to at least AD 10, interest rates on commercial loans fell once again to the 4 to 6 percent range.

The Roman coinage began to be debased under the rule of Nero (AD 54–68), with the content reduced from 100 percent silver to 90 percent. Trajan (98–117) reduced the coin to 85 percent silver, and Marcus Aurelius (161–180) reduced it to 75 percent. After the reigns of Commodus (180–192) and Septimius Severus (193–211), the silver content of the denarius had been reduced to 50 percent. These were rather minor devaluations, but during the string of puppet emperors during the third century AD, rampant devaluation began. By the reign of Gallienus (260–268) the silver content of the coin had been reduced to about 4 percent, implying an inflationary rise in prices of 25:1. Gallienus tried issuing as coinage masses of copper flakes known as "billions," but they were refused by the banks.

Aurelian (270–275), facing revolts and soldiers' demands for payment in commodities, discovered a new form of inflation—issuing coins at higher denominations—which allowed inflation to be unfettered by the difficulty of reducing the silver content of coins still further. The 20-denarii coin was solid copper with a light silvery wash. Rebellions broke out, and Aurelian was murdered in 275.

As Rome reeled under both hyperinflation and increasing taxation, its economic decline accelerated. Diocletian (284–305) strove to halt the inflation, even issuing reformed full-weight coins. However, he gave the coins a face value equivalent to the debased coins, and as a result his new coins were simply hoarded and disappeared

from circulation. Diocletian was surprised and dismayed by his failure—
as we are today, for he was so close to success! The proper solution
would have been to allow the new coins to trade at their intrinsic value,
many times that of the debased coins that they would eventually
replace.

Having failed to restore a reliable hard currency, as Alexander,
Caesar, and Augustus had done, Diocletian reached for price controls
in his famous Edict of Prices of 301, which simply exacerbated the
problem by introducing a new impediment to trade. Although the
death penalty applied to violations of the price controls, they were a
failure and had to be repealed after many had been executed. As
hyperinflation reached its ultimate stage and the monetary system
broke down completely, Diocletian abandoned tax payments in coin
for payment in goods and services, which resulted in the spread of a
Soviet-style planned economy to provide support for the military.
The mighty Roman government had been reduced to barter.[3]

In the mid-fourth century one record shows the Roman denarius had fallen 30,000,000:1 from its value under Augustus. The process of increasing taxation and further debasement of the currency
led to the complete breakup of the market economy and the creation
of the feudal system. The Dark Ages had begun.

Powerful landowners were able to avoid the crushing tax load
through legal and illegal means, in effect making themselves independent of the Roman state. Lesser landowners, driven into bankruptcy, signed on as tenants to the large landowners. Some even
signed on as slaves, since slaves paid no taxes. Indeed, so many farmers willingly signed themselves into slavery to avoid the tax collector
that in AD 368, Emperor Valens declared it illegal to renounce one's
liberty in order to seek protection with a great landlord.

It was during this time, as bankrupted farmers lost their land to
creditors, that the Christian church rose in popularity and imposed
its policy of no lending at interest. One of the earliest Christian
restrictions against lending at interest was made by the first general
council of the Christian church, the Council of Nicea, in the year
325, as the Roman economy collapsed. The council cited Psalm 15.

The term *usury* eventually applied to any attempt to extract financial gain from another's misfortune, such as asking a higher price for goods during shortages. Many aspects of the early Christian church were socialistic in nature, a reaction to the disintegration of Roman capitalism, and concentrated on providing for the needy. This offered a counterbalance to the more capitalistic focus of Judaism, which continued to condone hard-nosed commerce in general and lending at interest in particular. Finance was stifled in Europe by the Christian decrees until the fourteenth century, at which time Italy passed new laws permitting interest lending, thus allowing the reappearance of finance.

For another thousand years the European feudal system was based on self-sufficient estates that operated primarily without money. The system could be seen as a simple, diffuse form of communism, the statist reaction to the collapse of the Romans' capitalist empire. What trade existed was carried on in independent towns, each of which had their own tax and tariff systems, making trade with other towns difficult. Roman law, which had bound the entire Mediterranean world in one great circle of exchange, had been blown to bits. By 435, coins had fallen out of use in Britain, the outer reaches of the Roman Empire, and they were not adopted again there for 200 more years.

While Europe slept, the spirit of commerce was revived in China, where the world's first example of paper money (actually a sort of payment transfer device) emerged in the early ninth century. The Chinese used paper money for another 600-plus years, but the cycle of devaluation and reform was incessant. A true paper currency was developed in the early eleventh century by Szechwan merchants. The government monopolized the printing of money soon after, in 1016, and in 1020 note issuances had reached a point that historians have compared to the 1920s inflation in Germany. The monetary chaos of the period inspired Hung Tsun to write a *Treatise on Coinage* in 1149, possibly the first text devoted to monetary affairs. The country suffered another hyperdevaluation in the 1160s.

The fourteenth-century Chinese historian Ma Twan-lin later explained:

> Paper should never be money (but) only employed as a representative sign of value existing in metals or produce. . . . At first this was the mode in which paper currency was actually used among merchants. The government, borrowing the invention from private individuals, wished to make a real money of paper, and thus the original contrivance was perverted.[4]

Rampant devaluation under the Sung and Chin dynasties in the early 1200s preceded the invasion by the Mongols. The Mongol governments reinstated a hard silver currency, and under their rule Chinese paper money reached its zenith. Marco Polo, who lived in China from 1275 to 1292, described a Mongol paper currency that was redeemable in silver:

> Should any be desirous of procuring gold or silver for the purposes of manufacture, such as drinking cups, girdles or other articles wrought of these metals, they in like manner apply at the mint, and for their paper obtain the bullion they require.[5]

Marco Polo returned to Europe with knowledge of both the printing press and paper money. The first known use of the Chinese-inspired printing press in the Western world occurred in 1294, almost immediately after his return. The press was used, in fact, to print money, specifically unredeemable notes circulated by the king of Persia in the city of Tabriz. The king was suffering revenue difficulties and was no doubt inspired by the success of the Chinese alchemical magic, which apparently turned worthless paper into gold and silver. He demanded, under penalty of death, that the unredeemable paper be accepted at face value. But the citizenry refused to accept the notes, and instead deserted the marketplaces. The experiment was halted after two months.

The Mongols' finest expression of a currency freely convertible into silver began in 1260, and by Marco Polo's time the notes' redeemability had already become rather spotty. Hu Zhiyu (1227–1295) compared the inconvertible notes to "orphans who had lost their mother in childbirth" and blamed the resulting inflation on an excessive quantity of notes in circulation rather than, as some claimed, a shortage of goods or labor.[6]

After decades of relatively mild inflation, from about 1356 the Mongols' paper currency slid into extreme devaluation. Citizens abandoned paper money for copper coins and barter. In 1368, a massive uprising, led by the unlettered peasant Chu Yuan-chang, drove the Mongols from Beijing. The victorious Chu declared the beginning of the Ming dynasty.

The Ming bureaucrats revived paper currency, but it was never convertible and steadily lost value. In the 1430s, people once again began abandoning paper currencies and trading in silver instead. By 1448 the Ming note had been devalued from a nominal 1,000 *cash* (the Chinese word for their copper coins) to a market value of 3. Apparently disgusted with the difficulties of paper currencies, by 1455 the Ming government had officially abandoned paper money and engineered a return to a wholly metallic coinage that traded at commodity value, which lasted into the nineteenth century.

However, this introduced a new problem. Because Chinese citizens were now unable to use cheap paper as money, they were forced to carry out commerce with expensive silver coins. The country's need for monetary silver exploded. In 1500 the highly advanced and briskly growing Chinese economy already included as many as 100 million people, compared to about 60 million in all of Europe. Although China had exported silver when it had used paper currencies, from the mid-fifteenth century it imported silver in colossal quantities, first from Japan and later from Europe, which in turn would obtain it from the New World. The shortage of monetary metals in Asia and Europe (pepper was for a time used as money in some European cities) was a major motivation for the voyages of discovery that followed Columbus's voyage of 1492. Not only did the Chinese obtain silver in trade with the Europeans, but shipped huge

27

quantities directly from Acapulco, on the Pacific side of Mexico, to Macau and Manila, from where it traveled onward to China. According to certain studies, in some periods half or more of the total silver output of the Spanish mines crossed the Pacific, never even passing through Europe.[7]

While silver was plentiful, and the arrangement was acceptable enough, but especially after the mines of the New World ran out in the early seventeenth century, the incessant outflow of silver from Europe to China alarmed many, who interpreted the flow as a diminishment of wealth, though the Chinese traded all manner of luxury items in return. This probably helped inspire the mercantilist policies favoring trade restrictions and a retention of precious metals that lasted through the eighteenth century. Like their Chinese counterparts, the European governments loved to stockpile titanic quantities of bullion in their treasuries. The mercantilist confusion between a trade deficit and an outflow of precious metals continues to this day. The Chinese, whose own mines were relatively barren, in this way also exposed themselves to the danger of a reduction of the supply of silver from the West.

The Ming dynasty began its decline in the early seventeenth century, with a series of seven tax hikes between 1618 and 1636. The silver coin was dramatically debased beginning around 1620, throwing the economy into further turmoil. As mercantilist policies became ascendant in Europe and Japan, the silver supply was choked off beginning around 1640, which dealt a final blow to the already sputtering economy. The Ming dynasty ended in 1644.

Holland's great economic success in the seventeenth century can be traced in part to the establishment of the Bank of Amsterdam, in 1609, for the express purpose of producing a standardized gold and silver coinage that traded as a 100 percent commodity money. The Dutch did not try to hoard their precious metals, according to the mercantilist orthodoxy of the day, but instead allowed free import and export of bullion. Indeed, the Dutch produced full-weight coins specifically for export, which they used in all of their many international trading endeavors. The Dutch coinage became the premier international currency of its day. The result of maintaining a high currency quality was that long-term interest rates in Amsterdam fell to gold-standard levels of around 3 to 4 percent, a great boon to financing the many adventurous and highly profitable trading expeditions all over the globe, as well as domestic manufactures such as textiles.

The English, amazed by the Dutch success and aware of the relative turpitude of their own economy, understood the critical importance of low interest rates. Interest rates for loans in England were 12 percent or higher at the time, typical for countries today with poor-quality currencies and a history of devaluation. The mercantilist theorists in England, however, did not associate the low interest rates with the reliability of the Dutch currency and instead made numerous proposals and experiments to lower English interest rates by other means. Some suggested simply making higher interest rates illegal, but this merely made lending illegal as well. Others suggested making money plentiful. This was an impetus to devaluation and currency manipulation, and also the now-famous mercantilist edicts on the export of precious metal (reasoning that money would be "more plentiful" if it was prevented from escaping the country). None of these experiments enjoyed much success.

The solution was finally found by the philosopher John Locke, who argued for the establishment of a reliable, full-weight coinage to protect the relationship between creditors and debtors. His arguments convinced Parliament and also Isaac Newton, who, in addition to his scientific accomplishments, became the Master of the Mint and held the position for 27 years. In 1697–1698 a recoinage was made at a rate of 3 ounces, 17 pennyweight and 10.5 grains of silver per English pound. It was the first such recoinage since 1299.

Locke's idea was revolutionary. Before Locke, few people in England even entertained the idea that the value of coins should be stable and unchanging. Kings made coins to do with as they pleased, as they had for centuries. After Locke, the stability of monetary value was held paramount. In 1717, the pound's value was translated into gold at 3 pounds, 17 shillings, 10.5 pence per ounce of gold, putting England on a bimetallic standard with gold on top instead of silver. The Locke definition of the British pound persisted (with lapses) until 1931, a 233-year stretch of currency stability.[8]

Locke's insistence on a stable unit of account to protect the relationships between borrowers and lenders was no doubt intrinsic to the success of the Bank of England, which was created in 1694 in order to provide a huge £1.2 million loan to the government to fight the War of the League of Augsburg. The access to capital that the bank provided reduced the temptation to resort to currency devaluation for financing purposes, reduced the desire to stockpile warehouses of silver during times of peace to finance wars, and also strengthened the redeemable paper currency system, which greatly reduced Europe's demand for precious metals and the consequent competition for those metals with India and China. In this new environment mercantilism declined and the classical principles of low taxes, free trade, and stable currencies thrived, forming the basis for the Industrial Revolution and the final sweeping away of the feudal system.

After some initial difficulties, interest rates in England plummeted. For much of the eighteenth century, the British government was able to borrow at less than 4 percent and infinite maturity. The inherent conflict of the bimetallic standard was officially resolved in 1816, leaving Britain on a monometallic gold standard that eventually included the entire world. See Figure 2.1.

The Revolutionary War of the United States was largely a tax revolt, not only against the rather modest impositions already in force but also the looming threat of limitless future demands. Taxes in Europe consumed 40 percent or more of peasants' production at the time. The most adventurous crossed the ocean and faced the uncertainties of life at the edge of the great wilderness in order to enjoy a life that

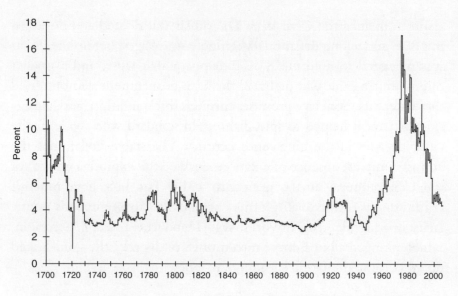

FIGURE 2.1   Britain: Yield on 2.5 Percent Consol Bond, 1700–2005

was almost tax free. They did not want to give it up. The war, however, was financed in large part by simply printing more money, and
the new country began its history with a hyperinflation. The Founding Fathers were appalled by the results, and in the Constitution of
1789, they explicitly forbade the issuance of an unconvertible fiat
currency. A bimetallic gold and silver standard was established in 1792.

The new country was founded not only on the ideals of democracy and congressional rule, but also on the classical economics
expressed by contemporary writers such as Adam Smith. As a result,
the United States, more than any other major country, abhorred the
encroachment of government on the private monetary sphere. For
much of the nineteenth century, the government had minimal influence on the monetary system, even going so far as to forbid the Treasury to deposit any cash in private banks, lest it play favorites or gain
a lever with which to influence the financial system.

The U.S. government, which was still minimal in size and dependent on tariffs for revenue, resorted to the printing press once

again to finance the Civil War. The dollar was floated and devalued in 1861, and a long deflationary struggle was waged before the dollar was repegged to gold in 1879. Except for that lapse, and a smaller offense during the War of 1812, the U.S. government demonstrated that it kept its monetary promises through thick and thin, and, alongside Britain, it helped to spread the gold standard worldwide in the latter decades of the nineteenth century. The stable dollar, and the almost complete absence of taxation, enabled the explosive growth of the U.S. economy in the period to 1914. The U.S. government's commitment to the quality of its currency led to the dollar's popularity worldwide. After World War I and the Great Depression, which plunged all of Europe into monetary disarray, the gold-linked dollar became the world's leading currency.

The first modern public bank in France was established in 1716 by John Law, born in Scotland to a banking family. The bank was a great success, and its profit from issuing banknotes lured the French government to nationalize the bank in 1718. Law was made the minister of finance, and in a bit of financial derring-do, he swirled together banknote issuances with an investment company (the Mississippi Company) and a plan to pay off the government's debts. Law was soon issuing gigantic amounts of banknotes, and the resulting inflationary fiasco was termed the Mississippi Bubble. In 1720, Law left France in disgrace (and dressed as a woman) to spend the remainder of his life in Vienna's gambling dens. The French abandoned paper money and returned to a wholly metallic currency.

In 1776, banking and paper currencies were again attempted in France by a Scotsman and a Swiss. For 10 years the new bank maintained the value of its paper money, but beginning around 1786 the bank began to make excessive loans to the heavily indebted government, which was accompanied by overissuance of banknotes. The French Revolution soon followed, but the revolutionary governments were even worse. They issued enormous quantities of fiat currency after 1789. Like the United States, modern France began with a hyperinflation. By 1795, 100-livre notes traded for only 15 sous in coin. Riots broke out in Paris in May 1795, which led ultimately to the rise of Napoleon. His Bank of France, established in 1800, put France on a sound currency convertible into gold.

The French Revolution, like the American Revolution a few years earlier, was, in essence, a tax revolt. Before the Revolution, as much as 80 percent of citizens' incomes were being confiscated by the state. Afterward, that ratio dropped to around 30 percent. Napoleon ignored his advisers and kept tax rates low. Combined with a sound currency, France's economy gained the might that allowed Napoleon to march across Europe, sweeping away the remnants of feudalism as he went and, like Caesar, reuniting the Continent in a great circle of commerce. As for Napoleon himself, he was so wildly popular after 1801 that he was voted consul for life, and in 1804 he dared to declare himself emperor, which stuck.

The outbreak of war with France in February 1793 incited a small banking panic in England, which the Bank of England helped the system weather, although the principles of central banking were still to be discovered. A French invasion of Britain was widely expected, and in February 1797 a small complement of French troops landed in Wales. They mistook a distant gathering of women in Welsh costume as British troops, and promptly surrendered. However, when rumors of the invasion reached London, it touched off a banking panic, as people redeemed their deposits for banknotes, redeemed their banknotes for gold, then took the gold and buried it in the ground. Gold is money under any government, but banknotes would be worthless.

The Bank of England botched its management of the panic, and its gold reserves were quickly depleted. On February 26, 1797, the bank suspended the redeemability of its banknotes. The step was expected to be of very short duration, but it was 24 years before Britain returned to the gold standard. The British pound became a floating currency, managed by the Bank of England. The bank had numerous special advantages conferred on it at its inception, which was common practice in the mercantilist era, and thus had an effective monopoly on banknotes. Although the bank had no intent to devalue the currency, the natural tendency, particularly since the bank profited from the issue of banknotes, was toward oversupply. For most of the next two decades the pound's value floated downward and Britain suffered inflation.

The inflation, averaging 3 to 4 percent per year, was mild by modern standards, but to a country that had enjoyed a century of sound money it was deeply disturbing. The debate raged between those who wanted a return to gold convertibility at the prewar parity, and those who wished to continue with the floating pound. The arguments of the latter were considered rather ridiculous at the time—they claimed the fall of the pound on the foreign exchange market, the fall against gold, and the persistent rises in prices had nothing to do with the quantity of money issued by the Bank of England—but to adopt the policy of the former group would have meant intentionally inducing a recessionary deflation even as Britain was fighting a war. The result was political gridlock. The defeat of France in 1815 provided the catalyst for action, greatly aided by large tax cuts in that same year as the wartime income tax was eliminated and other taxes reduced. From 1815, the pound gained value, and a resumption of full convertibility at the prewar parity was accomplished in 1821—two years ahead of schedule.

The deflation caused some hardship, particularly in the agricultural sector. But the tax cuts and return to sound money set the stage for an incredible economic expansion that lasted until the 1870s, a period in which Britain's government continued to cut taxes almost every year (as it enjoyed persistent budget surpluses), pay down its debts, promote free trade worldwide, finance investment all over the globe, and eventually solve one of the most vexing problems of banking, the liquidity-shortage crisis.

The tide turned back toward socialism and economic nationalism in the 1870s. A series of bad harvests during that decade pushed European governments to grasp at relief measures, and they turned away from free trade and back to protectionism. Laissez-faire ideology, which had left out any place in its theory for what has today become state welfare systems, offered no way to address the suffering of economic contraction. The danger of incredible suffering even during boom times was made apparent by events such as the Irish famine of 1846, and that decade also saw the rise of nascent socialism, including the publication of Marx's *Communist Manifesto* in 1849. But there was as yet little theory or experience of integrating welfare programs within a growth framework, and governments instinctively grasped at the protectionist and cartelist policies of preceding centuries. Protectionist tariffs are a poor system of welfare, for a decay of economic health is the inevitable result, leading to still more economic contraction. Worse yet, unlike domestic taxes, tariffs can also cause economic contraction in the country's trading partners, which too often leads to retaliation, more tariffs, and further contraction. Even after the poor harvests of the 1870s, the agricultural sectors of European economies were threatened by large-scale competition with imported foodstuffs, made possible in the 1880s and 1890s by improvements in railroads and steamships.

Germany began on the path of cartelization and protectionism beginning around 1869, which accelerated in the 1880s. Tariffs were pushed higher in 1879, 1890, 1902, and 1906. Between 1879 and 1885, 76 cartels were established. France raised tariffs after a terrible harvest in 1875—and raised them again in 1881, 1892, 1907, and 1910. The United States, which had raised protectionist tariff barriers at the beginning of the Civil War, raised them again in 1890 and 1897. Switzerland, Italy, and Russia joined in the game, with periodic rounds of rising tariffs.

As a result of the new trade barriers, the world economy's growth tapered off in the period from 1870 to 1914, and some industrial sectors in all countries suffered due to the convulsions in trade. Britain did not retaliate in the tariff wars, but the new recessionary pressure led Britain to adopt a series of welfare programs beginning in the 1870s, made possible in part by the adoption of an income tax. The higher taxes slowed Britain's growth rate, and many historians mark the beginning of the decline in British economic power at 1870, although the slowdown in growth before the World War I was trivial compared to what came afterward.

The agricultural difficulties and policies of economic nationalism that began in the 1870s caused increasing international friction, and in response, European governments steadily increased their military outlays. France spent 3.1 percent of gross domestic product on its military in 1873; by 1904, this had risen to 4.0 percent, and to 4.8 percent in 1913. British spending rose from 2.0 percent in 1873 to 3.2 percent in 1913; Germany's rose from 2.4 percent to 3.9 percent; Italy's rose from 1.9 percent to 5.1 percent. Germany's standing army steadily grew in line with its military expenditures, from about 400,000 men in 1874 to 750,000 in 1914.[9]

With the rise of economic nationalism and beggar-thy-neighbor trade and cartel policies, it is probably no coincidence that the years from 1884 to 1900 also saw an expansion of empires worldwide, as governments struggled to include sources of labor and raw materials within their empire's free-trade zone—or simply squabbled over then-useless land, which might become useful in coming decades and centuries. Governments hoped colonies would provide a "market for finished goods and a source of raw materials," in other words, everything they had lost as free trade was abandoned. If countries would not cooperate with each other, then each country would be led to establish an empire that could be economically self-sufficient. In those 16 years, the British Empire expanded by 3.7 million square miles and 57 million people; France annexed 3.5 million square miles and 36 million people; Germany built an empire of a million square miles and 17 million people. The United States government was relatively inactive in the rush to empire because it was still digesting its western territories and could find all the markets and raw materials it needed on the North American continent. Nevertheless, the U.S. government found time to grab Cuba, the Philippines, Alaska, Hawaii, Puerto Rico, and Guam, not to mention a few of the Solomon Islands and a piece of Panama. Belgium began developing the Congo. Italy went into North Africa. Russia and Britain dueled in central Asia. Japan took Korea, Taiwan, and a chunk of Mongolia. By 1914, the world had been completely divvied up, and the empires went toe to toe over already-accounted-for areas such as the Balkan remainders of the decaying Ottoman Empire.

The monarchs of Europe eventually resolved the growing economic conflict in the traditional manner—warfare. But industrial, mechanized warfare proved intolerable, and the ultimate casualties of the war were the monarchs themselves. Europe's crowned heads of state were swept away and replaced with parliamentary bodies that were more likely to find a way to resolve conflicts before they erupted into violence.

Though rising tariffs were suppressing free commerce between major European countries, from around 1865 to 1914 the world enjoyed a monetary and financial unification greater than had ever been achieved before. The Bank of England's gradual mastery over the issuance of convertible, gold-backed banknotes and its understanding of lender-of-last-resort operations drew admiration and imitation from around the globe. Beginning around 1870, the gold standard was adopted worldwide, and by 1900 every major economy in the world was on the gold standard except for China, which was still on a metallic silver standard. Trade within empires remained free, and Britain's great empire remained a free trading zone for all countries. As transportation and communications improved, the world was bound together in a circle of commerce that was not equaled again until the 1980s. It was the first great age of globalization, made possible by a hard-money system that encompassed the globe.

The unification of government implied by empire allowed a great expansion of trade and investment, much of it between the home country and the emerging markets of the empire's new territories. Joint stock companies were deregulated in Britain in 1863, and the 691 joint stock companies of 1863 expanded to 1,600 around 1882 and 7,000 in 1914. Investment trusts (mutual funds), developed in Britain in the 1880s and 1890s, became very popular, especially for foreign investments. Investors, particularly British investors, grew more willing to accept paper promises from foreign countries in exchange for goods rather than demanding other goods and precious metals in trade, and as a result foreign investment flourished. London became the world's banker and insurer, and British capital flowed around the world. Net foreign investment several times rose above 6 percent of British gross domestic product, and on the eve of World War I it climbed to nearly 9 percent. In 1914, 44 percent of total world foreign investment was coming from Britain, which was investing nearly as much abroad as it was domestically. Much of this fountain of capital was flowing to wholly undeveloped areas. In 1914, Britain was investing nearly twice as much capital in Africa as it was in European countries (due in part, no doubt, to European tariffs) and nearly four times as much in Latin American countries. From 1880 to 1914, British exports of goods and services averaged around 30 percent of national income, a stupendous figure. Britain had made itself rich; now it was setting about making the entire world rich.

This was made possible, of course, by the world gold standard centered around London and the Bank of England. Investors, importers, and exporters did not have to worry about foreign exchange fluctuations; tariffs within the empire were low; and Britain's legal system, which it exported to its colonies, reduced the legal and political uncertainties. The Bank of England's commitment to the gold standard was unwavering, and as a result it was able to hold together the world gold standard with only a pittance of gold in reserve. The enormous capital flows did not cause never-ending crises, as they are accused of today. The world monetary system remained unruffled. For decade after decade, hard money stayed hard; exchange rates stayed fixed; interest rates remained low; and gold remained the basis of it all. Though the period had its share of financial excitement, not to mention a number of wars—the Spanish-American War, the Boer War, and the Russo-Japanese war, not to mention the Balkan skirmishes and threats of war leading to the outbreak of violence in 1914—it was the world's finest expression of currency stability, before or since.

All of that changed with the outbreak of war in 1914. Britain never officially went off the gold standard, but in 1914 Britain's banks quietly suspended specie payments and removed gold coins from domestic circulation. This step, as in 1797, was conceived as a temporary emergency expedient, but it became permanent. Overseas movements of gold were prevented by the hazards of shipping during wartime. Once again, the pound had become a floating currency. Although, as was the case during the Napoleonic Wars, the Bank of England had no overt inflationary policy, the pound, freed from the discipline of convertibility, drifted downward. This pushed interest rates higher, and the British government, which had paid 2.5 percent for capital only a few years earlier, financed the war at an exorbitant 5 percent. Countries across Europe similarly floated their currencies at the onset of war. An era of soft money began.

After the war, the European powers once again moved back toward the prewar system of hard money that had been so successful. In 1920, after hostilities had ceased, Britain chose to deflate the pound back to its original parity of 3 pounds, 17 shillings, 10.5 pence per ounce of gold, just as it had after Napoleon's defeat in 1815. However, there was one major difference: In 1815 Britain's government undertook a gigantic tax cut, eliminating wartime taxes and giving the economy, and the currency, a tremendous boost. But after World War I, the government decided to retain wartime tax rates (which had been doubled from their prewar levels) to pay off war debts, and the combination of deflation and high taxes drove the economy into recession. The pound regained its redeemability at the prewar parity in May of 1925, though Britain suffered from the deflation and excessive taxes throughout the 1920s as the economy gradually adjusted to the new monetary conditions. The situation was so bad that in 1926 workers staged a general strike.

The rest of the world, left with floating currencies after the war, struggled along with Britain to rebuild the gold-based monetary system that prevailed before the war. The franc had lost 80 percent of its value during the war. A British-style return to prewar parity was unthinkable, as it implied increasing the franc's value by a factor of 5. After fluctuating wildly, the franc was effectively repegged to gold by the end of 1926 at prevailing rates, and in this way France avoided the deflationary effects that Britain was suffering at the time. France's government also cut taxes dramatically, and in the late 1920s the French economy roared alongside that of the United States. Many other countries took a similar course, and by the end of 1926 the world gold standard was again operating in 39 countries.

Germany did not follow Britain's example by returning the mark to its prewar parity of 4.2 marks per U.S. dollar after the war ended. In 1918, at the end of hostilities, the mark had fallen to around 8 marks per dollar, a devaluation similar to that of the British pound. However, the government then ran the printing presses to meet fiscal demands, which were especially great due to the crushing commitments required by the Treaty of Versailles. The value of the mark fell to 184 per dollar in 1921, 7,350 per dollar in 1922, and finally 4.2 trillion per dollar in November of 1923. One reason the government continued its devaluation policy to its reductio ad absurdum is that the printing presses managed to stay one step ahead of people's expectations, and the resulting money illusion actually produced low unemployment. In October 1922, when the hyperinflation was going full bore, registered unemployment in Germany was only 1.4 percent, compared with 14 percent in Britain. Low unemployment did not hide the impoverishment of the middle classes or the declining productivity of the economy, however, and as citizens were reduced to barter and revolution threatened, Germany was one of the first of the European countries to return to a semistable currency, in late 1923, and finally to the gold standard in 1924. The other countries that suffered hyperinflation after the war were also quick to readopt the gold standard: Austria in 1923, Poland in 1924, and Hungary in 1925.

The United States was the sole major power to stick to the gold standard through the war, although its commitment was rather shaky between 1917 and 1920. Also, unlike Britain, it slashed back its high wartime tax rates beginning in 1921. While much of Europe struggled through deflation and recession, the United States enjoyed a boom built on low taxes and hard money, which gained momentum throughout the decade as taxes fell further.

An intense worldwide trade war, touched off by the threat of the passage of the Smoot-Hawley Tariff Act in the United States in October 1929, and the tariff's imposition in 1930, brought an end to the economic expansion and pushed the world toward depression. Domestic tax hikes piled up worldwide, and under the strain, arguments for devaluation began to look attractive. During the summer of 1931, Austria and Germany devalued and floated their currencies, followed by Britain on September 19, 1931. The rest of the world followed, and the world gold standard, which had been painstakingly and laboriously re-created in the 1920s, again fell to pieces. In 1933–1934, Roosevelt devalued the dollar from its parity at $20.67 per ounce of gold, its rough value since 1792, to $35 per ounce. However, unlike other major currencies, the dollar did not float, but remained pegged to gold. Roosevelt suspended the convertibility of outstanding banknotes, and for good measure he also outlawed private holdings of gold for nondecorative uses.

Whatever the economic effects of this plan, it had certain attractions for the U.S. government: By confiscating citizens' gold at $20.67 per ounce and then devaluing the dollar to $35 per ounce, the government produced for itself a windfall of $2.8 billion, about equal to a year's worth of tax revenue.

The thrills of wholesale beggar-thy-neighbor devaluation soon wore off, and already by 1932 Britain was moving toward stabilized currencies. Nor did the dollar devaluation of 1934 produce the benefits its advocates promised, and afterward, Britain, France, and the United States began rebuilding the world monetary system. Beginning in 1934, Britain and France moved to construct a currency system based around the U.S. dollar, and in 1936 the three governments formalized the Tripartite Agreement to establish a system of stable currencies. The currencies of the three countries would be held stable to each other, and since the U.S. dollar was still linked to gold at

$35 per ounce, the system was linked to gold. Once again, a world gold standard had been reconstructed, but it was a rather crude and messy one, and it had only one tie to gold: the willingness of the U.S. government to keep the dollar pegged to gold at $35 per ounce. A meeting of leaders at Bretton Woods, New Hampshire, in 1944 served to formalize the system already in place and also to create the World Bank and International Monetary Fund to further add strength and stability to the system.

As a result of the reestablishment of the worldwide gold standard, World War II could be cheaply funded at gold–standard interest rates. Britain, which had paid 5 percent on its bonds during the floating-pound period of World War I, funded World War II at an average rate of around 2.25 percent. Twenty-seven-year U.S. war bonds yielded 2.5 percent. The U.S. dollar did slip somewhat against gold during this period, but both countries stuck close enough to gold that they were able to avoid both the turmoil of wartime currency devaluation and the bitter effects, after the war, of returning a devalued currency to its prewar parity. Wars are fought with munitions, not money, and the productivity decline caused by currency instability can only reduce the war-making effectiveness of an economy.

The defeated Axis powers were in somewhat worse shape after the war. Germany ended the war under high taxes, price regulations, and a rationing system that had all but destroyed the monetary economy. Cigarettes and chocolate circulated as currency. In 1948, Germany's brilliant economics minister Ludwig Erhard (who had read the works of Ludwig von Mises even as they were banned in Hitler's Germany) replaced the worthless reichsmark with a deutsche mark linked to gold—or, more properly, linked to the dollar, which was in turn linked to gold via the Bretton Woods arrangement. Erhard lifted regulations on prices and rationing and radically slashed tax rates. The three primary spheres of economic management—taxes, money, and regulation—were at last lined up in growth mode, and Germany's economic recovery after the war was soon dubbed a miracle.

Japan found its way onto the same growth path as Germany, aided by Joseph Dodge, a Detroit banker who was put in charge of monetary affairs by the U.S. occupation administration. (He had just finished helping Erhard in Germany.) The yen, which had traded near ¥2 per dollar in 1929, finished the war at around ¥4.5 per dollar, but was grossly devalued afterward under the oversight of the U.S. occupation government. Japan suffered hyperinflation. Dodge swept away rationing and price controls, and repegged the yen to the dollar at ¥360 per dollar in 1949, or ¥12,600 per ounce of gold. That rate lasted until the monetary turmoil of 1971.

Japan had been given an insanely repressive tax system by the U.S. occupation administration. Beginning in 1950 and continuing throughout the 1960s, Japan, like Germany, slashed away at taxes incessantly. Combined with the gold-linked yen, the result was an explosion of economic activity. The Japanese postwar economic miracle bettered even that of the Germans.

The Bretton Woods era was clouded by incessant turmoil as governments refused to abide by the passive discipline of the gold standard and currency boards and instead attempted to implement their own domestic monetary policy. The two came into constant conflict. Unwilling to acknowledge the source of their problems, governments reached for coercive measures such as capital controls and trade restrictions. The breaking point was reached when President Richard Nixon pressured the Federal Reserve to stimulate the economy with easy money in the face of impending recession and an upcoming presidential election. The Fed complied, and, as the dollar's value sagged, the dollar's gold convertibility came under increasing strain. In the second week of August 1971, the media reported that France and Britain planned to convert their dollar holdings into gold. On August 15, Nixon foiled their plans by suspending gold redeemability. Because the dollar was the Bretton Woods system's only link with gold, the act in effect separated the entire world monetary system from its gold foundation. The end of the world gold standard was the most significant economic event of the past 50 years. It was considered a temporary measure.

As the dollar was devalued, countries around the world broke their dollar links to keep from getting dragged down with the dollar.

(Britain was the exception, and took the opportunity to outdevalue the dollar.) By early 1973 the Bretton Woods system had disintegrated completely, and currencies everywhere floated. The United States led the world into inflation. The dollar, worth $\frac{1}{35}$ ounce of gold since 1934, was eventually devalued to a nadir of $\frac{1}{850}$ ounce at the end of the Carter administration. During the Bretton Woods period the dollar had become the world's primary currency, and with devaluationist rhetoric in the air all governments were ultimately sucked into the inflationary vortex. The inflation interacted with the steeply progressive tax systems in place worldwide to set off tax hikes in the form of bracket creep, if not outright tax hike legislation, as recession hobbled government revenues, and the combination of tax rate increases and inflation pushed countries everywhere into economic decline.

Once again, the citizenry searched for a hard-money champion and found one in Ronald Reagan, who was elected president in 1980. Reagan came close to including a return to the gold standard as part of his 1980 campaign platform, and he brought up the gold standard throughout his presidency, but he was repeatedly talked out of it by his anti-gold monetarist advisers. However, Reagan did manage to stop the devaluation trend of the dollar and currencies worldwide with the help of Federal Reserve Chairman Paul Volcker. Once again, the world started on the difficult path to hard currencies.

Although the one-way devaluation was halted, the dollar fluctuated wildly between $300 and $500 per ounce of gold during the 1980s. Volcker's successor, Alan Greenspan, tamed the volatility of the dollar still further, keeping it closer to $350 per ounce, and as a result spared the U.S. economy from monetary turmoil during much of the 1990s. However, Greenspan did little to halt a rise in the dollar beginning in 1997, which set off monetary crises around the world.

The European governments, who are more sensitive to exchange rate fluctuations due to the trade integration of their economies, have sought a return to a fixed-rate system since the breakdown of Bretton Woods. France never wavered from its commitment to fixed rates, especially with Germany. They began with the "Snake" in the 1970s, a crude and mostly unsuccessful attempt to maintain fixed rates without currency boards, a central monetary authority, or a gold link. Plans for a common currency began in the severe monetary turmoil and inflation of 1978. In 1979 the European Monetary System was developed, and enjoyed a little more success due to the relative monetary stability of the 1980s, but it was still not based on currency board–type pegs and was troubled by constant instability. Central rates were adjusted every 8 to 12 months. Faced with high unemployment due to tax and regulatory errors, European governments ached to fiddle with their currencies. In 1991 the Maastricht treaty to unify Europe under a single currency was ratified, and on January 1, 1999, the euro was born. The euro began as a commitment for eurozone countries to link their currencies through a currency board system guided by a single central bank, the European Central Bank, and in 2002 banknotes issued by the ECB replaced those issued by individual governments. A collection of central European governments are planning to adopt the euro within 10 years.

Dollarization is being seriously considered throughout Latin America and has already been implemented in Panama, Ecuador, and El Salvador. Japan has been quietly floating proposals to link together an Asian currency bloc, but mismanagement of the yen over the past two decades has scared off all takers. The euro project could also fail if mismanagement of the euro is so severe or unnecessary fiscal constraints so onerous that governments decide they would be better off on their own.

The world has been in a soft-money cycle since 1971, but since 1980, the world has been slowly inching back toward the kind of fixed-rate free market system it enjoyed in the 1750s, 1880s, and 1960s. The advantages of a hard currency have become clear to all, but the monetary authorities have held back, perhaps acknowledging on a deep level that they do not yet have the institutional knowledge to manage such a system. That is mostly a matter of time; the world will probably find its way back to a hard currency one way or another.

CHAPTER 3

SUPPLY, DEMAND, AND THE VALUE OF CURRENCY

How the Value and Quantity of Money Are Regulated by Central Banks

The value or purchasing power of money depends, in the first instance, on demand and supply.

—John Stuart Mill, *Principles of Political Economy*, 1848[1]

The relation between the demand for money and the supply of money, which may be called the money relation, determines the height of purchasing power.

—Ludwig von Mises, *Human Action*, 1948[2]

Monetary authorities can control the supply of a currency, but they cannot directly control the demand for the currency. If the market demands less currency than the authorities are cranking out, the value of the currency falls. That is exactly what is happening with the euro. To call the decline in the euro "irrational" simply evades the responsibility that the European Central Bank has in maintaining the value of the currency.

—Deutschebank foreign exchange analyst Ken Landon, 2000[3]

Despite claims to the contrary, proper currency management is simple. A currency's value is determined by the balance of supply and demand. The currency is supplied by the issuer of currency, which today are central banks. The currency is demanded by anyone world-wide who wishes to hold the currency.

Whenever supply is growing relative to demand, the currency loses value. Whenever supply is shrinking relative to demand, the currency gains value. When supply maintains an equal relationship with demand, stable currency value results.

Everybody knows that if a central bank increases supply (i.e., "prints money") willy-nilly and far in excess of demand, the currency's value will fall. However, this is not the only means by which inflation can take place. If demand shrinks and supply does not shrink accordingly, the result is that supply grows relative to demand and the value of the currency falls. It is possible for the currency's value to fall even when supply is shrinking—if demand is shrinking even faster.

A fall in supply relative to demand will push the currency's value higher. This can happen through a contraction of supply, but it is also common to find that the demand for a currency can increase sharply. This will raise the currency's value even if supply is stable or growing.

All fluctuations in a currency's value, which can be noted in the foreign exchange market and currency's exchange rate with gold, are the result of the mismatch of supply and demand.

Money is supplied by institutions with the power to create money. In the past, private commercial banks created money. At other times, money has been created by government treasury departments or ministries of finance. Today, money is created by central banks, although central banks were not created for that purpose.

Today, money is rarely printed in the first instance, but rather comes out of a very special checking account at the central bank that nobody puts any money into. The central bank will buy something on the open market, usually either domestic government bonds or foreign currencies, and will pay for the purchase with its magic checking account, creating an increase in the seller's bank account. In a normal transaction, A has a bond and B has $1,000, and afterward, B has a bond and A has $1,000. The amount of money in circulation does not change. However, if A sells the central bank a bond, A's account is credited with $1,000, but no account is debited. New money enters circulation. This money ends up as bank reserves, which can be redeemed for paper banknotes on demand. If the government does not have sufficient paper currency in its vaults, it prints new currency to meet this request. Thus, increasing the money supply by buying bonds with the magic checkbook is equivalent to printing money.

Supply can be reduced through the opposite process. If the central bank sells a bond to A, A's account is debited, but no account is credited. The money simply disappears. One can imagine the issuer of currency "running the printing press backward." Central banks today have enough bonds or other assets to buy back the entire supply of money available. The U.S. Federal Reserve, for example, can buy up every single dollar in the world. Thus, it can supply any amount of money, from zero to infinity.

Even if a central bank, or government, did not have enough assets to purchase currency, it could issue new bonds or eliminate currency taken in from tax revenues.

The central bank is in a nice position here. It can buy things with money it simply creates out of nothing. The profit inherent in producing money is known as *seignorage*, a word signifying that it has long been considered the right of kings. However, it does not have to be done by governments. Many of the early commercial banks, in eighteenth-century Scotland, for example, specialized first in printing paper money (replacing metallic coinage) and only later diversified into making loans. As private institutions, they profited from money creation in the same way that governments profit today. Today, the interest income from the roughly $800 billion of government bonds held by the privately owned Federal Reserve is remitted to the U.S. Treasury, after deducting the operating expenses of the central bank. (At least, that is the official story.)

The money that is created by the Fed's magic checking account is known as *base money* and consists primarily of Federal Reserve Notes (i.e., paper currency, dollar bills) and bank reserves, which are deposits of commercial banks with the central bank and are recorded electronically at the central bank. Only the Fed can create base money, and the

Fed can create no other type of money except for base money. Paper bills make up the majority of base money. At this time, the U.S. Federal Reserve counts about $812 billion of base money, with $750 billion in bills and coins, and $62 billion in bank reserves. During the 1990s, U.S. base money grew at an average rate of 7.14 percent per year.

The term *base money* is used because upon the base of base money sits a much larger pyramid of credit. A bank deposit is not money, but is actually a kind of debt instrument, a bond that must be repaid at the request of the lender, called the *depositor*. As a bond, it pays interest. While the amount of base money available is determined to the dollar by the central bank (at least insofar as bills are not destroyed or lost by their holders or created by counterfeiters), the amount of existing credit can change according to a nearly infinite number of factors.

Thus it is incorrect to say that "banks create money." Only the Federal Reserve creates base money. Banks can only create credit, which does not alter the supply of base money, but which may have an effect on the demand for base money. Actually, anyone can create credit, simply by making a loan. Credit is not money.

The money supply figures cited by economists today are usually statistics about a certain kind of credit, M2 + CDs, which consists of bank deposits and time deposits. This is just one, somewhat arbitrary, definition, a statistical fudge, chosen because certain theorists noticed a vague relationship between this figure and nominal gross domestic product, which is just another statistical fudge. These figures are largely irrelevant. The only purpose of the M statistics and their cousins is to guide the central bank's management of the supply of base money. But with the dollar in use all over the world, statistics about the United States alone are meaningless. A staff member of the International Monetary Fund estimated that as little as 10 to 15 percent of all the U.S. currency held outside of banks is used inside the United States. The rest is being used outside of the country—by foreign central banks, in dollarized countries and countries where business is conducted in dollars, by travelers, smugglers, drug cartels, tax evaders, and foreign commercial banks—as the international currency of the world.[4] Roughly two-thirds of all the dollars in the world are in the form of $100 bills, a denomination almost never seen in the United States.

The ideas of *money* and *credit* are easily blurred in discussions today, but they are very distinct. Credit is a type of contract denominated in money. Credit may expand whenever borrowers and lenders decide that it is in their mutual benefit to do so. The supply of money may expand to accommodate this new economic activity. Often, this is the case when economic conditions are good. This expansion of credit is not a "monetary expansion" and is not inflationary, because it does not alter the value of the currency. Likewise, a contraction of credit in the event of an economic downturn is not a "monetary contraction" and is not deflationary.

All monetary transactions take place with base money. It may seem that you can buy things with "money in your bank account," which is a loan to the bank (bond), or "money in your money market account," which is technically an equity shareholding in an investment fund that purchases short-term debt instruments, but that is because the bank automatically takes care of the messy details regarding the repayment of your bank credits in base money. Checking or other banking transactions take place with base money—specifically, banking reserves, which are maintained at the central bank.

The term *monetary* refers primarily to changes in the value of the currency, and the term *financial* refers primarily to changes in credit relationships. A crisis may have both monetary and financial characteristics. If you lose your job and cannot pay your mortgage, you are suffering a financial crisis, not a monetary crisis. If you are unfortunate enough to be caught in a hyperinflationary period, you are suffering the effects of a monetary crisis. However, one effect of hyperinflation could be to solve your financial crisis: It is much easier to repay debts with devalued currency. (This is one attraction of inflation.) Your lender, however, may suffer a financial crisis due to the monetary crisis, since its loans to you will become worthless.

The Federal Reserve, since it neither lends nor borrows today, also does not "create credit," which is another name for the same thing. The Fed has very little power besides its ability to create and destroy base money. The primary question it faces is how much base money to supply, and when. All of the statistical and policy structures in existence today are aimed at solving this question.

Demand for base money emerges from the citizenry's interest in holding money. Demand changes from minute to minute, second to second. It is inherently chaotic and unpredictable. Virtually every act involving money changes the demand for money in some way, large or small. By taking a coffee can of bills to the bank, the holder's personal demand for money falls. By collecting bills in a can, the holder's personal demand for money increases. There is no way to measure the demand for money directly.

It might seem that a person's demand for money is limitless, but that is not the case. A person's demand for the things that money can buy may be limitless, but the demand for money itself is limited. If you have $10 in your wallet, you may decide that this is insufficient for the expenses you might face over the day, and so you go to the bank to withdraw cash. You have personally demanded more base money. If the bank runs out of cash, it will request more from the Treasury, and if it runs low on reserves, it will acquire additional reserves from the Federal Reserve (that's how the Fed got its name). However, if you have $1,000 in your wallet, you might decide this is excessive and go to the bank to deposit the money in your account, thus reducing your demand for base money. You have traded your money for a bank deposit, which is a type of bond.

Every other person or corporation or government in the world is making similar calculations, and in aggregate this constitutes the demand for money. There is no money that is not held by someone or some organization. "The economy" as an entity does not demand money. Money is not some sort of hydraulic substance whirling through the economy's machinery. People demand money—and in the case of the U.S. dollar, people all over the globe, not merely those in the United States itself. Because it is based on the decision of individuals and individual circumstance, it is easy to see why the demand for money is variable and unpredictable.

Modern money can be recognized as the non-interest-bearing debt of the government. The citizenry decides how much government debt it chooses to hold as non-interest-bearing debt, for use in transactions, and how much as interest-bearing debt, as longer-term assets. Here the opportunity cost of using money—namely, the interest forgone—is apparent, which describes why the demand for money is limited. As a corollary, the opportunity cost increases along with the increase in nominal yields on government bonds. This implies that people will tend to be more willing to hold non-interest-bearing cash when interest rates are low and less willing when interest rates are high.

Notice how easily the aggregate demand for money can change due to any number of factors. For example, if people are accustomed to using paper money, but then adopt debit cards or credit cards or other techniques that reduce the need to carry paper bills, the demand for money can shrink, or at least not grow as quickly as before. If the central bank fails to accommodate this relative reduction in the demand for money, the result would be a fall in the value of the currency, or inflation. Likewise, a mania for keeping one's wealth in the form of banknotes in home safes (as happened recently in Japan) could well increase the demand for money, which must be supplied by the central bank if it is to avoid a deflation. Before the beginning of the year 2000, many central banks printed enormous supplies of paper bills, fearing that the demand for money would explode as people took precautions against a breakdown of the electronic payments system.

The demand for money tends to grow in sympathy with the economy. A larger, faster-growing economy tends to demand more money. A smaller, slower-growing or shrinking economy needs less money. The demand for money often moves in anticipation of future economic performance, so policy changes or even offhand comments by politicians and government officials can immediately affect the demand for money, and thus the foreign exchange market.

The demand for money often varies cyclically. For example, in Japan, where the use of paper money is high and banks are traditionally closed on weekends, people withdraw large amounts of cash on Fridays to pay for all their weekend expenses. The demand for paper bills rises. During the weekend, these bills move from people's wallets to the cash registers of shops and restaurants. On Monday the shops and restaurants deposit the money back in the bank, and the demand for money falls.

The demand for money also varies over the course of the year—for example, during tax time or anytime large numbers of transactions might be made, like the end of the month or the end of the fiscal year. Historically, harvest season in the autumn was a time when many monetary transactions were made, raising the demand for money and credit. The need to accommodate these large short-term changes in the demand for money led to the development of central banking in the nineteenth century.

A central bank, or other monetary authority, with a policy of currency stability will adjust the supply of base money in response to changes in demand. If the currency's value is rising, the central bank knows that its supply is insufficient. It buys bonds on the open market, creating new supply, until the currency's value again returns to its target value, such as a parity with gold bullion. If a currency's value is falling, the central bank can sell bonds on the open market, shrinking the supply of money.

If it wishes, the central bank can buy and sell currency on foreign exchange markets. In that case, the central bank ends up with debt of foreign governments instead of domestic debt. Except for that small technicality, the process is the same, and the effects are essentially the same as well.

Though this system of managing supply to meet demand may seem foreign at first, it actually served as the basis of currency management from at least the seventeenth century to the early 1970s, and it remains a common feature of monetary systems today. To illustrate how the system works, let's take an everyday example: the exchange rate between dollars and quarters.

There aren't just dollar bills in the U.S. monetary system, but actually several currencies: pennies, nickels, dimes, quarters, $1 bills, $5 bills, $10 bills, $20 bills, $50 bills, $100 bills, and electronic bank reserves. Each one has a supply (there are a certain number of pennies in circulation) and each one has a specific demand. You need quarters to pay parking meters, dollars to pay tips, twenties to buy clothes, and hundreds to make large illegal transactions. Each one also has a specific value and exchange rate: four quarters exchanging for a dollar bill, and 10 dollar bills exchanging for a $10 bill.

How does the government manage these 11 discrete currencies? How does it know how many dimes to produce and how many $10 bills? Why don't their exchange rates fluctuate? These are not trivial questions. There is nothing intrinsic to either the quarter or the dollar bill, such as their metallic content or commodity value, that forces one be exactly four times as valuable as the other. Nor can government edict alone force a fixed exchange rate. It would only cause a black market in coins and bills.

If there were a shortage of quarters relative to dollar bills, for example, eventually someone wishing to use a parking meter or Laundromat would offer three quarters for a dollar bill. Their exchange rates would fluctuate.

Instead, the U.S. government is willing to trade one for the other, and in this way adjusts the supply of each to meet its demand. The currencies are convertible, or redeemable. If you have four quarters and want a dollar bill, you can take it to a commercial bank. For you, at that instant, the value of four quarters was less than that of a dollar bill. Your personal supply of quarters exceeded your personal demand, and your personal supply of dollar bills was short of your personal demand.

The bank may later trade the quarters with someone who has an excess of dollar bills. But if the bank already has plenty of quarters and can't find anyone who wants to accept them in trade—in other words, if there is an aggregate surplus of quarters—it will take them to the government in trade for bank reserves or dollar bills. The government will accept the quarters and make the trade. The effect of the trade is to remove the excess quarters from circulation and add dollar bills. The supply of quarters shrinks and the supply of dollar bills increases. In this way, the values of quarters and dollar bills are held at a fixed rate of exchange.

It is a very simple step to extend this example to real-world currencies. If you substitute *yen*, *franc*, *mark*, and *pound* for *penny*, *dime*, *quarter*, and *$5 bill*, you get a rough description of the international monetary system of the 1950s and 1960s. From 1999 to 2001, the central banks of the eurozone fixed their currencies together through the same mechanism, while they awaited the issuance of universal paper bills and coins. Was this difficult? No problems were noted.

In the 1960s, a penny was worth $\frac{1}{100}$ of a dollar. A yen was worth $\frac{1}{360}$. Why should a yen be any harder to stabilize than a penny?

The Japanese government pays its employees in yen. But you can't buy U.S.-made goods with yen. You must have dollars. Because the Japanese government, the supplier of yen, does not trade yen for dollars, and thus does not manage the supply of yen in order to maintain a fixed ratio of value with the dollar, yen holders must turn to someone—anyone—willing to trade dollars for yen. The yen is a floating currency.

But imagine that the Japanese government agreed to trade yen for dollars at a fixed rate, just as the U.S. government is willing to trade pennies for dollar bills. Any excess yen would arrive daily at the government's doorstep, with hands outstretched for dollars. And if there were a shortage of yen, people would show up at the government's doorstep with dollars in exchange for yen. In this way the government would know whether its supply of yen was excessive or insufficient compared to dollars, relative to a certain exchange rate, or *parity*. As long as the Japanese government dutifully adjusted the supply of yen in accordance with the market signals it received at its *dollar window*

56

(the office where people came to exchange dollars and yen with the government), the exchange rate between yen and dollars would be fixed, just like the exchange rate between pennies and dollars. During the 1950s and 1960s, when the yen was linked to the dollar at a fixed rate of ¥360 per dollar, this mechanism was in active use.

Japan, in effect, used a currency board. Countries that use currency boards have no discretionary monetary policy. The system automatically adjusts to market conditions, just like the system that maintains dollars and quarters at a fixed rate. That is why fixed-rate systems such as currency boards are market-based systems, while a floating currency, in which a government determines the money supply through its policy boards, is a centrally planned system that is directly analogous to the central planning of industry practiced by the Soviet Union and other such communist governments.

Often a mistake is made here by people who confuse money and credit. It is not the responsibility of a currency board to guarantee the debt liabilities of banks. For example, Mexico, using a currency board with a 1:1 peso/dollar exchange rate, may have a monetary base of 10 billion pesos and currency reserves of 10 billion dollars. Mexican banks may have 100 billion pesos in deposit liabilities. If depositors choose to withdraw all their deposits from the banks and hold them as banknotes, then banks have to come up with 100 billion pesos in base money. The Mexican banks would borrow 100 billion dollars on the worldwide dollar money market and take the dollars to the currency board office for exchange into pesos. The Mexican monetary base would expand to 110 billion pesos, and foreign reserves would also expand to 110 billion dollars. In this case the U.S. Federal Reserve would act as the *lender of last resort* for the Mexican financial system.

It may seem at times that currency boards fail, as happened in 2001 in Turkey or Argentina, but actually the currency boards were abandoned voluntarily in the midst of crises that were caused by other factors.

A gold standard is simply a system that uses currency board–type mechanisms of supply adjustment to peg a currency, not to another country's currency, but to gold, the universal currency of human-kind. The exchange rate with gold, more commonly termed the *price of gold*, remains fixed.

Instead of using the system of convertibility, a peg could be based on currency market prices. When the peso falls against the dollar, from US$1.00 to US$0.98 for example, the Mexican central bank would sell peso-denominated Mexican government bonds on the open market, extinguishing the pesos received in trade and reducing the supply of pesos. When the peso rose against its parity (say, to US$1.02), the central bank would buy bonds, increasing the supply of pesos. In this way, the peg would be maintained even without convertibility. It is not necessary to have any foreign reserves at all to operate a currency board–type peg. A central bank maintains control over its currency even if it runs out of reserves, domestic or foreign, as long as it has some way of altering the supply of base money.

Since central banks have virtually no powers except to increase and decrease the supply of base money, all of the different policy frameworks that have been tried over the years—gold standard, currency board, monetary aggregate targeting, currency basket, interest rate peg, consumer price index targeting, and so forth—differ only in their targets, which are merely red–light/green–light signals that show when and how much to adjust the supply of base money. The present monetary system in the United States is almost identical to a currency board or gold standard in operation, differing only in its choice of policy goals. It uses short-term interest rates as a target rather than the value of foreign currencies or gold. When the short-term interest rate rises above the target level, the Fed buys government debt securities on the open market, creating new base money. This ends up as bank reserves and tends to increase the funds available for borrowing, thus pushing down the interest rate. When the short-term interest rate sags below the peg, the Fed sells bonds, taking dollars in return and extinguishing them. This reduces bank reserves, shrinking the funds available for borrowing, which tends to drive up the interest rate.

Of course, if a central bank is adding and subtracting base money in response to an interest rate peg policy, it cannot do so in response to a currency board or gold standard policy. To enjoy the benefits of a currency board or gold standard, governments must abandon the urge to manipulate the economy by twiddling interest rates.

Pegging a currency to another through supply adjustment is a fine and effective technique, but that alone does not produce a stable currency. You can't peg the yen to the dollar and the dollar to the yen and solve all your problems. A Mexican peso pegged to the U.S. dollar would mean the exchange rate between the two would be fixed, but that does not mean that the currencies would not fluctuate in value in absolute terms. They would simply fluctuate in parallel, just as quarters and dollar bills do. In the end, there needs to be some concept of an absolute standard of value. Having the quarter, dollar bill, and $10 bill pegged to each other, as they are today, does not prevent inflation or deflation. Though the notion of monetary value can sometimes seem abstract, the effects of changes in the value of a currency are a very real and tangible phenomenon.

The relative value of currencies can be seen in the free market for currencies. If the U.S. dollar is trading for 200 yen, and soon thereafter the dollar is trading for 100 yen, then the value of the dollar relative to the yen has fallen by half, and the value of the yen compared to the dollar has doubled. However, it is not possible to know from the foreign exchange market alone whether the dollar's absolute value has fallen or the yen's has risen, or whether there has been some combination of the two. It could be that the yen's value has fallen in half while the dollar's has fallen by a factor of 4 (as in the 1970s). Or perhaps both have risen (as in 1999–2000). When central bankers of different countries meet, they often argue about which country is responsible for changes in exchange rates. These arguments usually end unresolved.

How does the central bank know the absolute value of a currency? This is indeed a real problem. A perfect measure of absolute monetary value does not exist, but humans have decided over thousands of years of experimentation that gold is the best approximation of stable value available, and one that, despite its minor flaws, works rather splendidly in practice. Gold's value varies very little. Gold thus serves as the measuring rod against which the value of currencies can be measured. Gold has been used as a monetary benchmark for millennia, its stability confirmed by centuries of experience.

Even if the monetary authorities chose, for whatever reason, to ignore gold, or if gold didn't exist, nevertheless they would still need some way of gauging the value of their currencies—through observations of the bond market, foreign exchange rates, commodity prices, and so forth. Gold simply makes this conundrum quite a bit simpler than it would otherwise be.

The price (or value) of money is not expressed by interest rates. An amazing number of people to this day continue to confuse the price of money, which can be found in a relative sense in the currency market and in an absolute sense in the gold market, and the price of credit, which can be found in the short-term debt market, or *money market*. Actually, the rate of interest is the price of borrowing capital, which is not money per se but the time and labor, represented in money units, of the citizenry.

Here is John Stuart Mill, a great economist of his era, trying to straighten out this basic misunderstanding way back in 1848:

It is unfortunate that in the very outset of the subject we have to clear from our path a formidable ambiguity of language. The Value of Money is to appearance an expression as precise, as free from possibility of misunderstanding, as any in science. . . . But unfortunately the same phrase is also employed, in the current language of commerce, in a very different sense. . . . Borrowing capital is universally called borrowing money; the loan market is called the money market; those who have their capital disposable for investment on loan are called the monied class; and the equivalent given for the use of capital, or in other words, interest, is not only called the interest of money, but, by a grosser perversion of terms, the value of money. This misapplication of the language, assisted by some fallacious appearances which we shall notice and clear up hereafter, has created a general notion among persons in business, that the Value of Money, meaning the rate of interest, has an intimate connexion with the Value of Money in its proper sense, the value or purchasing power of the circulating medium.[5]

Mill is being careless when he equates the value of money with its "purchasing power." This is a crude generalization, easily misunderstood, and the better classical economists have always labored to distinguish the difference between the value of a currency and what it can buy in the moment. It is quite common that, immediately after a currency is devalued, its purchasing power is largely unchanged, as prices have not yet adjusted to the devaluation. On the other hand, if you get on a plane from New York City to dollarized Ecuador, you would find the purchasing power of your dollars changed dramatically, although of course their value is the same. As David Ricardo, a successful speculator who, in his early retirement, became one of the finest economists of the early-nineteenth century, explained in 1817:

> It has been my endeavor carefully to distinguish between a low value of money and a high value of corn, or any other commodity with which money may be compared. These have been generally considered as meaning the same thing; but it is evident that when corn rises from five to ten shillings a bushel, it may be owing either to a fall in the value of money or to a rise in the value of corn. . . .
>
> The effects resulting from a high price of corn when produced by the rise in the value of corn, and when caused by a fall in the value of money, are totally different.[6]

A hundred and thirty-two years later, Ludwig von Mises, one of the leading classical economists of the twentieth century, struggled against the same misunderstanding:

> It is a popular fallacy to believe that perfect money should be neutral and endowed with unchanging purchasing power, and that the goal of monetary policy should be to realize this perfect money. It

is easy to understand this idea as a reaction against the still more popular postulates of the inflationists. But it is an excessive reaction, it is itself confused and contradictory, and it has worked havoc because it was strengthened by an inveterate error inherent in the thought of many philosophers and economists. . . .

Changes in the purchasing power of money, i.e., in the exchange ratio between money and the vendible goods and commodities, can originate either from the side of money or from the side of the vendible goods and commodities. The change in the data which provokes them can occur either in the demand for and supply of money or in the demand for and supply of the other goods and services.[7]

Prices can change for all manner of reasons, one of them being a change in the value of the monetary standard. A price change alone does not imply a change in the value of the currency. To take a simple example, when a country institutes or raises its sales tax, the price of goods increases by the amount of the tax. Indexes such as the consumer price index will reflect the price rise. This is not a monetary phenomenon—though, unbelievable as it may seem, central bankers have often reacted as if it were, with predictably bad results.

There is no "price index" in real life, no "general price level," just specific prices for specific goods and services at specific times and places. The cost of a transistor has famously collapsed to near zero. Is this a change in the value of money? Of course not. At the same time, the cost of San Francisco real estate skyrocketed. This was not a monetary effect, either, although it is intimately related to the price of transistors.

Prices differ depending on where something is purchased, and this is the motivation for comparison shopping. Prices change dramatically in short periods of time—at an after-Christmas sale, for example. Prices even change depending on the amount purchased. Any visitor to a discount store knows that prices can fall dramatically if you buy in bulk, although a stockbroker has the opposite experience. None of these are monetary phenomena. The notion of comparing goods from different time periods is particularly dubious. What can be gleaned from comparing the price of a 1990 Toyota Camry automobile with a 2000 model? In the end, statistical efforts such as the consumer price index are more effective than should be expected, given the absurdity of their task, but they remain academic exercises that have no counterpart in the real economy. They are not "real." The common practice of taking a genuine, tangible market-generated artifact, such as an interest rate, and combining it with a statistical abstraction to create a "real interest rate" is an exercise in gross misrepresentation. Commodities indexes tend to be better, since it is easier to compare the prices of wheat or oil today with those of 20 years ago, and the commodities are internationally traded in broad, standardized markets. But commodities, too, have large nonmonetary price swings, caused by drought, flood, war, or countless other things.

Even the most basic commodities change over time. Beef today, grown with hormones and antibiotics and dubious feed substances, on government subsidy, is considerably different from the hormone-free, range-fed beef of the 1950s or 1880s. This difference is evident in the large premium paid for 1950s-style beef, now called "organic" beef, in supermarkets. The same holds true of genetically modified corn.

Prices are supposed to change. The information transmitted in changing prices organizes the market economy. Prices are an avenue of communication by which the citizenry cooperates in its productive endeavors. The great productive advantage the market economies have over the centrally planned economies is the efficiency with which information is transmitted through market price changes. "Stable prices" is a nonsensical goal. The real goal is a stable currency, which allows prices to form without being molested by monetary distortion (i.e., inflation and deflation).

Economic development itself can cause a general rise in prices. In a developing country, it may be possible to get lodging for $3 a night or a haircut for $0.50. Even if the currency of the country is pegged to the U.S. dollar (as has often been the case), one would expect prices to rise relative to those in the United States as the country becomes more wealthy, with prices eventually resembling those in fully developed countries. Even within a country, a region that is enjoying a boom may experience a general rise in prices, while prices might fall in regions that are losing appeal. When prices in Tokyo are supposedly 20 percent higher than in New York, endless commentaries appear about the exchange value of the yen and the balance of trade. Yet nobody thinks it out of the ordinary that prices in New York City might be 50 percent higher than those in Buffalo or Rochester.

The same thing, of course, happens to wages. Rising incomes is the whole point of economic development. At the beginning of its industrialization, a country has an average per capita income of $1,000 a year. Three decades of development later, the country's citizens are making $10,000 a year. This is not inflation.

Income or corporate taxes are cut, and the stock market rises. Real estate becomes more valuable. This is not inflation.

To straighten out the confusion between price changes that are due to monetary distortion and those that are not, *inflation* is defined here strictly as a fall in the currency's value (as would be reflected in the currency's exchange rate with gold) and *deflation* as a rise in the currency's value. In other words, inflation and deflation are defined as strictly monetary phenomena. Price changes due to other factors can be called a *noninflationary price rise*. Von Mises termed these "cash-induced" and "goods-induced" price changes. Odd as it may seem today, the terms *inflation* and *deflation* originally had strictly monetary meanings, as von Mises explains:

> The notions of inflation and deflation . . . were not created by economists, but by the mundane speech of the public and of politicians. They implied the popular fallacy that there is such a thing as a neutral money or money of stable purchasing power. From this point of view the term inflation was applied to signify cash-induced changes [declining currency value] resulting in a drop in purchasing power, and the term deflation to signify cash-induced

changes [rising currency value] resulting in a rise in purchasing power. . . .

The semantic revolution which is one of the characteristic features of our day has also changed the traditional connotation of the terms inflation and deflation. What many people today call inflation or deflation is no longer the great increase or decrease in the supply of money [causing a change in currency value], but its inexorable consequences, the general tendency toward a rise or a fall in commodity prices and wage rates. This innovation is by no means harmless. It plays an important role in fomenting the popular tendencies toward inflationism.

First of all, there is no longer any term available to signify what inflation used to signify. It is impossible to fight a policy which you cannot name. Statesmen and writers no longer have the opportunity of resorting to a terminology accepted and understood by the public when they want to question the expediency of issuing huge amounts of additional money. They must enter into a detailed analysis and description of this policy with full particulars and minute accounts whenever they want to refer to it, and they must repeat this bothersome procedure in every sentence in which they deal with the subject. As this policy has no name, it becomes self-understood and a matter of fact. It goes on luxuriantly.

The second mischief is that those engaged in futile and hopeless attempts to fight the inevitable consequences of inflation—the rise in prices—are disguising their endeavors as a fight against inflation. While merely fighting symptoms, they pretend to fight the root causes of the evil. Because they do not comprehend the causal relation between the increase in the quantity of money on the one hand and the rise in prices on the other, they practically make things worse. . . . Thus the confusion of inflation and its consequences in fact can directly bring about more inflation.

It is obvious that this new-fangled connotation of the terms inflation and deflation is utterly confusing and misleading and must be unconditionally rejected.[8]

Thus the concept of value is independent of any other single price in the economy, and certainly independent of statistical price indexes. Commodities price indexes, made up of goods that change little from decade to decade, such as wool or wheat, are observed to be stable in the long term under a stable currency, but of course may fluctuate greatly in the shorter term due to weather, wars, tariffs, economic conditions, or any number of other factors. Some thinkers have concluded that *value* is ultimately a representation of the most basic economic good, namely, the time, ability, and labor of humans: capital. Economies are ultimately manifestations of human effort. But it is not necessary to verify or quantify this claim to make use of the concept of value. Gold, the most monetary of commodities, has been chosen as the best existing measure of value available. It is difficult to say how accurate gold is as a measure of value, because if a more accurate measure existed against which gold could be compared, we would use that as a measure of value instead of gold.

When measuring things, the usual terminology is to denote the number of measurement units per the thing being measured. Thus we say that "Steve is 1.75 meters tall," not "Steve's length is 0.5714 Steves per meter." It would make sense to refer to currency values the same way: "$100 is worth 2.87 ounces of gold" instead of "$35 per ounce of gold." This book shall refer to currency values in the traditional terminology, but it must always be remembered that, in virtually all instances, due to gold's stability of value, changes in the currency/gold ratio represent changes in currency value.

Supply, demand, and *value:* These are the fundamental concepts of the classical view of money. They are simple, but their implications are far-reaching. The model implies that issuers of money, such as today's central banks, have full control over their currencies. No currency is at the mercy of "the market." If the currency is deemed too low, the central bank need only contract supply. If the currency is too high, the central bank need only expand supply.

This model ignores interest rate differentials, the balance of payments, capital flows, price levels, growth rates, differences in taxation systems, tariffs, government debts and deficits, unemployment rates, stock market movements, savings rates, or any other such thing. These things may affect the demand for money and are thus of interest to currency traders, but since virtually everything affects demand there is no reason to single out specific influences.

The ideal currency is as stable and unchanging in value as the meter, liter, or kilogram. The notion that currencies need to be adjusted to economic conditions is wholly erroneous, except to the extent that the adjustment may correct prior monetary error. California, for example, has 36 million people, more than most of the countries of Europe. If price, trade, or growth statistics were kept for California, they would often diverge from the rest of the United States. Does this mean California needs its own currency? Of course not.

All the currency fluctuation in the world is due to the actions of central banks. The monetary authorities' traditional responsibility is to match supply with demand, producing a stable currency. The fact that central banks have recently ignored this responsibility, indeed hardly know that it exists, does not absolve them of blame for all of the monetary disasters of the past 30 years—every single one. Incompetence is a poor excuse.

It is true that many countries have tried and failed to peg their currencies, with disastrous currency crises often the result. This is because such governments did not properly use supply adjustment to maintain the peg. Often the peg is maintained by some form of government coercion. The end result of this strategy is that either the government becomes extremely coercive, with draconian capital and exchange controls and the like, or the desire of the world citizenry to trade on its own terms overwhelms the coercive powers of the government. With a proper currency management system, no government coercion is necessary, because the government follows the dictates of the market by adjusting supply.

Instead, governments try to influence currency markets through large-scale sales or purchases of foreign currencies, thus "scalding the fingers of speculators." This is merely another form of government coercion, and the government's coercive powers are represented by its foreign exchange reserves, the "bullets" with which it "punishes" the currency markets.

Like all artificial price controls, these "foreign exchange interventions" are destined for failure. When combined with an interest rate peg policy, they typically do not alter the supply of domestic currency available and thus have little effect on the value of the domestic currency. The money that is taken out of circulation by the foreign exchange intervention is immediately returned to circulation by the interest rate peg, a process known as *sterilization*. The supply of money is no different than if there had been no intervention at all. The exchange rate is perturbed for a short period, but soon after reflects again the fact that the supply of currency is unchanged. Rather than supporting the currency, after the intervention, the currency's value may fall further, for it has become apparent that the central bank is incompetent. Speculators, betting on continued blunders by the monetary authorities, sell the currency short in enormous quantity. The monetary authorities soon run out of foreign reserves with which to conduct their short-term market perturbations, and the currency falls like a stone.

Central banks adopt this nonsensical approach because of a misguided attempt to separate domestic monetary policy from foreign monetary policy. Today they are even overseen by different departments—in the United States, the Treasury is in charge of foreign monetary policy and the Federal Reserve is in charge of domestic monetary policy. This bizarre arrangement has been replicated all over the world.

There is only one currency, and it has only one supply, one demand, and one value. It cannot be made to do two things simultaneously. Domestic monetary policy is typically based on interest rate targets. Foreign monetary policy is based on exchange rates. But in trying to accommodate these two policy frameworks, the central banks can do only one thing—adjust the supply of money, either in terms of the interest rate target or the exchange rate target. At some point the two come into conflict, in which case usually the interest rate target takes priority, the exchange rate target is abandoned, and the effects of foreign exchange intervention are sterilized. (If the foreign monetary policy takes precedence and the interest rate target is abandoned, the system in effect becomes a currency board–like mechanism.) To maintain the two impossibly contradictory policy goals, central banks intervene in currency markets in a losing battle, not with the market, but with their own domestic monetary policy, screaming in anguish as they bang themselves in the head and shoot themselves in the foot. This farce is a source of great hilarity for those who understand it, and for some speculators, a source of enormous profits.

Governments attempted to cleave monetary policy into two because, during the period from 1935 to 1980, they wished to incite an inflationary boom without suffering a fall in the currency's value. It is impossible to devalue and not devalue a currency at the same time, as those governments that have attempted it have amply proven. Although few major governments pursue devaluation actively and overtly today, having learned their lessons the hard way during the 1970s, nevertheless they have inherited an operational framework designed for devaluation. Most of the academic, intellectual, institutional, and policy structures in the world today are relics from the era of inflationism. They cannot be used to create a stable monetary system, and must be discarded.

CHAPTER 4

INFLATION, DEFLATION, AND FLOATING CURRENCIES

The Effects of Monetary Distortion on the Economy

Inflation is a persistent fall in the value of a monetary standard. National inflation is the fall in value of a specific national monetary standard. Multinational inflation refers to the decline in value of more than one national standard. . . . Contemporary understanding of the inflation issue is hardly better than it was several centuries ago, despite the sophistication of very large economic models involving great mathematical and statistical sophistication but very primitive economic understanding.

—Economist Robert Mundell, 1975[1]

If the Italians or Romans did in the end make such alterations [debasement], as appears from ancient bad money sometimes to be found in the country, this was probably the reason why their noble empire came to nothing. It appears therefore that these changes are so bad that they are essentially impermissable.

—Nicholas Oresme, *De Moneta*, circa 1360[2]

In theoretical investigation there is only one meaning that can rationally be attached to the expression inflation: an increase in the quantity of money . . . that is not offset by a corresponding increase in the need for money . . . so that a fall in the objective exchange value of money

71

must occur. Again, deflation (or restriction, or contraction) signifies a diminution of the quantity of money . . . which is not offset by a corresponding diminution of the demand for money . . . so that an increase in the objective exchange value of money occurs.

—**Ludwig von Mises, *The Theory of Money and Credit*, 1912[3]**

Inflation: 3. Undue expansion or increase, from overissue;—said of currency.
Inflationist: One who favors an increased or very large issue of money.

—***Webster's Dictionary*, 1913**

I.

Inflation is defined as a decline in the currency's value. It will first be noted in the currency's exchange rate with gold, and likely in the foreign exchange market and the international market for commodities. Inflation will eventually result in rising prices, but that is only one of its many deleterious effects. Inflations are sometimes accidental, but often they are intentional, in which case they are known as *currency devaluations*.

The temptation to devalue can be intense, and as a result inflation is common throughout history. Attention always focuses on those parties who will benefit from the devaluation, while those who suffer, inevitably a greater number, are easily overlooked. Inflation is sometimes perceived as a redistribution policy, a sort of welfare system. A brief illusion of economic health can be created. As a result, governments and their economic advisers have often reached for currency devaluation to cure apparent problems, though inflation doesn't solve the problems and instead creates new ones.

The submerged desire to devalue the currency, in a time of crisis, is the only real reason for government manipulation of the monetary system today. The private sector is perfectly capable of managing a stable currency on its own. In the nineteenth century, nonintervention in monetary affairs was a first principle of government in both Britain and the United States.

The dangers of inflation have been understood for a very long time:

> Lenin was certainly right. There is no subtler, no surer means of overturning the existing basis of Society than to debauch the currency. The process engages all the hidden forces of economic law on the side of destruction, and does it in a manner which not one man in a million is able to diagnose.
>
> —John Maynard Keynes, "Inflation and Deflation," 1919[4]

> [Currency devaluation] occasions a general and most pernicious subversion of the fortunes of private people; enriching in most cases the idle and profuse debtor at the expense of the industrious and frugal creditor, and transporting a great part of the national capital from the hands which were likely to increase and improve it, to those which are likely to dissipate and destroy it.
>
> —Adam Smith, *Inquiry into the Nature and Causes of the Wealth of Nations*, 1776[5]

> [Currency devaluation] discourages all prudence and thrift. It encourages squandering, gambling, reckless waste of all kinds. It often makes it more profitable to speculate than to produce. It tears apart the whole fabric of stable economic relationships. Its inexcusable injustices drive men toward desperate remedies. It plants the seeds of fascism and communism. It leads men to demand totalitarian controls. It ends invariably in bitter disillusion and collapse.
>
> —Henry Hazlitt, *Economics in One Lesson*, 1946[6]

Although there are countless scourges which in general debilitate kingdoms, principalities, and republics, the four most important (in my judgment) are dissention, [abnormal] morality, barren soil, and debasement of the currency. The first three are so obvious that nobody is unaware of their existence. But the fourth, which concerns money, is taken into account by few persons and only the most perspicacious. For it undermines states, not by a single attack all at once, but gradually and in a certain covert manner.

—Nicholas Copernicus, "Treatise on Debasement," 1517[7]

I say that a thing which tends to bring a realm to ruin is disgraceful and harmful to the king and his heirs, my first premise; that it extends and changes [the kingdom] to a tyranny, my second, and that it does so by alteration of the coinage, my third.

—Nicholas Oresme, *De Moneta*, circa 1360[8]

The first panacea for a mismanaged nation is inflation of the currency; the second is war. Both bring a temporary prosperity; both bring a permanent ruin. But both are the refuge of political and economic opportunists.

—Ernest Hemingway

What happens when a currency's value falls in half? The effects of inflation are myriad, and virtually all economic relationships are distorted. The notion that inflation is merely "rising prices" is laughably simplistic. Here we will suggest only a few of the most obvious phenomena.

For this example, imagine that a currency had a value of $100 per ounce of gold, then fell quickly to $200 per ounce, where it was restabilized.

The most obvious effect would be in foreign exchange markets, where the currency's value would fall in half compared with other stable currencies. Foreign holders of debt would see half of their principal vanish. Wages and expenses in the devaluing country would also fall by half, in gold terms, which would mean that companies would be able to sell their products for much less, thus undercutting international competitors. Imports would double in price. Any foreigners who had borrowed in the devalued currency would experience an instant windfall.

Other countries don't much like this competitive devaluation, as it is the epitome of unfair trade. They may react with protectionist tariffs or with devaluations of their own.

Prices in the devaluing country would eventually adjust to the devalued currency. In other words, something that cost $100 (equivalent in value to one ounce of gold) before the devaluation will tend to cost $200 (equivalent to one ounce of gold) afterward. However, this price adjustment process, in practice, can take a very long time to fully play out. Prices for internationally traded commodities will tend to adjust first, typically within a year or so of the devaluation. Other prices (medical expenses, rent, education expenses, etc.) can take up to two or even three decades to fully adjust. The slowness of adjustment is due in large part to the existence of long-term contracts. Anyone with a long-term lease, for example, will enjoy predevaluation rents for as long as 20 years. Homeowners with 30-year fixed-rate mortgages enjoy effectively the same advantage. Companies with long-term debt will find their debt obligations lightened. These companies can thus keep their prices lower, and the companies' customers thus enjoy somewhat lower costs as well. As leases expire and are renewed at postdevaluation prices, as homes are sold to new buyers, as corporate debt matures and fixed capital is replaced at postdevaluation prices, the higher costs are passed on to consumers, who in turn must ask for higher wages to maintain their standard of living, which in turn raises costs for their employers. We can imagine a large crowd of people shuffling from point A to point B while attempting to keep the relationships between each other unchanged. This is a rough sketch of how the multiyear adjustment process takes place.

Economies that have experienced regular devaluation, such as might be found in Latin America, will tend to have much shorter contract lengths, and the adjustment process can be much quicker.

This effect of rising prices is a typical target of public scorn, but it is a natural and benign process by which the citizenry renegotiates price relationships that were disrupted by the change in the value of the currency, in this way returning the economy to its highest productive state. The faster this price rise happens, the faster the economy can adjust and reach a new equilibrium.

As prices adjust to the new monetary conditions, they do not do so in parallel. Workers do not demand higher wages in perfect lock-step. There is no one "price level," represented by a single variable in economists' algebraic simplifications, but only billions of prices. Nor is there one "wage level," but only millions of individual contracts between employers and employees. Price adjustments take place on a piecemeal basis. Each change introduces an arbitrary alteration in the relationships between economic actors, and each alteration produces arbitrary winners and losers.

In the period after World War I, when the British pound had been devalued and floated, the young John Maynard Keynes wrote:

> Such changes [in the value of money] have produced in the past, and are producing now, the vastest social consequences, because, as we all know, when the value of money changes, it does not change equally, for all persons or for all purposes. A man's receipts and his outgoings are not all modified in one uniform proportion. Thus a change in prices and rewards, as measured in money, generally affects different classes unequally, transfers wealth from one to another, bestows affluence here and embarrassment there, and redistributes Fortune's favors so as to frustrate design and disappoint expectation.[9]

At this point it should be clear that basing central bank policy on the consumer price index (CPI) is purest foolishness, since this statistic, besides being subject to endless nonmonetary factors (including purposeful government manipulation), is absurdly insensitive and reflects changes in currency value from as much as two or three decades earlier. CPI indexes tend to be heavily weighted toward housing, health care, and education, three sectors that adjust to devaluation very slowly.

Monetary distortion also distorts profit and loss, and since profit determines the use of scarce capital, capital is misallocated. Some industries, possibly commodities industries, get too much capital, while others get too little. Perfectly good businesses go bust, and mediocre businesses enjoy an artificial success. Of course, this is wasteful and inefficient.

Since prices effectively fall in half if the value of the currency falls in half, demand for goods can increase. After all, who doesn't like a half-off sale? Devaluation often creates an artificial inflationary economic boom, which is much loved by devaluationists in government. In the United States during the 1970s, for example, official real gross domestic product growth was often over 5 percent. But this just illustrates the unreliability of official statistics: Everyone living at the time agreed that the economy was steadily worsening. This false boom effect is the infamous inflationary overheating.

Unfortunately, genuine economic growth is often mistaken for an inflationary overheating, with predictably bad results as the government attempts to correct for nonexistent inflation by crippling the economy through tax hikes and more monetary tomfoolery. Inflation can create a false growth, but genuine growth does not cause inflation. Translated into the terms of classical economics, "growth causes a decline in currency value" is nonsense. There is no known limit to how fast economies can grow with a stable currency. During the 1960s, on a gold standard (and thus a situation in which *nominal* equals *real*), Japan's economy experienced nominal growth rates in excess of 20 percent per annum. If this was possible with all the flaws in policy of that time, probably growth rates in excess of 30 percent per annum could be achieved under optimal conditions.

One of the most insidious effects of devaluation is on the tax system. If an income tax is *progressive* (i.e., higher tax rates at higher income), then the effects of devaluation will be to throw people into higher tax brackets. Rates intended for the superrich fall on doctors and lawyers; rates intended for doctors fall on middle managers; rates intended for middle managers fall on schoolteachers and tradespeople. Nominal capital gains are taxed, even as the real value of assets declines. Therefore, $1 must become $2 just to keep pace with currency devaluation. But this "capital gain" is taxed, eating away not only at real gains but at the principal itself. Corporate depreciation, based on predevaluation purchase prices, does not reflect that equipment will cost twice as much to replace. The effect is an increase in corporate taxes.

The effect of higher taxes is often to cause a further decline in currency value, first because economic contraction tends to cause a reduction in demand for money, and second because the offending government, faced with recession caused by currency devaluation's effect on the tax system, reaches for more devaluation, hoping again that the inflationary boom will get it reelected. Or perhaps the government finds that the economic problems caused by devaluation are increasing the need for welfare spending. The government spends more, finds itself in deficit, raises taxes, and causes more currency decline. This spiral of devaluation—welfare spending and tax hike—devaluation can quickly cripple even the healthiest economies, as virtually all countries discovered during the 1970s.

One effect of inflation is that it lightens debt burdens. Since bankruptcies are normally caused by inability to pay debts, bankruptcy is typically not a problem during inflation. This can mask the damage of inflation on an economy and is another effect that attracts devaluationists.

Lenders and bondholders are not much excited by the prospect of being paid back in money only half the value of the money they lent. Higher interest rates, to compensate for devaluation and the resulting price increases, are the natural result. Currency unreliability eventually prevents borrowers and lenders from working together effectively, and the financial system dries up and withers away. In countries that have had a history of devaluation, finance is virtually nonexistent, except for those large companies that are able to borrow in foreign currencies. Credit cards, consumer debt, home mortgages, and small business loans are unavailable, or available only at usurious interest rates. Not surprisingly, perhaps, the owners of large companies often conclude that devaluation is their friend, as it obliterates their smaller competition, slashes their employee wage costs, and makes hard assets available for sale at low prices. They become known as *oligarchs*. Often these "capitalists" are capitalism's worst enemy, as they seek to keep the economy in a constant state of semicrisis, boiling over every 5 or 10 years into full crisis.

Devaluation can have a tremendous effect on the stock market, though it is often masked by rising prices. In 1929, the Dow Jones Industrial Average hit a high of $381, or 19 ounces of gold when the dollar was worth $20.67 per ounce. The DJIA fell to 41 in 1932, or two ounces of gold. In 1966 the DJIA hit 1,000, or 29 ounces of gold at $35 per ounce. In 1980, the DJIA was around 800, or one ounce of gold with the dollar at its nadir of $800 per ounce—a decline of over 96 percent in gold terms and half the value it was in the depths of 1932! Most people still say the "stock market was flat" during the 1970s. The two-decade stock market boom of the 1980s and 1990s merely brought the DJIA back to where it was in 1966, or about 29 ounces of gold, a DJIA of 10,000 with the dollar around $350 per ounce. See Figure 4.1.

Devaluation has caused similar effects on per capita income in the United States. In 1970, just before the disaster of the 1970s, per capita income in the United States was $3,587, or 102 ounces of gold at $35 per ounce. It had risen from $2,022 (58 ounces) in 1960 and $1,385 (40 ounces) in 1950. In 2004, per capita income was $29,416,

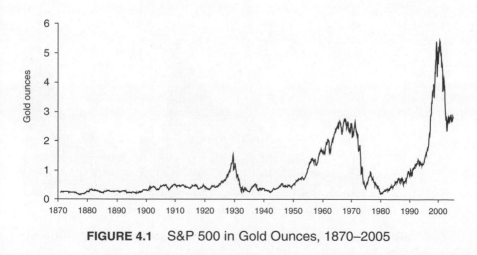

FIGURE 4.1   S&P 500 in Gold Ounces, 1870–2005

or 73.5 ounces of gold at $400 per ounce—or, to take a more chari-
table interpretation, 84 ounces at $350 per ounce, an approximation
of the equilibrium currency value for the economy at that time.
Despite new technology, the U.S. per capita income peak of 1970 has
never been bettered. Indeed, even the improvement since 1982 has
been due in no small part to the explosion in two-income house-
holds. Average weekly wages, in gold terms, never really recovered to
even half of their 1960s levels. See Figures 4.2 and 4.3.

Continuous inflationary periods are often accompanied by a conspicuous decline of morality and civility. Just as people cooperate in the
money economy, they cooperate in their daily lives, forming unspoken
agreements. The Golden Rule prevails: Do unto others as you would
have them do unto you. The money I'm borrowing from you is the
same value as the money I will use to repay you 10 years from now.
During inflation, all the monetary contracts between people are
warped and distorted. Creditors lose their shirts. Debtors gain unexpected windfalls. Real wages decline. Pensioners find their monthly
payments are inadequate. Taxes rise due to bracket creep and the taxation of illusory capital gains. The deterioration of monetary contracts is matched by a deterioration of social contracts, because
monetary contracts, in the end, are also agreements between people.

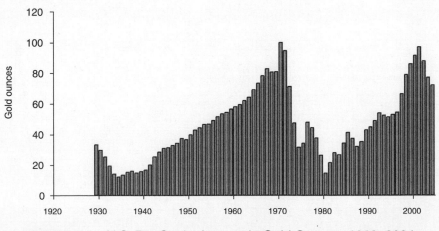

FIGURE 4.2   U.S. Per Capita Income in Gold Ounces, 1929–2004

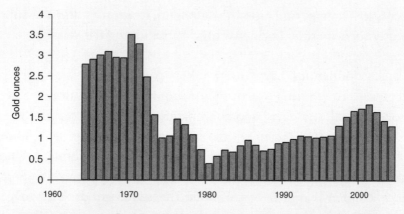

FIGURE 4.3   U.S. Weekly Wages in Gold Ounces, 1964–2004

Historians recount that civilizations fell into decadence as people lived for immediate gratification rather than saving and investing—and financial deterioration led to deterioration in their personal relationships. Such things are said of the decline of Rome, Weimar Germany in the early 1920s, and the United States in the 1970s. During Britain's great stretch of currency stability, between 1698 and 1914, the soundness of the currency was reflected in the ironclad propriety of Victorian society. Marriage was a commitment as strong and reliable as the Bank of England's everlasting bonds. It's no coincidence that the golden ages of Rome, Britain, and the United States were also eras when the currencies themselves were as good as gold.

During hyperinflation, the complete breakdown of monetary cooperation, often centuries-old ethnic hatreds will flare, and civil war may ensue. The centers of civil unrest in the world today are countries that have suffered radical inflations. Indonesia suffered price rises of 40 percent annually after a currency disaster in 1997, and East Timor decided to secede. The Russians, prodded by the inflationists of the International Monetary Fund and the Harvard Institute for International Development, devalued the ruble from 4 per dollar on the black market to roughly 29,000 per dollar; the Soviet Union splintered, and civil war erupted in Chechnya. After the inflationists of the IMF visited Yugoslavia in the 1980s, the country suffered the most horrible hyperinflation of the twentieth century and was subsequently torn apart by ancient ethnic hatreds and civil war.

Monetary inflations have often taken place during wartime, but prices can rise during wartime for nonmonetary reasons as well. Chocolate, silk stockings, and champagne become scarce. The workers who previously manned the factories producing such luxury items are off fighting. The champagne factories are bombed. Those lucky enough to have sufficient resources are willing to pay higher prices—higher real prices—to obtain the scarce goods. The government is in the same predicament. It needs 3 million pairs of combat boots, and to get them, it must outbid all the consumers who want the shoe factories to produce civilian shoes. Some boot factories are destroyed in the war. The government cannot wait. Necessity forces it to pay a higher price than it would pay in peacetime, when boots are plentiful and there's time to spare. Boots become scarcer, and the price rises. Handbag producers, seeing the extraordinary profits available from producing combat boots, retool their operations. Wages rise as boot manufacturers hire any available workers to make more boots. Just as rising prices are the market's way of adjusting to a currency devaluation, rising prices are the market's way of adjusting to the needs of a wartime economy.

Except for the rare example where the government is paying its bills by printing money, government deficit spending has no effect on the supply of money. Only the Fed (or other monetary authority) can create money. The government has to acquire it from present income (taxation) or borrow it from someone else, just as corporations or individuals do. Governments do not "inject money" into the economy. However, under the enormous government spending of all-out war, prices may indeed rise. This is perhaps the root of the notion that deficits create inflation. On a deeper level, over long historical experience stretching centuries, humans have learned that once a government's debts become excessive, it is inevitably tempted to devalue the currency, thus repudiating its debts.

To understand whether a general rise in prices is due to monetary or nonmonetary factors, it is necessary to look at changes in the value of the currency compared to gold or other currencies.

As David Ricardo wrote in 1817:

> When each country has precisely the quantity of money which it ought to have, [the "purchasing power" of] money will not indeed be of the same . . . in each, for with respect to many commodities it may differ 5, 10, or even 20 percent, but the exchange will be at par. One hundred pounds in England, or the silver which is £100, will purchase a bill of £100, or an equal quantity of silver in France, Spain, or Holland.
>
> In speaking of the exchange and the comparative value of money in different countries, we must not in the least refer to the value of money estimated in commodities in either country. The exchange is never ascertained by estimating the comparative value of money in corn, cloth, or any commodity whatever, but by estimating the value of the currency of one country in the currency of another.[10]

Rather than a one-time devaluation, it is perhaps more common to find open-ended inflation, a constant decline in the value of the monetary standard over years, as when Abraham Lincoln ran the printing presses in 1861 in order to pay for Civil War expenses and when Richard Nixon broke the dollar's link with gold in 1971 hoping that an inflationary boom would lead to reelection.

The artificial inflationary boom is short-lived. The money illusion lasts as long as people are fooled that more money equals greater wealth and greater productivity, not just an excess supply of paper chits. The illusion works only to the extent that it is unexpected. If the market expects further devaluation (i.e., annual price increases included as part of every businessperson's plans, cost-of-living increases written into workers' contracts, and high interest rates in the bond market), then further devaluation will have no boom effect at all. To sustain the artificial boom, the government must not only continue its devaluation, but must constantly increase the rate of devaluation. It must continually exceed inflationary expectations. This policy quickly ends in hyperinflation.

Even slowing the pace of inflation can have recessionary effects. If a company expects 10 percent CPI price inflation next year and expects to raise prices on its own products by 10 percent as well, then it may agree to raise workers' wages by 10 percent, to pay suppliers 10 percent more, and to pay bankers 14 percent on a loan. However, if inflation abates and is only 3 percent, then that company may find itself in some trouble.

Since stopping a continuous inflation can cause a recession, it is always best to combine monetary restraint with some pro-growth fiscal policy such as meaningful tax cuts.

II.

Deflation is a rise in the value of the currency, most easily detected in a rise in the currency's value versus gold. If it persists, falling prices are the likely result. Deflationary periods are historically rare. Inflation has all manner of temptations—the lure of a competitive devaluation, the effects of the artificial boom, the appeal of creating money out of nothing, the repudiation of government debt and so forth—but deflation is so obviously recessionary and unpleasant that no government undertakes it cheerfully, and political opposition is often intense.

The term *deflation* is often conflated today with the notion of economic contraction and the decline of real asset values. Sometimes, economies boom at the onset of monetary deflation, as was the case in Japan from 1985 to 1990 and in the United States from 1997 to 2000. In a particularly bizarre turn, some have recently taken to arguing that deflation can take place with hyperinflation! What they mean, apparently, is hyperinflation associated with economic

decline, which is exactly what one would expect during hyperinflation. Semantic confusion is all too often a mirror of conceptual
confusion.

Though the inflationary boom is illusory, the deflationary bust is
real: The economy "underheats," the rising currency leads to an
apparent decline in competitiveness, domestic demand evaporates,
and the government's debt burden increases as it struggles to pay off
its debts in an appreciating currency. Deflations were typically carried
out by governments to return the currency to its original value after
a wartime currency devaluation. Between 1800 and 1980, there were
only four deflationary periods in U.S. and English history, each one
undertaken through an official act of government: after the War of
1812 and the Civil War in the United States and after the Napoleonic
Wars and World War I in England. Only since 1980 has deflation
been so misunderstood that countries have suffered deflationary recessions by accident.

The recessionary effects of deflation can be experienced as a
shortage of demand, which is sometimes interpreted as a surplus of
goods, or overproduction. The shortage of demand is merely the result of the rise in the value of money. Prices effectively rise as the currency rises, and thus less is purchased. The same holds true of labor.
Goods and services go unsold. Production is suspended. Workers are
laid off. Eventually, companies lower their sales prices. To maintain a
profit margin, they must also reduce labor expenses, pushing down
wages. As long-term contracts expire and are renewed at lower
prices, corporations' and individuals' costs decline and they are able
to accept lower sales prices and wages. In this way, once again like a
large crowd trying to shuffle along together while keeping their relationships unchanged, market prices for goods and labor slowly adjust
to the new value of the monetary standard, sometimes taking as long
as 20 years to do so.

Markets do not always adjust by lowering prices. Instead, more
goods may be sold at the same price ("30 percent free"), or the quality
of goods may improve. Nominal wages may not fall, being protected

by contract or convention, but perks such as lavish expense accounts, subsidized housing, generous pension or medical benefits, or luxurious offices may be withdrawn.

The natural outcome of deflation, falling prices, tends to create worry and alarm, but this is merely the natural adjustment process of the economy. Just as with an inflationary price rise, the deflationary price fall represents a renegotiation by the citizenry to return the system to its most productive state. When the adjustment is complete, the recessionary effect of the deflation finally fades away.

Sometimes prices may be supported by nonmonetary factors such as tax hikes, shortages in specific commodities such as oil, or by an increase in the real value of labor, property, or equity. These factors do not cancel out the deflation, but merely mask it. The deflationary monetary adjustment, with all of its consequences, continues.

Like inflation, deflation creates artificial winners and losers. Creditors benefit, their credits paid back in an appreciated currency. Debtors suffer. But the benefit to creditors is limited, because debtors, struggling both to make debt payments in an appreciated currency and to make profits in the deflationary recession, go bankrupt. The creditors' investment is lost. The financial system sags under the weight of bad debts.

Just as there are nonmonetary reasons for rising prices, there are nonmonetary reasons for falling prices as well. After the higher prices caused by wartime—higher real prices, denominated in a stable currency—the end of the war can be accompanied by a return of prices to peacetime levels. Many say today that increasing productivity is being reflected in lower prices, and perhaps this is true.

A sharp economic contraction for nonmonetary reasons (e.g., due to tax, tariff, or regulatory blunders) may produce falling prices. A nationwide inventory liquidation and going-out-of-business sale begins. As prices and productivity decline, workers receive lower wages.

One reason for falling prices, ironically enough, is devaluation (i.e., inflation) by a foreign country. Companies must compete against those in the devaluing country that have had their prices cut by devaluation. This is often called a *deflationary effect*, but it is actually an *inflationary* effect.

While inflation can cause higher effective taxes, deflation tends to lower tax burdens. However, deflation tends to increase welfare burdens on the state, as the ranks of unemployed swell and as pensioners and the unemployed receive benefits paid in a more valuable currency. This can lead the government to legislate higher taxes. Also, more generous unemployment benefits reduce the impetus to seek a new job. To solve a deflation, the value of the currency must be depressed through an increase in the supply of base money. A well-placed tax cut or two can help boost the economy out of its deflationary recession, although one must be careful not to allow the currency-supportive effects of tax cuts to cause the currency to rise, creating further monetary deflation.

III.

Nothing places the farmer, the wage-earner, and all those not closely connected with financial affairs at so great a disadvantage in disposing of their labor or products as changeable "money." . . . You all know that fish will not rise to the fly in calm weather. It is when the wind blows and the surface is ruffled that the poor victim mistakes the lure for a genuine fly. So it is with the business affairs of the world. In stormy times, when prices are going up and down, when the value of the article used as money is dancing about—up to-day and down to-morrow—and the waters are troubled, the clever speculator catches the fish and fills his basket with the victims. . . . Hence the farmer and the mechanic, and all people having crops to sell or receiving salaries or wages, are those most deeply interested in securing and maintaining fixity of value in the article they have to take as "money."

—Andrew Carnegie, The "A B C of Money," 1891[11]

87

Floating currencies are the product of government manipulation, and fixed-rate currencies are market-based systems. When the citizenry is left to its own devices, it invariably creates a fixed-rate system. When governments today say they will leave their currency's value "up to the market," it means in effect that they do not wish to allow the market to determine the supply of money through the operation of an automatic currency peg of some sort and that they would rather take control of the supply of money themselves through the operations of a bureaucratic (and unelected) policy board. The market is free only to pass judgment on this monetary manipulation, and does so continuously.

In this case, the citizenry must still struggle to make its monetary agreements as reliable, stable, and predictable as possible, which it does by entering into a myriad of fantastically complex and expensive derivatives transactions. Derivatives amount to a sort of insurance scheme. They do not reduce the risk or damage of currency fluctuation, but they spread the risk to those who can bear it. Auto insurance does not prevent auto accidents. The more accident-prone a currency is, the more expensive it is to insure.

Federal Reserve Chairman Alan Greenspan, whose intellectual exposure to the gold standard as a young man infused his thinking throughout his tenure, is one of the few central bankers who understands that a floating currency is not a free market currency. In this exchange on July 22, 1998, at a meeting of the House Subcommittee on Domestic and International Monetary Policy of the Banking Committee, he spoke with representative Ron Paul (R-Texas), a longtime gold standard advocate:

DR. PAUL: A very quick question. You seem to welcome, and you have been quoted as welcoming, a downturn in the economy to compensate for the surge and modest growth in the economy. Is it not true that in a free market, with sound money, you never welcome a downturn in the economy? You never welcome the idea of decreased growth, and you don't concern yourself about this? And yet, here we talk about when is the Fed going to intervene and turn down the economy? It seems that there is a welcoming effect to the fact that the Southeast Asia has tempered, you know, price pressures. Couldn't we make a case that the free market would operate a lot better than the market we use today?

MR. GREENSPAN: I think you have to define what you mean by a "free market." If you have a fiat currency, which is what everyone has in the world . . .

DR. PAUL: That is not free market.

MR. GREENSPAN: That is not free market. Central banks, of necessity, determine what the money supply is. If you are on a gold standard or other mechanism in which the central banks do not have discretion, then the system works automatically. The reason there is very little support for the gold standard is the consequences of those types of market adjustments are not considered to be appropriate in the 20th and 21st century. I am one of the rare people who have still some nostalgic view about the old gold standard, as you know, but I must tell you, I am in a very small minority among my colleagues on that issue.[12]

An analysis of the floating currencies of today is somewhat complex, since it is necessary to understand what happens to an economy when a currency moves both up and down in an erratic fashion. The concept is in principle simply an aggregate of the concepts of inflation and deflation.

Strictly speaking, every fall in a currency's value is an inflation, and every rise is a deflation. The currency move will produce some sort of inflationary or deflationary effects, at the very least a relative profit or loss in the accounts of currency traders, importers, and exporters. The minor wiggles and jiggles will have insignificant effects on the economy as a whole.

But each currency movement still produces effects in the economy. Inflationary and deflationary symptoms coincide. If the swings are big enough, inflationary and deflationary effects can overlap dramatically. The economy may suffer from a deflationary recession at the same time that prices are adjusting upward for the inflation. This was the case in the United States during the 1982 recession. Or a deflationary recession can dissipate even as prices continue to adjust downward. This was the case in Japan in 2004.

In these conditions, price indexes become quite meaningless. Some prices are rising briskly (adjusting to inflation) while others are falling (adjusting to deflation).

An economy tends to have a center of gravity, a currency level at which the effects of inflation and deflation and the interests of creditors and debtors, the numbers of monetary winners and losers, are in rough balance. Various parts of the economy may be suffering from or adjusting to inflation or deflation, but on the whole the economy does not exhibit a preponderance toward one or the other. If half the contracts in the economy were made at a currency value of $100 per ounce of gold, and half were made at a currency value of $200 per ounce of gold, then a rough balance might be struck at $150 per ounce, which balances the adjustment difficulties of both groups, although it would not be ideal for any one single actor.

For most situations, a 10-year trailing moving average of the value of the currency (i.e., the price of gold denominated in the currency) is a good first approximation of the center of gravity. Sometimes, a 5- or 20-year average may be more appropriate. The characteristics of each economy are unique, and policymakers must not be too dogmatic when determining an appropriate currency value.

If a floating currency's value is higher than the center of gravity, the economy will tend to show deflationary effects. Likewise, if a currency's value is below the center of gravity, the economy will tend to show inflationary effects.

If a currency's value is inflationary with respect to the center of gravity, but returns toward the center of gravity, inflationary effects are reduced. This can be termed *disinflation*. If a currency's value is deflationary with respect to the center of gravity, but then returns toward the center of gravity, deflationary effects dissipate. This can be termed *reflation*. See Figure 4.4.

An economy will naturally function best when the currency's value is near the center of gravity and held there. This is true in an

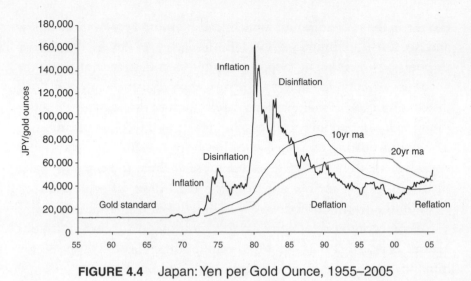

FIGURE 4.4   Japan: Yen per Gold Ounce, 1955–2005

environment of floating currencies, but it has special relevance for countries that intend to move to some sort of fixed-rate system. When the new rate, the price of gold in a new gold standard, for example, is at the center of gravity, the adjustment made necessary by the new currency regime is minimized.

If a government misjudges the center of gravity, and chooses to peg a currency to gold at an inappropriate rate (more than 20 percent from the center of gravity), a destructive inflation or deflation will result as the economy adjusts to the new currency value. This is no fault of the gold standard per se, but of the government's clumsy policymaking. In the long term, however, the economy will naturally accommodate the currency's new fixed value.

In an environment of floating exchange rates, feedback effects can form with all manner of surprising and disastrous results, a phenomenon the investor George Soros has called *reflexivity*. In the absence of coherent currency management by the monetary authorities, a change in the currency's value or exchange rate with another currency can lead to a change in other economic conditions, which in turn leads, through a change in the demand for money, back to a change in the exchange rate, which leads to more economic changes, and so forth ad infinitum. When monetary policy is conducted through an interest rate peg, as it often is today, the relationships become even more complex as the monetary distortion interacts with distortion of the capital markets. The system of interest rate pegging in use today is extremely chaotic, and reflexive effects are paramount. The era of floating exchange rates has been punctuated by a never-ending series of monetary disasters, most of them too small to make the front pages of U.S. newspapers, but some large enough to threaten the world economy.

We'll let Soros, one of the world's most successful currency speculators between 1973 and his semiretirement in 1989, speak for himself:

> While reflexive interactions are intermittent in the stock market, they are continuous in the market for currencies. I shall try to show that freely floating exchange rates are inherently unstable; moreover, the instability is cumulative so that the eventual breakdown of a freely floating exchange rate system is virtually assured.
>
> The traditional view of the currency market is that it tends toward equilibrium. . . . Speculation cannot disrupt the trend toward equilibrium—if speculators anticipate the future correctly, they accelerate the trend; if they misjudge it, they will be penalized by the underlying trend that may be delayed but will inevitably assert itself.
>
> Experience since floating exchange rates were introduced in 1973 has disproved this view. Instead of fundamentals determining exchange rates, exchange rates have found a way of influencing the fundamentals.[13]

Floating currencies were rare in the two centuries before 1973, but those who witnessed the occasional bout of currency fluctuation (e.g., in the 1920s), came to similar realizations. In a 1944 report for the League of Nations, the economist Ragnar Nurkse concluded that:

The post-war history of the French franc up to the end of 1926 affords an instructive example of completely free and uncontrolled exchange rate variations. . . . The dangers of . . . cumulative and self-aggravating movements under a regime of freely fluctuating exchanges are clearly demonstrated by the French experience. . . . Self-aggravating movements, instead of promoting adjustment in the balance of payments, are apt to intensify conditions of instability. . . . We may recall in particular the example of the French franc during the years 1924–26.[14]

France returned to the gold standard in December 1926, which it made official in 1928.

The regime of floating currencies today is characterized by unpredictability, the inchoate actions of central banks based on the vapid theorizing of governing boards following no clear rule or even framework of inquiry. In such an environment the reflexive effects can reach full bloom.

All such effects are in essence changes in the demand for money. A currency can only go up or down; a reflexive effect is one in which a fall in the currency tends to create a relative shrinkage of demand, leading to a further fall in the currency, or one where a rise in the currency tends to create an expansion of demand, leading to a further rise in the currency.

A falling currency is, of course, inflation, and in an inflation people's willingness to hold cash diminishes. The paper is losing its value. Prices are rising and are expected to keep rising. Interest rates rise, and as a consequence the opportunity cost of holding non-interest-bearing currency increases. People drop their cash holdings and move into goods and hard assets, even overseas assets or other currencies. This is a drop in demand for money. During the German hyperinflation of the early 1920s, workers were paid twice a day and spent all their money immediately. Overseas holders of assets are not cushioned by the slow adjustment of prices in an economy. The inflation hits them immediately by way of the foreign exchange market, so naturally their actions are quicker and more abrupt. The value of their assets is falling, so they drop their asset holdings for cash and then drop the cash in favor of another currency. Speculators sell the currency short to profit from the fall. This is a drop in demand. If a central bank takes no steps to adapt to the changing demand conditions and shrink supply, the currency will tend to fall further. As inflation pushes people into higher tax brackets, the economy goes into contraction and the demand for money shrinks. This puts supply in excess of demand, and the currency falls further still.

Because they cannot accommodate changes in demand, currency management systems based on the supply of money alone are doomed to failure. They assume that demand will be proportional to the size of the economy. Under monetary regimes that target the value of the currency, such as under a gold standard, this may indeed turn out to be roughly the case during certain time periods. However, when the monetary authorities ignore the value of the currency and concentrate only on its supply, reflexive effects take over and demand begins to vary unpredictably.

Though a currency is not a stock, particularly in the environment of floating currencies, it shows some of the same behavior. A currency is an asset. Like a stock, the free market price of a currency reflects not only the conditions, or so-called fundamentals, of the moment, but also expectations of future events. The stock and currency markets are similar in the sense that each one engages in a complex, never-ending discussion with itself about the present and the future as it places a value on the asset.

If the president of a cigarette company announced that, in response to antismoking activists, the company would no longer sell cigarettes but instead attempt to get into the mortgage lending business, the cigarette company's stock may plummet as investors conclude that the experiment would end in bankruptcy. No change in the material components—the factories, the contracts with workers, the price of tobacco—has changed, but the new information about the thinking of the leadership of the cigarette company has radically changed the value of the company's shares.

Likewise, remarks by the managers of currencies—central bankers, bureaucrats, and politicians—can radically affect the value of currencies. What if the government announced that it would undertake a devaluation six months in the future? Certainly nobody is going to wait around six months for their assets to be devalued. Demand for the currency would fall instantly—with today's information systems, likely within 30 seconds after the words were spoken. This would lead to downward pressure on the currency immediately, not six months in the future. Many would claim that the economic fundamentals hadn't changed. But of course they had.

Few governments would announce a devaluation ahead of time, but they often "worry that they might have to devalue," or they may say that they will leave the value of a sagging currency "up to the market," which amounts to the same thing. If a currency declines, for whatever reason, and the central bank ignores the fall, that in itself is a signal of the currency managers' attitude. The market will pass judgment on this reaction and may push the currency lower. If the central bank still shows no concern, the currency may be pushed lower yet.

CHAPTER 5

THE GOLD STANDARD

The Most Effective Means of Creating a Currency of Stable Value

And God created the two precious metals, gold and silver, to serve as the measure of value of all commodities. They are also generally used by men as a store or treasure. For although other goods are sometimes stored it is only with the intention of acquiring gold or silver. For other goods are subject to the fluctuations of the market, from which they [gold and silver] are immune.

—Ibn Khaldun, *Al Muquaddimah*, circa 1379[1]

The first chief function of money is to supply commodities with the material for the expression of their values, or to represent their values as magnitudes of the same denomination, qualitatively equal, and qualitatively comparable.

It thus serves as a universal measure of value. And only by virtue of this function does gold, the equivalent commodity par excellence, become money.

—Karl Marx, *Capital*, 1867[2]

An article is not first made valuable by law and then elected to be "money." The article first proves itself valuable and best suited for the purpose, and so becomes of itself and in itself the basis-article—money. It elects itself. . . .

[T]he one essential quality that is needed in the article which we use as a basis for exchanging all other articles is fixity of value. The race has instinctively always sought for the one article in the world which most resembles the North Star among the other stars in the heavens, and used it as "money"—the article that changes least in

97

value as the North Star is the star which changes its position least in the heavens; and what the North Star is among stars the article people elect as "money" is among articles.

—**Andrew Carnegie, "The A B C of Money," 1891**[3]

Gold still represents the ultimate form of payment in the world. Fiat money in extremis is accepted by nobody. Gold is always accepted.

—**Alan Greenspan, May 20, 1999**

[Gold is] the unalterable fiduciary value par excellence.

—**Charles de Gaulle**

Gold is money. That's it.

—**J. P. Morgan**

For most of the past three millennia, the world's commercial centers have used one or another variant of a gold standard. It should be one of the best understood of human institutions, but it is not. It is one of the worst understood, by both its advocates and detractors.

A *gold standard*, in any of its many forms, shall be defined as a system that ties the value of money to the value of a fixed quantity of gold. The simplest way to do this is to actually use metallic gold or silver as money, using full-weight coins, ingots, nuggets, and so on that trade at commodity value. As monetary systems became more sophisticated, the gold standard referred to paper currencies whose value was pegged to the value of a specified amount of gold. Commonly, paper money was legally redeemable for gold on demand. When the value of paper currency fell below its gold parity, paper money (base money) was returned to its issuers, who (ideally) would then remove it from circulation. Supply was reduced, supporting the value of the currency. When the value of the paper currency rose above the gold parity, supply was increased. The mechanism of the gold peg was the alteration of supply. In this fashion, a gold standard was, in effect, a currency board linked to gold.

The use of gold as the benchmark of monetary value is based on the premise and observation that the value of gold is more stable than

98

any other commodity or any statistical concoction or any string of guesses by a policy board. The purpose of a gold standard is therefore to produce the most stable currency value possible in both the short and long term.

A gold standard is a value peg, not a quantity peg. A gold standard is not, and never has been, a system by which the amount of base money is determined by the amount of gold held by the monetary authorities. From this it can be seen that importing or exporting gold, or other such actions, are generally of little concern, since moving gold from place to place does not change its value.

Indeed, during much of the twentieth century, major government gold holdings have been stored in the basement of the U.S. Federal Reserve. "International gold transfers" consisted of shuffling gold bars around the Fed's basement. These "gold movements" have been blamed for all manner of economic upheavals—oddly enough by people who criticize others for their supposed faith in gold's supernatural powers!

The use of token chits redeemable on demand for gold as a form of money is older even than the use of coins. Warehouse receipts for gold in the form of clay tablets date from the second and third millennium BC, and eventually these clay tablets traded among third parties. The gold standard, in its most rudimentary form, dates back literally to the beginnings of recorded history. The first known use of writing was to create clay tablets such as these.

Although the Chinese had created a paper currency redeemable for silver back in the eleventh century, the roots of the gold-linked paper currency system, which lasted until 1971, began in the seventeenth century. Before then, gold itself, along with silver and occasionally other metals such as copper, was used as money. After thousands of years of experimentation and elimination, gold and silver had been chosen as the most stable measures of value available in the imperfect world. For the most part, they worked quite well.

Gold-linked paper currency, in its most recent incarnation, was not invented in a flash of insight but developed in a slow, step-by-step progression in the private market, with little interference from governments. Many people at first opposed it (and many people still do today), arguing that paper is a poor substitute for the real thing. Once governments saw they could do little to stop it, and that in fact paper money had quite a few positive attributes, governments accepted the citizenry's innovation as official policy.

The modern gold standard, based on redeemable paper money, began when people decided not to hoard and protect their own gold holdings, fearing theft or other risks, and instead deposited their gold with private institutions, receiving a claim check in return. Deposit an ounce of gold; get a one-ounce claim check. It did not matter what form the check took—even a handwritten note would do—as long as it was legally binding. In Britain this began as a side business of the scrivener in the early seventeenth century. Goldsmiths, who had the facilities to store and protect large gold holdings, later took over this business, particularly after 1640. People deposited their bullion and coin with the goldsmiths and received claim checks. They gradually found that their claim checks circulated as well or better than the bullion they had deposited.

Metal money, used in hand-to-hand transactions, has a number of drawbacks. Its weight and purity may be in doubt. Over time, metal coins wear down and lose their value, thus suffering from natural devaluation, and they must be periodically reminted and returned to their original weight. Some coins may have been debased and devalued by the issuing body, usually the government, and don't contain the metal indicated by their face value. Coins are heavy and unsuited for large transactions. Early Chinese paper money grew out of the desire to do business transactions without having to transport hundreds or thousands of pounds of silver coins. Today the Chinese word for *bank* literally means "silver movement."

Because coins vary in their metallic content as a consequence of use and wear and thus vary in their commodity value, a proper gold-linked paper currency is, in practice, a more stable and reliable gold standard than even gold coins. All paper bills are redeemable, and thus all have the same value.

Also, paper money could be made as plentiful as needed, while new gold and silver had to be laboriously dug out of the ground. During the time of metallic monies, many people rarely used money at all, and often never saw high-value money such as gold. Much of the economy was still conducted within the sphere of the household (most people were farmers) or through barter. The barter might be done in a monetary context—$10 of rum for $10 of wheat—but it was still barter.

By the 1660s, goldsmiths were not only handing out claim checks to depositors, but to borrowers as well, and the modern era of banking began. Already by 1698 the value of redeemable paper (tallies, banknotes, bills, etc.) exceeded the value of metallic coinage in Britain.

By Adam Smith's time, the latter eighteenth century, there had been many unhappy experiments with unredeemable paper currencies, and some thinkers (Montesquieu, for example) had tried to relate the proper supply of money in a fixed proportion with the size of the economy overall. This is almost precisely the analytical model of the monetarists, who gained influence under the leadership of Milton Friedman in the 1960s. (This hypothetical fixed proportion is labeled *velocity* by the monetarists.) Smith lambasted the monetarists of his day. "What is the proportion which the circulating money of any country bears to the whole value of the annual produce circulated by means of it, it is, perhaps, impossible to determine," Smith said. "It had been computed by different authors at a fifth, at a tenth, at a twentieth, and at a thirtieth part of that value."

Smith insisted that the value of money was the important guiding principle, and that the monetary authorities' supply of currency should depend on the currency's market value and not on unreliable academic constructs. Ultimately, citizens, the users of money, do not care how much money is supplied or how much is demanded. They care only about the quality of the currency, not the quantity. Only a few specialists know the exact size of the Fed's monetary base, but all newspapers publish foreign exchange rates and report on price indexes for evidence of a change in the currency's value. Even today, financial media regularly report on the dollar/gold price, while ignoring metals more important to industry such as aluminum, steel, copper, or nickel.

Because the notes were convertible on demand for gold or silver, the value of the banknotes could never fall much below the value of the metal they represent. Any overissuance of money by the bank resulted in redemption of banknotes into gold or silver. The surplus of banknotes returned to the bank. On this point Smith is explicit:

> The whole paper money of any kind which can easily circulate in any country never can exceed the value of the gold and silver, of which . . . would circulate there, if there was no paper money. . . . Should the circulating paper at any time exceed that sum, as the excess could neither be sent abroad nor be employed in the circulation of the country, it must immediately return upon the banks to be exchanged for gold and silver. Many people would immediately perceive that they had more of this paper than was necessary for transacting their business at home, and as they could not send it abroad, they would immediately demand payment of it from the banks. . . . There would immediately, therefore, be a run upon the banks to the whole extent of this superfluous paper, and, if they showed any difficulty or backwardness in payment, to a much greater extent the alarm, which this would occasion, necessarily increasing the run.[4]

The mechanism of the system is an adjustment of supply. When the supply of banknotes is excessive, they return to the bank and are removed from circulation. Smith was not theorizing in a vacuum. At the time he was writing, this system had been the backbone of the British and Scottish monetary system for over a century.

In a situation of deflation, where the value of paper rises above that of gold and silver, people would rush to the bank with gold and silver and take out paper (if for no other reason than to buy more gold and silver, thus making an arbitrage profit). However, since banks profit from the issuance of paper money, there is a constant incentive to increase the supply of paper money as much as possible, and this condition is rare.

This is the free market in action. The gold standard was created by the free market, the citizenry, and it operates to manage the supply of paper currency under a self-adjusting market system. There is no central bank, no secretive policy board, no armies of statisticians churning out spurious indexes and aggregates, indeed no discretionary monetary policy at all. The government's contribution to the system is merely to ensure that banks abide by their legal contract to honor the redemption of their bills for specie.

Smith cites 20 percent as an adequate reserve of specie, but there is no reason the reserve can't drop to 10 percent or 5 percent as banks build trust that their currencies will remain convertible. As England's pound sterling grew to become the center of the entire world monetary and financial system in the latter nineteenth century and early twentieth, the reserves did not increase. Trust in the Bank of England's sound monetary policies was so great that not only did people happily accept the bank's *consols* (short for "consolidated," government bonds that never matured), but from the 1880s to 1914 the bank's gold reserves could be kept between £20 million and £40 million, while France and Russia kept over £100 million each. As a reserve bank, the Bank of England also held the reserve of banks of foreign countries, so in fact an even larger amount of currency and deposits were guaranteed by the Bank of England's modest gold holdings. The amount of gold in bankers' vaults does not determine the supply of paper money, but rather the value of gold in relation to the value of the convertible paper currency. If the Bank of England had taken the advice of Walter Bagehot, an influential writer for the *Economist* magazine, and increased its gold reserves to £200 million, it would have had no effect on the value or number of banknotes (nor did Bagehot intend it to), but would merely add security to the system in times of crisis. It is perfectly appropriate for the bank to increase or decrease the size of its reserves as it sees fit. An increase or decrease in reserves does not in itself imply a deviation of the currency from its gold peg, although it could be evidence of such. During the Bretton Woods period, 1944 to 1971, the entire monetary system of the world was backed by $12 billion in U.S. gold reserves.

However, there is often confusion on this point, because from the standpoint of a banker (and later central banker), the amount of gold in the vaults matters very much. The inflow and outflow of gold can show whether the value of banknotes is changing compared to gold, and it serves as a signal to expand or reduce the supply of money. This takes place at a national level as well; gold will flow out of a country whose currency is losing its value, as foreigners redeem their debts and banknotes in gold.

David Ricardo added an important corollary, that the value of the currency can be adjusted by managing its supply so that it is always equivalent to a given amount of gold, even if the paper is not redeemable and the monetary authorities hold no gold at all:

> It is on this principle that paper money circulates: the whole charge for paper money may be considered as seignorage. Though it has no intrinsic value, yet, by limiting its quantity, its value in exchange is as great as an equal denomination of [gold] coin, or of bullion in that coin. . . .
>
> It will be seen that it is not necessary that paper money should be payable in specie to secure its value; it is only necessary that its quantity should be regulated according to the value of the metal which is declared to be the standard.[5]

This does not imply that currency holders have no recourse. Even if the paper is not redeemable with the government, it can be traded for gold bullion on the private gold market. It does imply that even if central banks run out of gold reserves completely, or have none to begin with, they can still maintain a gold standard. Gold is a benchmark of monetary value, just as a yard is a benchmark of length. Central banks need not hoard gold, any more than carpenters need hoard yardsticks. The question is whether central banks know how to use gold properly to measure and manage the value of their currencies.

It is not necessary for the government to hold gold even under a system of redeemability. The monetary authority can always buy or borrow gold on the open market. Speculators regularly buy and sell gold that they do not own. If the value of banknotes is out of line with gold, then gold and banknotes will simply cycle around and around until the problem is corrected. Adam Smith recalls that many banks of the eighteenth century found themselves engaged in just such foolishness when they attempted to press upon the public more paper banknotes than the public wished to hold.

Let us suppose that all the paper of a particular bank, which the circulation of the country can easily absorb and employ, amounts to forty thousand pounds; . . . Should this bank attempt to circulate forty four thousand pounds, the four thousand pounds which are over and above what the circulation can easily absorb and employ, will return upon it almost as fast as it is issued. . . .

Had every particular banking company always understood and attended to its own particular interest, the circulation never could have been overstocked with paper money. But every particular banking company has not always understood or attended to its own particular interest, and the circulation has frequently been overstocked with paper money.

By issuing too great a quantity of paper, of which the excess was continually returning, in order to be exchanged for gold and silver, the Bank of England was for many years together obliged to coin gold [mint and distribute gold coins in return for banknotes] to the extent of between eight hundred thousand pounds and a million a year; or at an average, about eight hundred and fifty thousand pounds. For this great coinage the bank . . . was frequently obliged to purchase gold bullion at the high price of four pounds an ounce, which it soon after issued in coin at £3 17s 10.5d. an ounce, losing in this manner between two and a half and three per cent. upon the coinage of so very large a sum. . . .

The Scotch banks, in consequence of an excess of the same kind, were all obliged to employ constantly agents at London to collect money [gold] for them, at an expense which was seldom below one and a half or two per cent. This money was sent down by the waggon, and insured by the carriers at an additional expence of three quarters per cent. or fifteen shillings on the hundred pounds. Those agents were not always able to replenish the coffers of their employers so fast as they were emptied.[6]

Though redeemability is not necessary, in Ricardo's day, like any other, there were inflationists preaching the benefits of floating fiat currencies and the oversupply of money. Ricardo concludes:

Experience . . . shows that neither a state nor a bank ever have had the unrestricted power of issuing paper money without abusing that power; in all states, therefore, the issue of paper money ought to be under some check and control; and none seems so proper for that purpose as that of subjecting the issuers of paper money to the obligation of paying their notes either in gold coin or bullion.[7]

Ricardo's statements here have a particular poignancy, because at the time they were written the British pound had been a floating currency for 20 years. Ricardo later became a member of Parliament and helped reestablish the gold standard in Britain, setting the stage for a century of economic progress.

On the other side of the Atlantic the United States, which declared its independence in the same year as the publication of *The Wealth of Nations*, was getting started on the sound foundation of the gold standard. As Alexander Hamilton, the first Treasury secretary, argued in Congress:

The emitting of paper money by the authority of the Government is wisely prohibited by the individual States, by the national constitution; and the spirit of that prohibition ought not to be disregarded by the Government of the United States. Though paper emissions, under a general authority, might have some advantages not applicable, and be free from some disadvantages which are applicable to the like emissions by the States, separately, yet they are of a nature so liable to abuse—and it may even be affirmed, so certain of being abused—that the wisdom of the Government will be shown in never trusting itself with the use of so seducing and dangerous an expedient. In times of tranquility, it might have no ill consequence; it might even be managed in a way to be productive of good; but, in great and trying emergencies, there is almost a moral certainty of its becoming mischievous. The stamping of paper is an operation so much easier than the laying of taxes, that a government, in the practice of paper emissions, would rarely fail, in any such emergency, to indulge itself too far in the employment of that resource, to avoid, as much as possible, one less auspicious to present popularity. If it should not even be carried so far as to be rendered an absolute bubble, it would at least be likely to be extended to a degree which would occasion an inflated and artificial state of things, incompatible with the regular and prosperous course of the political economy.

Among other material differences between a paper currency, issued by the mere authority of Government, and one issued by a bank, payable in coin, is this: That, in the first case, there is no standard to which an appeal can be made, as to the quantity which will only satisfy, or which will surcharge the circulation; in the last, that standard results from the demand. If more should be issued than is necessary, it will return upon the bank.[8]

A gold standard among multiple countries is, in essence, a world currency. It needs no central governing bodies; it is not dependent on any sort of fiscal rules and restrictions; and any country that chooses to participate may do so unilaterally. It is the citizens' world currency. A dollar is simply a contract redeemable in gold; a pound or euro or yen is also a contract redeemable in gold. These contracts used to be issued by private institutions, and the only difference between a dollar bill issued by the private Bank of Tennessee and a pound note issued by the private Bank of Nottingham was the amount of gold the holder would receive when presenting the note to the bank. The

GOLD: THE ONCE AND FUTURE MONEY

terms *dollar*, *pound*, *franc*, and so forth were little more than specified weights, as easily convertible as gallons and liters. In the past, some have even argued for discarding the old currency names and simply using metric measurements—the 10-gram banknote, the 0.1-gram coin. The British *pound* originally referred to a literal pound of silver, and for many hundreds of years there was no coin or banknote that corresponded with that denomination.

There are those today who argue for a world currency, as if this were some sort of far-off utopian ideal like a unified world government. In fact, the world had a common currency for centuries, and discarded it only three decades ago. It was lost only due to carelessness, ignorance, and confusion, and it could be reinstated again, just as Britain, the premier economic and financial power of the time, reinstated the gold standard on May 1, 1821, after 24 years and two months of a floating pound.

Under a gold standard, the gold market is an open market free of government manipulation. The managing body does not intervene in the gold market to support or suppress prices. It used to be said that a devaluing government "changed the price of gold," but actually it was the value of the currency they were changing. The expansion and contraction of the supply of currency alters that currency's value in relation to gold, but has no effect on gold itself. Gold is the thermostat of the system. When the gold market says there's too much money, money is eliminated. When the gold market says there's too little money, money is created. Just as a thermostat guides the heating and cooling of a house, it does no good to deal with the problem of a hot or cold house by jiggering the thermostat.

All too often today, a gold standard is misunderstood as a system by which the gold market itself is manipulated, by buying or selling large amounts of gold in sterilized intervention (i.e., without a corresponding change in the supply of money) to create a short-term aberration in the market. This is totally ineffective. Without a change in the supply of money relative to demand, the gold/currency market will quickly return to an equilibrium point reflecting the discrepancy. If the central bank persists in buying or selling gold without adjusting its supply of currency, it will simply run out of gold reserves. This stupidity on the part of certain central banks is not the fault of the gold standard.

The gold/dollar market accumulates all the existing information about monetary conditions into one price, in a fashion similar to the manner in which a company's stock, if it is traded widely enough, will reflect all of the information available about the company. Like all market prices, the price of gold is one way the extended order transmits information. The gold market thus does away with the statisticians and bureaucrats in the same way that the stock market or the commodities market takes the place of Soviet system's central planners. The gold market, though it is a commodity market, is most similar to the foreign exchange market. It shows the market relation of a currency, not to another government's currency, but to the supranational currency of humanity, the world's sole nongovernmental monetary standard. As such, the gold market reacts more quickly to monetary changes than any other commodity.

The gold standard reinforces democracy; fiat money erodes it. Without the gold standard, the trillions of monetary agreements of the citizenry are made subject to the whims of a secretive, unelected, politically insulated policy board. The evolution of money has been toward a system that is not subject to political decision making. The bimetallic gold and silver standard had to be abandoned in the late nineteenth century because the questions of profit and loss, success and failure, solvency and bankruptcy were subject to a political decision of whether payment was allowed in gold or silver. It may seem trivial today, but it was a major source of contention for decades and had to be settled, ultimately, in a U.S. presidential election.

The same pitfall lurks for any sort of basket-type system, such as a commodities index. What will be the weightings in the index? What varieties or grades of commodities will you use? How does the market transmit information about monetary conditions through a basket of commodities? Any commodity that is not a simple chemical compound comes in a bewildering variety of grades, which may change or even disappear over time. By *crude oil*, do you mean West

Texas Intermediate, Brent, or Urals crude? Delivered or at the well-head? Cotton, corn, fish, and leather were important commodities in the past, while titanium, uranium, vinyl chloride, and DRAMs (memory chips) are more significant today. These may seem like minuscule issues now, but when fortunes hang in the balance they become the source of riotous contention. Interest groups lobby furiously to pressure governments into adopting changes that benefit them. When one commodity falls in price, the devaluationists will insist that the commodity's weighting in the basket increase. (There will always be devaluationists.) A basket system would also pose problems for redeemability. Under a monometallic system, there's no question of what the dollar is. It is not gold *or* silver, but gold alone. Gold is an element. It will not change 10, 50, or 100 years in the future. Contracts can be formed without the risk of future legal disagreements. Through history, the number of commodities used as money has steadily shrunk, not increased.

In practice, aggregate commodity prices tend to lag changes in currency values by about a year. In other words, when the value of a currency falls, the price of gold rises immediately, and the price of a broad basket of commodities tends to rise about a year later. This phenomenon has been seen in centuries of data, and it continues to the present day. It is hardly optimal to base a monetary system on such an imprecise and lagging indicator. Decisions to increase or decrease the supply of money must be made on a day-to-day and even hour-to-hour basis.

The strength of a gold standard is not a function of the amount of gold locked away in hoards. It is based, first and foremost, on the soundness of a promise between the government and the people. If the promise is good, as two centuries of experience had proven in Britain in the late nineteenth century, very little gold will be needed. If a government aims to break its promise with the people, it does not matter if gold has been piled to the rafters in Midas's treasury. With a stroke of the pen, as Roosevelt did in 1933 and Nixon did in 1971, the government can confiscate the gold and tear the gold standard to tatters. (The result of Roosevelt's decision, by the way, was a dramatic increase in the government's gold holdings.)

On the contrary, a large reserve can make the authorities lazy about adhering to the discipline of the gold standard. The colossal reserves of gold in the United States after World War II were an open invitation to bend the rules, a bad precedent that, when repeated chronically over the following two decades, ultimately led to the breakup of the world monetary system. The Bank of England of the late nineteenth century, on the other hand, maintained a minimal reserve, which is why it had to manage its affairs with legendary precision.

One reason governments have returned to the gold standard so many times over the course of history is that it is simply cheaper to do so. Because a gold standard lends monetary stability, which in turn allows economic stability, interest rates can fall to very low levels and stay there indefinitely. Interest rates that were common under the gold standard are impossible in today's environment of monetary chaos. Amsterdam had rates of around 3.5 percent during its heyday in the seventeenth century. In 1751, a large part of the British government's debt was refinanced at a 3 percent rate and an infinite maturity. After a surge in interest rates during and after the Napoleonic Wars, British interest rates again fell to the 3 percent range in the latter half of the nineteenth century, and World War II was financed at around 2.25 percent. All borrowers enjoyed the low interest rates, which encouraged brisk economic development. Corporate rates were routinely below 5 percent, even for 40- or 100-year bonds, which were common at that time. In 1957 a first-time homebuyer in the United States could get a mortgage at 4.57 percent. A 6 percent home mortgage was considered high. These low market interest rates are evidence of the stability of gold's value.

It is still possible today to get a gold loan. It is a preferred method of finance for gold-mining companies. The borrower borrows gold, not dollars, and repays the loan in gold. The interest rate on such gold loans (known as *leases*) has not changed much since seventeenth-century Amsterdam or nineteenth-century Britain, averaging about 1.5 percent over the past two decades. This discount rate on gold also shows up in the valuation of gold-mining companies, which, unique among metal miners, tend to be valued based on their reserves with a discount rate below 5 percent. See Figure 5.1.

One of the most pervasive and confusing claims about the gold standard is that it somehow balances out trade between countries so that there is never a persistent current account surplus or deficit. This is nonsense; a gold standard does no such thing, nor would it be desirable for it to do so.

This theory is generally attributed to David Hume, specifically his essay "Of the Balance of Trade" in the year 1752, and can be found today in virtually every academic treatise and college textbook about the subject, though it is a perversion of Hume's actual argument.

All of the financial arrangements possible with a floating currency are possible with a gold standard. If two countries' currencies are both pegged to gold, international trade and finance is made much easier, since the risks of currency fluctuation are eliminated. This can lead to large international capital flows, which today are mislabeled "current account imbalances." The large international capital flows of the late nineteenth century are a perfect example of this.

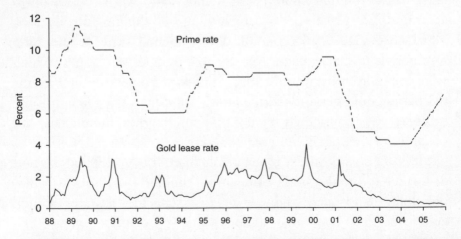

FIGURE 5.1 United States One-Year Gold Lease Rate and U.S. Dollar Bank Prime Rate, 1988–2005

The international trade in gold bullion is simply the process by which a good moves from where it is in relative surplus (a gold-producing country), to where it is in relative deficit (a country without mines). In this way the value of gold is, as Hume said, "like water," always finding an even level, always the same value everywhere.

Another reason for international gold flow is that one country or another has not been properly managing its gold standard.

Two countries using a gold standard are effectively sharing the same monetary system. The situation between countries is no different than the situation, for example, between the different states in the United States. Does anybody care about the balance of payments of New Jersey and whether it runs a trade surplus with Pennsylvania? It is completely irrelevant. Does New York ever suffer from a surplus of money while Connecticut suffers from a shortage of money? Never happens. If trade between New York and Honolulu or Miami and Anchorage is irrelevant when they share the same currency, the same must be true of trade between Boston and Montreal, or Seattle and Vancouver, or San Diego and Tijuana. Hume made the exact same argument:

> What happens in small portions of mankind, must take place in greater. The provinces of the Roman empire, no doubt, kept their balance with each other, and with Italy, independent of the legislature; as much as the several counties of Great Britain, or the several parishes of each county. And any man who travels over Europe at this day, may see, by the prices of commodities, that money, in spite of the absurd jealousy of princes and states, has brought itself nearly to a level; and that the difference between one kingdom and another is not greater in this respect, than it is often between different provinces of the same kingdom.[9]

The theories that are attributed to Hume are really variants of the monetary theories of the mercantilists and reflect the mercantilists' feverish fascination with fallacious "trade imbalances," which persists to this day. The great achievement of the classical economists, beginning with Hume, was to smash the grip of these erroneous notions and allow world trade to flourish.[10]

Unfortunately, quite a few gold standard advocates today propose what they call a "real" or "true" or "genuine" or "pure" or "100 percent" gold standard, something of a misnomer for a system that was always unusual and basically went extinct in the mid-eighteenth century. Any system that pegs a currency's value to gold, using market processes based on supply adjustment, is a gold standard. There is nothing purer. The "pure gold standard" advocates are motivated by ancient memories of governments' broken promises. In their efforts to create an unbreakable gold standard, one that is supposedly immune to political subterfuge, they have created a plan that is technically and politically impossible to begin with. Such arguments have been around since at least the Renaissance, a tradition of hard-money cranks providing a counterpoint to the even more pervasive tradition of soft-money cranks.

The stipulation of 100 percent gold reserve backing of banknotes (or a wholly metallic currency) alone is an insurmountable obstacle. At present there are about 4 billion ounces of gold in the world, a figure that grows by about 2 percent per year from new production. At a market rate of $350 per ounce, the world supply of gold is worth about $1,400 billion, compared to the U.S. monetary base of about $800 billion. In other words, to give a 100 percent gold reserve backing to U.S. dollar banknotes, roughly half the entire world gold supply—every wedding band, dental filling, Rolex, and Tutankhamen's coffin—would have to be locked up in Fort Knox! The rest of the world would have to fend for itself. Nor does this accounting make any provision for bank deposits, which under this scheme would also require 100 percent gold reserve backing. The amount of banknotes plus deposits in the United States was recently around $7.061 trillion, and that does not include dollar-denominated deposits in foreign countries.

Even if such drastic measures were possible, they offer no advantage. The strength of the gold standard is the strength of the government's promise to uphold the integrity of the monetary system, not a commitment to dig gold out of the ground and then bury it again in government vaults. If the promise is good, very little gold is needed. If the promise is broken, no amount of gold can put it back together.

Fixed reserve requirements, whether 100 percent, 40 percent, or 10 percent, have actually caused quite a bit of mischief over the years, for although the reserve is set aside for times of need, when the need arrives, institutions have often found that they are barred by law from using the reserve. This is analogous to a regulation that hikers must carry a rain jacket in their pack in case of rain, but when rain begins to fall, the regulation keeps them from taking the jacket out of their pack! In the long run, growth in the supply of world base money has tended to outrun the 2 percent average annual growth in world gold supply, leading to a series of steps throughout history to reduce the reserve backing of banknotes. This economizing on gold is perfectly natural, indeed unavoidable. The final expression of this trend was the Bretton Woods system, in which the world gold standard's sole reserve consisted of the gold holdings of the United States. European governments also held gold, but although this gold was termed a "reserve" it could not be accessed through redeemability and was merely a gold holding of the government.

Many of the criticisms directed at today's gold standard advocates are, alas, richly deserved.

Humanity settled on gold to serve as a worldwide standard of value after millennia of experimentation with other solutions. Scores of alternatives have been tried and abandoned. Cowrie shells once traded as money throughout Oceania, Africa, and the Middle and Far East. They were used in payment of taxes until the early twentieth century in Uganda. Other contenders have included cows, wheat, whales' teeth, giant stone disks, and strings of beads. In 1715 in North Carolina, 17 commodities were declared legal tender. Homer recalls the use of cauldrons and iron tripods as money in the ancient world.

Though alternatives persisted in the periphery, the world's commercial centers soon adopted metals as money. "Abraham was very rich in livestock, in silver, and gold," says the Bible (Genesis 13:2). Metal rings have apparently been used as money since the predynastic era in Egypt (fourth millennium BC) and have been found in Mycenae and in the Palace of Knossos in Crete. Copper and bronze were abandoned in favor of silver and gold in Europe in Roman times, though they lasted much longer in China. In the Zambezi River basin, there is archaeological evidence of underground gold-mining operations dating from 100,000 BC. In the New World, cocoa beans traded as small change, but gold and silver were hoarded as a grander store of wealth, much to the Spaniards' delight. The final challenger, silver, was abandoned throughout the world in the late nineteenth century (with China and India again laggards). Scores, if not hundreds, of systems managed by the forerunners of today's central bank policy boards have also been attempted, dating from at least the eighth century BC, but they have always failed, and the citizenry has always guided a return to systems based on precious metals.

The decision to use gold as the monetary Polaris, the universal standard of value, is not the product of a deductive process, a weighing of pros and cons, but the end result of millennia of trial-and-error experimentation. It is possible only to postulate, in hindsight, why this process produced the result it has. Nor does anyone claim that gold is a perfect and unchanging measure of value. It is simply the best measure available, the one that, if adhered to in the long run, least burdens the citizenry with the effects of inflation and deflation. The North Star itself has a bit of a wiggle, as do the Earth's magnetic poles.

Gold and silver were independently adopted as money in China, Japan, Africa, Europe, and the Americas. No mere superstition could produce such a result. It is only because few are able to explain this result that gold's functional supremacy takes on the air of superstition or faith.

The use of gold for monetary and quasi-monetary purposes dates back before the beginning of recorded history and predates the monetary use of silver, which takes some metallurgical skill to isolate, by several thousands of years. However, because of its rarity and high value, gold was not useful for smaller day-to-day transactions, and it long took a minor but persistent role behind more easily traded mediums of exchange such as cowrie shells and wheat, or later, bronze, copper, and silver.

Gold is an element; it comes in only one form and does not chemically combine with other elements. It does not tarnish or rust. It is highly malleable and can be pounded with hand tools into thin foils and then back into lumps. It is easy to melt, and it can be subdivided indefinitely. Because of its extraordinary density, it cannot be counterfeited, for all other common metals (except for platinum, which is more valuable) are less dense and thus easily discovered. Unlike a cowrie shell, it cannot be crushed or broken. It is found throughout the world and is present even in seawater.

Gold is a singularly useless metal. Except for a few uses such as in electronics and dentistry, there is little industrial demand for gold. Uses such as jewelry (including gold teeth) are quasi-monetary. Pure gold is too soft for use in jewelry, and it must be alloyed for such use. Silver, a much more chemically reactive metal, is useful for photography, for example, where much of it is now used. More than half of silver production now goes into industrial applications in photography, electrical products, catalysts, brazing alloys, dental amalgam, and bearings. Copper and bronze have multitudes of uses in the modern world and were much used in the ancient as well, and these metals tend to be of a value too small for any but the tiniest coins.

As a result, gold is hardly ever consumed, used up, or thrown away. The demand for gold for nonmonetary uses is trivial. There is no competition between monetary and industrial uses of gold. Electronics and dental uses, the two largest uses for gold today, together consume about 6 percent of annual production, or about 0.12 percent of the total supply. There is no utilitarian reason to use gold in dental work. New technologies are allowing ever smaller amounts to serve in electronics. Of the 125 million kilograms of gold estimated to have been mined from prehistory to 2001, humans still possessed

106 million kilograms, or roughly 85 percent of it.[11] Of that total, roughly 34 million kilograms were held by central banks, and 72 million kilograms were held by private citizens.

As a result, the gold market is not subject to the vicissitudes of either supply or demand in the same manner as other markets. Commodities such as steel, foodstuffs, and oil are consumed within a year of their production. For most commodities, *production* and *supply* are nearly synonymous, but annual gold production from mining is a tiny fraction of the total supply, averaging about 2 percent of supply per year, and final consumption is smaller yet. In an average year, the supply of gold grows from 100 units to 102; if production were to suddenly and inexplicably double, the supply would grow from 100 to 104. If gold production ceased completely, supply would begin the year at 100 and end at 100. Gold production is spread throughout the world, making a dramatic rise or drop in production due to political factors unlikely. The largest producer, South Africa, produced 450,000 kilograms in 1999, around 19 percent of the world total of 2.30 million kilograms. The United States was second, with 340,000 kilograms, and Australia was third with 300,000 kilograms. Countries not in the top eight producers accounted for 700,000 kilograms.

Unlike other commodities, the gold futures market is never *backwardated*, meaning that its future value is never less than its present value. In other words, the interest rate on gold lending is always positive. Gold futures trade like currency futures. Gold is money. The Chinese, Koreans, and Japanese have an especially direct way of expressing this concept: The ideogram for metallic gold (金) also means money in a generalized sense. Although these regions used silver extensively for smaller transactions, the ideogram for silver (銀) refers to metallic silver alone.

Gold does not have a magical intrinsic value. Gold is used because it has served well through the centuries as a monetary commodity and measure of value, just as steel has been used to make machinery and copper has served to conduct electricity. That is why humans continue to go to great effort to dig gold out of the ground.

There have never been breakthrough technical inventions that have made gold drastically cheaper to produce. The last two centuries have seen the development of many incremental improvements in gold-mining techniques, but these have been offset by the gradually diminishing quality of existing gold deposits, as 5,000 or more years of mining have tapped out the most easily accessible sources.

The most disruptive thing to happen to the gold market in the past millennium or so was the discovery and plunder of the New World by the Spaniards. This radically reduced the effort needed to produce gold, since often it had already been mined and merely needed to be stolen. The native Americans' lack of resistance to smallpox simplified the Spaniard's task. The result was a flood of gold and, especially, silver to Europe; and by some measures, during the sixteenth century, European commodities prices in terms of gold rose by a factor of 5. But a century is a long time. A fivefold increase in prices—if these figures are accurate—works out to an annual change of around 1.6 percent per year, a far more stable and predictable change than any actively managed currency has ever been able to produce.

Since 1492, the world supply of gold has not risen by more than 5 percent in any one year, and even that modest figure was hit briefly only during the feverish gold rush of the 1850s. A gold rush from the 1890s to 1910 brought production to 3 to 4 percent of supply. Since 1910, it has averaged around 2 percent.[12]

Many people have used commodities price indexes to get an idea of the long-term stability of gold, and Roy Jastram's *The Golden Constant* is a fine example of this sort of effort. However, there is no reason to assume that a commodities index is a better measure of value than gold. Gold has been chosen as the monetary Polaris because it is not subject to the kinds of market factors that affect other commodities, and long-term indexes are often heavily weighted with one commodity or another. There is no higher authority by which one can determine whether prices change due to what von Mises called "goods-induced" factors or "cash-induced" factors. The gold standard is not intended to produce stable prices according to one definition or another, but rather, stable money.

Indexes heavily weighted toward cotton, as some are, will be affected by boll weevils, crop cycles, and trade barriers. Others are heavily weighted with wheat. When looking at such price indexes, it is imperative not to compare them with today's consumer price indexes, which are extremely slow moving and consist largely of housing, health care, and education costs. A reader who notes that a 17 percent fall occurred in a certain commodities index in the 1840s, the 1890s or the 1930s is led to imagine an episode that would produce a 17 percent fall in today's CPI index, which would likely be quite dramatic. A better comparison would be with today's Commodities Research Board commodities index, which has had several moves greater than 20 percent in the past several decades. Between 1996 and 2000, for example, wheat prices in the United States—a large component of historical price indexes—fell over 60 percent.

In the longest term, gold's record is impeccable. Commodities prices were roughly the same in 1717, when Britain began the gold standard, as they were in 1931, when Britain left it. The same held true in the United States between 1800 and 1930.

The volatility of the gold market since 1971 is almost completely due to the volatility of the currencies in which gold is valued, primarily the dollar. Sales of gold by central banks or variability in annual production are very modest compared to the world supply of gold, and have little effect on the price. Predictions that gold would become a commodity after 1971 and trade below $7 per ounce did not pan out. Gold is the world citizenry's standard of value, and, as von Mises predicted, no government action can undo that fact, just as governments were not responsible for its creation.

There is no ultimate authority by which gold's value itself can be measured. If there were, humans would have adopted it as a standard of value and abandoned gold long ago. Yet it can be observed today that when a currency declines in value compared to gold, inflationary phenomena appear. When a currency rises in relation to gold, deflationary phenomena appear. This is true of whatever currency is measured against the golden benchmark.

Gold has been adopted as money because it works. It has defeated every challenger. Though it has been spurned by governments many times, this has never been due to a fault of gold to serve its duty as a standard of value, but because governments had other plans for their currencies beyond maintaining their stability. There is no reason to believe the great monetary successes of the past four centuries, and indeed the past four millennia, could not be re-created in the next four centuries.

CHAPTER 6

TAXES

Economic Miracle to Economic Disaster, and the Art of Statesmanship

There's only one way to kill capitalism—by taxes, taxes, and more taxes.
—**Karl Marx**

The hardest thing in the world to understand is the income tax.
—**Albert Einstein**

Duke Ai asked Yu Zo: "It has been a year of famine and there are not enough revenues to run the state. What should I do?"
   Zo said, "Why can't you use a 10 percent tax?"
   The Duke answered: "I can't even get by on a 20 percent tax, how am I going to do it on 10 percent?"
   Zo said, "If the people have enough, what prince can be in want? If the people are in want, how can the prince be satisfied?"
—***Analects of Confucius* (12:9)**

Perhaps the heart of the entire classical economic viewpoint is a concept known as Say's law, after the great French economist Jean-Baptiste Say. Say's law is utterly simple, yet it can be difficult to grasp. It is more often misunderstood. Say's law is also difficult to put into words.

In short, Say's law states that production and consumption are two facets of one overall act, which is *economic creation*—the manner in which the citizenry cooperates to create what it needs and wants to live. Therefore, excess supply or inadequate demand of the sort typically blamed for recession and decline are aspects of impaired production.

But such a brief description rarely suffices. John Stuart Mill gave one of the most lucid explanations:

> What a country wants to make it richer, is never consumption, but production. Where there is the latter, we may be sure that there is no want of the former. To produce, implies that the producer desires to consume; why else should he give himself useless labor? He may not wish to consume what he himself produces, but his motive for producing and selling is the desire to buy. Therefore, if the producers generally produce and sell more and more, they certainly also buy more and more. Each may not want more of what he himself produces, but each wants more of what some other produces. There will never therefore, be a greater quantity produced, of commodities in general, than there are consumers for. But there may be, and always are, abundances of persons who have the inclination to become consumers of some commodity, but are unable to satisfy their wish, because they have not the means of producing either that, or anything to give in exchange for it. The legislator, therefore, needs not give himself any concern about consumption. There will always be consumption for everything which can be produced, until the wants of all who possess the means of producing are completely satisfied, and then production will not increase any further. The legislator has to look solely to two points: that no obstacle shall exist to prevent those who have the means of producing, from employing those means as they find most for their interest; and that those who have not at present the means of producing, to the extent of their desire to consume, shall have every facility afforded their acquiring the means, that, becoming producers, they may be enabled to consume.[1]

In other words, overproduction and underconsumption, the topic of a debate that began centuries before Mill and continues to the present day, are not intrinsic features of the market economy. The global glut theories popular during the 1990s are just as flawed as the mercantilist theories that Say and Mill were criticizing in their time.

The deep insight behind Say's law has often been grotesquely twisted into the notion that "supply creates its own demand," supposedly the claim that recessions and economic decline are impossible. At times, Say's supporters have been as guilty of this as his detractors. Of course, no sensible economist would argue such a thing. It cannot be denied that recessions and indeed long periods of economic stagnation and decline occur. Even today, the vast majority of the hundred-plus countries of the world are economically moribund, and even the most successful are operating far below their potential. Say himself lived through a period of great economic upheaval that included the French Revolution, hyperinflation, and rise of Napoleon. He was as concerned with how economies fall apart as how they grow. Book I, chapter 15 of his *Treatise on Political Economy* of 1803, which explains the principle now known as Say's law, concludes with the following two paragraphs:

> In a community, city, province, or nation, that produces abundantly, and adds every moment to the sum of its products, almost all the branches of commerce, manufacture, and generally of industry, yield handsome profits, because the demand is great, and because there is always a large quantity of products in the market, ready to bid for new productive services. And vice versa, wherever, by reason of the blunders of the nation or its government, production is stationary, or does not keep pace with consumption, the demand gradually declines, the value of the product is less than the charges of its production; no productive exertion is properly rewarded; profits and wages decrease; the employment of capital becomes less advantageous and more hazardous; it is consumed piecemeal, not through extravagance, but through necessity, and because the sources of profit are dried up. The labouring classes experience a want of work; families before in tolerable circumstances, are more cramped and confined; and those before in difficulties are left altogether destitute. Depopulation,

misery, and returning barbarism, occupy the place of abundance and happiness.

Such are the concomitants of declining production, which are only to be remedied by frugality, intelligence, activity, and freedom.[2]

Production and consumption are two facets of the same act, but Say implies that it is best to focus on production, the supply side, rather than on consumption, the demand side. An analogy could be made to the debate about whether the earth revolves around the sun or the sun revolves around the earth. Technically speaking, both are true. The choice of a center point is arbitrary; if the earth is arbitrarily chosen as the center point, then the sun indeed revolves around the earth. And if the sun is chosen as the center point, then the earth revolves around the sun.

The reason we choose today to arbitrarily define the sun as the center point is that it is much easier to understand celestial mechanics that way. The reason the classical economists chose to understand the expansion and contraction of economies as a phenomenon of rising and falling productivity rather than of demand is that it is easier to understand economics this way. This understanding translates into power in the form of policy decisions that produce the desired results. Policies based on boosting demand often ignore ways to boost supply—and since the two are mirror images of each other, the demand-centered policies invariably disappoint. Quite often, the demand-boosting policies involve steps that cripple production, particularly tax hikes and currency devaluation. Of course, this cannot succeed.

This relativism goes only so far, however. One must produce before consuming. Economics is, fundamentally, the study of how humans make a living. We all now agree that the Earth actually revolves around the sun.

Productivity is often taken to mean the number of widgets a worker or a factory produces in a day, or some such thing, but this is a very narrow and ultimately confusing idea. The solitary human on a deserted island does not labor from dawn until dusk weaving hula skirts by the hundreds or harvesting thousands of coconuts and pineapples. This is not a productive use of his time and effort. The only reason such a man would make this decision is if he were able to trade his products for something he desired—because, in other words, it produced a "profit." Perhaps he traded the coconuts with someone on another island who built dugout canoes. If the ability for the two to trade productively were diminished—let's say by a hostile tribe that interfered with transport between the two islands—then the coconut harvester and the canoe maker would both experience a falloff in demand because of the difficulty each has in trading with the other. Consequentially, they would also produce fewer coconuts and canoes, having no use for them themselves. Although an economist might say that the two have a "supply glut," the problem is that a new trade barrier has prevented the two people from interacting productively.

Thus, many economic phenomena can be understood as changes in people's ability to trade, or in other words, to cooperate productively. Two individuals can face a myriad of trade barriers, which prevent them from cooperating most efficiently. When these barriers are removed, productivity tends to rise. When barriers become greater, productivity tends to fall. Barriers can be geographic, such as an ocean or a mountain range. They can be cultural, such as the difficulty of communicating in foreign languages or different management and communication styles. Storms and piracy threaten the shipping trade. Legal complexities or excessive paperwork can make trade difficult. Many trade barriers are informational and can be overcome by the telegraph, the telephone, or the Internet. Developments in financial technology can make trade easier between providers and users of capital. And government policies can improve or impede trade, through monetary policy, regulation, and taxation.

A decline in productivity can take place because of an increase in barriers to trade due to any reason. If the citizens of Japan, for example, were to suddenly find their islands surrounded by some natural barrier that neither ships nor planes could penetrate, the economy would surely collapse, since the Japanese economy is dependent on imports of raw materials and foodstuffs. Both Japanese exporters and foreign oil and commodities producers would experience an unpleasant decline in demand, which would immediately spread to other sectors of their economies. The productivity gains due to trade with the outside world would be lost.

This is a rather fanciful notion, of course. Realistically, when natural trade barriers are overcome, they do not return. Shipping, once invented, is not forgotten. Neither is air travel, or modern finance, or the online auction, or the telephone. The only kind of trade barriers that tend to both rise and fall over the course of time are those created by governments. This book is about trade barriers—between individuals, not abstractions known as "countries"—created by unstable currencies, but it will not suffice to look at those alone. Regulation can also create trade barriers, but these tend to be easier to comprehend. The trade barriers created by taxation have, historically, been among the most difficult to understand, the most often ignored, and the most dramatic in their effect.

The classical economists thus tend to look to the government when searching for reasons for economic advancement or decline. Today, this analysis has become highly refined.

Because the effects of poor regulation are more readily apparent, people often focus on regulatory reform or privatization as a means to enhance economic growth and productivity. This is by all means a worthwhile endeavor, but its effect is often not great. Most regulations deal with only a tiny segment of the economy. Deregulation of airlines, for example, may cause enormous productivity gains in the airline industry, but the airline industry is perhaps only 0.5 percent of the entire economy. Also, such regulatory reforms tend to be exceedingly complex, politically difficult, may take years to implement, and may be ultimately unsuccessful. Reforms of regulations that affect great swaths of the economy—broad price-fixing programs, for example—would have the greatest effect. The transition from centrally planned communism to a market economy is a kind of regulatory reform. Today, however, most developed countries have learned their lessons and no longer have these kinds of broad economy-stifling regulations. (Major exceptions could be made for the restrictive labor policies of the European countries and regulation of property such as rent control or zoning.)

Taxes, however, affect everyone. Income taxes directly affect everyone who has an income, who may have one in the future, or who provides one to someone else. Corporate taxes affect all corporations, their investors, and, ultimately, the corporation's employees. Capital gains taxes affect all investments—all corporations are someone's investment. Sales taxes involve all consumers and retailers. Monetary reforms affect anyone who uses money or has contracts denominated in money. Obviously, the potential gains to be had in this realm, or the potential consequences of policy error, are much greater.

Excessive taxes discourage production. It's the simplest and most obvious of principles, and yet its vast implications have eluded thinkers throughout history. Taxation is a pivot upon which economies, countries, governments, and empires rise and fall. It can mean the difference between war and peace, prosperity and ruin.

This principle has doubtless been in existence in some form or another ever since governments have been levying taxes. Chapter 57 of the *Tao Te Ching*, written in approximately the fifth century BC, reads:

> Run the country by doing what's expected.
> Win the war by doing the unexpected.
> Control the world by doing nothing.
> How do I know this?
> By this.
>
> The more restrictions and prohibitions in the world
> the poorer the people get.
> The more experts a country has

the more of a mess it's in.
The more ingenious the skillful are
the more monstrous their inventions
The louder the call for law and order
the more the thieves and con men multiply.

So a wise leader might say:
I practice inaction, and the people look after themselves.
I love to be quiet, and the people themselves find justice.
I don't do business, and the people prosper on their own.
I don't have wants, and the people themselves are uncut wood
[naturally virtuous].[3]

Today's libertarian might say: "The government that governs best is the one that governs the least."

The following passage is by the fourteenth-century Arab genius Ibn-Khaldūn, who held high office in several governments and knew firsthand the rise and fall of economies and empires. It is shockingly sophisticated:

In the early stages of the state, taxes are light in their incidence, but fetch in a large revenue; in the later stages the incidence of taxation increases while the aggregate revenue falls off.

This is because the state, if it rests on a religious basis, will exact only dues provided for by Islamic Law, such as the Benevolence Contributions, Land Tax, and Poll Taxes whose rates are low . . . and fixed. . . . Now where taxes and imposts are light, private individuals are encouraged to engage actively in business; enterprise develops, because business men feel it worth their while, in view of the small share of their profits which they have to give up in the form of taxation. And as business prospers . . . the total yield of taxation grows.

As time passes and kings succeed each other . . . they impose fresh taxes on their subjects—farmers, peasants, and others subject to taxation; sharply raise the rate of old taxes to increase their yield; and impose sales taxes . . . until taxation burdens the subjects and deprives them of their gains. People get accustomed to this high level of taxation, because the increases have come about gradually, without anyone's being aware of who exactly it was who raised the rates of the old taxes or imposed the new ones.

But the effects on business of this rise in taxation make themselves felt. For business men are soon discouraged by the comparison of their profits with the burden of their taxes, and between their output and their net profits. Consequently production falls off, and with it the yield of taxation.

The rulers may, mistakenly, try to remedy this decrease in the yield of taxation by raising the rate of taxes. . . . This process of higher tax rates and lower yields (caused by the government's belief that higher rates result in higher returns) may go on until production begins to decline owing to the despair of business men, and to affect population. The main injury of this process is felt by the state, just as the main benefit of better business conditions is enjoyed by it.

From this you must understand that the most important factor making for business prosperity is to lighten as much as possible the burden of taxation . . . [4]

There have always been political leaders, businesspeople, and historians who have grasped this concept and have seen that economic booms can be touched off by lowering taxes or ended by raising taxes. Economists have not been so perceptive; taxation was for a long time neglected by academics and intellectuals of every stripe, whether classical, Keynesian, monetarist, Marxist, or some eclectic combination. Only recently has that imbalance been remedied. The study of economic policy cleaves naturally into monetary and fiscal affairs, but like the two halves of the brain, they are also naturally connected, and in the end both are necessary to make sense of history and set effective policy.

The early classical economists had many valuable and enduring insights about taxation—for example, this passage from Jean-Baptiste Say:

> . . . A tax is not productive to the public exchequer, in proportion to its ratio [rate] . . . it had become a sort of apophthegem, that two and two do not make four in the arithmetic of finance. Excessive taxation is a kind of suicide, whether laid upon objects of necessity, or upon those of luxury. . . .
>
> Were it not almost self-evident, this principle might be illustrated by abundant examples of the profit the state derives from a moderate scale of taxation, where it is sufficiently awake to its own interests.
>
> When Turgot, in 1775, reduced to ½ the market-dues and duties of entry upon fresh sea-fish sold in Paris, their product was nowise diminished. The consumption of that article must, therefore, have doubled, the fishermen and the dealers must have doubled their concerns and their profits; . . . that very increase in production will, beyond doubt, augment the product of taxation in other branches. . . .
>
> We are told by Humboldt . . . that in thirteen years from 1778, during which time Spain adopted a somewhat more liberal system of government in regard to her American dependencies, the increase of the revenue in Mexico alone amounted to no less a sum than 100 millions of dollars; and that she drew from that country, during the same period, an addition in the single article of silver, to the amount of 14,500,000 dollars. We may naturally suppose, that, in those years of prosperity, there was a corresponding, and rather greater increase of individual profits; for that is the source, whence all public revenue is derived.[5]

Adam Smith devotes nearly 80 pages of the *Wealth of Nations* to taxation, and he mentions tax issues throughout. David Ricardo manages closer to 180 pages in his *Principles of Political Economy and Taxation*, which includes this passage:

Notwithstanding the immense expenditure of the English government during the last twenty years, there can be little doubt but that the increased production on the part of the people has more than compensated for it. The national capital has not merely been unimpaired, it has been greatly increased, and the annual revenue of the people, even after the payment of their taxes, is probably greater at the present time than at any former period of our history. . . .

Still, however it is certain that, but for taxation, this increase of capital would have been much greater. There are no taxes which have not a tendency to lessen the power to accumulate.[6]

Unfortunately, Ricardo and others of his era tended to treat individual cases in a somewhat haphazard way and did not integrate their insights into a larger theoretical structure. The study of taxation stagnated, even deteriorated.

Today, most discussion of taxation takes place in the zero-sum framework, which assumes overtly that taxation has no effect on production. In this view, the effect of taxation is to distribute the production of the country into the government's share and the people's share. Economic growth is treated as a mysterious aftereffect, an unpredictable act of God or his archangel, the "trade cycle."

By the latter half of the nineteenth century, mainstream economics had moved even further away from taxes and toward the relationships of price, interest rates, money, investment, and the market system. Many at the time aspired to make economics a science like physics or chemistry, and as a result tended toward concepts that could be reduced to numerical terms and tabulated in time series. There is no way to reduce the stupendous complexities of tax code to an index, and taxation is a facet of economics where human behavior takes center stage. Talking about taxation is often much like talking about management theory: It tends to produce broad generalizations backed by historical case study.

The Austrian school of classical economics, as it made extraordinary advances in understanding the market system and monetary issues, gradually scrubbed taxation issues out of its field of vision completely. Carl Menger's *Principles of Economics*, published in 1871 and considered one of the founding texts of the Austrian school, contains no discussion of taxation. *Human Action*, a 906-page book by Ludwig von Mises published in 1949 and an enduring masterpiece about the monetary and market system, contains less than 20 pages about taxation. His student, Murray Rothbard, called it "economics made whole." Rothbard's own magnum opus, *Man, Economy, and State*, first published in 1962, contains 20 pages about taxation in its 987 pages (the table of contents has 24 pages). Rothbard classifies taxation as a "binary intervention," one involving only the state and the citizen. Zero-sum, in other words.

Even the insights of two centuries earlier were lost. Monetarism, a school of economic analysis led by Milton Friedman since the early 1960s, has ignored fiscal issues almost as a matter of principle. The Keynesians of every variety tend to look at taxation as simply the corollary to their fascination with spending, or demand, and operate from a zero-sum framework. John Maynard Keynes's *General Theory of Employment, Interest, and Money* lacks a discussion of taxation altogether. The title alone tells the reader where Keynes intends to get his employment. This should be no surprise, for Alfred Marshall's influential *Principles of Economics*, first published in 1890 and the text from which Keynes doubtless studied as an undergraduate, also has no mention of taxes in its 858 pages. Keynesians occasionally propose tax cuts as a way to increase spending and economic activity. Policymakers become fascinated with "putting money in people's pockets." Oddly enough, if tax rates are reduced, the technique works, not because of changes in spending but because of taxation's effects on the efficiency and productive capacity of the extended order.

Rebate checks, which are sometimes labeled "tax cuts" but do not affect tax rates, have only the briefest effect on the economy. Why some government disbursements—checks in the mail—should be labeled "tax cuts" and others labeled "welfare payments" is a question of political expediency, not economic effect.

"Pocket theory" has often been used to justify tax hikes as a counterinflationary measure, since what is inflation but too much spending and, presumably, too much money in people's pockets? By neglecting to observe that inflation is a monetary phenomena, the policy simply piles a tax hike on an inflation, with recession and increased inflation the likely result. The policy of "cut taxes in a recession, cut spending in a boom" is consistent both with Keynesian and classical principles. However, this, too, often becomes "raise spending in a recession, raise taxes in a boom," which will lead eventually to economic ruin.

Despite the amazingly retrograde state of discussion today, the enduring principles of taxation have never really been forgotten. Keynes himself, the self-taught essayist whose intellectual flexibility is not shared by many of his descendants, once argued:

> Nor should the argument seem strange that taxation may be so high as to defeat its object, and that, given sufficient time to gather the fruits, a reduction of taxation will run a better chance than an increase of balancing the budget. For to take the opposite view today is to resemble a manufacturer who, running at a loss, decides to raise his price, and when his declining sales increase the loss, wrapping himself in the rectitude of plain arithmetic, decides that prudence requires him to raise the price still more—and who, when at last his account is balanced with naught on both sides, is still found righteously declaring that it would have been the act of a gambler to reduce the price when you were already making a loss.[7]

The following rather sophisticated passage is from *Newsweek* columnist Henry Hazlitt's *Economics in One Lesson*, which became an international bestseller in 1946:

> Taxes inevitably affect the actions and incentives of those from whom they are taken. When a corporation loses a hundred cents of every dollar it loses, and is permitted to keep only 60 cents of every dollar it gains, and when it cannot offset its years of losses against its years of gains, or cannot do so adequately, its policies are affected. It does not expand its operations, or it expands only those attended

with a minimum of risk. People who recognize this situation are deterred from starting new enterprises. Thus old employers do not give more employment, or not as much more as they might have; and others decide not to become employers at all. Improved machinery and better-equipped factories come into existence much more slowly than they otherwise would. The result in the long run is that consumers are prevented from getting better and cheaper products, and real wages are held down.

There is a similar effect when personal incomes are taxed at 50, 60, 75 and 90 percent. People begin to ask themselves why they should work six, eight or ten months of the entire year for the government, and only six, four or two months for themselves and their families. If they lose the whole dollar when they lose, but can keep only a dime of it when then win, they decide that it is foolish to take risks with their capital. In addition, the capital available for risk-taking itself shrinks enormously. It is being taxed away before it can be accumulated. In brief, capital to provide new private jobs is first prevented from coming into existence, and the part that does come into existence is then discouraged from starting new enterprises. The government spenders create the very problem of unemployment that they profess to solve.[8]

Many of the great insights into taxation have been made by generalists. Perhaps it has taken a journalist, writing for a general audience, to see the obvious, as the professional economists grew ever more blinded by their intricate mathematica and increasing specialization. Jean–Baptiste Say himself was a journalist by trade.

Today's political debate about taxation falls almost completely within the zero-sum framework. Left-leaning Democrats insist that government take a larger share of the pie to redistribute through various welfare programs, while Republicans insist that government allow a larger slice of the pie to remain in private hands. Some will propose raising taxes on the wealthy and cutting them for the less-well-off, and others will propose the opposite—all squabbles over shares of the imaginary pie. From time to time, a politician will emerge who will champion tax rate reduction and reform as a way to increase the size of the pie—Calvin Coolidge, John F. Kennedy, and Ronald Reagan—but these leaders have been the exception rather than the rule.

The wealth-generating effects of effective tax policy are still totally unappreciated by those who tremble with doubt about whether it is actually possible that tax revenues could increase as a result of a reduction in tax rates. When a country gets a succession of pro-growth leaders, as Japan did in the 1950s and 1960s, the results can be spectacular. In 1960, Japan's central government received ¥1.801 trillion of tax revenue. In 1970, after cutting taxes every single year, it had revenue of ¥7.775 trillion! These were gold-linked noninflationary yen. The central government's slice of the pie hardly changed—it was 11.2 percent of gross domestic product in 1960, and 10.6 percent in 1970—but the size of the pie increased enormously, with growth fueled by continuous tax cutting. During the 20 years from 1950 to 1970, in which taxes were cut incessantly, the Japanese government's tax revenues increased by a multiple of 16. Even Japan, though, has not been able to sustain its past focus on wealth creation, and today its leaders, operating in a strict zero-sum framework, are among the world's worst. Now the flame has been passed to Ireland, Estonia, and, most recently, Russia and the countries of Eastern Europe. See Figure 6.1.

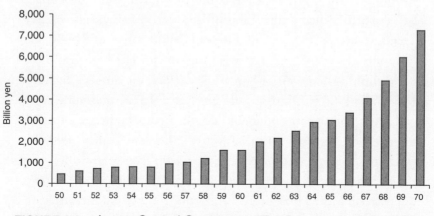

FIGURE 6.1   Japan: Central Government Tax Revenues, 1950–1970

Today, in the debate taking place in many countries about finding a way to finance their social security systems in the decades to come, hardly anyone has suggested a growth-oriented solution. Productivity-generating tax reform would allow the pie to be enlarged to such an extent that social security could be easily funded without hardship. At the end of all the financial analysis, the final demographic fact is that, under the present system, two workers will have to support one retiree. The only question is whether the two workers will be productive enough to support the retiree with 30 percent of their income, 20 percent, or 10 percent—with the additional complication that, if they are being taxed 30 percent of their income to support the retiree, the workers' productivity will be that much more impaired.

Every politician knows that the public wants tax cuts without cuts in government services. Politicians assume the public is behaving like an irresponsible child, but as it turns out, the public is smarter than the politicians. In government you really can have your cake and eat it, too—if you increase productivity enough to bake two cakes instead of one.

President Calvin Coolidge offered a more practical example:

Experience does not show that the higher rate produces the largest returns. Experience is all the other way. When the surtax on incomes of $300,000 and over was but 10 percent, the revenue was about the same as when it was at 65 percent. There is no escaping the fact that when the taxation of large incomes is excessive, they tend to disappear. In 1916 there were 206 incomes of $1,000,000 or more. Then the high rate went into effect. The next year there were only 141, and in 1918, but 67. In 1919, the number declined to 65. In 1920 it fell to 33, and in 1921 it was further reduced to 21. I am not making argument with the man who believes that 55 percent ought to be taken away from the man with $1,000,000 income, or 68 percent from a $5,000,000 income; but when it is considered that in the effort to get these amounts we are rapidly approaching the point of getting nothing at all, it is necessary to look for a more practical method.[9]

A full integration of taxation into economic theory had to wait until the 1960s and 1970s, with the supply-side school that was germinated by Robert Mundell and his student Arthur Laffer. (The term *supply side* refers to the classical focus on production.) After a century of ignoring tax issues, it is no surprise that academic orthodoxy has been slow to assimilate these developments. The breakthrough taxation discoveries of the supply-siders, the newest school of classical economics, when combined with the previous discoveries about money and the market system, offer an incredible promise: It apparently has become possible to explain all of economic history, booms and busts, the rise and fall of nations and empires, the onset of war and the return to peace, in economic principles, and not only that, as the result of specific government policies. There was no longer any need to appeal to psychological instability in the populace, the character of certain ethnic groups, moral and ethical decay, some sort of inevitable trade cycle, inexplicable long waves, inherent flaws in the capitalist system, technological change, or any other ad hoc deus ex machina, or even simple fate.

Arthur Laffer went so far as to claim there are only four major reasons for a country to suffer major economic decline: monetary instability (probably devaluation), high or rising taxes, high or rising tariffs, and excessive regulation, particularly wage and price controls. Since tariffs are simply a form of taxation, the list reduces to only three. And since wage and price controls are usually imposed in reaction to the problems created by monetary instability or destructive tax policy, the list reduces further to two points—*low taxes, stable money*. The principles of good economic management can be expressed in those four words. If there is some sort of major economic difficulty or disaster in the world, it can usually be traced to some government whose taxes were not low enough (and probably rose sharply) or whose money was not stable enough (and whose value probably fell sharply).

This theory of taxation is actually just a generalization of an argument that has been applied to the specific situation of international trade since the mid-eighteenth century and is now universally accepted. The mercantilist orthodoxy of the time held that exports were good and imports were bad. Thus every country tried to suppress imports by erecting punitive tariffs or other barriers to international trade. The purpose of the tariffs was not revenue, but protectionism. A protective tariff, if it is successful, naturally does not produce much revenue. The more effective it is at suppressing trade, the less revenue it generates. The effect of this policy was to create constant hostility and cripple productivity. The advent of the classical economists was in large part spurred by arguments against this destructive orthodoxy. The easiest way for England to acquire wine, they argued, is to sell woolens to France. The easiest way for France to acquire woolens is to sell wine to England. By engaging in unhampered trade, both England and France in the end enjoyed a greater amount of woolens and wine, the fruits of their increased productivity.

But "England" as an entity doesn't sell woolens, nor does the entity "France" sell wine. Only individual English people (or individual English corporations) sell woolens, and only individual French people sell wine. The Englishman, ultimately, doesn't care whether his trading partner is English, French, Belgian, Argentine, or Chinese. If the after-tax profits are acceptable, he'll sell woolens to anybody. On the individual level, nationality is irrelevant. People don't work for their governments, only for themselves. Today's national economies are merely regulatory jurisdictions for portions of the world economy. If there's an advantage to be had for the Englishman by trading with a Frenchman, or another Englishman, for that matter, then the trade will be made. The Frenchman likewise does not care about the nationality of his trading partner. In the hundreds and thousands and perhaps millions of trades the Frenchman engages in throughout the year as part of his daily life, some will be with English people, some with Belgians, and many with other French people. Individuals live in a country, but from the standpoint of commerce they have no nationalities.

Tariffs are taxes, and it can also be said that taxes are like tariffs.

Just as lowering tariffs between England and France allows greater trade and productivity between two foreigners, lowering tariffs (taxes) within England allows greater trade and productivity between two countrymen. An individual's life in the modern market economy consists of dozens, if not hundreds, of trades daily, both monetary and nonmonetary. Many of the monetary trades involve a tariff. The income tax is a tariff on trade between employer and employee. The sales tax is a tariff between retailer and consumer. The corporate income tax is a tariff between corporation and investor. If these tariffs are *protective tariffs* (i.e. with rates high enough to discourage trade), then they will cripple production and produce little revenue. It is sometimes illuminating to think of income tax rates the way tariffs or sales taxes are computed, as a percentage of the net transaction. A 10 percent income tax rate is an 11 percent tariff on income (the government gets 11 percent of what the employee gets). A 25 percent rate is a 33 percent tariff. A 50 percent rate is a 100 percent tariff. An 80 percent rate is a 400 percent tariff! It becomes easier to see why rates over 25 percent or so can quickly snuff out transactions.

Of course, if taxes were always bad, then humans would have long ago discovered a form of government without taxation. The fact is that if the citizenry wishes to have a government that will undertake communal endeavors and pay for them, the citizenry wishes to be taxed. At a minimum an economy will need some sort of judicial system and police force to enforce the laws of contract and private property on which a market economy depends. Probably a military force will be necessary, as will be some system of welfare, providing for those who momentarily are unable to provide for themselves. By providing the funding for such services, taxation indeed increases productivity and the general welfare.

By wishing to fund communal endeavors, the citizenry in effect desires government services more than the goods and services of the private market, up to a certain point. To the extent this is true, taxation will not deter production. If governments make excessive demands on their citizens, and citizens appreciate that their tax revenues will not be put to productive uses, then taxation becomes a deterrent to production. This is the principle expressed in the Laffer curve.

It is entirely possible for an economy to be undertaxed. Although this is practically nonexistent today, it is easy to imagine such a situation in, for example, the middle or late nineteenth century, when governments had rock-bottom tax rates but provided minimal government services. At that time, the citizenry as a whole likely sensed that productivity and general welfare would be increased by raising taxation to fund safety-net welfare programs or universal education.

Universal medical coverage, paid for via taxes, may be another situation in which the citizenry is happy to be taxed in return for the services received. Ideology aside, it is a measurable fact that countries that have universal medical care, such as Japan or Germany, spend less, as a percentage of GDP, on health care than the one holdout among developed countries, the United States, which continues to struggle with a largely private system. Health and longevity statistics suggest that the cheaper state-run systems are also more effective. In this case, both companies and individuals have apparently been better off paying the state to provide health care coverage, through payroll taxes, than paying private health insurance companies.

The government services desired by the citizenry and, correspondingly, the citizenry's desire to be taxed, will change—sometimes abruptly—through time. The great challenge of government leaders is to be sensitive to these changes. If the government is at war, and the citizenry believes that the war is worth fighting, it will demand a high level of war expenditures and will accept a high level of taxation. People will engage in productive activities, even though they are heavily taxed, so that the government will get the revenue needed to provide the services desired by the citizenry. The most zealous will even volunteer to go to the front lines, voluntarily "taxing" themselves, and many will pay the highest price.

If the war is not supported by the citizenry, it will refuse to "buy" war-making services by engaging in highly taxed activities. Seeing no advantage gained by taxes that divert revenue to the government and little personal gain because of the high tax rates, people will reject highly taxed activities. The effect of wartime taxes will be recession. If the citizenry is violently opposed to the government's policies and high tax rates, it may escape the taxation by joining the other side— as the Romans eventually learned. If there is no other side, the citizenry will create one and a civil war will ensue.

After a war, the citizenry's need for government services declines, as does its willingness to be taxed. If governments fail to be sensitive to the change in the citizenry's desires and lower tax rates accordingly, a recession will often result as people abandon over-taxed activities.

But this still remains too simplistic. Taxation is not a simple quantity or single rate that is raised or lowered. The tax code, covering thousands of pages, cannot be summed up in a single value. Governments and leaders must also be sensitive to how revenue is collected. They must ask themselves constantly: What taxation system will least detract from the forces of production while funding the desired government services? How can we get the most while losing the least? Should services be funded through debt instead of taxation? Sadly, only a minuscule fraction of the tens of thousands of politicians, analysts, bureaucrats, journalists, and others involved in the creation of tax policy today ever ask these questions, much less provide reasonable answers to them. One tax system that channels 20 percent of a country's gross domestic product to the government may encourage rapid growth. Another, which produces the same tax burden of 20 percent, may choke off development and drive the economy into deep recession.

Like so many basic taxation concepts, the notion of tax efficiency is not new. As Henry George put it in *Progress and Poverty* (1879):

> The mode of taxation is, in fact, quite as important as the amount.
> As a small burden badly placed may distress a horse that could carry

with ease a much larger one properly adjusted, so a people may be impoverished and their power of producing wealth destroyed by taxation which, if levied another way, could be borne with ease.[10]

A century earlier, Adam Smith wrote: "Every tax ought to be so contrived as both to take out and to keep out of the pockets of the people as little as possible, over and above what it brings into the public treasury of the state."[11] And a century before that, the legendary French finance minister Jean-Baptiste Colbert said: "The art of taxation consists in plucking the largest amount of feathers with the least possible amount of hissing."

It is not hard to think of tax systems that would be absurdly inefficient and destructive to an economy despite generating only a small amount of revenue. A 100 percent tax on corporate profits, for example, would cause the profit-driven capitalist economy to grind to a halt, even though corporate profits are a small fraction of gross domestic product. Businesses would either cease operations in that country or operate illegally, and the tax would produce no revenue. The tax revenue/GDP ratio would thus be 0 percent. In practice, taxes on the investment process—taxes on trading assets, capital gains, dividends, and interest income—tend to have the most intense negative economic effects in proportion to the modest revenue they generate. They are highly inefficient, and some of the wiser leaders in the world have thought it best not to tax these activities at all. Despite high income taxes and value-added taxes (VATs) in Europe, for example, taxes on corporations, assets, and investments are lower than in the United States. The United States, in fact, has some of the highest taxes on capital and corporations in the developed world. These differences between the European and the U.S. taxation systems are one reason why economic performance in both areas is not as divergent as one might otherwise presume.

Low, broad-based taxes such as sales taxes (below 10 percent) or taxes on employment income (below 25 percent) tend to have the fewest negative effects and generate large amounts of revenue.

Simple taxes, without a lot of exemptions, cause less economic distortion and can be set at lower rates.

Recent flat-tax proposals, advocated by both Republican Steve Forbes and Democrat Jerry Brown, are excellent examples of tax systems designed for maximum efficiency by eliminating exemptions and taxing at a low rate. Often mistaken for tax cuts, they are actually designed to produce an amount of revenue identical to that of the existing tax system, but being much more efficient, in practice they would generate more revenue—which could be used to fund government welfare programs if so desired. Flat-tax-like systems in Estonia, Russia, and Hong Kong have been wildly successful, inspiring Latvia, Lithuania, Slovakia, and the Ukraine to recently adopt such systems.

The thousands of pages of the national budget defy summarization, just like the tax code. The citizenry does not demand that the government spend, for example, "$100 billion dollars." It demands specific services. This is perhaps most apparent at the state or local level, where the electorate may vote for a bond issuance to build a museum (implicitly agreeing to be taxed to pay for the bond) and reject a bond for a flood control levee. The citizenry may wish to be taxed to provide welfare services, but not to fund a large military, or vice versa. Of course, no taxpayer wants to fund government waste. An education system that costs $1 billion may be better than no system, but a system that provides equivalent services and costs only $500 million is better.

The economist Alan Reynolds, observing statistics on taxpayer behavior in the United States over the past several decades, has in partial jest coined "Reynolds' law," which states: Americans will allow themselves to be taxed only at a net rate of around 10 percent of their income. In other words, whatever tax system is in place, whether rates are high or low, net tax revenues to the government will be around 10 percent of gross income. Like all so-called laws of human behavior, its future validity is not guaranteed, but this simple ratio has held up rather well in the past. Between 1951 and 2003, the ratio was never below 9 percent and never above 11.2 percent. When President Clinton pushed up top income rates to 39.5 percent in 1993, the ratio was 9.3 percent—down from 10.1 percent in 1988, when the top rate was 28 percent. Reynolds' law suggests that the zero-sum crowd might have it completely backward. Apparently, it is often difficult for a government to alter its slice of the pie, whether rates are high or low or whether deductions are generous or stingy. The government has only been able to alter the size of the pie, by adopting a tax system that encourages growth instead of one that suppresses growth. See Figures 6.2 and 6.3.

Efforts to tax the rich are often counterproductive—the so-called rich (usually the upper middle class) end up paying less tax, as a percentage of total tax revenue, than they had under lower tax rates. By attempting to make the wealthy foot the bill of government, in effect the policy shifts the burden to the lower income classes. In 1980, for example, when the top income tax rate was 70 percent, the top 1 percent of income earners paid 19.0 percent of all tax revenue and the lower 50 percent paid 7.1 percent. In 1988, after the Reagan tax cuts lowered the top tax rate to 28 percent, the top 1 percent paid 27.5 percent of all tax revenue and the lower 50 percent paid 5.6 percent.

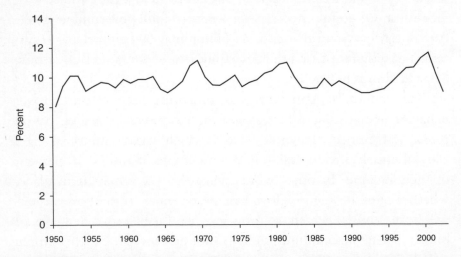

FIGURE 6.2 U.S. Income Tax Revenues as a Percentage of Personal Income, 1950–2002

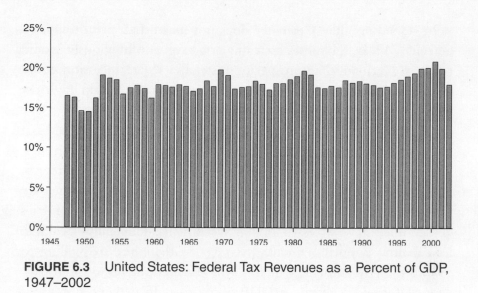

FIGURE 6.3   United States: Federal Tax Revenues as a Percent of GDP, 1947–2002

This was no fluke, for the United States had the same experience in the 1920s. In 1921 the top tax rate was 73 percent, and by 1926 it had fallen to 25 percent. In that period, the percentage of tax revenue paid by those with incomes over $100,000 (about $1.75 million today) rose from 28.1 percent to 50.9 percent. The percentage of tax revenue paid by those with incomes under $25,000 fell from 40.1 percent to 14.5 percent. A similar pattern can be seen during the 1960s, when taxes were first cut and later raised again. Britain had the same experience after the Thatcher tax cuts of the early 1980s. If by "taxing the rich," policymakers intend to have the higher income brackets fund a larger share of government services, experience shows the most effective technique is to lower top tax rates to no higher than 30 percent. High tax rates on higher incomes often serve only as a political justification for high taxes on moderate incomes. If high incomes are taxed at 50 percent, a 25 percent rate on moderate incomes does not seem as high by comparison.

Governments should be cautious before they raise taxes in an effort to emulate what they consider to be international standards. The fact that one country can be marginally prosperous with a high value-added tax, like Germany, does not mean that instituting a 15 percent VAT in a country that did not have one previously would result in Germany-like prosperity. Instead, a severe recession could result. Often, countries are able to manage under certain high tax rates because taxation of other activities is kept low.

Governments of developing economies, in particular, should not adopt the tax systems of the governments of developed economies. The developed countries are able to support generous welfare systems that the developing countries cannot, simply because they are wealthier. The citizenries of developed and developing countries desire different services of their governments. Generally speaking, less-wealthy populations have less revenue that they are willing to give to the government, which is why these countries so often have a ratio of total tax revenues/GDP of less than 15 percent, compared to over 30 percent in the developed countries. Taxing the rich to give to the poor makes sense, up to a point. Taxing the poor to give to the poor does not.

Tax evasion is caused by high tax rates. Citizens are perfectly happy to pay taxes if the tax rates are in line with citizens' notions of what the government should be paid. In Anhui Province in China, in 2001, tax evasion was rampant and tax collectors were regularly assaulted by irate citizens. After a major reduction in tax rates, the same citizens lined up at the tax office to pay their taxes.

A fine example is presented by the former West and East Germany. The result of reunification since 1990 has not been an outburst of prosperity for East Germany, despite the conversion from communism to capitalism and huge government spending in the region. Under the same government, the same laws, the same tax code, and the same currency, why should unemployment in eastern Germany continue at crushing levels of 18 percent or more, while the rate is 7 percent in western Germany? Why did China enjoy 10 percent growth rates as it converted from a centrally planned economy to market capitalism, while eastern Germany, formerly a center of industrial excellence, with every conceivable advantage, is a disaster?

One answer is simply that developing eastern Germany cannot tolerate the western German tax system. Eastern Germany also cannot tolerate the western German welfare system, which is far too generous and creates large incentives not to be productive.

The solution for a developing country is to accept that the citizenry wishes to devote perhaps 8 percent or so of GDP to government activities and *to design a tax system appropriate for this goal.* For example, a country like Bangladesh could prosper with a tax system that consists of nothing but a 10 percent VAT. Or, to give the poorest every advantage, a 15 percent income tax with a generous basic deduction, plus a modest tariff. The result, when paired with a stable currency, would be breathtaking economic growth, the natural disappearance of tax evasion (not to mention that a single tax would be far easier to enforce), and enormous increases in tax revenue. Although the developed countries now have much higher levels of taxation, of 30 to 50 percent of GDP, when they themselves were developing economies in high-growth mode, they often had tax systems even simpler and less intrusive than this. In 1930, for example, the first year such figures are available, U.S. federal government tax revenues amounted to 4.2 percent of GDP. In the century before the imposition of the income tax in 1913, the ratio was far less. When Japan was undergoing its first round of industrialization in the late nineteenth century, the government was funded almost entirely by a modest property tax and a tax on alcohol.

The U.S. example would have been highly praised by Mencius, a Chinese philosopher of the fourth century BC who tirelessly advocated low taxes to encourage prosperity. Mencius recommended that farmers be taxed at one-ninth of their produce and city dwellers at one-tenth.

The problem with high taxes and unstable money is that both cripple the productivity made possible by the extended order of trade, specialization, and investment. The extended order is the mechanism by which humans have enriched themselves beyond the hunting and gathering stage. Although it is quite robust, it takes only a relatively small drop in its overall efficiency to be felt as a major recessionary event. If the vast study of economics had to be boiled down to a single principle, a grand unified theory, it would be this: That which supports and encourages the smoother and more efficient working of the extended order will improve productivity and economic health; that which impedes, distorts, or prevents the smooth working of the extended order will cause recession and decline. This is the ultimate insight of Say's law. Virtually all the major economic problems of the world today can be quickly analyzed and solved by the application of this principle.

Part Two

A History of U.S. Money

CHAPTER 7

MONEY IN AMERICA

From Colonial Silver and Paper to the Turmoil of 1929

The American colonies that later became the United States quickly evolved along the same path the ancient world had taken thousands of years earlier. Beaver pelts, fish, and corn served as early forms of money. Wampum, a string of beads made from the inside shell of clams or mussels, gained a wide popularity. Rice was used as money in South Carolina, and tobacco was money in Virginia, where warehouse receipts for tobacco served as paper money. In time, gold and silver were imported to serve as monetary media and traded by their weight and fineness. English coins circulated, and also French, Portuguese, Spanish, and Brazilian coins. The leading coin was the Spanish silver dollar, which had become common all over the world as a product of the prolific Spanish silver mines in Latin America.

Massachusetts began an early soft-money cycle when it enacted laws in 1642 that set a value on the Spanish silver dollar higher than its weight in silver, in effect devaluing the coin, as part of a mercantilist plan to increase exports. Connecticut and other colonies followed, and a round of competitive devaluations swept the colonies. The English government halted the practice in 1707, only nine years after England itself had established a standardized metallic currency.

Unredeemable government paper money in the American colonies first appeared in Massachusetts in 1690 to pay soldiers after a failed plunder expedition to the French colony in Quebec. Massachusetts, which couldn't pay the soldiers, offered them notes that were supposed to be redeemable in specie after several years, but the redeemability date was repeatedly postponed. This was reasonably successful, so the government issued more money to pay off all its debts; the result was a devaluation of the paper currency. The inflationary policies met widespread opposition, and Massachusetts refrained from big issuances of government paper until 1744, when another failed expedition against Quebec led to huge issuances and a devaluation of 11:1 against metallic silver, the original par value. By 1750, every colony but Virginia had followed the example of Massachusetts, with the identical results: 9:1 devaluation in Connecticut, 10:1 in the Carolinas, and 23:1 in Rhode Island, for example.

The English government eventually stepped in and straightened out the wayward colonies and legislated a return to a metallic currency. In 1751, Britain prohibited further issues of legal tender paper in New England colonies, and in 1764 it had extended the prohibition and retirement of outstanding notes to all colonies. Government paper money had been outlawed. The New England colonies quickly retired their paper notes at the market rate and made a smooth return to a specie standard. The result was increased economic activity in the New England colonies, as a reliable and stable unit of measurement facilitated trade, investment, and production. Rhode Island lagged behind Massachusetts in the return to a specie standard, and as a result Boston became the region's major center of trade, while Newport's influence waned.

To finance the Revolutionary War that began in 1775, the Continental Congress soon began to issue huge amounts of unredeemable fiat paper. On top of an estimated $12 million total money supply in the United States at the time, Congress issued $2 million in June 1775 and a total of $6 million by the end of the year. In 1776 it added $19 million, $13 million in 1777, $64 million in 1778, and $125 million in 1779, a total of over $225 million, with the result that the fiat paper's value fell from its face value of 1:1 versus silver to 168:1 in 1781 despite all manner of price controls and compulsory par laws. The term "not worth a Continental" remained in popular use into the twentieth century. The governments of the individual colonies added their own unredeemable paper issues, totaling around $210 million. The United States began its history with a hyperinflation.

At the same time, the U.S. government had issued public debt totaling $600 million during the war, which also had depreciated on the open market. In 1779, it was trading at roughly 4 cents on the dollar. Some had been liquidated at the depreciated rate, but most remained as the beginnings of the U.S. federal debt.

Chastened by the colonies' long and unhappy experience with unredeemable fiat currencies, the framers of the Constitution in 1789, led by the first Treasury secretary, Alexander Hamilton (who studied Adam Smith closely), established that gold and silver would be the only money in the new United States. The intent was to outlaw the issuance of fiat currencies, explicitly by the states and implicitly by the federal government. Article I, Section 10 of the Constitution reads: "No state shall enter into any treaty, alliance, or confederation; grant letters of marque and reprisal; coin money; emit bills of credit; make anything but gold and silver coin a tender in payment of debts; pass any bill of attainder, ex post facto law, or law impairing the obligation of contracts, or grant any title of nobility."

Congress was given the power "to coin money, regulate the value thereof, and of foreign coin, and fix the standard of weights and measures." At the time, the dollar was simply considered a measure of gold or silver, just as the British pound had originally meant simply a pound of silver in any form. (The term *dollar* derives from the silver "thaler" coins produced from the mines of Joachimsthal in Bohemia, which served as a model for the silver coins made in Mexico and Peru.) In 1792, the dollar was defined as 371.25 grains of metallic silver or 24.75 grains of gold, or $18.65 an ounce of gold and a 15:1 silver/gold ratio. This was roughly the weight in silver of the popular Mexican silver dollar and its equivalent value in gold. It did not matter what form a dollar took. In 1793, all foreign coins were declared legal tender, and in 1800, an estimated 80 percent of all coins in circulation in the United States were of foreign origin. The congressional power to coin money primarily meant the power to issue a standardized full-weight metallic coinage, as England had successfully done a century earlier.

The restriction of money to gold and silver did not imply a wholly metallic currency. A redeemable banknote was not considered money in itself, but a contract redeemable in money, much like a bank check today. A bank check, a slip of paper with a scrawled signature and amount, can also be used in transactions because it is ultimately redeemable in the fundamental money of today, paper bills. See Figure 7.1.

A debate also raged about whether to default on the federal debt. Hamilton resolved the issue with a proposal to repay the entire debt, which had traded around 4 cents to the dollar, at face value, in gold bullion—even though the government held almost no gold at all. By honoring its agreements, Hamilton understood that the new government would create public confidence in both the government's bonds and the government itself and would create a large and influential group of people, bondholders, with a direct interest in the support of the new government and its policies of sound money.

By 1800, U.S. debt was trading at a yield of 6 percent. This is low

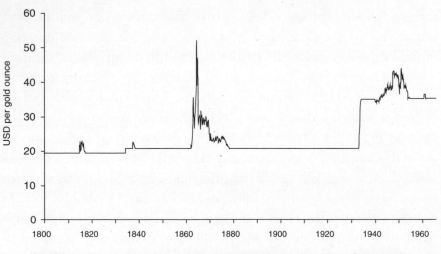

FIGURE 7.1   United States: Dollars per Gold Ounce, 1800–1965

by emerging-market standards of today, but as high-risk emerging-market debt it actually included a large premium over the 3 percent paid by longer-established governments. See Figure 7.2.

At the same time, Hamilton recommended the creation of a national bank, the First Bank of the United States. Hamilton saw the need for an institution of a sufficient scale, like the Bank of England, to address the financial needs of the new federal government. (The Bank of England itself had been founded to finance a war.) At the time there were only four chartered banks in the United States, all of them regional in scale. They each operated like an independent monetary system, their banknotes circulating in the immediate vicinity of the bank itself.

The plan met strong resistance from James Madison and others, who saw it as an intrusion of the federal government into the private sector and also into the affairs of the individual states (some states prohibited banking). The bill passed in 1791, and the First Bank of the United States began operations with a 20-year charter.

People who had crossed an ocean and fought a revolution to

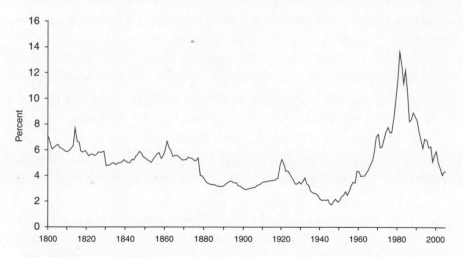

FIGURE 7.2   United States: Annual Average Yield on 10-Year Treasury Bond, 1800–2005

escape European taxation would gladly move a hundred miles farther west to escape the local tax collector. As a result, the new country remained largely free of taxes, and economic growth was at a maximum. Though the expansion of the British economy between 1815 and 1875 was one of history's great economic booms, the expansion of the U.S. economy was even more spectacular. By the end of the century, an experiment in government by a scruffy collection of outlaw farmers had become a world power comparable to Britain itself.

Throughout the nineteenth century the federal government derived most of its income from tariffs, and tariff blunders clouded the first 70 years of U.S. history. President Thomas Jefferson inaugurated this habit with the Embargo Act of 1808, which threw the economy into recession. Exports had grown briskly, from $19 million in 1791 to $49 million in 1807. Reexports increased from $1 million to $60 million. During the Napoleonic Wars, U.S. merchants were happily exporting war-making supplies to both sides, Britain and France, which naturally raised the ire of both and resulted in threats to U.S. shipping by the French and the British. Jefferson, who wished to keep the United States from being drawn into European wars, intended the embargo to keep U.S. merchant ships at home and out of danger. The policy worked, and a collapse of trade was the result—exports dropped to $9 million in 1808, and reexports dropped to $13 million. The economic contraction was so severe that the Embargo Act was quickly modified in 1809 as the Non-Intercourse Act, which forbade trade only with England and France. Trade recovered, as did the economy as a whole, although the rate of growth dropped off from its pre-1808 levels. British interference with U.S. shipping continued and led to the War of 1812 with Britain.

The outbreak of war touched off the first inflationary event of the new United States since the establishment of the gold standard in 1789. At the time, there was no national currency, and banknotes were issued by regional commercial banks. Fearing a run due to the war and sensing an opportunity to be free of their legal liabilities, banks in the Southern states suspended the redeemability of their banknotes, which in effect rendered them floating currencies. Suspension of redeemability was, of course, an illegal breach of contract, but the authorities were willing to turn a blind eye. The Bank of England itself was up to similar shenanigans at the time. The First Bank of the United States, which could conceivably have kept the Southern banks in line, had ceased operations as a result of the end of its charter in 1811. The federal government also issued Treasury notes to finance the war. These strange financial instruments paid interest and were declared legal tender in monetary transactions. Because they were usable as bank reserves, this amounted to an expansion of the monetary base, and since gold redeemability had been suspended, the result was inflation in the Southern states.

The banks of the Northern states maintained the gold redeemability of their notes, with the result that notes from Northern banks traded at a premium to notes from Southern banks. The federal government was soon trying to pay for Northern goods with notes from Southern banks, and Northern banks began to call for the redemption of the Southern banknotes into gold. In August 1814, the governments of the Southern states officially allowed the suspension of redeemability at Southern banks.

The Southern inflation prompted calls for another national bank, the Second Bank of the United States, which, among other tasks, would bring the Southern banks into line by beginning its operations with a nationwide policy of redeemability. The Second Bank was enacted into law on April 10, 1816, again with a 20-year charter. The Treasury also made wholesale retirements of the Treasury notes in 1816–1817, effectively shrinking the supply of money. A deflation had begun with the intent of raising the value of the Southern banks' banknotes back to their prewar value so that convertibility could be resumed. The deflation hit the economy, causing a recession in 1818–1820 and the Panic of 1819. In the western states, the monetary turbulence led to the adoption of grain and whisky as media of exchange. Prices fell, and gradually a full-scale return to redeemability and the gold standard was made possible at the prewar parity of $18.65 per ounce of gold.

After a stretch of prosperity, the Second Bank's decline began with the enactment of the Tariff of 1828, known as the "Tariff of Abominations." The government was running a surplus at the time, and the existing debt was modest. The protective tariff was pushed through by big northeastern manufacturing interests who wished to be protected from foreign competition. Many manufactured goods were consumed in the southern states, where the economy was dominated by cotton for export. While the North got its protection, the South faced higher prices and shoddier products, and it expected a falloff of cotton exports due to the increased trade barriers. South Carolina later essentially nullified the North's protective tariffs by refusing to enforce them, and talk of secession spread across the South. The North and South continued to do battle over the concept of protectionism versus free trade for the next three decades, which became inextricably entwined with antislavery debates (which were as much an economic issue as a moral one) and led to the Civil War.

The economy slid into recession in 1828 on expectations of higher trade barriers. Demand for imports expanded ahead of the enactment of the tariff, and the imports were financed by an expansion of credit by banks. Foreigners ended up in possession of U.S. banknotes, whose value was slipping, and brought them in for redemption. In response, the Second Bank put pressure on banks to restrict their banknote issuance and bring the value of banknotes back to their gold parity.

Andrew Jackson was elected president by antitariff elements of the electorate, and the tariff rates of 1828 were eventually lowered in 1832. In 1833, a nine-year series of tariff reductions began. Jackson, however, who despised banks of all kinds, blamed the Second Bank and its monetary restraint, not the tariff, for the contraction in 1828 and claimed the bank was unconstitutional. Didn't it wield power over the entire banking system? Indeed it did, and that was one of the rationales for its creation. Many banknotes of regional banks remained difficult for individuals to redeem in practice, especially those of the West and the South. The Second Bank had the clout to keep the banking system in line, as it had demonstrated first in 1816–1820 and later in 1828. Access to credit at the Second Bank could mean the difference between success or failure for a regional bank suffering from a seasonal liquidity shortage, as had happened in 1825. And because it had branches throughout the country (where banknotes could be redeemed), its banknotes traded widely and had gradually displaced the notes of competing regional banks. For these reasons, the Second Bank had more than a few opponents in the financial industry, including those in New York who were jealous that the country's premier financial institution should be headquartered in Philadelphia.

Though the Second Bank was essentially just a large commercial bank with few of the powers associated today with central banks, it was the first institution to acquire the kind of nationwide influence in its industry that would cause the railroad, steel, and oil companies to draw criticism in the 1890s. It did not help that foreigners owned more than a quarter of all the bank's outstanding shares.

The head of the Second Bank, Nicholas Biddle, aimed to resolve the conflict between the bank and President Jackson by asking for a decision on the bank's recharter in 1832, long before the existing charter's expiration in 1836. The bank was at the time very popular, and public sentiment sided with a recharter. Congress passed the re-charter bill, but Jackson vetoed it and Congress was not able to muster a sufficient majority to override the veto. Though the bank still had four years on its charter, it was a lame duck. Jackson moved immediately to curtail the activities of the Second Bank, including its ability to restrain the overissuance of banknotes by regional banks through redemption.

The Jacksonians claimed that they were trying to defend the integrity of the dollar from the manipulations of the Second Bank, but they had other things on their mind as well. In 1834 the economy was in recession. Not only that, the original bimetallic silver/gold ratio of 15:1, determined in 1792, was out of alignment with the bimetallic ratios of European countries and market values. France used a ratio of 15.5:1, and the market ratio was about 15.625:1. This tended to cause transactions to be undertaken in silver. In 1834, Congress changed the ratio to 16:1, although not by increasing the silver parity of the dollar, but by reducing the gold parity. In effect, the act was a small devaluation, and dropped the official gold value of the dollar from $18.65 per ounce to $20.67 per ounce, where it stayed until 1933. Because it was relatively cheaper than silver, gold became the primary basis of the bimetallic dollar. The United States was following the lead of Britain, which had begun gold monometallism in 1816.

Sales of government land had become a major arena of speculation, and though the revenue enabled the government to pay off the federal debt in its entirety, from around 1835 the value of many banknotes began to soften as banks expanded credit to fund land purchases, especially in western states, where the redemption of banknotes for bullion was spotty. (The Second Bank was no longer around to keep the banks in line by demanding redeemability.) Stock prices peaked in mid-1835 and headed downward as the inflation intensified in 1836. The open market value of banknotes fell against gold bullion. The government became worried about the quality of the banknotes it was accepting in trade for its land and demanded that all land sales (mostly in western states) should be paid in gold bullion (which was mostly in eastern states) beginning December 1836, a decree known as the Specie Circular.

Around the same time, it was also decided that the government's surplus revenues would be distributed from northeastern banks to banks in western and southern states. Both were highly destabilizing policies at a time when the transfer of gold or deposits from state to state could take days or weeks by wagon, canal, or horseback. Foreign banks, particularly in London, also began to doubt the quality of banknotes from U.S. banks, and in early 1837 began redeeming them for specie. The result of all this turmoil was the Panic of 1837, which was further intensified due to the removal of the Second Bank from its role as a lender of last resort, a stabilizing force for the financial system.

A secondary financial breakdown took place in 1839, due in part to the readoption of Treasury notes to fund deficits (the same odd device implicated in the inflation of 1812–1816), and in 1842 tariffs were pushed up.[1] The economy did not begin to recover properly until 1844, helped in 1846 by a tariff reduction, which produced one of the lowest tariff structures the United States had ever adopted. The period from 1844 to 1860 was a stretch of brisk expansion led by the development of railroad networks.

James Buchanan took office in March 1857 after being elected on a platform of prosperity and an end to strife over slavery. Tariffs were lowered again in 1857. A full-blown liquidity-shortage panic appeared around September of 1857, which sent the country into a brief recession. The downturn set off a debate about relief measures, which ranged from free land for settlers to river and harbor improvements, a railroad to the Pacific, and that oldest of economic antidotes, a protectionist tariff, which was particularly popular in northeastern manufacturing states such as Pennsylvania.

The economy recovered, but the Republican Party, which was staunchly antislavery, adopted all of these economic relief proposals into its platform for the 1860 election. The electorate chose to force a decision on the issue of slavery and elected Abraham Lincoln to the presidency. The South, infuriated by both the tariff and antislavery elements of the Republican Party's policy platform, seceded soon after. The Republican governments pushed tariffs higher throughout the war, beginning with the Morrill Tariff of 1861. An income tax was also instituted in 1861, the country's first.

On the eve of the Civil War, the federal government did not issue banknotes, and the currency of the country was issued and managed solely by private banks. However, the need for funding at the outbreak of hostilities in 1861 led the federal government to issue large quantities of U.S. notes, informally known as *greenbacks*, although this was in clear violation of the Constitution's prohibition against "bills of credit." The excess greenbacks and existing banknotes soon returned to the issuers in trade for gold, which would have put an end to this form of finance. Instead, the government and then the banks suspended convertibility on December 30, 1861, and the dollar became a floating currency. Issuance of greenbacks continued. The dollar headed lower until, in 1865, it momentarily sank to a nadir of $57.052 per ounce, or nearly a 3:1 devaluation. Commodity prices soared. The Confederate government pursued a similar strategy, but more aggressively, devaluing Confederate notes by a factor of around 28:1.

In December 1865, recognizing the sorry state of the monetary system, Congress passed a resolution to contract the existing supply of greenbacks, and the postwar monetary deflation began. This process proved to be painfully recessionary, however, and in 1868 Congress passed another act to halt the contraction of greenbacks, with the idea that a gradual deflation would be enacted as the economy slowly grew into the existing money supply. The act essentially fixed the base money supply at $656 million, and this inflexibility in the face of seasonal liquidity needs, combined with general economic weakness caused by the deflation, resulted in the Panic of 1873.

In January 1875, Congress passed the Resumption Act, which would finally return the dollar to its prewar parity and reestablish its convertibility into specie. The dollar was further deflated, with continuing recessionary effects, and redeemability in specie was indeed resumed in 1879 at the prewar parity of $20.67 per ounce. After 18 years of floating up and down, the dollar was again on the gold standard, and it remained on the gold standard, in one form or another, until 1971.

The wartime income tax was reduced in 1867, after the end of hostilities, and abolished in 1872. In 1880, with taxes lowered and the dollar finally repegged to gold after a long deflation, the United States was once again lined up in growth mode. By 1894, the United States, which had long been a dominant agricultural power, had also become the world's leading manufacturer.

Officially, the United States was still on a bimetallic standard, with debts payable in either silver or gold. Beginning in the 1870s, silver was abandoned in favor of gold around the world—in Germany in 1871, in the Scandinavian countries in 1873, and by the Latin Monetary Union in 1874—and the value of silver relative to gold dropped sharply beginning in 1872. In 1873, this was recognized in the United States, and an act was passed to end the coinage of silver at the mint. In 1792 the official ratio of silver to gold was set at 15:1, and in 1871 the market ratio was about 15.40:1. By 1900 the market ratio had fallen to 33:1.

Although it was mirrored by government acts, the demonetization of silver was intrinsically a decision of humanity as a whole. For millennia, silver had been necessary to serve as coinage for day-to-day transactions, for which gold was too valuable. Because of this, people had put up with the inherent difficulties of a two-pole standard. With the widespread use of redeemable paper money and token coins, silver and the problems of a bimetallic standard were no longer necessary. The adoption of monometallic gold standards worldwide represented a further improvement in the gold standard. The silver example has led many to claim today the gold could be, or has been, similarly demonetized. But humanity is not inclined to demonetize gold, since there is no alternative monetary benchmark available and doing so would offer no advantages. It is true that governments abandoned gold in the early 1970s in much the same way as they abandoned silver in the 1870s, but instead of losing value, as silver did, gold has held or increased its value against every benchmark.

The decline in the value of silver created two political pressures: first, pressure from the silver mining industry for the government to buy silver on the open market, thus supporting its price; and second, pressure from debtors, primarily farmers, to allow payment of debts in silver. In effect, this would have cut their debt burden in half. "Free coinage of silver" (i.e., permission to take 15 ounces of silver, worth 0.5 ounce of gold at prevailing market prices, to the mint and receive coins nominally worth 1.0 ounce of gold in return) was the term used at the time for what would have been an effective devaluation of the dollar. Both represented threats to the stability of the de facto monometallic gold standard and caused constant financial disruption, which came to a head in 1896.

Silver purchases began in 1878 under the Bland–Allison Act, but the influence of the pro-silver forces gained prominence with the Sherman Silver Purchase Act of 1890. This was considered a political trade-off, a concession to the western states for the protectionist McKinley Tariff Act of 1890, which was backed by northeastern industrialists. The effect of the Sherman Act was to sow doubts about the commitment of the U.S. government to maintain the gold standard. Foreign holders of U.S. securities began selling them off beginning in 1890 on fears of a devaluation. More and more banknotes were also redeemed for gold, touching off a panic in 1893. The fears forced banks and the Treasury to contract the supply of money to keep the dollar from falling in the foreign exchange market.

In the early 1890s, commodity prices declined under the pressure of big harvests, likely the result of increasing agricultural production efficiency. From 1894 to 1896, the production of corn increased by 65 percent, as the price dropped 53 percent. In 1895 alone, production of oats rose 23 percent, barley rose 41 percent, and potatoes rose 53 percent from the previous year. As productivity rose, the economy needed fewer and fewer farmers, and farmers were forced by falling prices into industry.

The Populist Party was officially formed in 1892, adopting "free coinage of silver" as a main part of its platform. The party was made up largely of farmers in debt to eastern banks and suffering from declining prices for agricultural products. In 1894, a bill permitting the coinage of silver then in the Treasury (the result of the silver purchase acts) passed House and Senate, but was vetoed by President Cleveland. (The bill would have constituted a devaluation.) The debate finally had to be settled in a presidential election, when silver advocates managed, in 1896, to get William Jennings Bryant nominated as the Democratic presidential candidate on a platform of free coinage of silver. The Republican candidate, McKinley, favored a monometallic gold standard. After Bryant's nomination July 10, the flight from U.S. assets by both U.S. and foreign investors intensified. Gold flowed out of reserves and interest rates rose on fears of devaluation.

The crisis passed instantly after Bryant lost the election. The citizenry of the United States had voted to maintain the gold standard. Silver would continue to be used in India and China, but in the major Western countries it had finally been abandoned. After thousands of years of experimentation, the global citizenry had, at the end of a long debate, finally whittled its monetary options down to one and one only. No longer would the United States, or any other major world financial power, allow itself to be wracked by the vagaries of bimetallism or any other basket standard. The United States formally adopted a monometallic gold standard with the Gold Standard Act of 1900.

The closure of the western frontier with the creation of the state of Arizona in 1912 was followed in 1913 by the Sixteenth Amendment, which legalized the federal income tax. There was nowhere left to run from the tax collector. However, this allowed the federal government to finally free itself from its dependence on tariff revenue, which had offered continuous temptation toward protectionism. Since 1861, protection of big business had become standard policy. The purpose of protectionism is to achieve what every big business desires, monopoly control and the suppression of competitors. In response, antimonopoly agitation arose in the latter decades of the nineteenth century. Democratic president Woodrow Wilson desired lower tariffs, but felt he had to make up for lost revenue by enacting an income tax, which began at 1 percent on personal or corporate income over $4,000 (about $70,000 today) and had a top rate of 7 percent on income over $500,000 ($8.750 million today). Though these rates may seem minuscule by today's standards, they were, except for during the Civil War, the first income taxes the country had ever seen. Even with the tariff reduction, the economy went into recession in 1913–1915 until the flood of overseas demand for war materials and domestic war spending counteracted the contraction in 1916. Northeastern business interests attempted once more, in

1929–1930, to reinstate the protectionist policies of the past, with disastrous results.

The last major monetary hiccup in the United States, before the tectonic shifts of the 1930s, was a brief cycle of inflation and deflation during and after World War I. The outbreak of hostilities in Europe in 1914 was soon followed by a flood of demand for U.S. products by all the combatants to fight the war. At the same time, exports of European goods were reduced as factories retooled for wartime. All in all, delivery of roughly $1 billion in gold, sales of $1.4 billion in U.S. securities (accumulated over a century of investment in U.S. industries), and $2.4 billion of borrowing in U.S. financial markets were undertaken by European countries to finance their imports of U.S. goods.

The gold flows were not in themselves inflationary, for it is the value of gold, not the amount of gold that happens to be located in the United States, that determines the value of the dollar. The skyrocketing demand for U.S. goods pushed up U.S. prices beginning in 1914. This was primarily what von Mises called a "goods-induced" change in prices, caused by the intense demands of wartime. The same thing had happened when the United States manufactured goods for use in the Napoleonic Wars.

That changed when the United States entered the war in April 1917. Gold inflows immediately stopped and were replaced by modest gold outflows, perhaps in anticipation of an end to gold redeemability (as every European government had done). In September 1917, President Wilson prohibited all gold exports without the permission of the Federal Reserve Board and the Treasury and brought foreign exchange transactions under explicit control. In September 1918, the gold embargo was broadened to prohibit private hoarding of gold, though the war would end only a few months later. The net effect of these two steps was to float the dollar, or at least make its link to gold highly elastic.

The Federal Reserve had been created in 1913 to prevent liquidity-shortage crises. The coalition majority that wrote the bill for the new system even claimed it was not creating a central bank.

In any case, the Fed was just starting operations when the Treasury pressured it into accepting a very contemporary central banking role—pushing down interest rates so that the government's wartime funding could be accomplished more cheaply. With the dollar's link to gold weakened, it was an invitation for inflation, which is indeed what happened.

When the gold embargo was lifted in June 1919, gold immediately flooded out, a sign that the dollar's value had dropped well below its gold parity. Wartime prices, pushed up by real demand, would probably have begun dropping in late 1919, as government spending contracted, but the Fed's expansion pushed prices higher into early 1920. Eventually, the outflows of gold could not be ignored, and the Fed, in 1920, began contracting the supply of base money. Combined with a natural retreat of wartime prices, the result was a violent drop in prices and wages of about 35 percent in the brief but intense recession of 1920–1921.

The recession was exacerbated by high wartime tax rates, which had not been lowered after the return to peace. The top tax rate of 7 percent in 1913 had gone to 77 percent during the war. Total federal debt had increased from $1 billion to $24 billion, at the time a staggering amount. In his 1919 State of the Union address, President Wilson argued for a lowering of wartime tax rates:

> The Congress might well consider whether the higher rates of income and profits taxes can in peace times be effectively productive of revenue, and whether they may not, on the contrary, be destructive of business activity and productive of waste and inefficiency. There is a point at which in peace times high rates of income and profits taxes discourage energy, remove the incentive to new enterprise, encourage extravagant expenditures and produce industrial stagnation with consequent unemployment and other attendant evils.[2]

Wilson did manage a small cut in taxes in 1919, and the top rate fell to 73 percent. However, in the 1920 election Wilson's Democratic

Party stuck with keeping the rates high to pay off war debts, while Wilson's tax-cut message was picked up by the Republican Party. Warren G. Harding won the presidency in a landslide on a platform of "return to normalcy" for the tax system, but managed only a reduction to 57 percent in the top rate and the elimination of the excess profits tax in 1921. It wasn't much, but it was enough to help bring the economy out of recession. Rates were lowered again in 1923 and 1924, which brought the top rate to 46 percent. The economic boom of the Roaring Twenties began to be felt.

The architect of the economic boom of the 1920s was Andrew Mellon, a wealthy industrialist who helped establish Alcoa, Gulf Oil, Union Steel, Pittsburgh Coal, and many other ventures. He became Treasury secretary under Harding in 1921. In April 1924, he published a wonderful little book, *Taxation: The People's Business*, which explained in detail how Mellon would put the U.S. economy into high gear. The book begins with this passage, which is quoted at length to give a flavor of Mellon's economic strategy:

> The problem of Government is to fix rates which will bring in a maximum amount of revenue to the Treasury and at the same time bear not too heavily on the taxpayer or on business enterprises. A sound tax policy must take into consideration three factors. It must produce sufficient revenue for the Government; it must lessen, so far as possible, the burden of taxation on those least able to bear it; and it must also remove those influences which might retard the continued steady development of business and industry on which, in the last analysis, so much of our prosperity depends. . . .
>
> Any man of energy and initiative in this country can get what he wants out of life. But when that initiative is crippled by legislation or by a tax system which denies him the right to receive a reasonable share of his earnings, then he will no longer exert himself and the country will be deprived of the energy on which its continued greatness depends.
>
> This condition has already begun to make itself felt as a result of the present unsound basis of taxation. The existing tax system is

an inheritance from the war. During that time the highest taxes ever levied by any country were borne uncomplainingly by the American people for the purpose of defraying the unusual and ever-increasing expenditures incident to the successful conduct of a great war. Normal tax rates were increased, and a system of surtaxes was evolved in order to make the man of large income pay more proportionately than the smaller taxpayer. If he had twice as much income, he paid not twice by three or four times as much tax. For a short time the surtaxes yielded a large revenue. But since the close of the war people have come to look upon them as a business expense and have treated them accordingly by avoiding payment as much as possible. The history of taxation shows that taxes which are inherently excessive are not paid. The high rates inevitably put pressure upon the taxpayer to withdraw his capital from productive business and invest it in tax-exempt securities or to find other lawful methods of avoiding the realization of taxable income. The result is that the sources of taxation are drying up; wealth is failing to carry its share of the tax burden; and capital is being diverted into other channels which yield neither revenue to the Government nor profit to the people.[3]

Mellon's plan was adopted by Calvin Coolidge in the 1924 election. Coolidge proposed to reduce the top income tax rate to 25 percent. The lowest rate, which had been 6 percent in 1918, would fall to 1.125 percent. Coolidge's plan became reality in 1925, with Mellon continuing as Treasury secretary, and once again the U.S. economy went into a high-growth mode. The Dow Jones Industrial Average had spent the previous four years moving sideways, but as Coolidge put his pro-growth plans into action, the market picked up. The index reached 120 at the end of 1924, 159 in 1925, 167 in 1926, 202 in 1927, 300 in 1928, and peaked at 381 in September 1929. Mellon was hailed as the greatest Treasury secretary since Alexander Hamilton.

The whole economy grew alongside the stock market. Automobile sales more than doubled during the decade, and between 1923 and 1929 industrial electricity use rose 70 percent. The United States was producing more electric power than the rest of the world combined.

Corporate earnings surged, and as investors forecast more earnings growth in the future, trailing price-earnings multiples expanded from around 12 at the beginning of the decade to around 20 at the market's peak in 1929. Radio Corporation of America, the era's premier growth technology stock, enjoyed one of the highest price-earnings multiples. RCA's stock price was $101 on September 3, 1929, translating into $505 before a 5-for-1 stock split. This price was 32 times RCA's 1928 earnings of $15.98 a share. Overvalued? Consider that RCA's 1927 earnings were $6.15 a share, and the 1925 earnings were $1.32. With earnings growing at well over 100 percent a year, a multiple of 32 times trailing earnings is very reasonable by today's standards.

In 1929, earnings and dividends were increasing at a stupendous rate. In the first nine months of 1929, dividends increased 29 percent from the previous year. For September 1929, dividends were 44 percent higher than the same month of 1928, even though the dividend payout ratio fell to 64 percent from 75 percent. U.S. Steel's third-quarter earnings of $51.575 million were $21 million higher than the third quarter of 1928. Analysts predicted $20 a share for earnings for 1929 (this number turned out to be too low). At its 1929 high of $261.75, U.S. Steel shares traded at 13 times earnings estimates for 1929. In August of 1929, the economist Irving Fischer estimated that the forward price-earnings ratio of the market was 13.

Tax revenues flooded into the Treasury, and by 1929 the national debt had been reduced from $24 billion to $16 billion. Coolidge had already fulfilled his tax cut promises, but the market saw the big government surpluses and predicted even more tax cuts. The market had priced in expectations—at the time rational expectations—that the boom would continue, even stronger than it had been. Hoover was elected to carry on in Coolidge's footsteps, and Andrew Mellon remained at Treasury.

As U.S. industry boomed, however, agricultural interests were relative laggards and once again sought a protectionist tariff on agricultural products. To win support for the tariff in Congress, the tariff's advocates steadily expanded the scope of the tariff to include a wide range of nonagricultural imports.

The prodigious economic expansion was stopped in its tracks in late 1929 by the threat of passage of the Smoot–Hawley Tariff Act, which touched off an explosion of tax hikes worldwide and threw the world into recession and monetary turmoil. The stock market quickly revised its view of the future, from one of tax cuts and roaring growth to one of tax hikes, international trade friction, declining corporate profits, and subdued growth prospects. It is often said that the stock market, due to the efforts of investors to predict the future, tends to precede changes in corporate profits by about six months. Profits began to decline in early 1930.

The brevity of the 1920–1921 recession, and intensity of the boom that followed, made a great impression on economists of the time, who apparently had proof of the economy's ability to quickly adjust to a new productive equilibrium at a lower price level. The unemployment rate, which hit 12 percent in 1921 (with nonfarm unemployment near 20 percent), was back under 5 percent by 1922. But even as lowering taxes became the subject of presidential debate and Treasury Secretary Mellon's personal crusade, the economics profession proved unable to incorporate taxation in its framework of analysis. Part of the problem was a long political tradition in which northeastern big business backed low domestic taxes and high protective tariffs, as offered by the Republican Party, while the Democratic party, with its support in the South and among the working class, had long backed low tariffs and high domestic taxes. Neither party was for lower taxes across the board. When faced once again in the 1930s with falling prices and rising unemployment, but this time with tax rates and tariffs shooting higher worldwide, economists confidently waited for a recovery that never came.

Until the introduction of the income tax in 1913, the U.S. government's taxation policy was restricted almost entirely to tariffs, where it could do relatively little harm. From 1789 to 1913, most of the economic and financial crises were primarily monetary in nature, due to either leaving, threatening to leave, temporarily deviating from, or inexpertly returning to the gold standard—as in 1812–1816, 1819, 1828, 1835, 1860–1865, 1865–1879, and 1893–1896—or liquidity shortage crises, as happened in 1810, 1825, 1838, 1857, and 1907. Some, such as the Panic of 1873, had both elements. Given this history, it is not surprising that economic thinking by the end of the nineteenth century had fixated almost completely on monetary and financial affairs.

Today is it often claimed that there were regular crises in the nineteenth century under the gold standard, but the gold standard cannot be blamed for crises caused by leaving the gold standard or for those that took place while the gold standard was not operating. Gold's performance as a benchmark of monetary value during the century was impeccable. Liquidity-shortage crises are not inherent to the gold standard, and the problem of the liquidity-shortage crisis was eventually solved within the gold standard framework.

After 1913 the income tax, even as it allowed the financing of wars and desired welfare programs, opened a whole new realm for policy error in the United States and in the countries around the world that mimicked the U.S.'s conventional wisdom. As governments attempted to solve problems caused by their poor tax and tariff policies, they reached for monetary manipulation and devaluation.

CHAPTER 8

A HISTORY OF CENTRAL BANKING

From Ancient Egypt and Rome to the Bank of England and the U.S. Federal Reserve

I am a most unhappy man. I have unwittingly ruined my country. A great industrial nation is controlled by its system of credit. Our system of credit is concentrated. The growth of the nation, therefore, and all our activities are in the hands of a few men. We have come to be one of the worst ruled, one of the most completely controlled and dominated Governments in the civilized world, no longer a Government by free opinion, no longer a Government by conviction and the vote of the majority, but a Government by the opinion and duress of a small group of dominant men.

—President Woodrow Wilson, in reference to the Federal Reserve Act of 1913, which he signed into law.

If the American people ever allow private banks to control the issue of their currency, first by inflation, then by deflation, the banks and corporations that grow up around them will deprive the people of their property until their children will wake up homeless on the continent their fathers conquered.

—President Thomas Jefferson

History records that the money changers have used every form of abuse, intrigue, deceit, and violent means possible, to maintain their control over governments, by controlling money and its issuance.

—President James Madison

Banking is older than coinage—much older. The Egyptians had sophisticated banking systems based on wheat, and some have claimed evidence of banking under the Assyrians. The Code of Hammurabi, the Babylonian leader who ruled from around 1792 to 1750 BC, contains rules of procedure for banking transactions. Sumerian records show that in the period from 3000 to 1900 BC, the standard rate of interest on a loan of barley was 33.3 percent annually, and the rate on silver was 20 percent—which neatly describes the relative monetary qualities of each commodity. (Considering that these loans were probably much like today's credit card loans, the rate was not particularly high.) The Sumerians were the first civilization recognized as such on the Earth; before them were only nomads and tribal agriculturalists.

Ever since the invention of banking, or more precisely *fractional reserve banking*, in which banks take deposits and make loans, banks have faced the danger of bank runs and liquidity shortages. A bank may loan out 90 percent of its deposits, keeping 10 percent in cash as a reserve against withdrawals. The bank's loans may be multiyear loans, home mortgages, for example, and thus illiquid. If, for some reason, the bank's reserves are depleted either by withdrawals or by requests for loans, people may fear that the bank may soon be unable to honor further withdrawals. To fail to do so is technically bankruptcy, and uninsured deposits in a bankrupt bank are lost.

The bank faces a shortage of liquidity, meaning cash and bank reserves, or base money. The bank is said to be *illiquid*, and faces a *liquidity crisis*. But as long as a bank's assets, its loans, are sound, the bank should have no trouble borrowing money from another institution, likely another bank, that has a surplus of cash. Because it will receive dependable future income from the repayment of its outstanding long-term loans, it will be able to repay the short-term loans, and thus its credit is good. A bank that is running low on reserves will simply borrow the money on the *money market*, the name given to the market for short-term loans between banks and large corporations, and the potential crisis is easily averted.

Corporations also have short-term liquidity (base money) needs, which are often seasonal. They may have to pay workers, suppliers, creditors, or shareholders before they receive revenue from sales. If they fail to honor their commitments, they, too, are technically bankrupt. But if their future revenues are certain, then their credit is good, and they will normally have no difficulty securing a short-term loan from a bank.

A bank can be described as a certain form of investment fund that invests the capital of its shareholders using a fixed strategy: Borrow from the short end of the yield curve (from depositors), buy the long end (its long-term loans), and profit from the difference in interest rates between the two. Banks use a large amount of leverage in pursuing this strategy; under the current Bank for International Settlements requirement of 8 percent capital, the bank uses leverage of 12.5:1. If it has net investment losses of 8 percent (i.e., if a large number of its loans threaten to go bad), then its liabilities to its depositors are greater than its assets. Depositors realize that the bank likely cannot pay all its obligations. It is *insolvent* and faces a *solvency crisis*. This, too, may cause a bank run, but for a different reason. In the first example, the bank is well managed, its assets are sound, and except for a short-term shortage of cash (which is not its fault) it is in fine health. In the second case, the bank was poorly managed or suffered from unfortunate investments, its assets are poor, and the bank is in weak health. Not only is it unable to repay its depositors in the short term, but possibly in the long term as well. Its credit is poor, and prudent lenders will not make loans to the bank. Unless it receives more capital from shareholders, it is bankrupt.

If you have insufficient money in your pocket to pay a restaurant tab, you face a *liquidity crisis*, which can be resolved, perhaps, by using a credit card. If you lose your job, have no ready cash, and are deeply in debt, you face a *solvency crisis*.

It is of utmost importance to distinguish between a liquidity crisis and a solvency crisis. Often, banks or corporations—not to mention the politicians that serve them—are eager to blur the distinction, since an insolvent bank will remain in operation if it is able to claim it faces a liquidity crisis (as opposed to a solvency crisis) and secure a loan from the government. Certain economists are equally eager to blur the distinction as a justification for excessive base money creation and currency devaluation.

It is possible that the declining health or failure of one bank (a solvency crisis) may cause a run on healthy banks (a liquidity crisis), since depositors are afraid of any more unwelcome surprises. A corporate failure, a crisis such as the outbreak of war, or a change in government policy can also cause a widespread withdrawal of deposits, or a desire to increase cash holdings. In such a situation, all the healthy banks experience a withdrawal of cash and a depletion of their reserves. Because they all have a shortage and nobody has a surplus, they are unable to borrow from each other to cover their shortages despite their good credit. Corporations, no matter how good their credit, are also unable to borrow since there is no money to be lent—it simply does not exist. In other words there is a shortage of liquidity (base money, cash and bank reserves) not only at one bank or corporation, but throughout the entire financial system. The interest rate on short-term loans rises to spectacular levels as borrowers scramble for remaining funds. Widespread bankruptcy looms. The stock and bond markets go into convulsions. This is a liquidity-shortage crisis.

The year AD 33 is remembered today primarily because in that year Pontius Pilate sentenced a young carpenter to death by crucifixion in the remote Roman province of Judea. But the great and the good of Rome were more concerned with a liquidity-shortage crisis taking place in the capital, described here by someone who experienced it, the historian Tacitus:

> Meanwhile an army of accusers broke loose on the persons who habitually increased their riches by usury, in contravention of a law of the dictator Caesar, regulating the conditions of lending money and holding property within the boundaries of Italy: a measure dropped long ago, since the public good ranks second to private utility. The curse of usury, it must be owned, is inveterate in Rome, a constant source of sedition and discord; and attempts

were accordingly made to repress it even in an older and less corrupt society. First came a provision of the Twelve Tables [Tacitus dates this measure from 450 BC] that the rate of interest, previously governed by the fancy of the rich, should not exceed one-twelfth per cent for the month; later a tribunican rogation lowered it to one-half of that amount; and at length usufruct was unconditionally banned; while a series of plebiscites strove to meet the frauds which were perpetually repressed, only, by extraordinary evasions, to make their appearance once more. In the present instance, however, the praetor Gracchus, to whose jurisdiction the case had fallen, was forced by the numbers implicated to refer it to the senate; and the Fathers in trepidation—for not one member was clear from such a charge—asked an indulgence from the prince. It was granted; and the next eighteen months were assigned as a term of grace within which all accounts were to be adjusted in accordance with the prescriptions of the law.

The result was a dearth of money: for not only were all debts called in simultaneously; but after so many convictions and sales of forfeited estates, the case which had been realized was locked in the treasury or the imperial exchequer. To meet this difficulty, the senate had prescribed that every creditor was to invest two-thirds of his capital, now lying at interest, in landed property in Italy (the debtor to discharge immediately an equivalent proportion of his liability). The lenders, however, called in the full amounts, and the borrowers could not in honour refuse the call. Thus, at first there were hurryings to and fro, and appeals for mercy; then a hum of activity in the praetor's court; and the very scheme which had been devised as a remedy—the sale and purchase of estates—began to operate with a contrary effect, since the usurers had withdrawn their capital from circulation in order to buy land. As the glutting of the market was followed by a fall in prices, the men with the heaviest debts experienced the greatest difficulty in selling, and numbers were ejected from their properties. Financial ruin brought down in its train both rank and reputation, till the Caesar came to the rescue by distributing a hundred million sesterces among various counting-houses, and facilities were provided for borrowing free of interest for three years, if the borrowers had given security to the state to double the value in landed property. Credit was thus revived, and by degrees private lenders also began to be found. Nor was the purchase of the estates practised in accordance with the terms of the senatorial decree, a vigorous beginning lapsing into a careless end.[1]

In the face of a systemwide shortage of liquidity (in this case, literally silver coins) caused by the convulsions of credit, the imperial treasury was the only actor around with a surplus of cash. It acted as what is known today as a *lender of last resort*. By providing loans— effectively increasing the supply of base money by taking it out of the treasury and putting it into active circulation—the liquidity shortage was resolved.[2]

A liquidity-shortage crisis can be understood as a sharp spike in the demand for money. By withdrawing their deposits from the banking system, depositors are increasing their desire to hold currency. Consider, for example, if everyone had $20 in their pocket and $100 in bank deposits, which aren't really money but loans to the banks. The banks hold perhaps $10 of reserves for each $100 of deposits. Therefore there is $30 of base money ($20 in pockets and $10 in reserves) in existence per person. Each person is entitled to withdraw $20 from their savings deposit and put it in their pocket, and the banks must honor their request or face bankruptcy. After the withdrawal, each person has $40 in their pocket and $80 in deposits, backed by $8 of bank reserves. Therefore, $48 of base money must exist per person. The extra $18 per person of base money has to come from somewhere. The money supply must be flexible enough to accommodate the change in demand. In Tiberius's case, the flexibility came from the imperial treasury's willingness to introduce new money into the system (or, if one considers the treasury to be part of the system, by reducing its demand for cash). When the crisis is passed, the loans from the government would be repaid, and the coinage would flow back into the imperial treasury, thus reducing the supply of money available. In this way, the money supply is more flexible than is allowed by the other means of its increase, in this case by mining and importing silver.

It does not take a business failure or economic crisis to incite a sharp rise in the demand for money. All manner of natural business developments and government policies can induce short-term changes in the demand for money. Historically, periods of high demand for money and credit often appear during harvesttime or the end of the fiscal year, when the number and size of transactions often increase. In the first century and a half of U.S. history, agricultural workers were customarily paid a full summer's wages in a lump sum at the end of the season, which is when farmers were paid for their crop. Workers were paid in cash, which of course meant that the cash had to be in existence. Even today, the need for liquidity increases at the end of the calendar or fiscal year. Fluctuation in the demand for money is a natural feature of a well-developed financial system.

A classic liquidity-shortage panic does not reflect irrationality on the part of investors, or herd behavior, or poor management by banks, or failures by corporations, or bad government policy, or a business cycle, or any other such thing. It is a problem that appears when the supply of money is not sufficiently flexible to accommodate short-term changes in demand. However, a liquidity-shortage crisis often takes place in reaction to greater economic problems, often precipitated by poor government policy—situations in which many people call in their loans and withdraw their deposits.

After the collapse of the Roman Empire and its advanced financial system, the Western world waited until the development of banking institutions around the seventeenth century before the issues of liquidity crisis and a lender of last resort again rose to the fore. London eventually became the world's financial center, and the private Bank of England took the lender-of-last-resort role that had been played by Tiberius's imperial treasury.

This time, however, the interpretation of liquidity conditions was complicated by the issue of paper money under the gold standard. By withdrawing deposits and taking paper bills, the depositor exhibits an increasing demand for base money. However, during a liquidity crisis, by demanding base money the depositor threatens to push the bank into bankruptcy. If the bank is bankrupt, it won't be able to honor redemptions of its paper bills for gold, so the depositor will often preempt this risk by asking to redeem the bills for gold. The drawdown of its gold reserves simply piles on a new threat of bankruptcy, which exacerbates the crisis.

From the bank's point of view, however, the crisis can be difficult to interpret. A liquidity-shortage crisis, when the supply of money is insufficient, can result in redemptions of banknotes for gold. But if the bank overissues paper bills (i.e., if there is a surplus of base money), the bank will again experience redemptions and an outflow of gold. In both cases, gold may flow out of the bank, but in one case the solution is to expand the supply of credit and banknotes, and in the other the solution is to contract it. In either case, if the bank chooses the wrong solution, it will worsen the crisis.

This is exactly what the Bank of England did in a series of crises in the late eighteenth century, especially the crisis of 1797 that threw the bank off the gold standard. In the following decades, the role of the bank during such crises became the subject of intense discussion. The Bank of England eventually learned to respond to liquidity crises by aggressively expanding its lending. It became the most conservative financial institution during normal times (it kept a large reserve and capital base), but during a crisis, it lent with generous abandon. This is the opposite of what a prudently managed commercial bank was expected to do. In recognition of its unique role and its dominance of the British financial system, the Bank of England was eventually termed a *central bank*, although it was functionally little different than any other bank.

During a liquidity-shortage crisis, short-term lending rates can climb to 50 percent or more. The problem is not the rate in itself—corporations won't go bust paying 50 percent annualized interest on a two-week loan—but the fact that the interest rate shows the scarcity of money available to loan. Many borrowers will return from the market empty-handed, with possibly dire effects on their business.

The interest rate, which is the price of borrowing capital, is, like any other price, perfectly capable of being set by the market. But governments, often in response to outcries from disenfranchised elements of society about the difficulty of obtaining capital, or perhaps in response to the inevitable outcome of their own currency manipulation schemes, have long introduced restrictions and limitations on the market's setting of interest rates. The Romans had legal maximum interest rates, and later, as the Roman economy and financial system broke down in the third and fourth centuries, the Christian edict against usury spread throughout Europe. Many governments forbade the collection of any interest at all.

The Christian prohibitions against lending at interest were overcome in Florence in 1403, which allowed the economic expansion of the Renaissance period. In Britain, they were overcome as a result of the Act of Supremacy of 1534, which broke England's religious ties with Rome. It is not too much of a stretch to say that Britain's later financial dominance was the outcome of Henry VIII's desire to divorce his wife. In 1545, Henry legalized the payment of interest, with a maximum rate of 10 percent. The legalization was repealed in 1552, but reinstated in 1571. In 1624, the maximum rate was set at 8 percent; by that point the stage had been set for the rise of banking in Britain. But Britain, eventually the world's primary financial power, had legal controls on interest rates until the latter half of the nineteenth century, and the short period of laissez-faire with regard to interest rates lasted only 45 years. Today, the active approach to interest rates continues in government programs that provide below-market-rate loans for students or first-time homebuyers.

The most extraordinary feature of the monetary systems of the nineteenth and twentieth centuries, however, is how governments' ancient desire to tamper with interest rates, typically through regulatory means, was slowly merged into a second concern, the prevention of liquidity-shortage crises in the banking system, which in turn was merged with a third, the management of the supply of money in accordance with the gold standard. The manipulation of interest rates eventually evolved into a fourth purpose, the primary focus of monetary policy to which all the previous aims would be held subordinate. This framework led to the inflation of the 1970s and the currency confusion of the 1980s through to the present day. The process began in the nineteenth century with the Bank of England.

The Bank of England eventually became a central reserve bank: It was the bank with which other banks deposited their major reserves, except for a small working reserve for daily use. The Bank of England also became the holder of most of other banks' gold reserves, such that the primary reserve of the English banking system, and later a significant part of the reserve of foreign banking systems as well, was kept with the Bank of England.

When a liquidity-shortage crisis threatened, the Bank of England was expected to tap into this central reserve by making loans to other banks and corporations. It did this through the mechanism of the discount rate, the rate it charged for short-term loans. In such a crisis the discount rate would be set significantly above the usual market rate for such loans, perhaps around 10 percent. By setting the rate so high during crises, the bank avoided introducing more base money than was necessary to deal with the crisis. As it made loans, new base money would enter active circulation. (For our purposes we will consider the bank's reserve to be "outside" the system. If one considers the bank's reserve to be "inside" the system, the effect of drawing down reserves is a decrease in the bank's demand for money.) By providing new liquidity through loans, the Bank of England effectively reduced the crisis-level interest rates. When the need for liquidity subsided, the market rate of interest would fall to its normal levels, the Bank of England's loans would be paid back, the reserve would be replenished, and the loaned money would quietly exit active circulation.

However, the Bank of England was not just a white knight waiting patiently for the onset of crisis. It, too, was a private profit-making institution, albeit a conservatively managed one. The division between private bank and central bank had not been formally defined. Lest it price itself out of business, the bank lowered its discount rate to market levels during normal times.

In the early nineteenth century, a legal maximum interest rate of 5 percent did not allow the bank to set its discount rate appreciably above prevailing market rates. In practice the discount rate was often at or below the market rate, in which case the Bank of England would supply large amounts of base money to the market in the form of loans, even though there was no liquidity shortage. This oversupply of base money would push down the value of the pound, resulting in outflows of gold.

In June 1822 the Bank of England lowered its discount rate from 5 percent to 4 percent, and its volumes of loans increased, including long-term loans. The bank's low discount rate and expansive policy of lending caused an inflation in which its gold reserves sank from £14.2 million in 1823 to £1.26 million in early December 1825. On December 13, 1825, the Bank of England raised its discount rate back to 5 percent. The loans were repaid, the reserves increased, and the active money supply was reduced. The contraction and deflation touched off a quick liquidity-shortage crisis, however, and the Bank of England had to again expand its supply of cash and credit to cope with the situation. When that rate proved to be too low, the 5 percent upper limit was eventually breached in a crisis in 1839 and caused a gold outflow.

Even as it used the discount rate and lending to cope with liquidity-shortage conditions and as part of its day-to-day operations, the bank also used the discount rate to manage the supply of liquidity in accordance to the gold standard. If gold was flowing out of the bank's reserves, it set about contracting the active supply of base money by raising its discount rate. At the higher rate, the bank would make fewer loans and its reserves would increase, effectively shrinking the supply of money. If it felt it should allow more money into the system, it would lower the discount rate and make more loans.

Nearly from the beginnings of the modern financial system, two distinct functions—first, the provision of short-term liquidity, and second, the management of supply in accordance with the gold standard—were thus combined in one instrument, the discount rate of the Bank of England. Smith makes no mention of interest rates in his description of the gold standard; neither does Ricardo, writing only a few years before such discount rate manipulation became standard policy. The discount rate was part of the mechanism by which supply was adjusted, but instead of focusing on supply and demand, everyone has since focused on the discount rate, and this misleading fixation on interest rates has continued to the present day.

It's not hard to see how this process came about. In the example of 1823 to 1825, the Bank of England had set its interest rate too low, thus overheating the economy through the devaluation of the currency. Perceiving its error and fearing inflation, it then induced a quick deflation and financial panic by raising interest rates. Superficially, the system hardly seems different from our own. And yet it was the complete opposite, anchored faithfully to a convertible gold standard, while ours today is a chaotic floating fiat currency. In the nineteenth century, the discount rate was a tool by which the supply of money was adjusted in accordance with the gold standard; today, the supply of money is the tool by which the interest rate is adjusted in accordance with an interest rate target. In that seemingly tiny difference lies the gulf between a hard-money system and a soft-money system.

The recognition of the Bank of England's influence in the British monetary system led to a series of reforms in 1844, in which the bank was split into a note-issuing division and a banking division. The issue department was supposed to manage the supply of banknotes in accordance with the gold standard, while the banking department was supposed to be free to carry on as a simple commercial bank. However, the issue department was conceived to be relatively sluggish about its issuance of banknotes, and it envisioned a slow growth of the supply of banknotes in line with the long-term growth of the economy as a whole. (The monetarist economists adopted a similar viewpoint in the 1960s and 1970s.) The demand for base money did not conform to the incrementalists' expectations, however, and in effect the banking department again took over the day-to-day management of the gold standard and the role of the lender of last resort. These two roles, and the Bank of England's third role as a private commercial bank, continued to be combined in its discount rate and lending policy. The inflexibility of its issue department resulted in a suspension of the 1844 rule during liquidity-shortage crises in 1847 and 1859, when the banking department nearly ran out of reserves and printed up new banknotes to meet demand.

A liquidity crisis in 1866 was the final test of the Bank of England's lender-of-last-resort abilities. By discounting freely at 10 percent, it dexterously weathered the storm. England never suffered another liquidity-shortage crisis again. After decades of struggle, it had mastered central banking.

In the latter decades of the nineteenth century, the Bank of England became less dominant in the financial system, and the effectiveness of its discount rate adjustment strategy as a means of managing base money via loan issuance, and thus of managing the value of the currency, waned. The bank then supplemented its discount rate and lending policy with open-market operations to adjust the supply of base money directly. If the pound sagged on the foreign exchange market, the bank would sell bonds on the open market and reduce the supply of money. If the pound was strong, the bank would buy bonds and expand the supply of money. *Making a loan* and *buying bonds* are virtually identical operations—both involve the acquisition of debt assets—but the government bond market allowed the Bank of England to operate with considerable more scale and finesse.

For a long time the United States, for the most part, did without a central institution like the Bank of England to give its financial system the flexibility it needed to adapt to liquidity shortages. Liquidity-shortage crises plagued it throughout the nineteenth and early twentieth centuries, until the creation of the Federal Reserve in 1913.

The First Bank of the United States, often cited as an early central bank, was essentially a simple commercial bank. Because it was large and conservatively run (i.e., had an ample reserve), it was able to help resolve a liquidity-shortage crisis in 1810, just before its charter expired in 1811 without being renewed. The bank's opponents criticized the bank's monopoly on the holding of government deposits and the possibly dangerous influence of its contingent of British shareholders. Thomas Jefferson, a leading opponent of the bank's charter renewal, argued that banking was not listed in the Constitution as a power of the government.

If the First Bank has continued its operations, it would have had the clout to keep the Southern banks in line and prevent the inflation that began with the War of 1812. The Second Bank of the United States took this role beginning with its charter in 1816, and afterward continued to make sure the financial system didn't stray from the discipline of the gold standard. The head of the Second Bank, Nicholas Biddle, paid close attention to the foreign exchange market, and if the dollar's free market value slipped against other gold-backed currencies like the pound, the bank would redeem the banknotes of other banks for specie, shrinking the supply of money and maintaining the currency's value—which was no more than private citizens were supposed to be able to do. Otherwise, the Second Bank, like the first, was primarily a large and conservatively run commercial bank, as befitting an institution in which the government kept its deposits. Because of its ample reserves, it was able to address a liquidity-shortage panic in 1825. With offices in all the states, it was also able to issue a uniform national currency, the only one to trade at its face value throughout the country, since most other banknotes would not be accepted at face value a long distance away from the issuing bank.

The Second Bank was crippled after the recharter debates of 1832 and lost its national charter in 1836. The hard-money advocates had railed against the Second Bank's influence over the financial system, but it was followed immediately after by a period of quiet influence by the supposedly independent Treasury. Beginning in 1837, the Treasury once again began issuing Treasury notes, the non-interest-bearing bonds usable as currency that it had issued during the War of 1812. In effect, the Treasury was issuing banknotes and influencing the supply of money. By altering the ratio of its issuances of normal deficit-financing bonds and Treasury notes, the Treasury could, in effect, adopt a lender-of-last-resort role.

In the face of criticism that the issuance of what were effectively banknotes was unconstitutional—it was exactly the sort of action the Constitution explicitly forbade—the Treasury began recalling its outstanding Treasury notes beginning in 1847, and by 1851 they had disappeared from circulation.

The Treasury thus gave up whatever lender-of-last-resort services it provided by the issuance of Treasury notes. Beginning in 1851, seasonal liquidity shortages intensified. In 1851 the Treasury acted to relieve the pressure by buying bonds on the open market. Like Tiberius, the Treasury in this way introduced its own government cash reserves into circulation (which at this time could not be held in commercial banks), quietly ignoring its obligation to remain independent. It did so again in 1853, but the danger of crisis did not abate until a regular disbursement of Treasury funds later that year. A similar pattern was repeated each year following. In 1857, a new pressure was added: Legislation in July 1857 lowered tariffs, with a greater demand for liquidity the likely result. In August of 1857 a classic liquidity-shortage panic developed that spread even to Britain and Europe. The crisis ended when the Treasury stepped in with a whopping new issuance of $20 million of Treasury notes, reintroducing the instrument it had eliminated six years earlier. Only four years later, the Treasury began issuing unredeemable fiat banknotes, the infamous greenbacks, to fund the Civil War.

In contrast to the centralized financial system that developed in Britain in the eighteenth and nineteenth centuries, particularly after the demise of the Second Bank, the U.S. monetary system was decentralized and a laboratory for all manner of experiments. The period from 1789 to 1860 is a favorite of many free-banking advocates who see it as a time when the monetary and financial system was most independent of government control, although if they had lived during that time they would no doubt favor the sounder, redeemable notes of New England banks over the less reliable and often, in practice, unredeemable notes of banks in the frontier states. But the free-banking system had become cumbersome when applied to such a large country, especially without nationwide banking institutions or advanced communications systems. The *Hodges Genuine Bank Notes of America, 1859*, a reference work on the desk of every person engaged in trade at that time, listed 9,916 notes issued by 1,356 banks, all of which were acceptable legal tender, and even then, hundreds of legitimate notes were omitted. Most notes traded at a discount, further complicating matters. The wildcat banks of the time, which issued banknotes and then disappeared in the middle of the night, were little more than quasi-legal forms of counterfeiting.

Beginning in 1863, the federal government took control over the issue of notes, which offered the advantage, as did the Second Bank of the United States, of providing a uniform currency that was accepted at face value throughout the country. The national banknotes were issued by private banks that were members of the National Bank System. From 1865, banknotes issued by nonmembers of the system were taxed at 10 percent, and almost immediately disappeared. Because gold redeemability had been suspended and the dollar had been floating since the beginning of the Civil War, the federal government had to decide how many national banknotes to allow into circulation. This duty fell to politicians, and the Congressional records of the time contain many lively debates about the supply of banknotes, complicated by the desire to deflate the currency back to its original value and reinstate gold redeemability. The management of the supply of banknotes was once again left to the free market after gold redeemability was restored in 1879.

As a result of the national banknotes system, the fact that the notes were not redeemable for gold, and that the supply of money was determined by Congress, the supply of notes was inflexible and individual banks could no longer print notes to meet periods of extraordinary demand. As a result, the risk of liquidity-shortage crises increased. The Treasury was pushed again into the lender-of-last-resort role and, when needed, purchased bonds on the open market to allow government-held cash into active circulation.

In 1873, the dollar was floating and the supply of money was held absolutely rigid by an act of 1868 that prescribed precisely $356 million of greenbacks and $300 million of national banknotes. (The act was intended to cause a gentle deflation as the economy grew into the fixed money supply.) In the autumn of 1873 banks did not have adequate reserves to meet the seasonal increase in demand associated with harvesttime, and on September 8 the Panic of 1873 began. The Treasury did nothing, and the panic ended when a government budget shortfall in November and December of that year was resolved by the issuance of $26 million of new greenbacks.

Individual banks had begun in the Panic of 1857 to remedy the liquidity-shortage problem by using *clearinghouse currency*, a kind of temporary currency that could be created on the spot to resolve liquidity-shortage panics. Its influence grew in the Panic of 1873, and later throughout the 1880s and 1890s. This system was in many ways highly successful, and it has admirers today as a sort of "decentralized central bank" that accomplishes the task of providing a short-term increase in the effective supply of base money without the presence of any sort of central governing body. However, because of the ban on issuing unauthorized banknotes, the clearinghouse system was considered rather shady, if not outright illegal, and because of its somewhat arcane workings was thought by nonbankers to be a confusing and potentially dangerous shell game. Though the system functioned well in many ways, it was not allowed to develop to its full potential, and in practice it did not prevent the onset of liquidity-shortage panics with the same success as the centralized Bank of England.

During this time, fixed reserve requirements also created the problem of making reserves unusable. Both of these factors exacerbated a liquidity-shortage panic in 1907, in which J. P. Morgan famously secured an agreement among frightened bankers to draw down reserves and expand credit, thus resolving the crisis. The 1907 crisis provided the final political impetus for the eventual creation of the Federal Reserve System in 1913.

A wonderful account of the liquidity-shortage crisis of 1907 is given by Jesse Livermore, fictionalized as "Larry Livingston" in Edwin Lefevre's classic *Reminiscences of a Stock Operator*, published in 1923. Livermore was one of the greatest speculators of his generation, which is why his account is both thrilling and, unlike many histories, focuses on the important details:

> You remember that money loans used to be made on the floor of the [New York Stock] Exchange around the Money Post. Those brokers who had received notice from their banks to pay call loans knew in a general way how much money they would have to borrow afresh. And of course the banks knew their position so far as loanable funds were concerned, and those which had money to loan would send it to the Exchange. This bank money was handled by a few brokers whose principal business was time loans. At about noon the renewal rate for the day was posted. Usually this represented a fair average of the loans made up to that time. Business was as a rule transacted openly by bids and offers, so that everyone knew what was going on. Between noon and about two o'clock there was ordinarily not much business done in money, but after delivery time—namely, 2:15 P.M.—brokers would know exactly what their cash position for the day would be, and they were able either to go to the Money Post and lend the balances that they had over or to borrow what they required. This business also was done openly.
>
> Well, sometime early in October [1907] the broker I was telling you about came to me and told me that brokers were getting so they didn't go to the Money Post when they had money to loan. The reason was that members of a couple of well-known commission houses were on watch there, ready to snap up any offerings of money. Of course no lender who offered money publicly could refuse to lend to these firms. They were solvent and the collateral was good enough. But the trouble was that once these firms borrowed money on call there was no prospect of the lender getting that money back. They simply said they couldn't pay it back and the lender would willy-nilly have to renew the loan. So

any Stock Exchange house that had money to loan to its fellows used to send its men about the floor instead of to the Post, and they would whisper to good friends, "Want a hundred?" meaning, "Do you wish to borrow a hundred thousand dollars?" The money brokers who acted for the banks presently adopted the same plan, and it was a dismal sight to watch the Money Post. Think of it!

Why, he also told me that it was a matter of Stock Exchange etiquette in those October days for the borrower to make his own rate of interest. You see, it fluctuated between 100 and 150 per cent per annum. I suppose by letting the borrower fix the rate the lender in some strange way didn't feel so much like a usurer. But you bet he got as much as the rest. The borrower naturally did not dream of not paying a high rate. He played fair and paid whatever the others did. What he needed was the money and was glad to get it.

Things got worse and worse. Finally there came the awful day of reckoning for the bulls and the optimists and the wishful thinkers and those vast hordes that, dreading the pain of a small loss at the beginning, were now about to suffer total amputation—without anaesthetics. A day I shall never forget, October 24, 1907.

Reports from the money crowd early indicated that borrowers would have to pay whatever the lenders saw fit to ask. There wouldn't be enough to go around. That day the money crowd was much larger than usual. When delivery time came that afternoon there must have been a hundred brokers around the Money Post, each hoping to borrow the money that his firm urgently needed. Without money they must sell what stocks they were carrying on margin—sell at any price they could get in a market where buyers were as scarce as money—and just then there was not a dollar in sight.

My friend's partner was as bearish as I was. The firm therefore did not have to borrow, but my friend, the broker I told you about, fresh from seeing the haggard faces around the Money Post, came to me. He knew I was heavily short of the entire market.

He said, "My God, Larry! I don't know what's going to happen. I never saw anything like it. It can't go on. Something has got to give. It looks to me as if everybody is busted right now. You can't sell stocks, and there is absolutely no money in there."

"How do you mean?" I asked.

But what he answered was, "Did you ever hear of the classroom experiment of the mouse in a glass-bell when they begin to pump the air out of the bell? You can see the poor mouse breathe faster and faster, its sides heaving like overworked bellows trying to get enough oxygen out of the decreasing supply in the bell. You watch it suffocate till its eyes almost pop out of their sockets, gasping, dying. Well, that is what I think of when I see the crowd at the Money Post! No money anywhere, and you can't liquidate stocks because there is nobody to buy them. The whole Street is broke and this very moment, if you ask me!"

It made me think. I had seen a smash coming, but not, I admit, the worst panic in our history. It might not be profitable to anybody—if it went much further.

Finally it became plain that there was no use in waiting at the Post for money. There wasn't going to be any. Then hell broke loose.

The president of the Stock Exchange, Mr. R. H. Thomas, so I heard later in the day, knowing that every house in the Street was headed for disaster, went out in search of succor. He called on James Stillman, president of the National City Bank, the richest bank in the United States. Its boast was that it never loaned money at a higher rate than 6 per cent.

Stillman heard what the president of the New York Stock Exchange had to say. Then he said, "Mr. Thomas, we'll have to go and see Mr. Morgan about this."

The two men, hoping to stave off the most disastrous panic in our financial history, went together to the office of J.P. Morgan & Co. and saw Mr. Morgan. Mr. Thomas laid the case before him. The moment he got through speaking Mr. Morgan said, "Go back to the Exchange and tell them that there will be money for them."

"Where?"

"At the banks!"

So strong was the faith of all men in Mr. Morgan in those critical times that Thomas didn't wait for further details but rushed
back to the floor of the Exchange to announce the reprieve to his
death-sentenced fellow members.

Then, before half past two in the afternoon, J. P. Morgan sent
John T. Atterbury, of Van Emburgh & Atterbury, who was known
to have close relations with J. P. Morgan & Co., into the money
crowd. My friend said that the old broker walked quickly to the
Money Post. He raised his hand like an exhorter at a revival meeting. The crowd, that at first had been calmed down somewhat by
President Thomas' announcement, was beginning to fear that the
relief plans had miscarried and the worst was still to come. But
when they looked at Mr. Atterbury's face and saw him raise his
hand they promptly petrified themselves.

In the dead silence that followed, Mr. Atterbury said, "I am
authorized to lend ten million dollars. Take it easy! There will be
enough for everybody!"

Then he began. Instead of giving to each borrower the name
of the lender he simply jotted down the name of the borrower and
the amount of the loan and told the borrower, "You will be told
where your money is." He meant the name of the bank from
which the borrower would get the money later.

I heard a day or two later that Mr. Morgan simply sent word to
the frightened bankers of New York that they must provide the
money the Stock Exchange needed.

"But we haven't got any. We're loaned up to the hilt," the
banks protested.

"You've got your reserves," snapped J. P.

"But we're already below the legal limit," they howled.

"Use them! That's what reserves are for!" And the banks
obeyed and invaded the reserves to the extent of about twenty million dollars. It saved the stock market. The bank panic didn't come
until the following week. He was a man, J. P. Morgan was. They
don't come much bigger.[3]

The immediate result of the events of 1907 was the Aldrich-Vreeland Act of 1908, which formalized and legalized the existing clearinghouse system. The clearinghouse system, now made respectable, nicely averted a potential liquidity-shortage crisis stemming from the outbreak of war in Europe in 1914, before the Federal Reserve system was functional.

The purpose of the Federal Reserve System was, once and for all, to establish a formal institution to take the role of the lender of last resort in liquidity-shortage crises. In the terminology of the time, the money supply was to be *elastic*, able to expand or contract in response to changes in demand. (This in no way implied that the value of money, expressed in gold, was to vary.) During the previous century this role had been informally passed around, from the First Bank of the United States, to the Second Bank of the United States, to the Treasury, to Congress, to the clearinghouse associations, and even to J. P. Morgan. Although the decades-long political debates that led to the creation of the Federal Reserve are complex, it was conceived, at least by its noblest supporters, as the capstone of a monetary system based on gold. It would finally combine stability in the financial system, by solving the problem of liquidity-shortage panics, and stability in monetary value, which the gold link provided, just as had been accomplished in Britain a half century earlier to great success. The Fed would accomplish this by printing its own currency, Federal Reserve Notes, which it would then disburse through commercial loans during liquidity shortages. The United States was the last major country to adopt a centralized lender-of-last-resort institution.

> A . . . feature of the new institution on which both its sponsors and its opponents agreed was its scope. They did not create the Federal Reserve System to usurp the functions of the gold standard and become an omnipotent central bank. Their intention was only to provide for form-seasonal elasticity in the economy's money supply, and to do so on the basis of bona fide, self-liquidating, short-term commercial loans. . . .

Congress intended the Federal Reserve System to be a self-regulating adjunct to a self-regulating gold standard. The Fed was to do at short term what the gold standard did secularly, namely, to provide seasonal money commensurate with seasonal productions of commodities. It would also become a system-wide clearing house for banks; and it would take over the erstwhile clearinghouse function of issuing "emergency" currency in a crisis, and put it on an official, legal basis.[4]

The Fed's detractors worried about the presence of a centralized governing bureaucracy and what it might become in the future. As representative Frank Mondell of Wyoming argued in the House:

The Federal Reserve Board under this bill is an organization of vastly wider power, authority, and control over currency [and] banks . . . than the reserve associations contemplated by the National Monetary Commission. . . . It is of a character which in practical operation would tend to increase and centralize. . . . It will be the most powerful banking institution in all the world. . . . In your frantic efforts to escape the bogey man of a central bank, . . . you have come perilously near establishing in the office of the Comptroller of the Currency, under the Secretary of the Treasury, the most powerful banking institution in the world.[5]

The fear of centralized control caused the Federal Reserve System to be conceived as a system of 12 regional banks instead of a single central bureau. When the Federal Reserve Act was signed by president Woodrow Wilson in September 1913, a clause was included as a precaution against future misunderstandings of the Fed's purpose. It said: "Nothing in this act . . . shall be considered to repeal the parity provisions contained in an act approved March 14, 1900," which referred to the Gold Standard Act of 1900.

By separating the lender-of-last-resort function from the operation of the gold peg (notes were redeemable at banks and the Treasury) and giving the Fed the power to print money as needed to respond to a crisis, in many ways the new U.S. system was superior to the British system. No longer would both functions be tied in a single mechanism, the discount rate, and confused with a third function, commercial lending for profit. The Treasury and individual banks, via the national banknotes system, would handle the gold peg, the Fed would handle liquidity-shortage crises, and commercial banks would take care of day-to-day commercial lending.

The Fed would be what the Bank of England was not, a white knight waiting patiently for the onset of crisis. The heads of the regional reserve banks would set a discount rate well above the normal market rate, perhaps 10 percent, and then the Fed would wait until a liquidity-shortage crisis pushed up the short-term rate of interest so high that borrowers would appear at the Fed's window asking for loans. When the crisis passed and the demand for money and credit had subsided, the borrowers would pay back their high-interest loans, the supply of money would naturally contract, and the Fed would then wait until the next crisis. It might have to wait years, even decades.

And that's it. That's all the Fed would do.

But that's not the way it worked out—and in retrospect it is hardly surprising that a quasi-governmental body with such potentially awesome powers would be content with the role of placidly waiting for some impending crisis years in the future. The outbreak of World War I, and the subsequent breakup of the gold standard in Europe, naturally inclined the Federal Reserve to take a more active role. Socialist central-planning ideologies, which led to the establishment of a communist government in Russia only three years later, were reaching, especially among intellectuals, a heady peak still untempered by bad experience. Almost immediately the Fed set about redefining its role and expanding its powers. As economic historian Richard Timberlake describes:

> The Board in its 1914 report added other norms for Reserve Bank operations. A Reserve bank should not be merely an emergency

institution, argued the report, "to be resorted to for assistance only in time of abnormal stress . . . its duty . . . is not to await emergencies but by anticipation, to do what it can to prevent them." If interest rates—the indicators for policy—get too high, the report continued, it will be the duty of the Reserve Board, "acting through the discount rate and open market powers, to secure a wider diffusion of credit facilities at reasonable rates."

A natural reaction to a careful reading of the passages quoted here is, 'Wait a minute!' Was this report outlining a policy for the Reserve banks or the Reserve Board? . . . By a subtle shift of substantives, the Board is suddenly in the role of a policymaker— judging whether interest rates are too high, and exercising open market powers.[6]

The Federal Reserve Board, which had been conceived as little more than a liaison committee between the 12 regional banks and Congress, also asserted the Federal Reserve's right to conduct open-market operations, which were "to give the Federal Reserve Board the necessary economic control of the domestic money market and to preserve a proper equilibrium in international relations." In just 13 months since being signed into law, and long before beginning full operations, the Fed had already traveled a long way from simply giving bankers a short-term loan during the rare crisis.

The Fed never got a chance to function as it was intended. From 1917, just about the beginning of its full operations, the Fed was pressed by the Treasury to keep its discount rate low so that the Treasury could issue bonds to the market at artificially low interest rates to finance the U.S. entry into World War I (the discount rate was an effective cap on market interest rates). The Fed accomplished this task by expanding its supply of liquidity for short-term loans. The gold standard had been rendered ineffectual by the wartime gold embargo, and the result was a small currency devaluation and inflation. The institution that had been conceived as a self-adjusting adjunct to the gold standard only four years earlier was already managing an effective fiat currency through the operation of an interest rate peg and was being pressured by the Treasury to maintain low interest rates and expand the supply of money. A half century later, this same combination destroyed the world monetary system.

But the Fed pulled back in 1920, after the gold embargo was lifted, and retreated to take a secondary role alongside the gold standard, although it continued to fuss with market interest rates. Open-market operations became routine soon after their first use in 1922. From then on the Fed was influencing the short-term loan market on a daily basis.

In the worldwide economic contraction of the early 1930s, the inflationist arguments that appear during any economic crisis once again came to the fore. Countries worldwide devalued their currencies in hopes of solving a problem they did not understand, but their main effect was to shatter the world monetary system that had been painfully reconstructed during the 1920s. The devaluations of the 1930s were bald-faced acts of intentional manipulation—the Fed had nothing to do with the dollar devaluation of 1933–1934—and soon fell into disfavor. Beginning in the latter 1930s, when the world had for the most part already abandoned its inflationist policies and yearned once more for a system of stable currencies, the arguments of the inflationists came to be disguised as "lowering interest rates."

Wasn't the Fed created to solve economic crises? And didn't it solve these crises by "lowering interest rates?" Apparently so, but only liquidity-shortage crises, not crises caused by the tax and currency disasters of the 1930s. But this distinction was already lost. The publication of Keynes's *General Theory* in 1936 gave academics a justification for inflationist arguments that had been burbling for decades, if not centuries. Keynes, in the *General Theory*, cites at length the influence of Silvio Gesell, who, writing in 1906, recommended an interest rate eventually of zero. But the idea dates from far earlier than that. In 1809, in a pamphlet titled *The High Price of Bullion, Proof of the Depreciation of Bank Notes*, David Ricardo excoriated his contemporaries who wished to "lower interest rates":

To suppose that any increased issues of the Bank [of England] can have the effect of permanently lowering the rate of interest, and satisfying the demands of all borrowers, so that there will be none to apply for new loans, or that a productive gold or silver mine can have such an effect, is to attribute a power to the circulating medium which it can never possess. Banks would, if this were possible, become powerful engines indeed. By creating paper money, and lending it at three or two per cent under the present market rate of interest, the Bank would reduce the profits on trade in the same proportion; and if they were sufficiently patriotic to lend their notes at an interest no higher than necessary to pay the expenses of their establishment, profits would be still further reduced; no nation, but by similar means, could enter into competition with us, we should engross the trade of the world. To what absurdities would not such a theory lead us![7]

Keynes, and the hordes of young economists who followed in his footsteps, had a new vision of a government solution to an apparently unstable capitalist system. The problem of recession and unemployment could be solved, they thought, by "lowering interest rates," and the mechanism by which this would be accomplished was the open-market operations of the Federal Reserve and institutions like it that had been created around the world.

Keynes himself had long been steeped in the classical system, as his earlier writing shows, and adopted his inflationist tendencies primarily as a reaction to the immediate economic conditions of the mid-1930s. He later returned somewhat to his classical roots. His friend and intellectual sparring partner throughout the 1930s, Friedrich Hayek, recalled:

It was early in 1946, shortly after he [Keynes] had returned from the strenuous and exhausting negotiations in Washington on the British loan. . . . A turn in the conversation made me ask him whether he was not concerned about what some of his disciples were making of his theories. After a not very complimentary remark about the persons concerned, he proceeded to reassure me by explaining that those ideas had been badly needed at the time he had launched them. He continued by indicating that I need not be alarmed; if they should ever become dangerous I could rely upon him again quickly to swing round public opinion—and he indicated by a quick movement of his hand how rapidly that would be done. But three months later he was dead.[8]

The low interest rates common during times of stable money are a genuine economic advantage, but the effects of "lowering interest rates" through the oversupply of base money and the devaluation of the currency amount to little more than the inflationary boom, malinvestment, and the money illusion. The money illusion could indeed temporarily lower unemployment, but only at the cost of eventual hyperinflation, as had happened in Germany in the early 1920s. The persistence of such fallacious ideas through the decades after World War II was mainly due to the fact that their supporters were not able to carry them out. The international gold standard, still operating through the Bretton Woods system, prevented such policies from reaching their natural conclusion.

This did not prevent the inflationists from trying, however, with the result that countries around the world became involved in monetary games like the "stop-go" policies of Britain, in which an attempt to "lower interest rates" (the "go" period) would result in a small inflationary boom and a sagging value of the pound. At that point, to maintain the Bretton Woods system's fixed exchange rates, the central bank would then have to engineer a monetary contraction (the "stop" period) to support the currency. It was the same thing that the Bank of England had done in 1825. But while the Bank of England had recognized its accidental mistake in 1825, the young inflationists did the same thing on purpose. The stop period would of course tend to be recessionary, which only created an impetus for another go period of excessive monetary expansion and fueled the inflationists' dreams of what would be possible if they weren't bound by the "golden fetters" of the Bretton Woods system.

As a result, the entire period from 1940 to 1971 was marred by continuing crises in which the domestic interest rate policies of central banks came into conflict with the external policy of fixed foreign exchange rates linked to gold. All manner of restrictions on trade and capital movements were imposed in response to the currency confusion. The gold flows at the time, the result of the conflict between the interest rate policies and the gold standard, were misinterpreted as problems of trade. A breaking apart of world trade and international finance also served the inflationists well, since the conflicting desires of domestic currency devaluation and fixed exchange rates could only be resolved in a situation without trade between countries. At that point the "official exchange rate" would simply be a fiction, there being nobody left to make exchanges except for the occasional tourist.

Rather than blame themselves, however, the inflationists blamed the market for reacting to their inflationist policies in the only sensible way. The myth grew that, to create monetary stability, the market had to be tamed by all sorts of government coercion. This myth persists to the present day, its believers oblivious to the fact that the great period of worldwide currency stability from 1870 to 1914 was a time when capital flowed freely among countries.

The inflationists at times gained the upper hand over the discipline of the Bretton Woods peg. In the late 1940s in Britain, the authorities argued that "lowering interest rates" would make it cheaper to service the national debt, and they embarked on a program of keeping short-term rates at a tiny 0.5 percent. This is almost exactly the game the Federal Reserve had been pressured into playing in 1919. The Fed called a halt to the charade—it was involved in similar foolishness in the late 1940s as well, before pulling back again—but the Brits carried it through to its logical conclusion. The pound was devalued from $4.03 to $2.80 on September 18, 1949. The existing national debt did indeed become cheaper to service, since the government essentially defaulted on much of it through the mechanism of devaluation.

The end result of all this "lowering interest rates" throughout the world was in fact a persistent rise in interest rates after World War II, as lenders demanded an extra premium to protect themselves against the risk of devaluation and inflationary default (which is exactly what happened).

Despite unceasing attacks on the gold standard, it still worked to keep money relatively stable, and the inflationary trend of the 1950s and 1960s was modest compared to what followed. Business for the most part was good in the United States and around the world, and the period would later be seen as a sort of golden age, in which inflation and unemployment were both low, economic progress was impressive, particularly in Germany and Japan, and the moral and civil foundations of society were sound.

The result of the continuing dominance of the gold standard through the Bretton Woods system was that the inflationist doctrine of "lowering interest rates" was never fully debunked, and instead completely saturated the academic economics establishment. The principles of economics upon which the gold standard was founded were scrubbed clean from textbooks after World War II. Frustrated by the inability to carry out their policies to their conclusion, the descendants of Keynes instead strengthened their position by indoctrinating two generations of economists to their way of thinking.

The postwar inflationists developed all manner of intellectual constructs in favor of their arguments to "lower interest rates." One of the most enduring has been the Phillips curve, which is the assertion that more inflation leads to less unemployment. It's merely the inflationary malinvestment boom rendered graphically.

The Keynesian inflationists set about "lowering interest rates" in earnest beginning in 1970, leading to the break of the dollar's link with gold in 1971. The result, of course, was that U.S. interest rates skyrocketed to levels not seen in nearly two centuries. The resulting turmoil caused the Bretton Woods system of fixed dollar exchange rates to finally shatter in 1973, leaving each country free to "lower interest rates" as they saw fit. The era of floating fiat currencies had begun.

The predictions of the Phillips curve never did pan out. As the inflation combined with progressive tax structures to drive economies around the world into sharp contraction, inflation and unemployment rose in tandem, a condition that was known as *stagflation*. From the classical perspective, this was blandly predictable—currency instability and rising taxes are always the primary suspects in any serious economic downturn—but from the standpoint of a theoretical structure that touted the virtues of inflation, it was shockingly converse. Unable to conceive of the idea that 40 years of indoctrination into inflationism would deprive them of the tools for dealing with an inflationary recession, the inflationists piled on more of the same bad medicine: more inflation to take care of the unemployment and higher taxes and price controls to take care of the inflation. In the United States, this policy mix was touted by James Tobin of Yale University.

The notion of inflation itself had become queerly divorced from any concept of monetary mechanisms. By disguising the devaluation as "lowering interest rates," the Keynesians eventually fooled themselves. It wasn't their fault that the market value of their currencies fell. That was the market's fault. The inevitable price rises following devaluation weren't their fault either. Blame that one on the Arabs. Blame it on excess demand from the irrational citizenry. Blame it on pushing costs and pulling wages. Blame it on anything, in short, except a fall in the currency's value.

All of the Keynesian tools—primarily devaluation and expanded government spending—had failed. In the late 1970s, governments (particularly in the United States and the United Kingdom) eventually turned to the monetarists, who had revived some of the classical concepts about money. Inflation, the monetarists claimed, was a purely monetary phenomenon and could only be solved by monetary means, namely adjusting the supply of money. So far so good, but the monetarists defined the supply of money not as base money, which could be adjusted directly, but as deposit money, which could not. They also focused on the supply of money directly, instead of seeing supply as the tool by which the value of money is stabilized, the principle on which classical monetary economics and the gold standard were based. As a result of these two methodologies, monetarism, like Keynesianism, required a policy board and the attendant armies of statisticians. It was not a self-adjusting system.

The monetarist experiments of the early 1980s eventually succeeded in stopping the inflation of the 1970s (helped by tax cuts in both the United States and the United Kingdom), but currencies, if anything, became even more unstable, experiencing wild swings in value up and down. Interest rates went on a roller-coaster ride, keeping up with the currency chaos. This was intolerable—a far cry from the dependable stability of the gold standard, even the embattled gold standard of the Bretton Woods years. But by then the academic economics profession had fought the gold standard for 50 years and, after generations of inflationist indoctrination, had completely forgotten how it worked. The monetarists, who shared the Keynesian fondness for monetary policy by philosopher-kings, had in fact joined hands with the Keynesians in calling for the gold standard's demise in 1971. The few calls for a return to the gold standard fell on deaf ears. The gold standard advocates themselves had largely forgotten how the gold standard worked, and though they remembered the ancient principle that a gold standard was a good idea, they couldn't properly say why it was a good idea or the practicalities involved in putting one together.

Monetarism was abandoned and gave way to a new sort of Keynesianism, in which the inflationist theories of the 1940s to the 1970s were pressed into service once again—this time, not to sing inflation's virtues but to fight inflation! This neo-Keynesianism remains the conventional wisdom of the economics establishment at this time.

The Fed's open-market rate, the mechanism by which currency devaluation had been disguised as "lowering interest rates," was now a tool to fight inflation. The Phillips curve, by which the inflationists argued that more inflation would bring lower unemployment, was turned on its head. Now they argued that lower unemployment causes higher inflation.

The peculiar blind spot between money and inflation, the blind spot that was necessary to believe that "lowering interest rates" wasn't a method of currency devaluation, remained. The monetarist assertion that inflation is a purely monetary phenomenon was pushed to the background. Growth caused inflation. Rising wages caused inflation. The rising cost of imported goods (evidence of currency depreciation if there ever was one) caused inflation. Excessive demand caused inflation. An overheating economy caused inflation. It was all aspects of the inflationary malinvestment boom, the money illusion, the effects of currency devaluation, looked at from another angle. And the solution to the problem was to "raise interest rates."

The goals of the postwar Keynesian inflationists, particularly the goal of full employment through currency devaluation, had all been abandoned by 1980. The ancient warnings against the perils of currency devaluation were proved once more. But the Keynesian inflationists themselves, often the very same people, and their theoretical structures continued to dominate. Often they would revert to their old ways when giving advice to governments of developing countries, who became duly impressed at the success of the U.S. economy after it returned to an antidevaluation policy. After spending much of the Bretton Woods period trying to figure out how to "lower interest rates" without devaluing the currency (they failed), the neo-Keynesians struggled in the 1980s and 1990s to devalue other countries' currencies without causing inflationary price rises (they failed again).

The neo-Keynesian system of "raising interest rates" has, for the most part, managed to keep currencies from veering dramatically into either inflation or deflation. Though a far cry from the stability offered even by the embattled gold standard of Bretton Woods, it provided a monetary foundation reliable enough to support economic expansion in the United States and around the world. It was helped in part because no neo-Keynesian had yet headed the Federal Reserve's Open Market Committee. After Paul Volcker, an eclectic monetarist, the reins were handed in 1987 to Alan Greenspan, who is one of the very few central bankers in the world with a genuine grasp of the gold standard and how it works. Ben Bernanke is the first academic at the Fed, and we will see how history treats him.

The result of all this raising and lowering of interest rate targets is that nobody is paying any attention to the traditional focus of currency management, the value of the currency, or the traditional means of managing a currency, the supply of base money. From an international standpoint, the neo-Keynesian system is pure chaos, with currency values endlessly waggling up and down in response to central banks' interest rate policies. The value of stable exchange rates is obvious to any businessperson and most politicians, although economists still struggle with the concept. The desire to calm the foreign exchange chaos has led to endeavors such as the creation of the euro and the currency boards of various countries. This in itself isn't stability, but it binds large economies together such that their currencies fluctuate in parallel, eliminating at least the maddening uncertainties of variable exchange rates. The neo-Keynesian claim that currency stability isn't possible is true within their framework—neither lowering nor raising their interest rate targets, nor the meaningless sterilized foreign exchange intervention they sometimes indulge in, will produce currency stability. There is a growing understanding that such stability can be produced if one is willing to give up central banks' interest rate manipulations, but after 70 years now of attacking currency stability and the gold standard, the urge to "lower interest rates" in the case of a recession remains strong among the economics establishment.

A recent threat to neo-Keynesian orthodoxy is, ironically enough, the genuine economic growth that the anti-inflation policies of the 1980s and 1990s have helped create. In the 1990s, all manner of ad hoc theories about a "new economy" were brandished to describe how economies can grow without inflation—all of them rather silly attempts to explain away the obvious failures of the neo-Keynesian theoretical structure. Technology has nothing to do with it, nor do supply shocks or all the other angels and demons conjured up by confused economists. The economics establishment still has not been able to absorb the rather simple idea that inflation is bad for economies (and thus employment), and a stable currency is good. After the experience of the 1970s and the battle to halt currency devaluation in the early 1980s, this would seem a rather obvious conclusion, but it has yet to find a place in today's conventional wisdom.

For all its failings, the Fed from day one has successfully dealt with the problem of liquidity-shortage crises. No major liquidity-shortage crisis has emerged since 1907. There is no conflict between a lender of last resort and the gold standard. The Bank of England championed both, and the Fed worked alongside the gold standard for most of the period from 1914 to 1971. The problem is that the Fed has adopted a new task, manipulating the value of the currency, and an operating system, the open-market interest rate peg, which is inappropriate for that task. Until these innovations are abandoned, true currency stability will remain elusive.

CHAPTER 9

THE 1930s

A Failure of Monetary and Fiscal Policy Causes a Capitalist Collapse

Much of the history of monetary theory reduces to a struggle between opposing mercantilist and classical camps. Mercantilists, with their fears of hoarding and scarcity of money together with their prescription of cheap (low interest rate) and plentiful cash as a stimulus to real activity, tend to gain the upper hand when unemployment is the dominant problem. Classicals, chanting their mantra that inflation is always and everywhere a monetary phenomenon, tend to prevail when price stability is the chief policy concern.

Currently, the classical view is in the driver's seat. By all rights it should remain there since it long ago exposed the mercantilist view as fundamentally flawed. It is by no means certain, however, that the classical view's reign is secure. For history reveals that, whenever one view holds center stage, the other, fallacious or not, is waiting in the wings to take over when the time is ripe.

—Thomas M. Humphrey, Federal Reserve Bank of Richmond annual report, 1998

"The effect of [Keynes's] *General Theory*," [John Kenneth] Galbraith explained, "was to legitimize ideas that were in circulation. What had been the aberrations of cranks and crackpots became now respectable scholarly discussion."

—Quoted in William Greider's *Secrets of the Temple: How the Federal Reserve Runs the Country*[1]

In 1928 the world monetary system had been rebuilt in the shape of the glorious successes of 1870 to 1914. Britain, which had purposefully deflated the pound back to its prewar parities after wartime inflation, had suffered years of recession in the name of rock-solid long-term currency stability. The principle of a pound at £3 17s per ounce of gold was over 200 years old, and the monetary authorities expected the gold peg to last another 200 years. All of that would change by 1932, however, and though the major powers would very soon rebuild the international gold standard once again in the form of Bretton Woods, the fundamentally mercantilist theoretical structure that had been revived in the 1930s, with John Maynard Keynes becoming its leading standard-bearer, remains dominant today in academia, the media, and government. The gold standard of the Bretton Woods era was ultimately abandoned not because of any intrinsic weakness, but because there was nobody left who remembered how it worked or what it was for.

Most people who read newspapers today are aware that in the end, Keynesian policies typically boil down into two counterrecession measures: government spending (often on public works) and "lowering interest rates," which often (though not always) amounts to a devaluation of the currency. Keynes can hardly take credit for inventing these. They are ancient. Pericles of Athens is said to have ordered public works projects to offset unemployment, and the famous roads of the Roman empire were funded for similar reasons. The question of how to address the poor, unemployed, unfortunate, and disenfranchised is as old as government itself, and political leaders throughout history have hit on the idea that, rather than simply handing out welfare distributions, it would be more beneficial to hire the unemployed in the service of the state. In this way, the public benefits from new facilities, and workers stay employed, which promotes a sound morality and makes them less likely to revolt.

The problem arises when counterrecessionary government spending is not considered simply a welfare policy, but a means to resolve the recession itself. Such spending can create more economic activity for as long as the money is flowing. But real growth is a result of the improving efficiency and productivity of the extended economic order, which welfare-directed public works spending typically does little to improve. If productivity has been impaired by tax hikes, regulatory burdens, or monetary instability, public works spending can do nothing to fix the problem.

The notion that government spending creates economic growth became a central tenet of the mercantilist theorists between roughly 1600 and 1750, who appeared partly in reaction to the wars and economic difficulties of the period. The brisk growth of the Industrial Revolution, beginning in the latter half of the eighteenth century, and the classical economics that helped make it possible, swept away the mercantilists' consumption-centered doctrine. John Stuart Mill wrote the following criticism in 1830, 106 years before Keynes published his *General Theory*:

> Before the appearance of those great writers whose discoveries have given to political economy its present comparatively scientific character, the ideas universally entertained both by theorists and by practical men, on the causes of national wealth, were grounded upon certain general views, which almost all who have given any considerable attention to the subject now justly hold to be completely erroneous.
>
> Among the mistakes which were most pernicious in their direct consequences, and tended in the greatest degree to prevent a just conception of the objects of the science, or of the test to be applied to the solution of the questions which it presents, was the immense importance attached to consumption. The great end of legislation in matters of national wealth, according to the prevalent opinion, was to create consumers. A great and rapid consumption was what the producers, of all classes and denominations, wanted, to enrich themselves and the country. This object, under the varying names of an extensive demand, a brisk circulation, a great expenditure of money and, sometimes totidem verbis a large consumption, was conceived to be the great condition of prosperity.
>
> It is not necessary, in the present state of the science, to contest this doctrine in the most flagrantly absurd of its forms or of its applications. The utility of a large government expenditure, for the purpose of encouraging industry, is no longer maintained. Taxes

are not now esteemed to be "like the dews of heaven, which return again in prolific showers." It is no longer supposed that you benefit the producer by taking his money, provided you give it to him again in exchange for his goods. There is nothing which impresses a person of reflection with a stronger sense of the shallowness of the political reasonings of the last two centuries, than the general reception so long given to a doctrine which, if it proves anything, proves that the more you take from the pockets of the people to spend on your own pleasures, the richer they grow; that the man who steals money out of a shop, provided he expends it all again at the same shop, is a benefactor to the tradesman whom he robs, and that the same operation, repeated sufficiently often, would make the tradesman's fortune.[2]

The other notion, managing consumption and the economy through monetary manipulation, is as old as devaluation itself. The Chinese thinker Kuan Tzu, who died in 645 BC, wrote:

> When money is high goods are low; when goods are high money is low . . . the ruler should manipulate the values of grains and money and gold, and the empire can thereby be stabilized.[3]

This idea, too, was revived by the mercantilists. In his 1601 work *Treatise on the Canker of England's Commonwealth*, Gerard de Malynes wrote: "The more ready money, either in specie or by exchange, that our merchants should make, the more employment would they make upon our home commodity, advancing the price thereof, which price would augment the quantity by setting more people to work." Mercantilists had always tended to favor discretionary control over the money supply. Inducing an inflation by keeping an excess of gold and silver within their borders was one of the intents of their restrictive trade policies. The idea was expressed perhaps most overtly by John Law, who sought ways to deal with the depressed Scottish economy of the time. In his *Money and Trade Considered; with a Proposal for*

Supplying the Nation with Money of 1705, he argued that issuances of banknotes would solve the problem of a shortage of money, drive down interest rates, and increase production and employment. These ideas Law put into practice as the finance minister of France in 1718, and his Mississippi Bubble ended in an inflationary bust.

The mercantilists' idea of managing the economy by managing the currency and credit perhaps reached its most sophisticated expression in the writings of James Denham Steuart, who is known as the "last of the mercantilists." Steuart, writing in 1767, envisioned a near-superhuman statesman, a wise and incorruptible government bureaucrat, to look over the country's monetary conditions:

> He ought at all times to maintain a just proportion between the produce of industry, and the quantity of circulating equivalent [money], in the hands of his subjects, for the purchase of it; that, by a steady and judicious administration, he may have it in his power at all times, either to check prodigality and hurtful luxury, or to extend industry and domestic consumption, according as the circumstances of his people shall require one or the other corrective, to be applied to the natural bent and spirit of the times. . . .
>
> A statesman who allows himself to be entirely taken up in promoting circulation, and the advancement of every species of luxurious consumption, may carry matters too far, and destroy the industry he wishes to promote. This is the case, when the consequences of domestic consumption raises prices, and thereby hurts exportation.
>
> A principal object of his attention must therefore be, to judge when it is proper to encourage consumption, in favour of industry, and when to discourage it, in favour of a reformation upon the growth of luxury.[4]

Steuart's statesman didn't stop there. He would also manage the rate of interest on loans and offset the chilling effect of higher taxes by applying a monetary boost:

A statesman when he intends suddenly to augment the taxes of his people, without interrupting their industry, which then becomes still more necessary than ever, should augment the circulating equivalent in proportion to the additional demand for it.[5]

Two centuries later, in 1971, the world gold standard was blown up by exactly this method, when Richard Nixon attempted to counteract a recession caused in large part by his 1969 capital gains tax hike with a big dose of monetary expansion. This catapulted Steuart's "statesman," today's central bank governor, to the pinnacle of influence, where he mismanages currencies with vague and fallacious principles that have hardly changed since the mercantilists' day.

Adam Smith found Steuart's writings abhorrent. In direct response to Steuart's work, Smith wrote a book of his own in which mysterious and omnipotent "statesmen" and their all-too-visible hands have no role in monetary affairs. Smith and the classical economists that both preceded and followed him hewed to Locke's doctrine: The best currency is a stable currency, the most stable monetary benchmark is gold, and there is little more to be said about it.

Given the high interest rates, often in the midteens for business borrowers, that prevailed during the floating-pound era of the seventeenth century, it is not at all surprising that the mercantilist writers would become fascinated with the idea of lower interest rates. The strange thing is that Keynes would revive this tired notion during the 1930s, an environment when the yields on long-term U.S. and British government bonds were below 4 percent and on their way to multidecade lows.

Mercantilism is merely the leading edge of a much greater dialectic, between *statism* and the laissez-faire theories of what used to be called *liberalism*. At the extremes of statism lie command economies that are run like corporations or militaries, in which everyone has a fixed predetermined role in a hierarchical power structure. The twentieth-century equivalents were the communist states of the Stalinist Soviet Union or Maoist China. At the other extreme lie the great liberalist experiments, of which the United States of the nineteenth century was perhaps history's greatest expression. At this time, the torch is perhaps carried best by Hong Kong or financial havens such as Bermuda or the Cayman Islands.

The dialectic between statism and liberalism has stretched over millennia, and, like so many perennial issues of statecraft, has echoes in the ancient Chinese philosophers. The Confucians and the Taoists were the liberals of the day, with the Taoists insisting that if governments did little, the result would not be chaos but an exquisite order. "Overseeing a great empire is like frying a small fish," reads a Taoist aphorism still popular today. (If you poke at it too much, it will fall apart.) A famous Confucian fable concludes that "an oppressive government is more terrible than tigers." The Chinese liberals, which also included Mencius and Hsun Tzu, faced off against the ancient statists, the Mohists and the Legalists, who were quick to recommend price fixing, government coordination of agriculture and industry, and currency manipulation. The thinking in this quote from Sang Hung-yang, a Mohist of the third century BC who also advocated the establishment of government offices of *chun-shu* ("equal distribution"), is virtually undistinguishable from Maoism:

> Let orders be given that, in all places far distant, those products which merchants and traders buy up and transport for resale when prices are high, should be transported to the capital in lieu of taxes. In the capital there should be established an office of p'ing chuan [standardization of prices] which shall receive all the goods submitted from throughout the realm. Call upon the office for artisans to manufacture carts and all kinds of equipment; for all of the above the Ministry of Agriculture shall provide the means. Let the Ministry of Agriculture through these various offices achieve a total monopoly on all the money and goods of the empire. When prices are high, it shall sell; when goods are cheap, it shall buy. In this way rich merchants and great traders shall have no access to vast profits; the people will return to the "fundamental purpose" [agriculture] and the prices of goods will no longer rise wildly. In this way

commodities throughout the realm will be held down in price; the name for this system shall be p'ing-chuan.[6]

How little is new under the sun! If either statism or liberalism were universally superior to the other, the dialectic would not have continued into the twentieth century in the form of the cold war standoff. At the simplest level, the great debate between statism and liberalism over the centuries has been driven by the fact that *good socialism is better than bad capitalism*. When the exquisite order of capitalism disintegrates into chaos, as it did in the 1930s, socialist ideas, ranging from increased welfare spending to government currency manipulation to price controls to industrial central planning, come to the forefront. A centrally planned communist economy is essentially public works spending taken to its ultimate, where the entire economy becomes a "public work" (i.e., a jobs-creation program) and people's incomes are taxed at 100 percent to pay for it. (In practice, the Soviet economy of the 1960s was indeed better than the capitalist disasters of the 1930s.)

It is perfectly possible to have a liberal capitalist economy run by a dictator or monarch. Hong Kong, Korea, and Taiwan have been under a militarist or externally appointed government for most of the past 50 years. Today's capitalist China has a mandarinate government not much different than the governments that have run China for at least the past 13 centuries. (A mandarinate government is essentially a large bureaucracy, in which decision makers are hired or promoted rather than being selected in a general election.) A king is merely a hereditary dictator. As Friedrich Hayek argued in his classic book *The Road to Serfdom*, it is difficult to manage a statist economy with a democracy, although it has happened for short periods, such as the United States during World War II.

The liberal values of the nineteenth century were swept away after the 1930s, even in Britain and the United States, their greatest strongholds. In time, the champions of liberalism regroup and demonstrate that when capitalism and liberalism are working at their best, the results are superior to virtually any form of socialism. The

Mohists and Legalists are not well remembered today. The pendulum swings back toward liberalism, as it has throughout the world since the 1980s.

The primary difference between the free-market liberals of today and those of the past is monetary policy. The principles of low taxes, free trade, modest regulation, and open entrepreneurialism are well understood. Socialist ideas are in decline everywhere, and the great central-planning experiments in the Soviet Union and China have been voluntarily and peacefully abandoned. Today's liberals, unfortunately, do not understand classical monetary policy. That knowledge was lost during the 1930s. Many do not understand fiscal policy, either, and hew to the same disastrous conservative fiscal nostrums that created the Great Depression. As a result, liberalism today does not live up to anywhere near its promises, and as monetary disasters continue to plague the world, leaders often react by piling on new fiscal errors such as price controls, tax hikes, nationalization of industries or exchange restrictions. Bad capitalism, still very much with us, continues to undermine the liberals' arguments and to drive governments toward statism. The dialectic will continue until, sometime in the future, leaders at last understand what causes capitalist economies to flourish or fall apart.

Classical economic thinking, as it was commonly understood in the 1920s, had reached extraordinary heights in terms of monetary policy, markets, and trade, but it was extremely crude with regard to fiscal policy, particularly taxation. The world was thrown into depression in the 1930s due to gross fiscal errors, most of which were pushed on governments by the conservative economists of the day. The first error of many was that of the purportedly pro-business Republican Party, which had slashed tax rates during the 1920s in a successful bid to increase the economy's productive capacity. The Republicans, however, still clung to the idea that a protective tariff, which favored large existing interests, would also be a boon to business in general, although it was plainly a tax hike.

The initial downturn of 1929–1930 was caused by the threat and eventual passage of the Smoot-Hawley Tariff Act in the United States, which was mirrored worldwide by equally drastic retaliatory tariffs. The Smoot-Hawley tariffs, and many similar tariffs enacted worldwide, were a major setback, but did not by themselves cause the Depression. However, the result of the economic downturn was a drop-off in government tax revenues worldwide, accompanied by budget deficits. The conventional wisdom of the time (much like the conventional neoliberal wisdom of today) generally considered the deficits a problem in themselves and recommended that they be closed by raising more revenue through higher taxes.

Governments in the United States, Britain, and Germany raised domestic taxes dramatically in an effort to close the deficits. The result of the higher taxes was, of course, more economic contraction and depressed tax revenues. In September 1931, a specially assembled British government, whose sole purpose was to protect the gold standard, announced that it would raise taxes to reduce the deficit. The move was supposed to increase confidence in the pound. The result of the act, of course, was downward pressure on the pound, and the pound's link to gold was broken a week later. The devaluation and floating of the pound, which was the world's premier currency at the time, was immediately followed by dozens of competitive devaluations worldwide, including one by Japan in December 1931. This added a new aspect of monetary turmoil to the crisis. The United States devalued the dollar in 1933–1934.

More than 1,000 economists signed a petition protesting the Smoot-Hawley Tariff Act, adding their voices to the complaints of 30 foreign governments. After all, Adam Smith had been remembered mostly for his free-trade arguments. But when the act was passed and trade predictably shriveled, not one of those economists drew the connection! Unaware of the fiscal policy catastrophe swirling around them, their excellent monetary training told them that, with currencies solidly pegged to gold and no evidence of a liquidity-shortage crisis, a swift return to economic health should be soon forthcoming. When their predictions and policy prescriptions didn't work out, they were cast aside to make way for the Keynesians. Keynesianism was something of a mess intellectually—Keynes's *General Theory* was so obtuse that it was impossible to argue against—but nevertheless it sanctioned deficits, opposed tax hikes during a recession (in principle, at least), and justified welfare-type spending that was very welcome at the time.

It was, in essence, the return of mercantilism. Keynes was well aware of what he had created. A whole chapter in his *General Theory* is devoted to the celebration of the mercantilists. In the preface to the German translation of the *General Theory*, published in Hitler's Germany, Keynes wrote that his policy proposals were more easily adopted to the conditions of a totalitarian state than those in which production is guided by free competition.

The classical economists did not react to the failure of their incomplete economic models by struggling to understand the fiscal policy disaster. Instead, they began to contort their excellent monetary theories into bizarre new forms in an effort to explain the onset of the Depression as a failure of monetary policy. This eventually resulted in the creation of monetarism, led by Milton Friedman, as a response to the statist and devaluationist ideas of the post–World War II Keynesians. Monetarism wasn't new, of course; it was another aspect of mercantilist thought that had been long dormant. The theoretical structure of Friedman's monetarism focuses almost entirely on monetary factors. Monetarists typically give their support to all of the other causes of the liberal economists—free trade, small government, low taxes, minimal government intervention, free markets, and so forth—but only on an anecdotal level. When asked to diagnose an economic event, give recommendations, or predict the future, they inevitably return to their monetary models.

There were no rising currencies during the Depression, and thus no monetary deflation. Prices fell due to "beggar thy neighbor" devaluation and general economic difficulties. But that hasn't stopped people from trying to blame the Fed for deflation for most of the past 50 years.

A popular theory today holds that the Depression was caused by some flaw in the post–Word War I gold standard. Since currencies' values were linked to gold, the only way this could happen is if gold rose in value quickly and dramatically, causing a monetary deflation. Realistically, it would take at least a doubling of gold's value within the space of a few years—something that has never happened before or since. The blame-gold theorists typically claim that the Depression was caused by gold purchases by the Bank of France, although total central bank gold purchases worldwide at the time were in line with—actually slightly less than—long-term averages and could not have caused such a sudden and unprecedented rise in gold's value.

To explain the Depression as a wholly monetary event, the *value theory* of the classical economists was contorted into *quantity theory*. The classical economists always focused on the value of the currency, which is related to the intersection of both supply *and demand* for the currency. In practice, this means the currency's value in relation to gold. Quantity theory tends to ignore both value and demand and is dependent entirely on the supply of a currency, or more commonly, the supply of some arbitrary definition of "money," which tends to shift to whatever measure best supports the author's arguments. Quantity theory has been around for centuries and had already been proven fallacious by Adam Smith's time. Indeed, one of the accomplishments of the early classical economists was to cast away the quantity theory of many mercantilist writers.

Economists of the 1920s and 1930s generally did not blame the events of the time on monetary errors. Keynes did not blame the Fed or the Bank of England; he saw them as tools for economic improvement for a collapse that seemingly came out of nowhere and refused to heal itself. Today the Depression is almost universally conceived as having been a monetary episode, but this phenomena dates from the 1950s and 1960s. In his 1962 book *Monetary Policy in the United States, 1867–1960*, Friedman revived quantity theory in a big way, blaming the Depression on a fall in what he calls the "money supply" between 1929 and 1933, hinting rather heavily, but never stating outright, that a rise in the dollar's value caused a terrible deflation. Friedman defines money not as base money, but as base money plus demand deposits. When banks went bankrupt, depositors' deposits were lost, and in addition many withdrew their deposits to pay liabilities and expenses. The total amount of deposits, which Friedman calls "money," not surprisingly, fell. None of this had any effect on the value of the dollar, which remained pegged to gold until 1933. Friedman conveniently ignored the gold standard to make his theories work—he never explains how such a destructive and historically unique deflation could have taken place with the dollar pegged to gold—and as a result of his blaming the Depression on the U.S. Federal Reserve, he suggests that the United States should have, like Britain, floated and devalued the dollar. The further implication is that, instead of the market mechanism of the gold standard, currencies should be manipulated by governments. Indeed, Friedman and his followers aided, abetted, and cheered the destruction of the gold standard in 1971, the classical economists' greatest success, arguing that it interfered with the proper government management of the supply of money.

The primary inheritors of the classical monetary tradition, the Austrian school, were likewise forced into contortions by the failure of the 1930s. Although Ludwig von Mises and the other early Austrians made specific critiques of the fallacies of the monetarists of their day, the post–Word War II Austrians lapsed into quantity theory themselves in an effort to explain the collapse of 1929–1932 as the failure of monetary policy. In his 1962 book *America's Great Depression* (1962 was a big year for quantity theory), Murray Rothbard set out to explain the Depression as a case of the "Austrian Theory of the Trade Cycle," which was a perfectly good explanation of what happens when governments bend or break the gold standard and devalue their currencies. This theory was appropriate for the 1970s, but wholly mistaken for the 1930s.

To argue that there was a terrible inflation in the 1920s, while the dollar was pegged to gold and price indices were dead flat, Rothbard, like Friedman, had to discard classical value theory and adopt a mistaken quantity theory. The definition of inflation was changed to mean, not a fall in the value of the currency as the result of an excess of supply relative to demand, but any increase at all in the supply of currency! Even this proved insufficient (base money in the United States was almost unchanged between September 1925 and September 1929), so Rothbard adopted Milton Friedman's M2 as his definition of "money." In an astounding intellectual somersault, Rothbard claimed that an economic collapse in which many prices fell 20 to 30 percent was caused by a disastrous monetary inflation. The abandonment of value theory for quantity theory changed the Austrian school completely, and for years the Rothbardians, despite their insistence otherwise, bore little resemblance to von Mises or their other classical forebears, at least regarding monetary theory.

Like the monetarists, the Austrians' support of low taxes, free markets, small government, and all the other libertarian rallying points remains at the anecdotal level. Most of Rothbard's book consists of an extensive exposition of poor fiscal policy—it's a splendid reference for this—but nevertheless he concludes by blaming the Depression on a monetary policy failure. Unlike the monetarists, the Austrians remain advocates of a gold standard today, but by blaming the Depression on the Fed they effectively blame the gold standard of the time as well, since the obvious implication is that it was insufficient to prevent an inflation of the most destructive proportions. Rothbardian quantity theory is inherently contradictory to a value-oriented gold standard, which is a basic reason why, although the Rothbardians claim to advocate a return to what they call a "gold standard," their specific proposals bear little resemblance to any gold standard of the past two centuries and are essentially unworkable. (Their chief argument for gold's virtue is not that the value of gold is stable, but that it is difficult to increase the supply of gold via mining.)

Thus, the two main competing monetary theories of the 1930s claim, on the one hand, a disastrous deflation and, on the other hand, a disastrous inflation, both of which were completely invisible to people living at the time. There does not seem to be any such confusion regarding the 1970s (has anybody claimed it was an era of deflation?) or the 1990s in Japan (an era of inflation?).

Keynesianism, as a school in itself, was largely discarded after the failure of the 1970s. Nobody now believes that it is possible to fine-tune the economy with the judicious application of public-works spending and interest rate manipulation/currency devaluation. The world has moved back toward a classical viewpoint, now commonly termed neoliberal. But this neoliberal consensus, as it is called, is often a combination of the very worst intellectual failures of the past century. On monetary policy, its laissez-faire approach typically involves complete neglect of the currency, which then fluctuates wildly and often falls like a stone. On the fiscal side, the threadbare conventional wisdom of the 1930s—raise taxes to balance the budget—that caused the Depression lives on as the International Monetary Fund (IMF) pressures one government after another to raise taxes to close deficits, or, if the government is running a surplus, to run a larger surplus.

The fiscal explanation of the 1930s wasn't properly presented until 1978, after the supply-side branch of classical economics had finally managed to integrate fiscal policy into classical theory in the 1970s. One of the more vexing questions of the Depression was: If the Smoot-Hawley Tariff Act was passed in June 1930, why did the U.S. stock market fall in October 1929? The market, it was argued, reacted to the fact that the majority in Congress who had been opposed to the tariff act was changed into a majority in favor of the act, virtually ensuring its passage. The market began its plunge on precisely that day. Indeed, tariff supporters accomplished their victory by radically expanding the tariff, which had originally applied primarily to agricultural products, to include industries found in the opposing Congressmen's home districts. The stock market recovered substantially in early 1930, on hopes that Congress might back off or that Hoover would veto the bill. Indeed, the market rally brought share prices nearly to the point at which they had started 1929.

No luck; the tariff was signed in June 1930, and the market began its long descent into the abyss. Laissez-faire had been the principle by which the early classical economists such as Hume and Smith had knocked down the trade barriers and high taxes created by the mercantilists and enabled a worldwide economic expansion. But in the 1930s, as tariff barriers and domestic taxes exploded higher around the world, laissez-faire was interpreted to mean "Let it be."

In its final form, the Smoot-Hawley tariff imposed an effective tax rate of 60 percent on more than 3,200 products. The retaliatory tariffs enacted by infuriated governments worldwide were equally severe, which only added to the world's sudden tax increase. Some of them had been enacted before the passage of Smoot-Hawley, with the understanding that they would be lifted if the tariff bill didn't pass. Japan, a nearly resource-free country that depended on trade to maintain its industrial economy, was particularly troubled by the contraction of world commerce. In the aftermath of the crash, the civilian government was replaced by a military government whose leaders almost immediately set about finding ways to become less trade dependent by incorporating raw-materials-producing areas within the Japanese state. Just as the rising tariffs and the increasing economic nationalism of the late nineteenth century pushed governments into empire building, especially by those governments whose economies were the most trade-dependent (Germany, Japan, Britain), so did those of the 1930s. China's new tariffs touched off a bitter trade dispute with Japan, whose territories in Manchuria and Korea (acquired from Russia in the 1904 Russo-Japanese War) were tightly trade-integrated with China. Japan's military leaders saw a simple solution to breaking down the trade barriers. On September 18, 1931, they began military expansion into Chinese territory in Manchuria, which also gave them further access to the oil shales of the region and other raw materials. (The invasion probably contributed to downward pressure on the British pound, which was devalued two days later.)

The breakdown of the stock market sent President Hoover into recession-fighting mode. He called for increased public-works spending in November of 1929, almost immediately after the stock market crumbled. Total federal spending rose from $2.9 billion in 1929 to

$3.1 billion in 1930, excluding government enterprises. In 1931, Hoover pushed through a mammoth 42 percent expansion of government spending, to $4.4 billion, excluding government enterprises (much of this consisted of transfer payments and grants-in-aid to states). By the end of his term in office in 1932, Hoover had engineered an expansion of public-works projects by state and federal governments of $1.5 billion, and he claimed proudly that during his four-year administration, more public works were built than in the preceding 30 years! Hoover Dam on the Colorado River is a relic of this round of spending, as is San Francisco's Bay Bridge and the Los Angeles Aqueduct.

Treasury Secretary Andrew Mellon stepped in with a surprise income tax cut in November 1929, with the top rate falling one percentage point, to 24 percent. This gave the market some support, but it was weak medicine against the disasters brewing worldwide. Perhaps because Mellon was a Philadelphia industrialist, a member of the group that had pushed for protectionist tariffs for decades and were a major force behind the Smoot-Hawley Tariff Act, Mellon did not see the consequences of a worldwide explosion in protectionism or the consequences of domestic tax hikes in foreign countries. He assumed that the capitalist system was in fundamental fine health and that the system would naturally take care of any investment excesses that had accumulated. As the economy crumbled, his advice for President Hoover was, famously: "Liquidate labor, liquidate stocks, liquidate the farmers, liquidate real estate." The word *liquidate* today, after the Stalinist purges, has connotations of "eliminate," but Mellon meant simply to encourage businesses to adjust to the new conditions by letting go of unneeded workers, selling unused assets, reducing inventories, and so forth. This is conventional wisdom today, and it would have been fine advice if economic policy worldwide had been fundamentally sound, but it was not, and it was rapidly getting worse.

Especially during 1931, economic policy in Europe and Japan (and thus the rest of the world, since the world was largely composed of European colonies at the time) worsened badly, overwhelming any tendency for the U.S. economy to improve and undermining

Mellon's rosy forecasts. Mellon and the increasingly interventionist Hoover did not get along, and Mellon's resignation in early 1932 cleared the way for Hoover to imitate the disasters in Europe by undoing Mellon's revolutionary tax cuts.

The breakdown of the economy and expanded government spending resulted in huge budget deficits, then the largest ever seen in peacetime. To address the deficit (of $462 million in 1931), caused in no small part by his explosive increase in public works spending, in 1932 Hoover pushed a giant tax hike through Congress. The top income tax rate went from 25 percent to 63 percent. The lowest rate went from 1 percent to 4 percent. Exemptions were sharply reduced. The estate tax was doubled. A new gift tax was introduced with a top rate of 33⅓ percent. Business taxes were increased. Hoover also tried to impose a sales tax, but this was defeated. The bill was passed on April 1, 1932, grandfathered to apply to the 1932 tax year. Hoover thought that attempting to reduce the government's deficit would improve business confidence; instead the change just increased the tax barriers in the economy. The U.S. economy turned from bad to worse. The tax hike did nothing for government tax revenues, which declined from $2.2 billion in 1931 to $1.9 billion in both 1932 and 1933. The budget deficit for 1932 was $2.7 billion, and it expanded to $3.5 billion in 1934.

During his campaign in the 1932 presidential election, Roosevelt criticized Hoover both for his budget deficits and his tax hike. In a speech in Pittsburgh on October 19, 1932, he said:

Taxes are paid in the sweat of every man who labors because they are a burden on production and are paid through production. If those taxes are excessive, they are reflected in idle factories, in tax-sold farms, and in hordes of hungry people, tramping the streets and seeking jobs in vain. Our workers may never see a tax bill, but they pay. They pay in deductions from wages, in increased cost of what they buy, or—as now—in broad unemployment throughout the land. There is not an unemployed man, there is not a struggling farmer, whose interest in this subject is not direct and vital. It comes home to every one of us![7]

Roosevelt, the Democrat, also backed tariff reductions, rejecting the economic nationalism of the Republican Party, which had led to Smoot-Hawley. For the United States and the world, the tariff was the most dangerous of the taxes because it had worldwide implications, which led eventually to World War II. Roosevelt's secretary of state, Cordell Hull, who believed that the Smoot-Hawley tariffs and the international conflict they created lay at the heart of the world's economic problems, was devoted to its repeal.

Hull steadily pushed tariffs lower for the rest of the decade, but after his election Roosevelt's attention soon turned elsewhere. Roosevelt had campaigned on vague promises of a sound currency, but one of his first acts in 1933 was to suspend dollar convertibility, rendering the dollar a floating currency, although it did not at first lose much value.

In 1933, Britain and France were already anxious to reestablish a sound world monetary system, after the monetary disasters that followed the floating of the pound in 1931. In 1933, a World Economic Conference was held in London, whose purpose was to resolve the world monetary problem and strike an agreement on quick reductions in tariffs worldwide. The United States, whose currency was still near its 1929 level when the conference was scheduled, was expected to lead the European governments back to the world gold standard. At the conference, however, Roosevelt shocked the participants by announcing that he would devalue the dollar. The act, in the eyes of foreigners an unpardonable act of economic nationalism, torpedoed Cordell Hull's attempts to achieve quick agreements on tariffs. In that situation, who wanted to open their markets to a country that was about to devalue and undercut them with cheap imports? In late 1933, Roosevelt devalued the dollar from $20.67 per ounce to $35 per ounce of gold—in essence mirroring the European devaluations and bringing exchange rates roughly in line with their pre-1931 levels—and repegged the dollar at that figure in January 1934. The dollar remained officially pegged at $35 per ounce until August 1971.

Roosevelt also forgot about his stated opposition to the Hoover tax hikes, and instead set about imitating them in an effort to fund his spending programs. He raised taxes in 1935, and in 1936 pushed taxes higher again. The economy deteriorated in 1937, and unemployment approached the highs of 1932–1933. Roosevelt probably could not have kept the presidency if the Republicans had admitted their errors. But in the 1936 election, the Republicans backed further tariff hikes, and they continued to do so until the end of World War II. Roosevelt won in a landslide, but the new Congress elected that year stopped the trend toward higher taxes and in 1938 enacted a capital gains tax cut, against Roosevelt's criticism, although he did not veto the plan. The economy began to recover.

The breakdown of Europe's monetary order began when Austria, in an attempt to reduce trade barriers, organized a customs union with Germany on March 21, 1931. France opposed the move, and the Bank of France and other major French banks suddenly called in their considerable loans and deposits in Germany and Austria. The strain on Austria's financial system, which was already severely weakened by the economic downturn, was too great, and in the midst of a banking panic that May, Austria went off the gold standard. Germany was similarly destabilized in July. This provided just the excuse Britain's devaluationists were looking for. As pressure grew on the pound's link with gold, the Bank of England made no attempt to defend the gold standard through a rise in the discount rate, the mechanism by which the bank effectively reduced the supply of base money. (The head of the Bank of England was on vacation at the time, recovering from a nervous breakdown caused by the strains of defending the pound's link to gold, leaving the reins in the hands of underlings with more "modern" ideas.) It was argued that the rise in interest rates would be an additional burden on the deteriorating economy, although the Bank of England raised its discount rate soon after the devaluation as it struggled to keep the pound from depreciating into oblivion. Keynes had recommended a devaluation for Britain only a month earlier.

More than 20 other countries, including British commonwealth countries, followed Britain's lead by the end of the year. This incensed the Japanese, who competed closely with the British in the export market. (In 1933, Japan usurped Britain as the world's leading exporter of cotton cloth.) Japan had waged a deflationary struggle to put the yen back on the gold standard in January 1930, but faced with a competitive devaluation by Britain, among its other mounting problems, Japan floated and devalued the yen in December of 1931. After the devaluation, the yen/pound rate returned to roughly its predevaluation level of the late 1920s.

The negative effects of Britain's devaluation, and the "beggar thy neighbor" devaluations that were set off in response, are underappreciated today. If one small country devalues, it can be safely ignored by the rest of the world. However, when the world's leading currency is devalued, and several other major governments devalue alongside, the consequences are almost impossible to resist. The pound's devaluation put immediate competitive pressures on all other countries who were getting "beggared" by Britain. Not devaluing after Britain and dozens of other countries, including Germany and Japan, had devalued would mean competing against dramatically lower prices in other countries, which would increase hardship and downward price pressures at home. To avoid this beggaring effect, countries had to devalue in line with the pound.

Certainly this is one reason why the gold standard is blamed for so-called deflation and economic contraction during the 1930s, although the problem was that Britain, and many other countries, had left the gold standard! In this light, Roosevelt's choice to devalue the dollar in 1933–1934 should come as no surprise—nor should Britain's attempt to get the United States to stick with the gold standard at $20.67 per ounce while Britain repegged to gold at a devalued rate, which would allow the beggaring of U.S. industry by

Britain, and the other countries that had devalued, to continue. The same thing happened during the 1970s, when even those countries that had no interest in imitating the devaluationist policies of the United States were sucked into the inflationary morass to avoid the trade consequences of dollar devaluation.

Even for those governments that decided to devalue in response to worldwide devaluation, it was not necessary to abandon the gold standard. The U.S. government devalued, but immediately repegged to gold at a new parity. The economic superiority of this solution, compared to a floating currency, is one reason the United States and the U.S. dollar rose to world prominence soon afterward.

The economic deterioration in the United States in 1931 was due largely to bad overseas policies. Britain pushed up income tax rates in 1930 and 1931, which drove it into hard recession much like the United States. The tax hikes prompted the following outburst from the Federation of British Industries, the largest and most influential business organization:

Heavy expenditure on social services and on general administration and the crushing load of direct taxation has undoubtedly seriously accentuated the difficulties inevitably imposed upon the country by the world crisis. In the opinion of the Federation the country has been attempting to work an economic system based on private enterprise under circumstances which made the successful conduct of such a system impossible. Private enterprise can only function efficiently and afford good employment and a good standard of living for the people if it is allowed to operate with reasonable freedom from Governmental restraints and is given the essential conditions for success. The most essential of these conditions is a plentiful and cheap supply of capital. Great Britain must therefore again become a country in which it is easy to accumulate capital and attractive to invest. Heavy direct taxation, especially of the present type, e.g. Income Tax, Super Tax, and Death Duties, all at high rates, is peculiarly inimical to the accumulation of capital and a serious deterrent to its investment. It is also psychologically a serious discouragement to the enterprise and initiative which is essential to the wellbeing of an industrial and trading nation.[8]

Britain's government took these arguments to heart and resisted further tax hikes on the grounds that they would exacerbate the recession. In 1934 and 1935, it enacted modest tax cuts. As a result, Britain's economy began to recover earlier than that of the United States, and the downturn of the 1930s was less exaggerated. Britain raised taxes again in 1936–1938 as part of a rearmament plan, however, and suffered a second downturn in 1937–1938, along with the United States.

Japan had been in a slump throughout the 1920s as it struggled with a floating yen and steadily pushed up income tax rates. The yen had been floated in 1917, and the decision to return the yen to gold in 1930, at its prewar parity, meant piling a small deflation atop the economic crisis of that time. (Although the yen floated, it remained within 15 percent of its prewar parity.) Much has been written about finance minister Koreikyo Takahashi's apparently proto-Keynesian program of yen devaluation and public-works projects during the 1930s, but little attention has been given to the fact that Takahashi refused to raise taxes, as virtually every other major government had done, arguing that tax hikes would worsen the economic downturn. Despite agitation by some industrialists, Japan also did not reciprocate in the worldwide tariff wars until modest hikes were made in 1935. As a result, in the early 1930s Japan avoided the self-punishing tax hikes that most of the rest of the world had undertaken, and the Japanese economy had one of the mildest downturns during the 1930s. In 1933, Japan had the lowest tariffs in the world. The devaluation of the yen relieved the small genuine deflationary pressure from the economy created by the return to the prewar gold parity, but more significantly, it compensated for the effects of the competitive devaluations of Britain and the many countries that followed Britain's example. It would have been better if the yen had been repegged at a lower rate rather than left to float. Japan's government actually undertook a series of tax cuts in the mid-1930s.

Britain raised tariffs dramatically in 1932, ending a commitment to free trade that had lasted a century. The move further enraged Japan, which had considerable trade with Britain's colonial territories, especially in Asia. However, Britain offered special, lowered tariffs to its territories, another step that moderated the intensity of Britain's recession. The Japanese government learned a lesson here as well: If you want to preserve trade and protect your economy from the whims of foreign governments, make your trading partner part of your empire.

Japan was late to the empire-building game, however, and to expand its empire it would have to take over territories from the Western powers. Many of Japan's trading partners, especially in Asia, were already parts of the British, French, Dutch, and U.S. empires. Japan's aggressive postures toward the West's colonial interests in Asia in the early 1930s worried the European powers. (Japan was also successfully expanding its influence in China, which the European powers had been muscling over since the mid-nineteenth century.) Bowing to European pressure, in 1934 the U.S. State Department threatened oil sanctions on Japan, which at the time were considered one step from military action. Japan's economy was almost entirely dependent on oil imports. The United States backed down, and the Japanese leaders, if anything, were even more convinced of the need to secure reliable oil (and rubber) supplies within their empire, notably from the Netherlands East Indies, now Indonesia. Japanese militarists trumpeted a "greater East Asian co-prosperity sphere" based on "economic self-sufficiency." After the disastrous management of the world economy by the United States and Britain from 1929 to 1934, it was reasonable for Japan to argue that Asia would be better off under Japanese leadership.

The tension built between Japan and the Western powers throughout the rest of the 1930s. On January 26, 1940, the United States canceled the 1911 American-Japan Commercial Treaty, which opened the door to sanctions. Despite criticism, Roosevelt at first continued to allow the export of oil. In 1940, 60 percent of Japan's total oil usage came from the United States, and that dependency increased to nearly 100 percent after the Netherlands East Indies cut off oil exports to Japan in June 1941. In mid-July 1941, the Japanese army moved into French Indochina, now Vietnam, Laos, and Cambodia, seeking raw materials and putting the army in position to take the oilfields of Burma, then a British colony. On July 26, 1941, Roosevelt ordered a freezing of Japanese assets in the United States, which brought U.S.-Japanese trade to a halt. In September, an oil embargo was laid on Japan, essentially a death sentence for the Japanese economy. In the following months, Japan's ambassador to the United States made numerous concessions to the U.S. government in an effort to have the sanctions lifted. Prince Konoye told Roosevelt that he would offer to meet anywhere in the Pacific, and that if Roosevelt agreed to resume oil exports to Japan, the Japanese army would pull out of Indochina. The Japanese government was shocked when Roosevelt refused—although the United States had apparently broken the Japanese diplomatic code and knew that its refusal would provoke the Japanese into military action. After a meeting with Roosevelt on November 25, Secretary of War Henry Stimson wrote in his diary that the main question is "how we maneuver them into the position of firing the first shot without allowing too much danger to ourselves."

Numerous historians have concluded that Roosevelt's refusal was a deliberate attempt to provoke a Japanese attack on U.S. naval forces in the Philippines at Subic Bay, which blocked Japan's ability to ship oil from Burma and the Netherlands East Indies. Roosevelt, who had promised in the 1940 election that he would not get involved in the war in Europe, had little interest in Japan but wanted to take advantage of Japan's ill-considered defensive alliance with Germany to allow the United States to save lonely Britain from being overrun by the Third Reich. Roosevelt had already tried to provoke the Germans into shooting first by attacking German submarines with military ships disguised as unarmed merchant freighters. The ploy, however, was exposed in the U.S. press. In the summer of 1941, U.S.

public opinion was very strongly against involving the United States in a war in either Asia or Europe.

The Japanese leaders calculated that, under the oil embargo, their economy would crumble and their military strength would dwindle to nothing within two years. The resulting act by the Japanese army has been called a "surprise attack," but it was baldly predictable. In December of 1941, well aware of their inferior military strength but seeing no other option, the Japanese military put their empire-building plans into action, taking over Western colonies in the Philippines, Hong Kong, Malaya, Borneo, Guam, and Singapore, clearing a way through East Asia to secure the shipping lanes between Japan and the oilfields of the Netherlands East Indies. Japan's military also made a daring long-distance attack on the U.S. naval base in the U.S. territory of Hawaii (like Guam today, it was not a state at the time, merely an outpost of the U.S. empire), where Roosevelt had moved the U.S. Pacific fleet from its base at Subic Bay. The attack on Hawaii was not the first step toward an amphibious invasion on the California coast, but the capstone of a plan to kick the meddling Western governments out of Asia once and for all.

As it turned out, Roosevelt's ploy was unnecessary, because Germany, in a totally unexpected move, declared war on the United States only four days after the Japanese attack on Pearl Harbor. This was very good luck for Roosevelt, who faced an uphill struggle convincing Congress that the Pearl Harbor attack justified entering the war in Europe.

Germany was the weakest of the weak economies of Europe in 1930. Britain and France had pressured Germany to keep its taxes high to pay the war reparations required by the Treaty of Versailles, which had kept the German economy grinding along in a constant state of recession. It had suffered a debilitating hyperinflation only a few years before. Germany reacted to the worldwide contraction with more protectionist tariffs, and in June of 1930, with a major tax hike. The Weimar government's support disintegrated along with the economy, and Adolf Hitler took power in the spring of 1933. Hitler ceased the payment of onerous World War I reparations, which lifted that burden from the German economy. Unemployment fell, the economy recovered impressively, and Hitler's popularity soared.

Despite the statist overtones of fascism in Germany, Italy, and Japan, all three fascist governments actually reduced government tax burdens, which allowed these economies to make a recovery in the 1930s. Hitler's finance minister Hjalmar Schacht steadily drew down tariff barriers and domestic taxes. Schacht's "New Plan" of September 1934 arranged 25 bilateral trade agreements with countries producing raw materials, which would receive credits to purchase German manufactured goods. By 1935, unemployment had declined from around 20 percent to 12 percent. Within the new environment of economic nationalism and colonialism, Germany, like Japan, was pushed into a search for land and raw materials to feed its industrial economy. As Germany became more industrial, the country depended more on imports of raw materials and foodstuffs, which had to cross over the tariff and currency barriers from outside Germany. This led Hitler to develop his idea of *Lebensraum*, the notion that Germany's intellectual and industrial prowess needed to be combined with Polish and Russian agriculture and raw materials within the German empire, eliminating all trade and currency barriers in the process. One of Hitler's first expansionist acts was to annex Austria in 1938, thus snapping the trade barrier that the two countries had first tried to lower in 1931. When Germany invaded Russia, the army advanced immediately upon Stalingrad, the gateway to the oilfields of the Caspian Sea.

Strangely, the result of the blame-the-Fed theories of the past half-century is an even greater fascination with currency manipulation. Whether the Fed is painted as a potential economic savior (by the Keynesians and the devaluationists of the 1930s) or as a dismal failure (by the monetarists or the Austrians), the conclusion either way is that proper manipulation of the currency would have allowed the world to avoid the disaster of the Great Depression. Neither is correct. Nothing the Fed could have done would have solved the problem of explosive worldwide increases in tariffs and domestic taxes, or the devaluations in Europe or Japan. The Fed did exactly what it should have done in the 1930s: assuage potential liquidity-shortage problems while remaining solidly fixed to the gold standard. This was the conclusion of economists at the time as well.

The devaluationists have little to complain about. Currencies around the world were indeed devalued, most of them at the relatively early date of 1931. It didn't do much good. Unemployment remained in double digits seven years later, and governments soon abandoned the tactic. The one possibly valid argument that could be made is that competitive devaluations worldwide reached such a point that a compensatory devaluation of the dollar became attractive. The 1933–1934 devaluation accomplished this task rather expertly, and the U.S. economy enjoyed about as much benefit from this strategy as was possible.

The myth that the Fed would save us from the next depression seized the minds of generations of economists, and remains a fundamental motivation today. The legacy of central bank interventionism since the 1930s, however, is not a good one. Libraries could be filled with a record of monetary disasters caused over the years by currency manipulation, neglect, and general incompetence, whereas it is difficult to find even one example of success. Governments have learned from this bad experience, but the final steps to the re-creation of a proper monetary system continue to be frustrated by the empty hope that the myriad challenges of economic leadership can be reduced to the twiddling of interest rate targets and currency values.

CHAPTER 10

THE
BRETTON WOODS
GOLD STANDARD

The Postwar Golden Age and the
Beginning of Monetary Chaos

There is need to remember that the policies of the American government and the Bank of England of maintaining on the London gold market a price of 35 dollars for an ounce of gold is the only measure that today prevents the Western nations from embarking upon boundless inflation.

—Ludwig von Mises, *Human Action*, 1949[1]

The way to crush the bourgeoisie is to grind them between the millstones of taxation and inflation.

—V. I. Lenin

While academic economists are still creating ever-more elaborate tales of the Great Depression, the world's leaders seemed to understand pretty well what had gone wrong in the 1930s and, in 1944, set about trying to fix it. In a meeting at the Mount Washington Hotel in Bretton Woods, New Hampshire, they reestablished the world gold standard and formed three international bodies to prevent what had happened in the 1930s from taking place again. The International Monetary Fund (IMF) was created to help keep countries pegged to gold, so that a breakdown like that of Austria and Germany in 1931 would not again spread around the world. A World

239

Bank was to maintain financial stability. An International Trade Organization was to avoid another round of tariff warfare. The ITO ran into difficulties and morphed into a weaker form, the General Agreement on Tariffs and Trade.

Given that the "beggar thy neighbor" devaluations of the 1930s disadvantaged those countries that stuck to the gold standard, it is perhaps no surprise that the Bretton Woods gold standard did not begin with the religious fervor for stable money that had been common in the nineteenth century. Besides, monetary manipulation was just too intriguing. Britain, represented by John Maynard Keynes, wanted a universal world currency managed by a world central bank. It would be a soft currency, manipulated to effect policy goals. The United States, represented by Harry Dexter White, wanted a hard currency based on gold. In the end, a sort of compromise was reached. The Bretton Woods system would be a hard-currency system based on gold, in which countries would be able to adjust exchange rates to allow for domestic monetary manipulation. Countries could also enact capital controls, which would theoretically allow countries more leeway in their domestic monetary policy while maintaining an official fixed exchange rate. Bretton Woods, in other words, was compromised from the beginning.

The Bretton Woods agreement laid an internationalist veneer over the fact that the world monetary system was controlled by and dependent on the United States. The governments of the world pegged their currencies to the dollar, with currency board–type mechanisms, and the dollar was pegged to gold on the London gold market. Private holdings of gold had been outlawed in the United States since 1933; U.S. citizens could not convert the dollar into gold, but foreigners could, and in this way the gold standard was maintained. London became the center for dollar/gold redeemability, and the European central banks became the watchdogs for the U.S. government's gold standard policy. See Figure 10.1.

Almost immediately, the inherent tensions of the Bretton Woods era—between domestic monetary manipulation and external fixed currencies—rose to the surface. Britain did not roll back its high tax

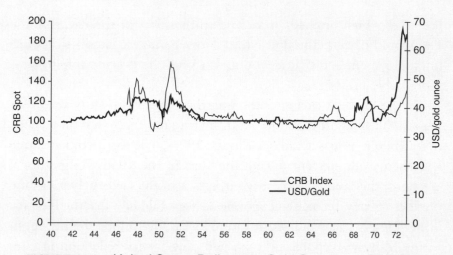

FIGURE 10.1 United States Dollars per Gold Ounce and CRB Spot Commodity Index, 1940–1972

rates after World War II, and as the economy sputtered the government reached for currency devaluation. The 1949 devaluation of the pound from $4.03 to $2.80 was accompanied by devaluations in 23 other countries, mirroring the British devaluation of 1931. France had already gone down a similar route, and in early 1948 had devalued the franc from 119 per dollar to 214. It was soon devalued again to 264. The Fed itself was under pressure from the Treasury to keep long-term bond yields below 2.5 percent during the war and the years afterward, leading to conspicuous weakness in the dollar's market value versus gold. But, as in the early 1930s, the thrills of devaluation quickly wore off, and Europe eased back into a stable currency framework. In the United States, the Treasury agreed to stop pressuring the Fed in an accord from March 1951, and the dollar's value returned to its $35 per ounce parity.

The tension between the Bretton Woods gold standard and the ever-increasing number of soft-currency advocates was embodied in the U.S. Employment Act of 1946, which stated that the "continuing policy and responsibility of the Federal Government [is] to use all practicable means . . . to promote maximum employment, production, and purchasing power." The act was applied to the Federal

Reserve, which implied, according to the ideas of the day, that the Fed would devalue the dollar (i.e., "lower interest rates") to reduce unemployment and that it would also keep the dollar stable to promote stable prices.

In the United States after the war, the Republican Party was rallying around an effort to reduce wartime tax rates and touch off an economic boom, just as it had done in the 1920s. The top income tax rate had risen to 86 percent during the war. In the 1946 Congressional elections, the Republican Party enjoyed a major victory. Democratic president Harry Truman's economic advisers told him that the Republicans' big tax cuts would be inflationary, and he vetoed the measures. In the end, the Republicans managed only a small reduction in rates and a few new exemptions.

The small tax cuts gained the economy some relief. But the Republicans had been cowed by the defeat of their ambitious tax cut plans and did not press the issue in the 1948 election. Truman managed a slim victory against Republican candidate Thomas Dewey. Truman, however, assumed his narrow win gave him a mandate to increase taxes. As the Korean War got under way, in 1950 Truman managed to push through a tax hike. The top rate went to 91 percent on income above $200,000, and an excess-profits tax of 77 percent was instituted.

In 1952 the Republican Party once again focused on tax cutting and gained control of both Congress and the presidency for the first time in 24 years. The Republican Congress soon delivered a bill to reduce personal income tax rates by 30 percent to President Dwight Eisenhower. But Eisenhower, who had been elected on a platform of tax cuts, had changed his mind upon entering the presidency. The cuts, he argued, would be inflationary, and besides, the government not only had huge debts from the war, it was running deficits. Eisenhower nixed the plan, burying it in committee so it did not even receive a vote. Congressional Republicans were infuriated. The economy slid into recession. Democrats proposed their own plans for a modest tax cut and took control of Congress in 1954. The Republican Party thereafter became the party of debt and deficit reduction rather than the party of economic expansion, and it did not regain control of Congress until 1994, when Republicans rallied in criticism of the Clinton tax hikes and offered their own capital gains tax cut plan. The GOP did not win both Congress and the presidency until 2000–2002, supported by the tax cut plans of George W. Bush.

Much of the Bretton Woods period was overseen by William McChesney Martin Jr., who was appointed head of the Federal Reserve's Open Market Committee in July 1951. Central banking was in his blood. His father had been a Fed governor and president of the St. Louis Fed from 1914 to 1940. It was Martin who asserted that the Fed's role was to "take away the punch bowl just as the party got going." In other words, the Fed would allow the dollar to weaken until it threatened the gold parity, then the Fed would pull it back up. In this way, the Fed maddened everyone, both the few remaining hard-money advocates, who wondered what the point of this binge-hangover cycle was, and the Keynesian devaluationists, who wondered what would happen if you didn't take away the punch bowl.

Martin's first task at the Fed was to clean up after the 1951 Accord (which restored the Fed's independence) and return the dollar to its $35 per ounce parity. After an expansion in late 1957 and early 1958 led to large gold outflows, Martin once again raised the Fed's rate targets in late 1958 and 1959. In early 1960, the Fed was still taking away the punch bowl, pushing short-term rates to a peak of 4.0 percent. Vice President Richard Nixon, who was campaigning for president against John F. Kennedy, urged Eisenhower to pressure the Fed to give the economy a monetary goosing.

As Nixon wrote in 1962:

Early in March [1960], Dr. Arthur E. Burns . . . called on me. . . . [He] expressed great concern about the way the economy was then acting. . . . Burns' conclusion was that unless some decisive government action were taken, and taken soon, we were heading for another economic dip which would hit its low point in October, just before the elections. He urged strongly that everything possible be done to avert this development . . . by loosening up credit and . . . increasing spending for national security.[2]

After all, what was wrong with a little monetary push? Official consumer price indexes rose only 1.5 percent in 1960. But Martin was not looking at the CPI. The outflow of gold through London was chronic. Eisenhower brushed off Nixon's appeals to put pressure on the Fed, and Nixon blamed the Fed for his narrow defeat against John F. Kennedy.

In the election, Kennedy pledged to "get the economy moving again" in the face of recession and a $7 billion budget deficit. But Kennedy did not have a specific strategy in mind, and spent most of the next two years testing the waters with different ideas. His own advisers could come up with nothing substantive. In May 1962, Kennedy made a visit to Germany, where he spoke with the great German finance minister Ludwig Erhard. Erhard had ignited the German postwar miracle economy with big tax rate reductions.

From Erhard, Kennedy learned what had been fueling the roaring economies of Germany and Japan. As Kennedy explained later in 1962:

It is a paradoxical truth that tax rates are too high today and tax revenues are too low, and the soundest way to raise the revenue in the long run is to cut the rates now. The experience of a number of European countries and Japan has borne this out. This country's own experience with tax reduction in 1954 has borne this out. And the reason is that only full employment can balance the budget, and tax reduction can pave the way to that employment. The purpose of cutting taxes now is not to incur a budget deficit, but to achieve the more prosperous, expanding economy which can bring about budget surplus.[3]

It wasn't until mid-1963 that Kennedy managed to put together a package that would pass Congress, and the measure was still up in the air when Kennedy was assassinated in November of that year. His successor, Lyndon Johnson, pushed the tax bill through in Kennedy's name and signed it into law in February 1964. The plan called for an

244

immediate 30 percent across-the-board reduction in income tax rates.

The recession ended, and the outflow of gold on the London market eased as the tax cuts led to increased demand for dollars, which supported the dollar's value. In 1965, revenues were flooding into the Treasury, as Kennedy had predicted. That year, the government was on track to run a $3 billion surplus, until it was hit with Vietnam-related expenses. The Republicans, which had opposed the Kennedy tax cuts, even though it was exactly the 30 percent reduction in tax rates that the Republicans had asked for in 1953, lent no support to further tax cuts. The Republicans lost political support, and Johnson took advantage of the political opportunity and bounteous tax revenues to implement his Great Society programs, including the introduction of Medicare.

The Dow Jones Industrial Average, which had sputtered around 600 throughout Kennedy's term, climbed to 1,000 in February 1966. Adjusted for rises in the consumer price index, it didn't regain that peak again until 1995. Adjusted for the dollar's 90 percent devaluation against gold during the 1970s, it did not regain that level until 1998. See Figure 10.2.

In fact, 1966 was such a fine year that the Keynesian economists,

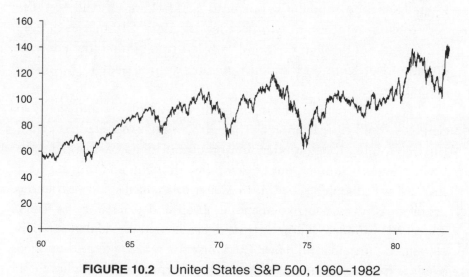

FIGURE 10.2   United States S&P 500, 1960–1982

who were happily taking credit for the Kennedy boom, began to fret about inflation. They thought the economy was beginning to "over-heat" and encouraged new tax measures to slow it down. Johnson added a 10 percent surtax on income to pay for Vietnam expenses, cheered by Republicans who were at this time more concerned with reducing deficits than cutting taxes.

The combination of Great Society spending obligations, Vietnam, and the contraction caused by the new taxes created expanding federal deficits, and from 1967 on the Treasury once again put pressure on the Fed to lower its interest rate targets so that the debt could supposedly be funded more cheaply. All of this pressure to lower short-term interest rates simply worried bondholders that the value of their invest-ments would be lost through currency devaluation, and long-term interest rates instead rose throughout the 1950s and 1960s. The mar-ket yield on the 20-year Treasury bond, 2.6 percent in 1954, had risen to 6.9 percent in late 1969.

The United States had $22.8 billion of gold at the end of 1950, or 652 million ounces at $35 per ounce. It did not need such a colos-sal hoard to operate the gold standard, which is merely a signal show-ing whether the Fed's supply of dollars is in line with demand. Instead of strengthening the gold standard under Bretton Woods, the United States government's enormous gold holdings had allowed the Fed to bend the rules for two decades. By 1965, $10 billion of gold had flowed out through the London gold market due to the constant downward pressure on the dollar, ending up primarily in European central banks.

The remaining $12 billion of gold was still plenty, and the gold outflows could have been easily halted by a little monetary restraint. But economists had forgotten how the gold standard worked. The United States is running out of gold, they thought, and thus the gold standard was doomed. Instead, President Johnson slapped restrictions on overseas investment, voluntary in 1965 and mandatory in 1968. These did nothing to lift the sagging dollar; if anything, like the 10 per-cent surtax, they made the problem worse. By refusing to give up their overly expansionary monetary stance, governments throughout the world were pushed once again into economic isolationism. Increasing restrictions on capital and trade were laid on all over the world to address the conflicts between domestic currency manipulations and fixed exchange rates. Kennedy had already slapped an Interest Equalization Tax on U.S. holders of overseas securities in 1963.

In March 1968, the dollar had sagged to $40 per ounce of gold on the open market, embarrassingly far from its promised $35 per ounce. Gold flushed out of the United States to Europe via London, until the U.S. government twisted the Europeans' arms into accepting instead a new concoction, Special Drawing Rights, which was a basket of currencies, instead of gold. The SDRs consisted of dollars and European currencies linked to dollars. They were touted as "paper gold," but they were merely paper. The United States was in essence allowing redemption of dollars for dollars, which was not redeemability at all.

The European governments were in a bind. Officially, they could still get gold, but there was the distinct risk that, if they had actually asked for gold, the U.S. government would officially shut the door in their face and throw the world monetary system into disarray—which, in the end, is exactly what happened. From 1968, the gold standard was essentially maintained by the good faith of Bill Martin, still at the Fed since 1951, who made efforts to prop up the dollar whenever it sagged against gold in the open market. The U.S. government still had many tons of gold in reserve, but it was operating the gold standard much like David Ricardo had suggested—as if it had no reserves at all.

Just as was happening in the United States, foreign governments were attempting to excite their sagging economies with monetary stimulus, in turn driving their currencies lower. Britain, still choking to death under high tax rates dating from World War I, devalued again in 1967, and France in 1969. While the European governments were begging the United States not to devalue the dollar, they were devaluing themselves, once again beggaring the United States as in the 1930s. This did not go over pleasantly, especially among the devaluationists in Washington.

Nixon won the 1968 election on a promise to balance the budget, withdraw from Vietnam, and eliminate Johnson's 10 percent income surtax. Like Eisenhower, however, Nixon quickly forgot about his tax cut promises after the election, and decided to extend the surtax in an attempt to balance the budget.

Nixon also convened the Business Roundtable, which consisted of the heads of America's largest corporations, for their views on what would help the economy. The Business Roundtable told Nixon that the best thing for the economy would be a repeal of the investment tax credit and a near-doubling of the capital gains tax. It was textbook Marx: Capitalism's worst enemies were the capitalists themselves. Not capitalists exactly, but the entrenched managerial elite, the heads of the big businesses that were threatened by the true capitalists, those who started small, risky ventures with the wild hope of rendering existing big businesses obsolete. By taking away the gains that are the reward for risk, the capital gains tax stifled entrepreneurs in the cradle.

Nixon repealed the investment tax credit, and the capital gains tax ranges rose from 25 to 27.5 percent to 32.3 to 45.5 percent. The capital gains tax is practically a tax on capitalism itself and is one of the most destructive taxes governments can levy. This was quite a bit different than the tax cuts promised in the election. The economy slid into recession in 1969 in anticipation of the new taxes. The effect on high-risk entrepreneurial businesses was dire. In 1969, there were 1,298 initial common stock offerings. The number dropped to 566 in 1970, the first year the tax was in effect. In 1978, as inflation multiplied the effect of the capital gains tax, the number had fallen to 18.[4]

For all the political energy that has been expended over the federal budget over the years, in the end the budget has little effect on the country's economy. Some claim that a big budget deficit is stimulative, while others are certain that a balanced budget is necessary for economic health. Most of the time, neither one matters very much. Consider what would happen if the government—horrors!—piled up so much debt that it actually defaulted. Bondholders would lose their investment, of course, but little else would necessarily happen. The end result would likely be that the government would find it difficult to issue bonds in the future, and would therefore be forced to balance the budget! As it happened, bondholders lost almost all of their investment in the 1970s anyway, through the invisible default of currency devaluation.

All of Nixon's tax hiking, in the name of a balanced budget, naturally put further downward pressure on the dollar. When Nixon arrived in the White House in 1969, he found Bill Martin still at the Fed, the same man he blamed for his 1960 electoral defeat. Martin and the Fed spent 1969 trying to prop up the sagging dollar and keep the $35 per ounce promise that was at the heart of Bretton Woods. In doing so, overnight interest rates rose to over 9.0 percent. The dollar averaged $43.46 per ounce in May 1969, and in December 1969 the dollar averaged $35.17 per ounce, back at its proper parity. (Martin's efforts, though effective, were clumsy. Such high interest rates were not really necessary, as proper direct contraction of base money would have more likely resulted in lower interest rates.)

Once again, Nixon blamed Martin for the recession caused by his own tax hikes, and when Martin's term expired in January 1970, he was replaced by Arthur Burns, an econometrician and Nixon's friend from Eisenhower days. Burns had formerly headed the National Bureau of Economic Research and was part of the Council of Economic Advisers under Kennedy.

Burns was specially picked to refill the punch bowl and keep the party rolling, which is exactly what he did. At his first Federal Open Market Committee meeting, Burns argued forcefully for a substantial shift toward monetary expansion, and the FOMC went along. Nixon got what he wanted. The 8.98 percent average Fed funds rate of January 1970 fell to 3.72 percent in February 1971.

By this point it was becoming apparent that the world was going to enter a period of widespread currency devaluation. As Friedrich Hayek, Keynes's old debating partner in the 1930s, said in a lecture given on May 18, 1970, titled "Can We Still Avoid Inflation?":

In one sense the question asked in the title of this lecture is purely rhetorical. I hope none of you has suspected me of doubting even for a moment that technically there is no problem in stopping inflation. If the monetary authorities really want to and are prepared to accept the consequences, they can always do so practically overnight. They fully control the base of the pyramid of credit, and a credible announcement that they will not increase the quantity of bank notes in circulation and bank deposits, and if necessary, even decrease them, will do the trick. About this there is no doubt among economists. What I am concerned about is not the technical but the political possibilities. Here, indeed, we face a task so difficult that more and more people, including highly competent people, have resigned themselves to the inevitability of indefinitely continued inflation.[5]

Hayek, who had been marginalized since the 1940s, was awarded the Nobel Prize in Economics in 1974.

The economy, recovering somewhat as the Burns-led Fed lowered its interest rate targets, was still disappointing as it labored under the pressure of the Nixon tax hikes and the inflation's bracket-creep effect on the progressive tax system. Price indexes rose 5 percent, while unemployment rose to 5.6 percent. The stagflation had begun, and economists everywhere were puzzled. In the end, they grasped at the remedies they had been taught to apply in recessions: deficit spending and monetary expansion.

Nixon was sold on economist Herbert Stein's "full employment budget," whose $15 billion deficit was supposed to raise employment and ultimately "pay for itself," with the deficit spending creating so much growth that the deficit itself would disappear. Stein's 1969 book *The Fiscal Revolution In America*, which celebrates the Kennedy's Erhard-inspired tax-cut success, begins with these lines:

> Herbert Hoover recommended a big tax *increase* in 1931 when unemployment was extremely high and a large budget deficit was in prospect.

John F. Kennedy recommended a big tax *reduction* in 1962 when unemployment was again a problem, although a much less serious one, and a large budget deficit was again in prospect.

The contrast between these two Presidential decisions symbolizes the revolution in fiscal policy that occurred in the intervening thirty-one years. . . . Hoover proposed a tax increase *both* to raise employment and balance the budget. Kennedy proposed a tax cut *both* to balance the budget and raise employment. [Stein's emphasis.][6]

If Stein, the head of Nixon's Council of Economic Advisers, had grasped the significance of what he had written a whole book about only one year earlier, it is quite possible that the worldwide economic contraction of the 1970s never would have happened and the world would still be on a gold standard. Unfortunately, despite writing this precocious passage, Stein and the Nixon administration could not distinguish between Kennedy's pro-growth tax cut and Keynesian government spending. They expected their deficit-spending plan, which contained no tax cuts, to have the same growth-enhancing effect as Kennedy's brilliant move. The plan gave Nixon an intellectual fig leaf to cover his failure to balance the budget as promised.

The Nixon economists also decided that nominal gross domestic product would have to rise to $1.065 trillion from $977 billion—a rise of 9.0 percent—for the economy to meet the administration's employment targets. This goal, following monetarist doctrine of the day, was to be achieved by running the printing press. The task of computing how much new money this would require fell, strangely enough, to Arthur Laffer, Mundell's protégé, then the young chief economist of the Office of Management and the Budget. Laffer, a staunch defender and advocate of the gold standard, did as he was told and thus handed to the Nixon economists the dagger that they would drive through the heart of Bretton Woods. See Figure 10.3.

Burns got his marching orders and opened the money spigots in the first two quarters of 1971. Because the rest of the world was pegged to the dollar, Burns set off not only U.S. inflation, but world inflation. Overseas central banks took their excess dollars to the Fed

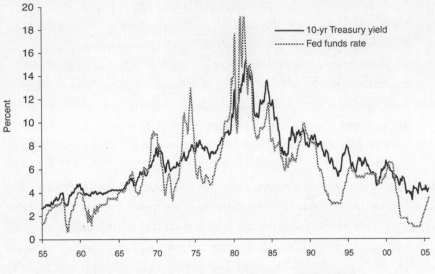

FIGURE 10.3   U.S. Interest Rates, 1955–2005

and, though they wanted gold, demanded Treasury bills, which was all they could get since 1968. The Fed would expand the base money supply in the morning, the dollars would zip around the world, and in the afternoon the unneeded dollars would show up back on the Fed's doorstep, exactly as Adam Smith described, with pleas from European central bankers to stop the monetary expansion, for the good of the international monetary system.

Their cries fell on deaf ears. Instead, U.S. economists asked: Why are we letting the Europeans influence our economic policy? Wasn't trade only about 5 percent of our economy? Why are we letting the excess dollars slip away overseas when they should be at home fooling people into thinking they're wealthier than they really are? All the other countries stopped converting their currencies into gold, why not the United States as well? Predictions abounded that gold would be "demonetized" and trade "like pork bellies" at a price of around $7 an ounce.

The internal conflicts of Bretton Woods continued to lead countries into economic isolationism. The next step was to break up the world currency so that every country had a currency of its own to play with.

The Keynesians wanted a floating dollar so Burns could keep interest rates low and start an economic recovery. Fred Bergsten, who later became an adviser to president Carter, was a leading Keynesian advocate of devaluation. The monetarists wanted basically the same thing, couched in different terms—an independent board of wise leaders who would manipulate the currency for the good of the economy. The few people who had reservations about floating the dollar saw only European central banks with bushels of excess dollars ready to demand gold in return, and they assumed that nothing could be done about the situation, although the solution was as simple as reducing dollar base money supply.

In early August 1971, Britain's government had $2 billion it wanted "protected against devaluation"—converted into gold. France also had bales of excess dollars. Capital was flushing out of the United States on devaluation fears. Price indexes were rising. The economy was in recession. Nixon went off to Camp David, in the mountains of Maryland, to formulate a response. On August 15, 1971, Nixon came down out of the mountains and blurted out a cornucopia of quick fixes: a 90-day freeze on prices; increased tax exemptions for individuals; an investment tax credit for businesses; the repeal of a 7 percent excise tax on automobiles; a 10 percent surcharge on imports; a temporary suspension of gold convertibility; a 10 percent cut in foreign aid; a 5 percent cut in government personnel; a six-month postponement of government pay raises.

At first it appeared that things had improved. Taxes were being cut, and so was government spending. Nixon was apparently returning to his election promises. The less desirable measures—the price regulations, the tax on imports, and the end of gold convertibility— were billed as temporary. At first, it was not particularly clear that things had changed much. Gold conversion hadn't happened since the SDRs had been introduced in 1968.

It was the end of the gold standard in the United States, the principle by which the U.S. government had abided since it was mandated by the Constitution in 1789. Dollars were never again pegged to gold, and the resulting inflation prompted price controls, especially on oil, throughout the following decade.

As the U.S. government abandoned gold, other countries' governments abandoned the dollar. Why should they be sucked down the sinkhole of devaluation along with the United States? Why should they link their currencies to what was obviously becoming a piece of junk? The German government, which still held bitter memories of the hyperinflation of the 1920s, had already broken the deutsche mark's ties with the dollar in May of 1971, when it was becoming clear that Arthur Burns had other things on his mind than keeping the $35 per ounce peg. The dollar averaged $40.52 against gold that month. The mark rose from around 3.63 per dollar in April to 3.40 per dollar in August and 3.27 per dollar at the end of the year. Japan's government dropped the dollar after the August 15 bombshell. The yen traded at 357 per dollar in early 1971, the upper end of its Bretton Woods trading band around 360 per dollar. In the first day of trading after the closing of the gold window, it traded at 340 per dollar, and at the end of 1971 it traded at 315 per dollar. The currencies of the world floated.

The United States had blown apart the world monetary system, much like Britain did, for similar reasons, in 1931. All the leading economic theoreticians had gotten what they wanted, just as they had in 1931. And just as in 1931, the governments of the world almost immediately realized that something had gone terribly wrong. It dawned on the stock market that the "temporary measure" of closing the gold window wasn't so temporary after all and that this step was a lot more important than the myriad other Band-Aids that had been laid on Bretton Woods over the years. It ground downward throughout the year.

The money bureaucrats of the United States and Europe huddled together, and in December of 1971, only four months after August 15, they had come up with a new world monetary system that attempted

254

to put the Bretton Woods system back together again. At European insistence, the devaluation of the dollar would be limited to only 8 percent, or $38 per ounce of gold. Other major currencies were repegged to the dollar around their recent market rates. However, the United States was not obliged to accept dollars and deliver gold in exchange. The gold window remained closed. The final bargain became known as the Smithsonian Agreement. It was the first official meeting of what later became known as the G7. Nixon proclaimed it "the most significant monetary agreement in the history of the world." The stock market boomed. The chaos of floating currencies had been avoided.

In principle the Smithsonian Agreement could have been a fine example of David Ricardo's assertion that a government needs no gold at all to maintain a gold standard. The European governments certainly intended it that way. At the Fed, Chairman Burns had actually backed away from his inflationist stance in the latter part of 1971 and was making strong anti-inflation statements in public. If the United States had been willing to abide by its agreement with the European governments to keep the dollar at $38 per ounce by adding and subtracting base money appropriately, the system could have held together to the present day even without gold convertibility.

But the U.S. government had no such intentions. In December 1971 the dollar averaged $43.48 per ounce on the gold market, and nobody in Washington was in a mood to deflate the dollar down to $38. Hadn't that caused the 1969 recession? Besides, who cared about the gold market? It had been illegal to own gold in the United States since 1933. See Figure 10.4.

The gold link of the Smithsonian Agreement was a fiction. In early 1972, Burns once again adopted an easy-money stance, aiming to juice up the economy in time for the presidential elections that November. The dollar slipped further against gold. In May 1972 it averaged $54.62 per ounce. In December it averaged $63.91 per ounce. The dollar's value had been cut nearly in half since Burns took office.

The U.S. government was not the only one playing this game. The same inflationist arguments that had become popular in the

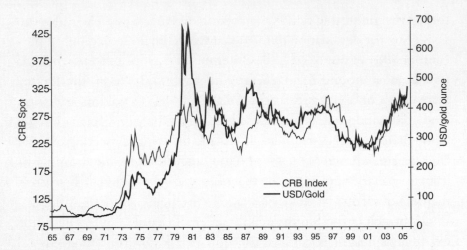

FIGURE 10.4   United States Dollars per Gold Ounce and CRB Spot Commodity Index, 1965–2005

United States had become popular all over the world. Britain had already devalued in 1967, and in 1972, it devalued again, against even the sinking dollar. In a race to the bottom, Britain seemed intent to win, even if it meant weakening the Smithsonian Agreement.

But most countries were pegging their currencies to the dollar, which meant they were being dragged down as the dollar sank. As dollars became relatively less valuable, dollars were traded for more-valuable European currencies at the fixed exchange rates, and European central banks ended up with masses of unwanted dollars, which were not convertible. Unwilling either to devalue along with the United States or to allow their currencies to break out of their fixed bands and appreciate relative to the dollar, Germany, Switzerland, and Japan imposed exchange controls and forms of credit allocations.

Despite these details, in November of 1972 Humpty Dumpty had apparently been put together again. The central bankers of the world once again were a chorus in support of fixed exchange rates, and the dollar was nominally pegged to gold at $38 per ounce. The Burns plan had apparently worked: the punch bowl had been spiked to an unprecedented degree, the economy seemed to be booming in 1972, and the stock market soared higher, at least in nominal terms, though its gold value fell. Nixon promised no tax hikes. His Democratic opponent, George McGovern, campaigned on broad tax hikes through the elimination of supposed loopholes, including taxing capital gains as regular income (at a top rate of 70 percent plus state-level taxes), and 100 percent taxation of inheritances over $500,000. McGovern also proposed a program of giving a $1,000 "demogrant" to all citizens, regardless of income. Nixon won in a landslide.

In early 1973 the U.S. government promised to repeg the dollar at $42 per ounce of gold. It was a sham; the dollar had never traded at the previously promised $38 per ounce, and already it was over $65 per ounce on the open market. The United States had shown no concern about bringing its base money supply in line with the official dollar/gold parity. The government of Switzerland, a country of bankers, saw where this was leading, and once again broke the Swiss franc's ties with the dollar. The other European governments followed, and in the spring of 1973 the Smithsonian Agreement dissolved into the air. Once again the currencies of the world floated, and they continue to float to this day. The U.S. stock market headed into a long decline, harrowing in nominal terms and murderous in terms of gold.

In the 1930s, the governments of the world had been able to rebuild the world monetary system around the dollar, the sole remaining major currency with a link to gold. As a result, the dollar replaced the British pound as the world's foremost currency. Now no major currency was available to take that role.

The gold standard was gone and it wasn't coming back. The significance of the breakup of the Smithsonian Agreement wasn't lost on the Organization of Petroleum Exporting Countries, which was paid in increasingly worthless dollars for its oil. They had been concerned since the closing of the gold window in August 1971. In September 1971, in an extraordinary session, they had adopted conference resolution XXV.140, which read in part:

> [OPEC resolves] that Member Countries shall take necessary
> action and/or shall establish negotiations, individually or in groups,
> with the oil companies with a view to adopting ways and means to

offset any adverse effects on the per barrel real income of Member Countries resulting from the international monetary developments of 15th August 1971.[7]

Oil had traded around $2.90 per barrel, or ½ ounce of gold, at $35 per ounce. On the eve of the "oil shocks," with the dollar around $100 per ounce and OPEC still accepting about $2.90 per barrel for oil, the OPEC producers were getting only ⅟₃₅ of an ounce of gold for their oil. After they pushed the price to around $10 a barrel in early 1974, with the dollar around $120 per ounce and falling, they were once again getting around ½ ounce of gold for a barrel of oil. OPEC was simply raising its prices, like every other shopkeeper, in response to currency devaluation. It was actually rather late to the game; prices of most other internationally traded commodities had been rising in response to the sinking dollar since the late 1960s. There had already been sharp rises in food prices in 1972–1973. But the oil shock gave the country a popular foreign scapegoat when its elites weren't quite ready to accept the fact that they had brought the disaster upon themselves.

As workers demanded higher salaries in reaction to the currency devaluation, they entered higher and higher tax brackets, which weren't indexed to inflation. Bracket creep was rampant. As the prices of tangible goods, such as corporate inventories, equities, or property rose, the already-high capital gains tax (raised to nearly 50 percent by Nixon in 1969) became even higher as it applied to inflationary gains. These automatic tax hikes stifled the economy further, which led to less demand for money, which led to a sinking currency and more inflation.

In July of 1973, Burns pushed up the Fed's short-term interest rate target, and short-term rates, which had been below 4 percent in early 1972, rose from an average of 7.84 percent in May to 10.40 percent in July. At last, here was evidence of willingness at the Fed to support the value of the currency. The dollar rose on the foreign exchange markets, and against gold. The rising interest rates did their usual damage to the economy, particularly in rate-sensitive areas such as real estate, but the policy had its intended effect. After falling to an average of $120.17 per ounce in July, the dollar rose to an average of $94.82 per ounce in November.

In early 1974, however, the dollar's value once again began to sink. The adjustment of oil prices to dollar devaluation increased the rate of inflationary adjustment in other prices as well. The wholesale price index was rising at a 27.1 percent rate, the consumer price index at a 13.3 percent rate. The Fed's short-term rate, now around 9 percent, didn't seem so high anymore. As a result, the Fed's policy seemed to be one of easy money. As Burns later explained: "Although money was commonly described as tight the rate of monetary expansion had in fact been quite ample so far this year and . . . interest rates were high because the demand for credit was high, particularly in view of inflationary expectations."[8] The increased supply of base money just pushed the dollar down further, and the demand for dollars was shrinking as people rushed to drop the depreciating currency for hard assets.

It was hardly all Burns's fault. He pushed interest rates higher through 1974, to an average of 13 percent in July, even as the economy sank into grave recession. The Fed came under increasing attack from Congress, in particular from Wright Patman, the chairman of the House Banking Committee, who wanted lower interest rates and actually blamed Burns's high interest rate targets for inflation.

The Watergate break-in had been in the news since June 1972, but it didn't really gain impetus until after the Nixon reelection and especially after the breakup of the world monetary system that spring. Nixon had lost what the Chinese called "the mandate from heaven." He stepped down in scandal in August 1973, and Gerald Ford entered the Oval Office with inflation near the top of his agenda. (The electorate was ultimately able to find a solution to the lack of good options in the 1972 election.) In October 1974, Ford presented his first inflation-fighting plan: a one-year 5 percent surtax on corporate and upper-level incomes, a $4.4 billion cut in federal spending, and a "Whip Inflation Now" program which consisted of little more than distributing buttons with the WIN logo.

Once again the threat of tax hikes did nothing to halt inflation, and instead made it worse. The dollar reacted appropriately, falling to an average of $183.85 per ounce in December, the lowest it had ever been. The dollar's value had fallen by a factor of 5 from its $35 per ounce Bretton Woods value. Democrats criticized the tax hike bitterly and, in the 1974 Congressional elections, gained a large victory.

Ford ultimately gave up his tax hike plan, perhaps because of advice from Donald Rumsfeld, his chief of staff, and Rumsfeld's deputy, Dick Cheney. In December 1974 Arthur Laffer first drew the Laffer curve for Cheney on a napkin in the bar of a Washington hotel. The Laffer curve, a visual representation of the idea that there are two tax rates, one high and one low, that produce the same amount of tax revenue, became popular in the 1980s as a symbol of the growth-enhancing power of tax cuts.

Ford retreated to his "winter White House" in Vail, Colorado, to come up with a new plan. In January 1975 he presented it: a one-time tax rebate, a $3 tariff per barrel of imported oil, lifting of price controls on domestic oil producers, and a windfall profits tax on the oil producers. A tax rebate isn't really a tax cut, but simply a government handout better classified as spending. But Ford had clearly dropped his tax hike plans and was moving in the opposite direction. The stock market bottomed in December 1974 and began a ferocious rally.

The Democratic Congress saw Ford's direction change and ran with it. The Democrats came back with an alternative tax cut bill, which involved a sizable permanent reduction in tax rates and an expansion of domestic spending. The dollar began to rise in anticipation. It averaged $176.27 per ounce in January 1975 and continued to rise until it reached an average of $109.93 per ounce in August 1976. But in 1975, the balanced budget–crazed Republican Party could not accept the Democrats' plan. In the final compromise, the Revenue Adjustment Act of 1975, only a small tax cut was managed. Ford was seen nixing the Democrats' tax cuts, one factor in his defeat in the 1976 election against Jimmy Carter.

As the dollar appreciated against gold in 1975 and 1976, it also

260

rose against the deutsche mark, the yen, the Swiss franc, the French franc, and the British pound. Commodities prices fell. During this time, broad price indexes continued to rise, as they continued to adjust to the previous devaluations, but at a much slower pace. The 12.2 percent CPI rise of 1974 moderated to 7.0 percent in 1975 and to 4.9 percent in 1976. The wholesale price index, which is more sensitive to monetary conditions and adjusts more quickly, rose 21.3 percent in 1974, 4.4 percent in 1975, and 3.4 percent in 1976. The first round of dollar devaluation was over, and the economy began to recover from the deep recession of 1974.

While tax-cut talk was bouncing around Washington, Arthur Burns of the Federal Reserve had switched hats again and had become a rabid inflation fighter. Throughout 1975, Chairman Burns held the line against critics from all sides who wanted more monetary expansion. Some congressmen went so far as to introduce a bill requiring the Fed to expand the money supply at a rate of no less than 6 percent.

During the 1976 campaign, Jimmy Carter made vague statements that suggested that he would tackle the country's tax and monetary problems. He called the tax system a "disgrace to the human race," and promised to remove the price controls on oil and gas that Nixon had imposed and that had caused artificial shortages. Ford had proven to be a do-nothing, and the electorate chose Carter.

In the end, Burns couldn't resist the temptation to play politics with monetary policy. His term at the Fed ended in 1978, and he wanted to be reappointed. Burns apparently aimed to ingratiate himself to the new president Jimmy Carter by turning expansionary almost immediately after Carter's election. In late 1976, the dollar once again began to sink against gold and foreign currencies. In December 1976, it averaged $133.88 per ounce and steadily sank in value throughout the Carter administration. The Carter administration wanted monetary easing to relieve unemployment. As the dollar sank against other currencies, the Carter administration practiced benign neglect, despite complaints from foreign governments that the policy was not so benign, for either the United States or the world. On the fiscal side, Carter's vague election campaign talk about tax reform evolved into nothing more than a $50 giveaway, a meaningless plan that was ultimately abandoned. Carter did nothing about the oil and gas controls, either.

Burns didn't get the nod in 1978. Carter instead chose G. William Miller, who had little background in monetary economics. He had been the chairman of Textron, Inc., and was willing to play along with the Carter administration's economic plans, which included an accommodative—inflationary—role for the Fed.

When Burns handed the reins of the Fed to Miller in March 1978, the dollar had sunk once again to an average of $183.66 per ounce of gold, about the lowest it had ever been and less than one-fifth of its Bretton Woods value. Miller let the horses run. If everyone in the economy expected 7 percent price rises, the reasoning went, then enough money would have to be supplied for prices to indeed rise 7 percent, or a recession would occur. The result was continuous devaluation. Not only that, Miller aimed once again for full employment through currency devaluation. Wall Street complained bitterly that the Fed was once again driving down the dollar.

For the only time in history, the head of the Council of Economic Advisers and the Treasury secretary campaigned for the Fed to pull in the monetary reins. Even a groundbreaking capital gains tax cut, led by Congressman William Steiger in 1978, only slowed the dollar's fall. The tax cut, however, marked a turning point in how those in Washington thought about fiscal policy. The U.S. government was finally feeling its way out of the inflation/tax hike disaster.

In June of 1979, the dollar averaged $279.06 per ounce of gold. Its value had been cut in half again since the beginning of the Carter administration, and it had continued to drop against the deutsche mark and the yen. Oddly enough, oil prices had doubled again. Newspapers bemoaned a "second oil shock." The Fed funds rate was over 10 percent. The consumer price index was once again rising at a double-digit rate. Workers were being forced into higher tax brackets, and the higher taxes were forcing the economy into contraction; the contracting demand for money was sinking the dollar, the Fed was trying to solve the economic contraction with more money creation, and OPEC demanded more of the increasingly worthless dollars in trade for oil. In July 1979, Carter retreated to Camp David to come up with a plan.

But even now, the political system was unable to grasp that the problem had always been monetary. After 10 days of study and deliberation, Carter gave a momentous speech to the country and the world. He blamed a "crisis of confidence." He blamed "politics as usual." He blamed self-indulgence. He blamed materialism. But most of all, he blamed the Arabs, and his only policy proposal was a six-point energy plan including import quotas and standby gasoline rationing. The markets sank, and the dollar sank, too, its value dropping below ⅟₅₀₀ ounce of gold for the first time.

Carter did one other thing after coming down out of the mountains. In his first week back he replaced several members of his cabinet. He offered the job of Treasury secretary to Chairman Miller of the Fed, and Miller took it. Paul Volcker, a lifetime monetary bureaucrat who was then head of the New York Federal Reserve, was chosen as his replacement.

Somehow Carter, who never did figure out that the inflation that was destroying his presidency was coming from the Fed, managed to oust his errant Fed chairman in the middle of his term by the only possible way and replace him, almost by accident, with one of the best men available for the job.

Despite the promises that floating currencies would allow countries to set economic policy as they pleased, it didn't quite work out that way. The United States and Russia (or, more properly, the Soviet Union and its communist satellites) are about the only two countries large and diversified enough that they could consider economic autarky, let the rest of the world be damned. The countries of Europe and Asia had always been inextricably enmeshed in trade, and they always knew it.

Fixed exchange rates had long lay at the heart of trade, and although currencies floated beginning in 1973, governments were loath to let them float very far. If the yen had remained pegged to gold at its Bretton Woods value of ¥12,600 per ounce of gold, then the yen/dollar exchange rate would have gone from 360 per dollar in 1970 to 14.8 per dollar when the dollar hit its low of $850 per ounce in 1980. The deutsche mark would have been worth $6.69. One could imagine the effects on trade competitiveness. Export industries would have immediately collapsed, and domestic industries would have been overrun with a flood of cheap imports. This is the beggar-thy-neighbor effect that flared up so virulently during the 1930s. The only means to stop the process would have been extreme trade re-strictions, which could not be borne by the trade-dependent Japan-ese, German, or French economies. Such action would not be much appreciated by trading partners, either, and deep memories remained of the results of the trade warfare of the 1930s. When the primary currency of the world is devalued, the downdraft is almost impossi-ble to resist.

All the countries of the world got sucked into the inflationary morass of the 1970s, just as Britain set off a round of devaluations in the 1930s from which no one was ultimately spared, not even the United States.

Even if the European and Japanese governments had wanted to set up an independent gold standard and allow the dollar to fall on its own, they were hampered by rules left over from Bretton Woods. The International Monetary Fund forbade governments from buying or selling gold except at the fixed parity prices. After the end of the Smithsonian Agreement, no country would do this, of course, be-cause by then the market price had diverged so much from the par-ity price. As a result, they were unable to trade gold with each other, which would have been the heart of a system based on convertibility. In 1975, a new agreement was reached whereby countries could sell gold at the open market price, but were barred from trying to fix the price of gold. The IMF is essentially a branch of the U.S. Treasury, and Washington had long wanted to minimize the use of gold, lest it lead to the decline of the dollar as the international medium of exchange.

All of this was taking place within the context of the cold war.

Both Europe and Japan were under the U.S. nuclear and military umbrella, which kept them safe from Soviet incursion. They found it difficult to remain military underlings and at the same time to usurp the U.S. government's dominance of monetary affairs.

The European governments had been tossing around the idea of monetary unification since the late 1950s, but they were not able to organize themselves as the world monetary system fell into disarray in 1971–1973. In time, they formed a plan that would help insulate them from future policy errors made by the U.S. government. The euro was conceived in the dark days of 1978.

CHAPTER 11

REAGAN AND VOLCKER

Monetarism Fails, but the Tax Cuts Succeed—and the 1980s Boom

The crisis was resolved, I argue, because the Mundell policy mix worked. This is not to say the diners at Michael I made it happen, or that anyone in power planned the policy mix or even understood it. But in its own mysterious, stumbling way, the system found it. Volcker's tight money killed the inflation; Reagan's tax cuts revived growth.

—**Robert Bartley, *The Seven Fat Years*, 1992**[1]

The international money system—regardless of which nations won and which lost—was a financial system that did continuing violence to the real producers. Since "floating" exchange rates were adopted in 1973, letting the free markets set the price of currencies, the dollar had moved through a series of what Lee Iacocca rightly called "violent swings" in value, destabilizing trade relationships each time. As long as the present free-market system was preserved, the extreme swings would continue.

Money was meant to be the neutral agent of commerce. Now it had become the neurotic master. . . . Trade wars were fought through currencies, the mercantile combat among nations that was as old as capitalism itself.

—**William Greider, *Secrets of the Temple*, 1987**[2]

In 1971, Richard Nixon proclaimed that "we're all Keynesians now." In 1977, the *Wall Street Journal* announced that Keynes was dead. Keynesianism could do nothing to explain, much less deal with, the recession of 1974. Indeed, Keynesianism, specifically the notion that currency devaluation would lead to lower unemployment and create economic expansion, was the cause of the problem.

People looked for new answers, and the members of the *Wall Street Journal*'s op-ed page staff found them in economist Robert Mundell and his former student Arthur Laffer. In May 1971, while the Bretton Woods gold standard was still hanging by a thread, Mundell wrote in an obscure publication:

> The correct policy mix [for 1971] is based on fiscal ease to get more production out of the economy, in combination with monetary restraint to stop inflation. The increased momentum of the economy provided by the stimulus of a tax cut will cause a sufficient demand for credit to permit real monetary expansion at higher interest rates.[3]

Today his tax-cut/sound-money proposal may seem obvious, but at the time it was radical. Didn't tax cuts cause inflation by overstimulating the economy? Wouldn't monetary restraint cause recession? A popular view at the time called for more monetary expansion (to solve unemployment) and more tax hikes (to stifle inflation). But by 1978, popularized by the *Wall Street Journal* and a handful of economists and politicians, Mundell's ideas were gaining force.

The 1978 capital gains tax cut, led by Republican congressman William Steiger, was a precision strike at the most destructive element of the increasingly destructive tax code. The old conventional wisdom, at least the Republican flavor that Nixon had followed, was that the tax was needed to close the chronic budget deficit. The Democratic conventional wisdom was that a high capital gains tax was needed to moderate the distribution of income. But this time the Democrat-dominated Congress passed Steiger's amendment, while giving a thumbs-down to Democratic president Carter's attempt to make the tax system more "fair" by limiting certain business deductions. The Steiger cut reversed the Nixon tax hike of 1968. The capital gains tax rate fell to 25 percent from nearly 50 percent, though it remained, as today, unindexed to inflation.

The year 1978 also saw the passage of the controversial Proposition 13 in California, which capped rises in property tax payments. The proposition, put on the ballot by the signature-collecting efforts of 75-year-old Howard Jarvis, was viciously opposed by every element of the California elite: the media, top businesspeople, government officials, and academics. The proposition passed anyway, and when the doomsday scenarios of its opponents failed to materialize, and instead California enjoyed a relative economic improvement, the intelligentsia began to admit that perhaps they had been wrong.

Perhaps most important of all was the return of the Republican Party to its tax-cutting roots, led by representative Jack Kemp. In early 1977, representative John Rousselot announced the beginnings of change by proposing, not a balanced-budget amendment as had become the habit of the Republican Party, but "a simple across-the-board tax cut for every American." By the end of the year, Kemp and Senator William Roth had introduced the Kemp-Roth bill, which proposed an immediate 30 percent cut in income tax rates. To deflect criticism from the Democrats, who were in a majority in Congress, the Kemp-Roth bill was specifically designed to mimic Democrat John F. Kennedy's 1963 tax-cut plan. It was narrowly defeated, but in October 1978 Democratic senator Sam Nunn revived the idea and combined it with limits on the growth of federal spending to create the Nunn amendment. Nunn's "Kemp-Roth-plus" passed both houses of the Democratic Congress but was killed in conference by the Carter administration.

Soon after, in 1979, the Joint Economic Committee, headed by Democratic senator Lloyd Bentsen and Republican representative Clarence Brown, endorsed an overtly pro-growth policy of tax cuts, the first unanimous annual report in 20 years. In 1980, the Mundell policy mix was embodied in the election of president Ronald Reagan, who promised, essentially, to remain faithful to the policies of Democrat Sam Nunn and the Carter-appointed Paul Volcker.

Volcker had been appointed almost as an afterthought. If Carter had thought about it a little more he might not have appointed Volcker at all, because Volcker represented the antithesis of the cheap money policies favored by the Carter administration and enacted by Volcker's predecessor, Bill Miller. But even after ascending to the top of the Fed, it was not at all clear that Volcker would be able to persuade the Open Market Committee to make a U-turn, with the danger of inducing a recession.

Volcker's term did not start auspiciously. He managed to get a unanimous FOMC decision to raise the discount rate—a mostly cosmetic change since the Fed now made few direct loans. A second rise in the discount rate was accomplished with only a marginal four to three majority. It seemed Volcker could barely persuade his own institution to take baby steps toward monetary tightening.

The dollar continued to fall in value. In October 1979, Volcker went off to an IMF meeting of central bankers in Belgrade, where they outlined for him the dire consequences of continuing dollar devaluation, not only for the United States but for the entire world. Volcker left the meeting early and called an emergency meeting of the FOMC. See Figure 11.1.

By the time the emergency meeting ended, a revolution had taken place. Somehow, Volcker, who had been barely able to get the committee to agree on a small rise in the discount rate, managed to get full cooperation on a plan to change the way the Fed worked entirely. The Fed began what is now known as the "monetarist experiment."

"The world is moving toward a floating regime," Mundell predicted in 1969. "The experience will be so painful that by 1980 it will begin moving back to fixity."[4] In October 1979, three months before Mundell's deadline, it began to happen.

Monetarism was a kind of warped, mutated classicalism. The classical economists had also asserted that inflation was a monetary

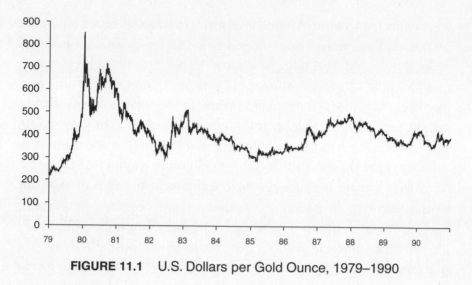

FIGURE 11.1   U.S. Dollars per Gold Ounce, 1979–1990

phenomenon and that the proper way to manage a currency was with direct management of the supply of base money. The difference was the target; the classicalists, from John Locke onward, always advocated a "price rule," the price of gold, which was really the value of the currency itself. This was a definite price generated by the dollar/gold market on a moment-to-moment basis. The monetarists targeted a statistical abstraction they had dreamed up that they called the "money supply," which could be derived only once a month or so, and completely ignored the fact that the dollar was being used worldwide, not just within the political boundaries of the United States. Short-term interest rates would no longer be targeted directly, but would be allowed to fluctuate like the rest of the credit market. The value of the currency would also be allowed to float.

Monetarism was supposed to stop inflation, but its initial effect was to make it worse—much worse. After all, if inflation is caused by excess money, how much is "excess"? Since the monetarists would not heed the value information provided by the gold market, they relied instead on the academic daydreams fashionable at the time. The initial plan was to moderate inflation gradually by gently slowing the rate of monetary expansion. In other words, if the economy were expected to grow 3 percent in real terms and to have 10 percent of inflationary price rises, the money supply, as the monetarists defined it, would have to grow around 13 percent. If the Fed were to provide only 11 percent money growth, for example, the inflation would gradually be tempered, according to monetarist theory. But in the autumn of 1979, Volcker told Congress that the economy would grow faster than had been anticipated in 1980, and to accommodate the extra growth, the Fed would provide more money! At the same time, the demand for money was collapsing in the face of rampant devaluation.

The market's opinion of Volcker's hypothesis was clear: The dollar, which had averaged $392 per ounce in October 1979, took a sickening dive to $850 per ounce in January 1980, once again losing over half its value in just a few months, before Volcker got his horses pointed in the right direction. While this episode is still regarded by many as a "mania for gold," it was actually a mania for dumping dollars, while gold remained essentially inert. A rise in gold's absolute value would not affect much of anything except jewelry and dentistry. A decline in the dollar's value results, ultimately, in more dollars being required to buy everything. The consumer price index for January 1980 marked its fastest rise ever, at an 18 percent annualized rate, and the producer price index rose at a 21 percent rate. Foreign exchange rates remained somewhat stable, which can be attributed to the commitment of foreign central banks to stabilize exchange rates. Interest rates, however, rose throughout the industrialized world.[5]

The dollar rebounded in February 1980, and the consumer price index moderated its rate of increase. In March 1980, the Carter administration, still stumbling around for an anti-inflation program, found an overlooked piece of legislation, the Credit Control Act of 1969. It had never been used. Volcker opposed the Carter plan, but eventually went along with the proposal to require banks to post new reserves for so-called bad loans, such as outstanding credit on credit cards, bank overdrafts, and money market funds. So-called good loans, for mortgages or autos, would not require the special reserves. Faced with such a vague and complex set of regulations, bankers stopped making loans altogether, and the economy lurched into recession. The growth of the monetary aggregates slowed, and to compensate for the recession and meet its aggregate targets (according to the monetarist voodoo of the day), the Fed expanded its money creation beginning April 22. In July, the Fed eliminated the credit controls, and the recession ended. The dollar went from an average of $517 per ounce in April 1980 to $673 per ounce in September. In September, the Fed once again went into tightening mode, which lasted until mid-1982.

While this was happening, Reagan was campaigning for president. During his campaign, Reagan outlined what has become known as the Rosy Scenario, in which inflation would be defeated while the economy would boom. The idea irked many whose sense of morality demanded a period of penitence for the mistakes of the past—whether by paying off the debt, by accepting greater government control over citizens' lives, or by accepting a recession so horrid that it would "break the back of inflation." Reagan had a different view. A policy that was good for the economy, he thought, should result in a better economy, not a worse one. (This is correct: A positive economic policy should produce positive results almost immediately. The effects of a very good policy will often be felt even while the plan is still passing through the lawmaking process. The effects of economic policy error are their own punishment.)

If government spending could be limited, perhaps to the rate of inflation plus 1 percent, as Sam Nunn had proposed, the extra economic growth might even make it possible to balance the budget by 1984, Reagan said. The Nunn amendment had forecast a balanced budget by 1982. Given the expectations—immediate tax cuts, fiscal restraint, and no monetary goofs—it was considered ambitious but not impossible. In March 1981, just after Reagan's inauguration, two-thirds of the economics forecasting profession predicted a balanced budget in 1984.[6] The most concerned economists were the supply-siders who had advocated the tax-cutting plan in the first place, who foresaw the risk that deflation and high interest rates caused by the Fed would overwhelm the tax-cutting benefits and drive the country into recession.

Reagan had one other expectation in mind when creating his Rosy Scenario. From the beginning of his campaign, Reagan was convinced that to return to full economic health, the country needed to return to a gold standard. Reagan intended to make it part of his election platform. In the primaries in 1980, when he broadcast his famous "talking head" television commercials outlining his economic plan, he had also recorded a commercial promising a return to the gold standard, which at the time had been gone for only nine years.[7] With a gold standard, the country would avoid monetary screwups, interest rates would collapse, and there would be an even more dramatic boom as the difficulties of exchange with a floating currency evaporated.

The ad didn't run. As was the case many times both before and after, he was talked out of it by his monetarist advisers. The official 1980 Republican platform ultimately read: "The severing of the dollar's link with real commodities in the 1960s and 1970s, in order to preserve economic goals other than dollar stability, has unleashed hyperinflationary forces at home and monetary disorder abroad, without bringing any of the desired economic benefits. One of the most urgent tasks in the period ahead will be the restoration of a dependable monetary standard—that is, an end to inflation."[8] No mention of Arabs.

Unlike the other tax cutters of U.S. history, whether Andrew Mellon in the 1920s or John F. Kennedy in the 1960s, Reagan would have to bring the economy back to health with a floating currency. The dollar's wild swings during the 1980s, particularly at the beginning of the Reagan administration, and the high interest rates resulting from Volcker's monetarist experiment, did not make this easy. Nor were Reagan's expenditure-reduction plans as politically feasible as was at first imagined. Reagan planned an expansion of military spending while shrinking nonmilitary outlays by 3 percent per year in real terms. No administration since the end of World War II had been able to make those kind of cuts in nonmilitary spending. In the end, Reagan, sensing the realm of political possibility, agreed to give up his gold standard and balanced budget goals in order to concentrate on lower taxes, an expansion of military spending, and a program of deregulation. See Figure 11.2.

If the dollar devaluation was halted by monetary steps alone, there was a danger of recession due to relative deflation caused by built-in expectations of future price rises. But if the monetary restraint was paired with significant productivity-enhancing tax cuts, the economy would be able to recover even as the dollar rose. In fact, the Fed might not have to contract at all, with all of the monetary restraint coming from increased demand for money due to economic expansion. The Reagan plan, just as Mundell had envisioned, was all gain and no pain. The economy would start improving from day one. No sacrifices would be necessary. Nobody would be left behind. The government's finances would even improve.

This scenario, as attractive as it was, nevertheless irritated many people. To solve the world's economic problems with such ease and flair would deeply embarrass everyone who had been proclaiming

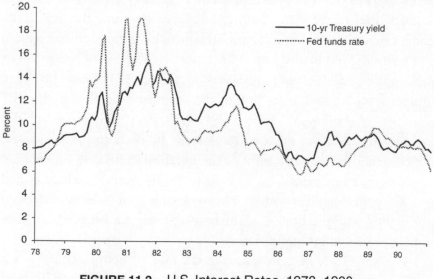

FIGURE 11.2 U.S. Interest Rates, 1978–1990

loudly, as was the intellectual fashion at the time, that the world was in an irrevocable process of decline due to shrinking natural resources. It *couldn't* be that easy. Besides, it smacked of irresponsibility. Short-term pain was supposed to be necessary for long-term gain. Reagan's plan sounded like a free lunch, and everybody was certain that there were no free lunches. The hunt was on to find some hidden disaster lurking in Reagan's plan. Economists, especially, were prone to assigning themselves a role as dour realists. With grim pride, they labeled their profession the "dismal science." Mundell's policy prescription was insufficiently dismal.

The world will tend to manifest whatever people imagine in their heads. This is as true of countries as it is of individuals. As it passed through Congress, under all manner of loopy rationalizations, Reagan's plan was tweaked to produce the desired amount of short-term pain.

Kemp originally proposed an immediate 30 percent reduction in income tax rates, a plan that produced instant improvement (and ample tax revenues) when Kennedy and Johnson had tried it. The proposal that cleared both houses of Congress in 1978 had spread the tax cuts over three years, the "10–10–10" plan. Reagan planned to adopt the "10–10–10" plan retroactive to January 1, 1981. But as had happened so many times before, after the election, the balanced-budget maniacs of Washington went to work on the president's plan, and when the bill finally passed, it set forth a 25 percent reduction in three stages, "5–10–10," beginning October 1981. Since taxes are ultimately computed according to the calendar year, the "5–10–10" plan was effectively a "1.25–8.75–10–5" plan. The final bill did include an important measure to link tax brackets to price indexes, which would help negate most of the inflation's effect on income tax brackets (but not capital gains). However, by now Washington had grown to like bracket creep. The indexing provision was delayed until 1985, with the hope that the bracket creep tax hikes would help reduce projected budget deficits.

The tiny 1.25 percent effective tax rate reduction in 1981 was hardly enough to offset bracket creep in a year when the CPI rose

10.3 percent. Not much tax relief would be coming in 1982, either. Also, a measure passed in 1977 caused automatic rises in payroll taxes in both 1981 and 1982; payroll taxes are simply another form of income taxes. Taking the payroll tax hikes into account, most taxpayers would see no net cut in their income taxes until 1983. And in 1982 the deficit mania that was convulsing Washington ensnared even Reagan, who signed a small corporate tax hike that year.

The Fed had always said it intended to gently moderate the rate of inflation over a period of years, not slam on the brakes. The monetarist construct, however, ignores the possibility of rising demand for a currency, and in 1981 demand was likely increasing both because of expectations for future tax cuts and the fact that, since the dollar wasn't losing value anymore and was in fact gaining in value, it made more sense to hold onto a greater number of dollars—not only for citizens of the United States, but for people around the world. The dollar, which averaged $557 per ounce of gold in January 1981, rose to an average of $410 per ounce in December, doubling in value from its 1980 lows. Volcker and the Fed were probably happy that monetary conditions turned out to be more restrictive than they had expected, since the CPI was still rising at a double-digit rate to adjust to the Fed's errors of the 1970s. Also, Volcker was convinced that the Reagan tax cuts would be inflationary and therefore had to be compensated for by monetary restraint.

A rise in the dollar is, of course, deflation. The dollar deflation of 1981 had only a moderate effect on the domestic economy, since the fall of the dollar to over $800 per ounce of gold and the deflation afterward had been so swift. It could be called a *disinflation*, a compensatory deflation. Unemployment crept higher in 1981, from 7.5 percent in January to 8.6 percent in December. In 1982, however, the recessionary effect of the dollar deflation became more intense. Disinflation became outright deflation. That year, unemployment climbed over 10 percent as the economy went into a downturn that some said was the worst since the 1930s. Short-term interest rates were often above 14 percent as the Fed sucked reserves out of the economy.

The conventional wisdom didn't blame the Fed for the contraction, however, but Reagan's tax cuts, which in any case had been mostly postponed to 1983–1984. The government had been in deficit for 20 years, but in 1982 the blame for the recession fell on the deficit that was supposedly created by Reagan's tax plan. Rather little attention was put on the expansion of spending, as if that was immutable.

Somewhere along the line, as the worst excesses of postwar Keynesianism were discarded, Keynes's important lessons from the 1930s were also lost. Only a few years earlier, accepting deficit spending during a recession (instead of hiking taxes) was considered the "Lesson We Learned in the Thirties." Part of the reason for the deficit mania of 1982 was that the years of inflation had produced nominal deficit figures that were larger than had ever been seen, although as a portion of GDP the projected deficits were about the same as the average deficit of 2.1 percent of GDP from 1971 to 1980. In 1975, a recovery year, the deficit had been 4.1 percent of GDP. In 1979, while the economy was apparently on the verge of collapse, Carter had managed one of the smallest federal deficits of the 1970s. Including state and local governments, in 1979 there was a small government surplus!

In 1982, the U.S. government threatened to wander into full-blown Hooverism, raising taxes in the midst of recession in the belief that balanced budgets would cure the country's economic ailments. Roosevelt had been guilty of the same errors, of course, so it is fitting that the 1982 tax hike bill split both parties, with a vote of 103 to 89 among the Republicans and 123 to 118 among the Democrats.

The dollar continued to rise in early 1982. In June, the dollar averaged $315 per ounce of gold. The Fed's G10 currency index rose from 106.96 in January to 116.97 in June. Deflation harms debtors at the expense of creditors, since debtors must pay back their borrowings in a more valuable currency. The advantage to creditors is limited, however, because the debtors threaten to go bankrupt and default altogether. This was happening in a big way all around the world in 1980–1982. Domestic borrowers are at least cushioned somewhat by the lag of general prices. Foreign borrowers, who typically borrow in dollars, feel the full force of deflation instantly as a change in exchange rates. During the 1970s, governments and corporations in a number of developing countries borrowed large sums, particularly to develop their commodities production. In the 1970s, the commodities-producing countries enjoyed a relative advantage, since commodities prices adjusted to dollar devaluation more quickly than general prices. Huge profits were made, and even at high interest rates companies and governments could borrow in expectation of further dollar devaluation and still higher commodities prices in the future. Borrowers had enjoyed a huge advantage during the 1970s as they paid back their loans in devalued dollars.

Banks were eager to make loans overseas, given the scarcity of good investment opportunities in the United States and the seemingly certain future profits from commodities production. In the late 1970s, many thought that the industrialized world would be practically held hostage by commodities-producing countries as the world "ran out of everything." But after Volcker began the dollar's deflation in 1980, these all turned out to be losing bets. Commodities prices peaked and headed lower in early 1980, and oil prices in 1981. (OPEC, as usual, was a bit behind the curve.) The profits from exporting commodities dried up, and the rising dollar made repayments ever more burdensome. Commodities producers everywhere were in a bind, as were their bankers in the United States and other developed countries.

In the 1970s, Mexico discovered it had large reserves of oil, and throughout that decade set about expanding its extraction capacity, funded by loans from U.S. banks. In 1981, as oil prices fell, the rising dollar put increasing pressure on the peso's dollar peg. There were no Reagan-like tax cuts in Mexico to boost peso demand. Instead, as the Mexican government scrambled for solutions, it ended up nationalizing the banks, which almost certainly resulted in a further drop-off in peso demand. In February 1982, the peso's dollar peg broke, and the peso sank to about 40 pesos per dollar, from 27. The devaluation spelled doom for Mexican oil producers and other industrialists who had borrowed in dollars. In April 1982, Grupo Industrial Alfa, Mexico's largest corporation, said it could not meet payments on $2.3 billion of loans. Citibank and Continental Illinois had each lent more than $100 million to the company. The top nine banks had loans in Mexico equivalent to 44 percent of their capital. That was just the tip of an iceberg of foreign loans held by U.S. banks that were looking increasingly rotten. Soon after, Drysdale Government Securities, a small brokerage, went spectacularly bust, followed by the collapse of Penn Square Bank in Oklahoma.

On June 28, the dollar hit $303.75 per ounce on the London market. The financial systems of the United States and the world could take no more dollar deflation. The dollar's value had nearly tripled from its 1980 low.

Volcker eased slightly on July 1, but the real relief came in mid-August 1982 when Volcker bailed out the U.S. banks by buying $600 million of Mexican debt and monetizing it, expanding the monetary base. The act ended the streak of Fed contraction that began in September 1980. The dollar mercifully sank from its highs. In September, it averaged $436 per ounce. On October 6, 1982, exactly three years to the day after beginning the monetarist experiment, Volcker told Congress he was no longer targeting the monetary aggregates. Monetarism was a failure.

In the end, the monetarist aggregates didn't mean much of anything at all by themselves. M1, one of the most widely watched statistics, expanded at an average annual rate of 6.35 percent during the 1970s, years of rampant dollar devaluation. During the 1980s, a time of tight money and a stable-to-deflating dollar, M1 grew at an average of 7.78 percent. See Figure 11.3.

The record of base money growth in the United States tells a similar tale. During the 1970s, the average annual increase in base money was 8.13 percent per year, or an increase of 119 percent for the entire decade. The value of the dollar fell by approximately a factor of 20, showing that the dollar collapse was caused primarily by a collapse in dollar demand (prompted by wild mismanagement), not grossly excessive money printing per se. During the 1980s, a decade

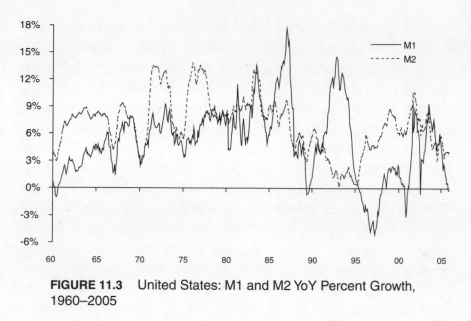

FIGURE 11.3   United States: M1 and M2 YoY Percent Growth, 1960–2005

in which the dollar's value rose, base money grew at an average annual rate of 7.52 percent. See Figure 11.4.

The monetarist experiment resulted in incredible volatility in the value of the dollar and in interest rates, which was completely intolerable. The Keynesian interest-rate-targeting system had already been

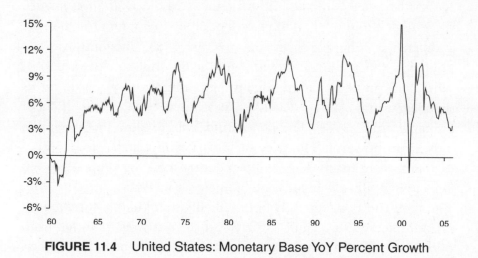

FIGURE 11.4   United States: Monetary Base YoY Percent Growth

abandoned in 1979. What next? In 1981–1982 attention turned again to the classical system of targeting some measure of value, preferably gold but possibly an index of commodities. In 1979 Congressman Ron Paul, with the help of Jesse Helms, attached a rider to an IMF appropriations bill that would create a government commission to study the feasibility of a new gold standard. Reagan okayed the commission, and it began to meet in the early 1980s. The gold advocates on the commission, Paul and Lewis Lehrman, did not make a good case for a gold standard, however, relying on impossible Rothbardian "pure gold standard" ideas. (They were coached by Murray Rothbard.) In 1982, when the commission gave its final report, the inflation of the 1970s had been reversed. Instead of presenting something appropriate to the 1980s, like a tuned-up Bretton Woods gold standard, the gold advocates offered instead a sort of hard-money fantasia. It was perhaps no surprise that a pragmatist member of the commission, Alan Greenspan, and the commission as a whole, concluded that a gold standard was "not appropriate at this time." The gold standard advocates had blown it, and since then, they have not had another chance to make their case.

At last the deflation was relieved, and beginning in 1983, the meat of the Reagan tax cuts was finally phased in. Finally, six years after Jack Kemp had put together his tax-cut plan and nine years since Robert Mundell had proposed his remedy in the *Wall Street Journal*, the Mundell solution was in place—or at least enough of it to make a difference. The economy boomed in 1983, showing an eye-popping 7.6 percent real growth, and the expansion continued until 1990. Reagan never did manage to get Congress to put a lid on its spending extravagances; deficits of more than 3.0 percent of GDP continued until 1986. The deficits did little to slow the economic expansion, however. The pace of CPI rises moderated to a degree that astonished many. The 10.3 percent rise of 1981 dropped to 6.2 percent in 1982 and an amazing 3.2 percent in 1983.

Stock and bond markets both rallied when Volcker finally loosened the screws in August 1982. Short-term interest rates fell from over 14 percent in June 1982 to around 9.0 percent in December.

Long-term rates fell from over 14 percent to around 10.6 percent. A two-decade bull market began.

But as the year drew to a close, long-term rates started inching up. The FOMC got the hint from the markets and quietly went into tightening mode again. The dollar exceeded $500 per ounce in February 1983 and then began to climb once again. Traders cited a comment by Volcker for a sharp move upward in the dollar in late February. Volcker, who rarely made statements about interest rates, said he expected interest rates to decline, which was interpreted as a change of policy toward tightening.

The economy continued to boom in 1984. Democratic presidential candidate Walter Mondale's insistence on the necessity of raising taxes inspired Reagan to press for further tax reform, with a lowering of top rates, in the 1984 election. Jack Kemp even managed to get a line about the gold standard in the official Republican platform, which read:

> The Federal Reserve Board's destabilizing actions must . . . stop. We need coordination between fiscal and monetary policy, timely information about Fed decisions and an end to the uncertainties people face in obtaining money and credit. The Gold Standard may be a useful mechanism for realizing the Federal Reserve's determination to adopt monetary policies needed to sustain price stability.[9]

Reagan's victory in the electoral college was the greatest in history, and wildly bullish for the economy. Reagan eventually pushed through a tax reform package that lowered top income tax rates to 28 percent in 1986. The tax plan would have been even more effective if the capital gains tax hadn't also been raised to 28 percent from 20 percent in the name of supposed "fairness," giving the United States one of the highest capital gains taxes in the developed world. (The capital gains rate hike was effective January 1, 1987. The income tax rate cut was delayed six months.) At the time, Japan didn't tax capital gains at all, nor did Germany, Belgium, Singapore, Switzerland, or

Hong Kong. Even socialist Sweden taxed capital gains at only 18 percent. Britain had a 30 percent rate, but it was indexed to inflation.

The dollar had plateaued at around $345 per ounce of gold in the latter half of 1984, but after the 1984 election it sailed higher. In late February 1985, it rose as high as $284.25 per ounce. The Fed's dollar/G10 currencies index had risen from an average of 117.73 in January 1983 to 158.43 in February 1985. Deflation threatened once again, as it had in 1982. Foreign debtors, domestic exporters, and domestic commodities producers were feeling the deflationary pressure. The dollar was too high. Unemployment, after falling steadily to a low of 7.1 percent in November 1984, started to creep back up again. Commodity prices sank. In February 1985, a delegation of legislators from 13 farm states met with Volcker in Washington to plead for monetary relief. Willie Nelson and other performers undertook a huge "Farm Aid" concert on September 22, 1985. Also in 1985, members of the Reagan administration, observing the dollar's rise on the foreign exchange markets and its damage to U.S. industries, began to argue with Volcker for a moderation of policy. Nobody wanted a replay of 1982.

The rise of the dollar was temporarily halted with heavy foreign exchange intervention in late February 1985, which was followed in early March 1985 with talks in Paris about a new monetary order that included a lower dollar.

As the dollar sank, unemployment once again headed lower, ending 1985 at 6.9 percent. In September 1985, representatives of the major governments gathered to formalize the plans they had been making since February. The United States, Japan, Germany, France, and Great Britain joined together at the Plaza Hotel in New York to sign the Plaza Accord, which was an agreement to prevent further dollar appreciation. In effect, it put a ceiling on the dollar. At the time, the dollar was trading around $320 per ounce of gold, 225 yen, and 2.7 marks.

The dollar went into a phase of relative stability beginning around 1985, which was reinforced by the Plaza Accord. Until mid-1986, the dollar remained roughly between $310 and $350 per ounce of gold, a band of around 13 percent, its most stable period since the end of Bretton Woods. During this time, the bond market finally rallied and the double-digit interest rates that had prevailed since the beginning of the 1980s broke. Interest rates of 11 percent or more in April 1985 moderated to 9.8 percent by the end of the year, and 7.3 percent by the end of 1986, even as Congress continued to pass large budget deficits.

During 1986, a number of members of the Fed's board of governors who had supported Volcker's monetary restraint resigned. Henry Wallich, J. Charles Partree, Emmett Rice, and Preston Martin were replaced by four Reagan appointees, who tended to favor a more accommodative monetary stance. Their opinions were influenced more by the deflationary troughs of 1982 and 1985 than by the inflationary meltdown of the 1970s. And though Reagan was a hard-money man to the core, his economic program and political support had been severely undermined by Volcker's deflation in 1982, to the degree that his tax-cutting program had been in grave jeopardy. Volcker was losing authority at the Fed.

Volcker and the Fed were being prodded in 1986 by the Treasury to continue pushing the dollar lower. After already being cut in March and April, the discount rate was lowered further in July and August as the Fed attempted to stimulate the economy. Many Fed watchers expected further rate cuts.

Fed expansion was a good idea in early 1985; by late 1986, the dollar had already been pushed low enough. The dollar took a sharp drop against gold in August and September of 1986, bottoming around $438 per ounce before recovering to around $390 per ounce.

In October 1986, the European governments once again jumped in to try to prop up the sagging dollar, setting in motion steps toward a second formal agreement between governments. As it appeared that the United States would agree to put a floor under the dollar, abandoning inflationism, the stock market, which had stagnated through 1986, began to rise in earnest. In February 1987, the G7 governments got together once again, at the Louvre Museum in Paris. The Louvre Accord effectively put a floor for the dollar at $400

per ounce, 150 yen, and 1.7 marks. The world was once again creep-
ing back toward a system of fixed, or at least less volatile, exchange
rates, and the United States was slowly taming the roller-coaster
swings of the dollar to a rough band around $350 per ounce, bounded
by the Plaza and Louvre accords. After the failure of both the Keynesian and monetarist ideas, the United States and the world stumbled
groggily back to a price rule, the foundation of the Bretton Woods
system.

The Fed was helped along this direction by Wayne Angell, who
was appointed to the Federal Reserve's board of governors in 1986.
A Kansan with a background in farming, he developed a commodity
basket to guide monetary policy and won increasing influence as he
used it in his decisions on the Open Market Committee. H. Robert
Heller, who joined the FOMC in August 1986, also supported the
idea of using commodity prices as a guide to monetary policy. At an
IMF meeting in Washington in October 1987, Treasury Secretary
Baker suggested that the G7 governments base their coordination on
"the relationship among our currencies and a basket of commodities,
including gold." At the same meeting, Britain's Nigel Lawson (chancellor of the exchequer and head of British monetary policy) urged
that "special attention should also be given to the trend of world commodity prices," and suggested "a more permanent regime of managed floating."[10]

The European and Japanese governments certainly intended the
Louvre Accord to mean that the Fed would not allow the dollar's
value to fall beyond around where it had been during the signing of
the agreement. If the U.S. government took responsibility for the
dollar and kept it within the broad bands outlined by the Plaza and
Louvre accords, then the governments of Germany and Japan, which
were much warier than the United States about currency devaluation
and inflation, would be able to keep their currencies roughly in line
with the dollar. The U.S. government had a slightly different interpretation: The United States government would do what it wished,
and the responsibility fell on Europe and Japan's governments to
manipulate their currencies to stay in line with the dollar, whether

the dollar rose or fell in value. It was the same difference of opinion that had scotched the Smithsonian Agreement 14 years earlier.

The Louvre Accord naturally implied that the Fed would now practice more restraint with its liquidity creation. Volcker was certainly for monetary restraint, but he was now outnumbered on the FOMC by weak-dollar fans. The Fed made only the smallest moves toward supporting the dollar; it didn't raise the discount rate until September. Treasury Secretary Baker and a somewhat reluctant Volcker instead spent early 1987 berating the German Bundesbank and especially the Bank of Japan to devalue their currencies along with the dollar. In April, the Fed was even reported to be putting off rate hikes with the express purpose of forcing the Bank of Japan to devalue![11] Baker was convinced that a devalued dollar would reduce the U.S. current account deficit. The situation was not helped by U.S. threats of trade sanctions, heightened by a trade bill passed April 30 that threatened retaliation if its trading partners did not lower their trade barriers. The dollar, which had been around $400 per ounce when the Louvre Accord was signed in February, fell to around $460 per ounce.

Volcker's calls for monetary restraint became lonelier. When his term ended in August 1987, he declined to be reappointed. The problem of the sinking dollar and the tattered Louvre Accord was left to his successor, Alan Greenspan.

In the 1980s the Reagan success and the Mundell policy solution was mirrored throughout the developed world. Yet if one had to choose a European counterpart to Ronald Reagan, it would surely be Margaret Thatcher, who became prime minister of Britain in 1979 on a platform of marginal tax rate reductions and an end to the devaluation of the once-respected British pound.

Upon becoming prime minister, Thatcher immediately pushed through a reduction in top income tax rates from 83 percent to 60 percent. However, just as Reagan was forced to accept delays in his tax cuts and indeed signed a tax increase in 1982, Thatcher was prodded by her chancellor of the exchequer to include a major hike in Britain's value-added tax from 8 percent to 15 percent, a bolt out of the blue that was never part of Thatcher's original plan and that many considered ridiculous. The VAT hike canceled out many of the economic advantages of the marginal rate cuts, and Britain's economy stumbled badly in the early 1980s as it dealt with deflation along with the United States. Tax revenues amounted to 34 percent of GDP in 1978–1979. In the mid-1980s they had expanded to more than 39 percent.

By 1986, Britain's economy was flexing its muscles for the first time in decades, and Thatcher had accomplished a long list of pro-growth steps. Top income tax rates were further lowered to 40 percent, with the basic rate falling from 33 percent to 25 percent. A further cut to 20 percent was planned. An investment income surcharge of 15 percent was abolished. The corporate tax rate was cut from 52 percent to 35 percent. Capital gains taxes were simplified and indexed to inflation, and the top rate was reduced from 75 percent to 30 percent. Industry had been freed from thickets of regulation and controls. Dozens of state-owned industries were privatized. As was the case in the United States, lowering tax rates did not lower tax revenue. In 1978–1979 the top 5 percent of income earners accounted for 24 percent of income tax receipts. In 1987–1988 they paid 28 percent.

Thatcher lost her popularity when she began to experiment with tax hikes, not only a new poll tax, but a hike in the capital gains tax rate to 40 percent from 30 percent. In Japan, a 40-year stretch of above-average economic performance ended with a flurry of tax hikes in the late 1980s and early 1990s, the first major episode of tax hiking since the Liberal Democratic Party came to power in 1955. The first half of the Reagan boom ended when George Bush, who had been elected on a platform of "no new taxes" and a cut in the capital gains tax, somehow ended up raising income taxes instead.

The savings and loan industry had been created in the 1930s to address a market, home mortgages, that tended to be neglected by the big banks. The flip side of specialization, of course, is a lack of diversification. S&Ls had all their eggs in a tiny basket: Their assets tended to be long-term fixed-rate mortgages, all backed by real estate within a small geographic area, and they were funded solely by savings account customers, whose deposits are effectively short-term variable-rate instruments. Commercial banks, in contrast, tend to have a more diversified portfolio of shorter-term corporate loans.

An S&L can survive and flourish only in an environment of relatively stable money. The S&L borrows short and lends long, and profits from the interest rate spread between the two. During the Bretton Woods era of stable money, this was a simple, even sleepy business. It was, however, a business guaranteed to self-destruct in the inflation of the 1970s. The interest income it receives from a mortgage made in 1960, for example, must be more than the interest it pays out to a savings deposit account in 1975. The explosion of the interest rate derivatives business over the past 20 years or so has been mostly to spread out this duration risk.

Already by the late 1960s—in the midst of Bill Martin's attempts to keep Bretton Woods stuck together—the S&L industry was beginning to totter. Congress stepped in with regulatory tweaks that gave S&Ls an artificial advantage over normal banks. That supported S&Ls for a little while, but by the late 1970s the entire S&L industry was in crisis. Regulators attempted to solve the problem by allowing S&Ls to diversify into other investments and also by raising the upper limit on federal deposit insurance from $25,000 to $100,000. The changes were an incentive to gamble; many S&Ls were doomed if managers did nothing, but if they made some high-risk investments that paid off, there was a chance the bank could be saved. If not, nobody got hurt since the government would bail out the depositors. After thrifts were further deregulated in the early 1980s, the riskiest and most aggressive thrifts could offer the highest interest rates, which naturally attracted more depositors since their deposits were insured by the government.

An institution goes bankrupt when it can't honor its obligations. An S&L's obligations are to its depositors, who can ask to have their money back at any time. Before the 1930s, banks often went bust as depositors caught a whiff of financial problems and withdrew their deposits. The financial collapse in the 1930s, which certainly deepened the Depression in the United States, led to the invention of depositor insurance, but as is so often the case, the new regulation demanded still more regulation to deal with the side effects. Banks would no longer go bust on their own, because depositors, assured that they would get their money back, had no reason to withdraw it. That was the whole point of deposit insurance. Banks weren't taking risks anymore with depositors' money, but with the government's money, and the government would have to decide when it would step in and shut down the bank.

All of this was worsened in the recession of 1982, when the government's S&L regulators eased various accounting procedures to allow S&Ls to weather the recession. The regulators were afraid, justifiably, that a wave of S&L implosions would send the economy on a new downturn. By wallpapering over the problems, the government could postpone the S&L cleanup to a time when the government and the economy could more easily bear the strain, but the final cost would be higher.

By 1985, no amount of wallpaper could cover the losses at some S&Ls, and the economy was easily healthy enough to brush off a round of S&L closures. Regulators pleaded to be allowed to shut them down, but influential Congressmen, who were backed by the S&Ls, stayed their hand. The S&Ls had enjoyed a never-ending supply of Band-Aids from Congress since the 1960s, and the cozy relationships between the S&Ls and influential Congressmen remained. By the late 1980s, a third of the industry was unprofitable. The final cleanup began with the Financial Institutions Reform, Recovery and Enforcement Act of 1989, and when the job was finally completed, around 1994, the total cost was about $200 billion.

There remains the myth that Reagan and deregulation caused the S&L crisis. Reagan had nothing to do with it—indeed, Reagan's sound money policies made S&Ls a viable business again. Certainly the problem festered under Reagan's watch, as crooked S&L managers played "double or nothing" with federally insured deposits, but that had little effect on the economy itself, which boomed. The S&L crisis was really a crisis of the 1970s, so it is quite a stretch of the imagination to believe that it somehow caused the recession of 1990–1991. Likewise, the final cleanup procedure, which did take place in the early 1990s, had little ultimate effect on the economy, good or bad.

The S&L debacle is today used, quite erroneously, as an example to other countries that if they "clean up their bad-debt problems" their economies will improve. If anything, the S&L experience is an example of not cleaning up bad-debt problems, and nothing particularly bad came of it during the 1980s. This is not to say that the government should not have acted sooner, but rather that the supposed advantages of bad-debt liquidation, recently pressed upon Japan, Korea, Thailand, and so forth, are vastly exaggerated. The real problem in these economies is to stop the process of bad-debt creation—in other words, to solve broader economic problems causing corporations to default on their debts. This has little to do with banks directly. One reason governments are flogged again and again, by Western advisers, with this myth is that it causes governments, recently in Japan and China, for example, to force local banks to sell assets to U.S. banks and other foreign vulture investors at ridiculously low prices. (They have to be forced because they are, unsurprisingly, unwilling to do it voluntarily.) This has turned out to be quite profitable for the U.S. banks. The investment bank Goldman Sachs is now one of Japan's largest real-estate owners, after the Japanese government forced Japanese banks to sell collateralized debt at "market" prices. (If it were a real market, there would be no need for government coercion.) Buyers of this debt usually do very well; after all, that is the point of buying it in the first place, at a price at which success is virtually assured. It normally makes little difference who owns debt. Whatever profit is made by the purchaser would have been made by the seller if they had not sold.

The S&L blowout was small beer compared to the disasters suffered by the big U.S. commercial banks as a result of the giant monetary swings of the 1970s and 1980s. The commercial banks had been able to weather the inflation that nixed the S&Ls, but were sunk by the rise of the dollar and the end of inflation in the 1980s. The Mexico debt blowout of 1982, a consequence of the radical turnaround in the dollar beginning in 1980, was just one of dozens of similar cases. Fifty-seven countries, with about 60 percent of the total external debt of the developing countries, incurred payments arrears or re-scheduled their debts between 1981 and 1984. Much of this was in Latin America. In 1982, the world's top 100 banks had $182 billion of exposure in Latin America alone, and they had only about $146 billion in capital to cover their losses. About a third of the debt was held by U.S. banks. By 1987, the banks' Latin American exposure had ballooned to $237 billion.

In the nineteenth century, when the United States was itself a developing country with an economy focused on raw materials, the Europeans poured a river of capital into risky ventures in the New World, much of it through bank loans. Bankruptcy and default were common, a natural feature of high-risk/high-return investing. When the United States became the creditor, however, the big banks ran to the International Monetary Fund to get bailed out, and the IMF then broke the legs of the debtors to get them to repay their loans.

When bankruptcy and default are due to simple business failure, it presents less risk for banks because their loans are naturally diversi-fied. At any given time, banks will have a large portion of good loans and a small portion of bad. When dramatic tax or monetary errors hit an economy, however, a whole sector of the economy can go bust simultaneously. Banks cannot withstand a shock of this sort, whether in 1930 or 1980, and they naturally call on the government to save the financial system from collapse.

The IMF would give the government of the distressed country a loan of U.S. taxpayer dollars to repay the money borrowed from U.S. commercial banks. The money spent no time in Mexico, Brazil, or Argentina, but immediately sailed back to New York. The govern-ments of the distressed countries were left owing just as much as before, to the IMF instead of the U.S. banks. In return for loaning them money, the IMF saddled the indebted countries with austerity programs that typically included government spending cuts and tax hikes. A horrendous currency devaluation was deemed necessary to produce a "current account surplus" with which to (according to this bizarre calculus) repay the IMF loan. By 1988, most of Latin America was operating under IMF economic programs.

What advantage did the governments of developing countries see in owing money to the IMF instead of U.S. banks? Probably they expected the IMF technocrats to help their country enjoy the kind of economic boom that was taking place in the United States. Instead, the worst of Hooverist deficit mania and devaluationist ideology was exported in its most virulent form. Double-digit inflation had thrown the developed countries into crisis during the 1970s, but by some contorted sequence of rationalizations, the IMF determined that what the Latin American countries really needed was triple-digit inflation. From 1983 to 1988, Argentina had average annual CPI increases of 370 percent, Brazil 295 percent, Mexico 92 percent, Peru 221 percent. Such radical currency devaluation had all the usual effects: galloping tax hikes through bracket creep, destruction of the savings of ordinary citizens, and gross distortion of the price structure. People, in short, became dramatically poorer, which made it even more difficult for them to pay their debts to foreign bankers and the IMF, creating a justification for even more tax hikes. While the 1980s were a decade of tax cuts, stabilizing currencies, and economic recovery for the developed world, many in Latin America remember it as a lost decade of tax hikes and endless devaluation. In 1990, one Western observer noted: "Now austerity has joined the IMF as one of the two most hated terms in Latin America."[12]

Despite the IMF bailouts, U.S. commercial banks suffered badly from their developing market loans, and in 1990 they were hit further by difficulties in the U.S. real estate market and high-yield bond market. This was the real banking disaster of the 1990 recession, not the puny S&Ls. The largest U.S. banks, including Citibank and Bank of America, teetered on the brink of default—in fact, they were probably bust—and their share prices tumbled toward zero. Did the U.S.

government rush in to liquidate the banks and their bad debts, as it recommends to so many other governments? It did not. Instead, it turned a blind eye, allowing the banks to operate, just as it had allowed the S&Ls to operate. The banks were eventually saved by the economic recovery of the early 1990s (and an extrasteep yield curve courtesy of the Fed).

The difficulties suffered by the commodities producers of developing countries were suffered identically by commodities producers in the United States. Deflation tends to favor those at the top of the economy—high-level services and high-tech manufacturing—at the detriment of commodities producers and low-tech fields. In the inflationary Carter years, the real equity of the agriculture sector rose at a 4.9 percent rate while that of the financial sector fell at a negative 2.9 percent rate. During the Reagan years, agriculture fell at a negative 10.3 percent rate while finance rose at a 6.5 percent rate.[13]

Farmers had taken out loans at double-digit interest rates to expand production; faced in the 1980s with falling commodities prices, a rising dollar, and huge interest payments, farmers went bust en masse. Farm credit institutions began slipping underwater during the second round of Volcker deflation in 1984. Not only agriculture, but a wide swath of traditional blue-collar industries such as steel, oil, mining, tire manufacturing, and forestry suffered during the 1980s. Economic growth in developed countries has always tended to lead to the expansion of leading-edge high-value-added industries and the contraction (in terms of the number of workers, at least) of older industries such as agriculture. That trend had been a rule throughout U.S. history. But in the 1980s that natural phenomenon was magnified by deflationary effects. The tendency for deflation to favor white-collar over blue-collar industries has intensified criticisms that Reagan's rising tide didn't lift all boats. But John F. Kennedy, who coined that term in support of his own Reaganesque tax-cut plan, didn't have to deal with a floating dollar.

CHAPTER 12

THE GREENSPAN YEARS

The 1987 Stock Market Crash, a Recession, Recovery, and Monetary Deflation

An almost hysterical antagonism toward the gold standard is one issue which unites statists of all persuasions. They seem to sense— perhaps more clearly and subtly than many consistent defenders of laissez-faire—that gold and economic freedom are inseparable, that the gold standard is an instrument of laissez-faire and that each implies and requires the other.

—**Alan Greenspan, "Gold and Economic Freedom," 1967**[1]

The only seeming solution is for the U.S. to create a fiscal and monetary environment which in effect makes the dollar as good as gold, i.e. stabilizes the general price level and by inference the dollar price of gold bullion itself.

—**Alan Greenspan, "Can the U.S. Return to a Gold Standard?" 1981**[2]

Whatever its successes, the current monetary policy regime is far from ideal. Each episode has had to be treated as unique or nearly so. It may have been the best we could do at the moment. But we continuously examine alternatives that might better anchor policy, so that it becomes less subject to the abilities of the Federal Open Market Committee to analyze developments and make predictions.

Gold was such an anchor or rule, prior to World War I, but it was first compromised and eventually abandoned because it restrained the type of discretionary monetary and fiscal policies that modern democracies appear to value.

A fixed, or even adaptive, rule on the expansion of the monetary base would anchor the system, but it is hard to envision acceptance for that approach because it also limits economic policy discretion.

—Alan Greenspan, 1997[3]

Would there be any advantage, at this particular stage, in going back to the gold standard? And the answer is: I don't think so, because we're acting as though we were there.

—Alan Greenspan, 2005[4]

The dollar was sliding lower as Greenspan entered office in August 1987, pushed down by the endless jawboning of Treasury Secretary James Baker. That month, it took around $460 to buy an ounce of gold, compared with around $400 per ounce at the signing of the Louvre Accord in February. The dollar had also sagged against the deutsche mark and the yen, contrary to the intent of the Louvre Accord. The Treasury and the Fed were constantly arguing with the German and the Japanese central banks about whether the agreed-upon dollar/yen and dollar/mark rates should be accomplished by supporting the dollar through monetary restraint in the United States, as the Germans and Japanese wished, or by pushing down the mark and yen by way of an easier-money stance, as the United States wanted. Baker was also mesmerized by the growing U.S. current account deficit and succumbed to arguments that the solution to the imaginary problem was a lower dollar.

A falling dollar (i.e., inflation) would have been particularly destructive because of the rise in the capital gains tax, beginning 1987, that was a concession to build Democratic support for the 1986 tax cut. Although income tax brackets had been indexed to the official CPI since 1985, the capital gains tax was not indexed (it still is not), which means that not only must higher taxes be paid on real capital gains, but also on illusionary gains caused by inflation. Memories were still fresh about how this combination had crippled the stock market in the 1970s.

But the Treasury does not conduct monetary policy. The real question was whether the Fed would play along with the Treasury.

The Fed hiked discount rates on September 4, 1987, a cosmetic change but the first such discount rate hike since 1984 and a sign that the Fed was bent on supporting the dollar's value. At an FOMC meeting September 22, Greenspan argued for maintaining the present monetary policy and leaning toward further restraint. Apparently the Fed wasn't going to play ball with Treasury. The stock market rose, and many expected further monetary restraint from the Fed in the future.

In an October 4 interview on ABC-TV's *The Week with David Brinkley*, however, Greenspan hinted that more rate hikes would not be coming. Not only that, many thought Greenspan's performance showed a dangerous streak of wishy-washiness. One analyst said Greenspan sounded more like a Fed watcher (his former occupation) than the head of the Fed itself.[5] Was this a sign that Greenspan would concede to Baker and the Treasury? The DJIA fell 159 points the week after Greenspan's televised interview. Bond yields headed higher. It was the last television interview Greenspan ever gave.

The next week was no better. On Tuesday, October 13, House Ways and Means chairman Dan Rostenkowski announced a measure to eliminate the tax benefits associated with corporate leveraged buyouts and raise taxes on profits made by so-called corporate raiders. The corporate restructuring had been a major engine of wealth creation and a force behind the rising stock market.

On October 15, yields on 10-year Treasury bonds broke above 10 percent. The same day, the dollar fell to $466.60 per ounce of gold, its lowest since February 1983. Markets were preparing for a return to 1970s-style dollar devaluation. Baker said the rise in yields was not consistent with a "fundamentally sound" economy, and blamed the market's "overblown" inflation fears. The Treasury, in other words, was not concerned. On Friday, October 16, the DJIA fell 108.35 points, at the time the largest nominal fall ever. That week, the DJIA fell a total of almost 225 points.

On Sunday, October 18, Baker stepped up his weak-dollar rhetoric and his attacks on the Bundesbank in an interview on NBC's *Meet the Press*. "We will not sit back in this country and watch surplus countries [Germany and Japan] jack up their interest rates and squeeze growth worldwide on the expectation that the United States will somehow follow by raising its interest rates," Baker declaimed. Just that morning, Wall Streeters had read on the front page of the *New York Times* that the Treasury would be willing to see a fall in the dollar against the deutsche mark, contrary to the wishes of the Bundesbank. There was no question—the Treasury wanted the weak dollar to go even weaker and was ready to blow up what was left of the Louvre Accord to do it.[6]

After entering office, Greenspan had also given an interview to *Fortune* magazine.[7] The resulting article's oft-repeated theme was that Greenspan wasn't leaning toward Volcker-style restraint as much as many in the markets believed, and wasn't that concerned about the falling dollar. "He has argued in the recent past that import prices could climb almost 10 percent a year without generating dangerous inflationary pressure," the article said. "Chances are that he will be willing to let the economy grow faster than many observers expect." Greenspan said he expected that the dollar would fall about 3 percent a year against the yen. The article began appearing in mailboxes just before the weekend of October 17–18. Did Greenspan forget about the Louvre Accord? Probably he was just verbalizing some of the many ideas passing through his mind, a harmless enough activity when he had been part of the Council of Economic Advisers. In the wild currency swings of the 1980s, the notion of the dollar falling "3 percent a year" was slightly absurd. But it apparently showed that the trend of Greenspan's thinking had been turned from monetary restraint to acceptance of a weaker dollar. Many billions of dollars are won and lost depending on the activities of the Federal Reserve, and market participants weigh the probabilities of future Fed actions based on the tiniest of comments. The Fed, it appeared, was going to go along with the Treasury. In the past, when the Fed and the Treasury have agreed on a weaker currency, no political force has ever been able to stop them.

Greenspan never gave a media interview again.

Stock markets around the world declined in advance of the opening of the NYSE on Monday, October 19, 1987. The world's first major market to open, the Tokyo Stock Market, started the decline with a 2.5 percent fall in the Nikkei average. London followed suit, down 10 percent at midday, before the opening in New York, with heavy selling of shares of U.S. companies listed in London. Stock index futures, traded in Chicago, opened with heavy selling.

The Dow Jones Industrial Average ended the day down 508 points, or 22.6 percent. The dollar, which had traded at $465.25 per ounce of gold on Friday, gapped down to $481.00 per ounce that Monday. The stock market fell to roughly the levels that had prevailed in late 1986, before the Louvre Accord had been signed.

Baker was flying to Stockholm that day to take a hunting trip with the king of Sweden, but stopped off unannounced in Frankfurt to meet with the German finance minister and the head of the Bundesbank, with whom Baker had been having his very public tiff. The three patched things up somewhat, and later issued a statement that they had agreed to "foster exchange rate stability around current levels." The Louvre Accord was back in play.

Greenspan was left with the question of how the Fed should deal with the market crash. Before the start of trading Tuesday, October 20, he issued a one-line statement: "The Federal Reserve, consistent with its responsibilities as the nation's central bank affirmed today its readiness to serve as a source of liquidity to support the economic and financial system."

None of this was particularly surprising, since this is exactly what the Fed had been created to do—serve as a lender of last resort. In the confusion of October 19 and 20, trading systems became overloaded. Clearinghouses and banks needed more short-term funds to meet their obligations. If a systemwide shortage of short-term funds available to borrow appeared, the Fed agreed to provide whatever additional funds were necessary.

The myth surrounding the Fed's actions that week was that the Fed "flooded the market with liquidity," thus avoiding a catastrophe of the kind that befell the United States and the world in 1929–1930. Actually, the Fed was taking exactly the same role as it did in 1929–1930: as a relatively passive lender of last resort. The myth is fueled by the theory that a quick devaluation of the dollar by the Fed in 1929–1930 would have headed off the ensuing contraction and the Great Depression. To devalue the dollar, of course, the Fed would provide a greater amount of liquidity than was necessary. Devaluationists are always quick to point to 1987 as a justification for their theories and, by extension, a justification for monetary manipulation and floating currencies in general. Didn't the Fed save us from capitalism's inherent instability?

But the dollar wasn't devalued on Tuesday, October 20, 1987. On the contrary, the dollar went up! After its sickening drop to $481.00 per ounce on Monday, the dollar snapped back Tuesday to close London trading at $464.30 per ounce. The dollar rose from 141.83 yen and 1.7777 marks Monday to 143.90 yen and 1.8078 marks Tuesday. The yield on the 30-year Treasury bond plunged to 9.48 percent

The dollar rose when news of Baker's agreement with the Germans hit the media. As Wall Street woke up Tuesday morning, wondering what would happen after Monday's disaster, they were greeted with the *Wall Street Journal*'s October 20, 1987, headline:

DOLLAR SURGES IN LATE TRADING ON REPORT U.S. AND GERMANY RESOLVED DIFFERENCES

Baker and the rest of the G7 spent Tuesday and the rest of the week constantly reassuring markets that they were "cooperating closely," meaning that the Louvre and Plaza accords were still in effect. Baker publicly patched up his relationships with the Germans and Japanese. A weak dollar became a focus of G7 concern for the rest of the year. The DJIA closed up 102.27 points on Tuesday and another 187 points on Wednesday. Long-term bond yields, which had risen to around 10.5 percent early Monday, finished the week at 9.1 percent.

Greenspan and the FOMC tilted back toward monetary restraint. Worries that a weak dollar would cause problems were foremost in FOMC meetings after October 19, and for the rest of the year the Fed decided to keep its monetary policy unchanged rather than concur with demands for a lower Fed funds rate target. Greenspan himself was no longer wishy-washy, but had settled firmly on the side of monetary restraint: He painted nightmare scenarios of a dollar collapse to convince his colleagues who tended toward further Fed easing.

Baker, however, turned out to be unrepentant. Once again he pressured the Fed to ease, and in late November the dollar once again began to sink against the yen, the mark, and gold. Interest rates headed higher. The stock market fell along with the dollar. On December 14, the dollar hit a low of $500 per ounce of gold. The S&P 500 hit a low of 224.45 on December 4, almost exactly the same as the 225.47 level at which it finished on the day of the October crash. The yield on the 30-year Treasury bond peaked at 9.465 percent on December 11. See Figure 12.1.

The weak-dollar problem was not properly resolved until the end of 1987, with another agreement among the G7 worked out over the phone on December 22. Baker agreed to tone down his weak-dollar proselytizing, and instead used the G7 agreement to pressure Congress into reducing its budget deficits and its protectionist pressure—which had been behind Baker's weak-dollar drive in the first place.

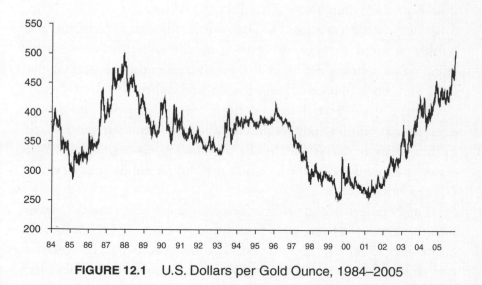

FIGURE 12.1   U.S. Dollars per Gold Ounce, 1984–2005

The markets were understandably skeptical, but gave the agreement greater weight after the G7 governments intervened simultaneously in foreign exchange markets on the first trading day of 1988 to push the dollar higher. Here was action, not just words, in evidence of a new policy direction for the dollar, in the United States and around the world. The dollar climbed through 1988, and the stock market edged higher. The DJIA ended 1988 at 2168.57.

The Fed, now converted to fighting inflation, began tightening in earnest beginning March 30, 1988, and didn't stop until the Fed funds rate neared 10 percent in February of 1989. The dollar headed higher throughout the period, from a low of around $500 per ounce of gold in December 1987 to a high of about $355 per ounce in September 1989. It was in January–February 1989 that the dollar finally rose definitively above its Louvre Accord value of $400 per ounce.

The dollar was helped higher in 1988 and 1989 by the nomination and election of George Bush as president of the United States. Bush promised "no new taxes" and a reduction of the capital gains tax from 28 percent to 15 percent, nearly cutting the tax in half. Even more important, Bush promised to index capital gains for inflation, a move that would have wiped out enormous tax liabilities for homeowners and others with huge illusory long-term gains due to inflation. Indexing would also reduce the risk and consequences of future inflation. As the tax most closely connected with investment and wealth creation, changes in capital gains tax rates can have a large effect on the demand for money. A much smaller capital gains tax cut in 1997 led to a dramatic rise in the dollar's value.

After his presidential victory, Bush quickly presented his capital gains tax cut bill to Congress, and it passed the House. It was favored by a majority of the Senate, but in late 1989 it was turned back by a series of maneuvers ending in a filibuster by Senate Majority Leader George Mitchell.

The National Bureau of Economic Research dates the downturn into the 1990–1991 recession from July 1990, the month Bush officially reneged on his "no new taxes" promise. Still-high Fed interest rate targets did not help, either. The economy sank further with the budget deal between the president and congressional leaders in late September. The final agreement excluded the capital gains tax cut the president had sought and raised the top income tax rate from 28 percent to 31 percent, with complexities that raised the top effective rate further to more than 34 percent. At first it was easy enough to blame the Gulf War for the downturn and the accompanying spike in oil prices. After a few months, however, it became clear that the economy was headed for a more serious period of recession.

The government committed the classic Hoover blunder: raising taxes in the face of recession. And they did it for the same reason Hoover did, to reduce the budget deficit that was supposedly threatening the economy. Yet strangely enough, the deficit mania that had gripped Congress and the Treasury evaporated once Bush had been prodded into reneging on his campaign promises. Few seemed to care that, as the economy sank into recession, a recession made worse by the tax hikes, tax revenues sagged and the deficit increased! The $152 billion deficit of 1989 expanded to $221 billion in 1990, $269 billion in 1991, and $290 billion in 1992—the largest ever. See Figure 12.2.

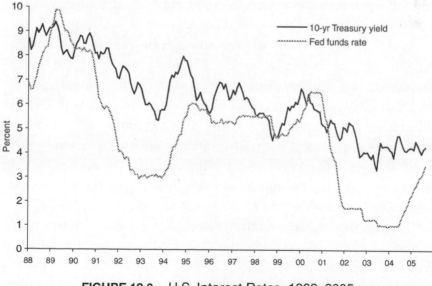

FIGURE 12.2   U.S. Interest Rates, 1988–2005

In no small part the tax hikes and recession of 1990–1991 were caused by the fact that many believed that the Reagan boom, then in its seventh year, could not continue. And by believing it could not continue, they forced it to end. Bush had promised smaller budget deficits in his campaign, by which he meant, like Reagan, restrained government spending combined with pro-growth measures that would increase tax revenues. Reagan had passed on to Bush a budget that projected a deficit of less than $100 billion in 1990, with an assumption of a 3.2 percent real growth rate. But many people, like House Budget Committee Chairman William Grey, considered this projection a fantasy. "[The budget proposal] makes two economic assumptions I've found no support for," Grey said in December 1989. "It says that, after six years of economic growth we'll have another five years of economic growth even higher than the six years we've had, and it calls for interest rates to drop two percentage points below their August level and stay there for the next five years."[8]

Ten-year Treasury yields did drop more than two percentage points below their August 1989 level of 8.20 percent, hitting 5.23 percent in September 1993, and averaged 6.39 percent through the entire decade of the 1990s. The economic expansion that eventually followed the recession, from 1991 to 2001, demonstrated that an 11-year expansion was indeed possible.

If Bush had been able to push through his capital gains cut and hold the line on tax rate increases, as he had promised, these projections could well have become a reality. Instead of recession, the economy would probably have enjoyed a greater boom, just as it did after the smaller capital gains tax cut in 1997, and the boom could have turned the government's accounts unexpectedly into surplus, just as it did following the 1997 capital gains tax cut. The tax cuts would also have supported the dollar, allowing lower long-term yields and making it easier for the Fed to reduce its rate targets drastically.

Instead, the tax hikes reduced Greenspan's ability to lower interest rates further, so although the Fed continued to make gradual reductions in its Fed funds rate target, a cut in December 1990 reduced the target to only 7.0 percent, still rather high. Despite pleas from the Bush administration, the Fed had spent 1990 in an inflation-fighting mode, with short-term rates above 8 percent—levels that leaned toward contraction, even as the tax hikes did the same.

Actually Greenspan, a long-term deficit hawk, had used his position of influence to pressure the Bush administration into the tax hikes, by being unwilling to reduce the Fed's interest rate targets further without evidence of a better-balanced budget, which to Greenspan meant tax hikes. In Greenspan's mind, high long-term interest rates and a weak dollar were caused by budget deficits, and the solution was a high Fed funds rate. (This fallacious line of thinking remains common.) But if the Bush tax cuts had gone through, the dollar would probably have soared so high that the Fed would have been forced into reducing its rate targets, just as Volcker had been forced into easing in 1982.

The Fed continued to lower its rate targets throughout 1991 and 1992, now apparently unconcerned about the large budget deficits caused by the recession. Its last cut in September 1992 left the Fed funds rate target at 3.0 percent. The Bush administration, however, spent 1991 and 1992 whipping the Fed for more. Bush continued to advocate his capital gains tax cut, although somewhat halfheartedly. Treasury Secretary Brady, however, put blame for the recession squarely on the Fed, and consistently spooked the bond markets with his weak-dollar rhetoric and Fed bashing.

Bush had broken his tax promise and had steered the Reagan boom into recession. If Bush had shown some awareness of his mistake, for example by apologizing for his errors and firing his budget director Richard Darman, who had advocated the tax hikes, he might have had a better chance in the 1992 elections.

Bush faced a new kind of Democrat in 1992. After traditional Democratic Party tax-and-spend redistributionists had been easily defeated in 1984 and 1988, the Democratic Party was feeling its way toward a different path. Bill Clinton ran on a platform of "middle-class tax cuts" and a "reinvention of government" that was supposed to leave it leaner and more effective. Also, in contrast to a tradition of easy-money "full-employment" Democrats, including Jimmy Carter, Clinton and his administration were in support of a strong dollar. Clinton, the Democrat, was apparently willing to carry on Reagan's sound currency/tax cut/lean government policy mix, where Bush, the Republican, had been an unrepentant failure.

Greenspan and the Fed naturally got along better with the Clinton administration than with the Bush administration. Greenspan resumed weekly breakfasts with Treasury Secretary Lloyd Bentsen, which Brady had abandoned, and their friendship later expanded to regular games of tennis on the White House courts. Greenspan had good reason to get along with the Clinton team—he wanted to be reappointed—and Clinton had a good reason to get along with Greenspan. He wanted to keep the current 3.0 percent Fed funds rate. Clinton's praise of the Fed was matched, in good-cop/bad-cop fashion, by threats from the Democratic Party in Congress to reduce the Fed's political power and require more transparency if the Fed started raising rates.

Many thought Greenspan got altogether too chummy with Clinton in the early days of the administration. Some suspect that Greenspan took the opportunity to push Clinton toward Greenspan's own brand of deficit-hawk conservatism and struck a deal with Clinton that the Fed would keep rates low if Clinton would do something about the deficit. Greenspan and the Fed denied that such a deal existed. However, at Clinton's first State of the Union address, on February 17, 1993, Clinton ditched the "middle-class tax cut" he had promised during the election only a few months earlier. Instead, he proposed a combination of tax hikes and spending cuts aimed at reducing the federal deficit. Fed watchers nearly fell out of their chairs when they saw, on national television, the supposedly independent Alan Greenspan listening to the president's State of the Union speech from the front row of a gallery box seated between First Lady Hillary Clinton and the wife of the vice president, Tipper Gore. Two days later, in his Humphrey-Hawkins testimony before the Senate Banking Committee, Greenspan read a special three-page statement in praise of Clinton's budget proposals.

Like Eisenhower, Nixon, Reagan, and Bush, Clinton had been corralled by the forces of Washington, in the form of deficit-mania, into turning back on his election promises. The dollar fell in reaction to the tax hike. It had been stable around $330 per ounce of gold in early 1993, but it tumbled below $400 per ounce before stabilizing at around $385 per ounce in 1994. Clinton was soon stumping for a government health insurance system, an old favorite of the Democratic Party, that would have meant a vast expansion of government bureaucracy and influence, not to mention still higher taxes to pay for it. Clinton had embraced the worst excesses of both parties, and his popularity plummeted.

The tax hike was supposed to lead to lower interest rates. The Clinton administration had convinced itself that each $10 billion of deficit reduction would lead to a 0.1 percentage point drop in yields. Greenspan told Clinton that each 1 percent fall in interest rates would lead to $50 billion to $100 billion more economic activity. They had fooled themselves into thinking that higher taxes would lead to more economic growth.

The yield on the 30-year Treasury bond was around 5.80 percent when the tax hike passed in September, with no Republican votes. As the dollar fell in response to the tax hike, bond yields shot up, gaining around 60 basis points by November 1993, when Clinton's boasts of "the lowest interest rates in 20 years" began to ring hollow. The tax hikes never led to lower interest rates: Yields on the 30-year Treasury bond soared above 8 percent in 1994 and didn't return to the 5.80 percent level until 1998, and then only briefly.

Corporations had undertaken a wave of productivity-enhancing restructuring steps whose benefit was beginning to be felt. Clinton had also done some significant tax cutting in the form of the North American Free Trade Agreement, which was approved by Congress in November 1993 and became effective January 1, 1994. The economy had enjoyed one other thing over the previous few years—a more stable dollar. After Greenspan had rescued the dollar from its lows in 1987, boosting its value once again above ¼₀₀ ounce of gold in early 1989, he managed to keep the dollar roughly within its

Plaza-Louvre-accords band. From 1989 to 1997, the dollar fluctuated between $320 and $400 per ounce of gold—still a rather wide range, but a much more stable currency than had been attained under Volcker.

The dollar's stability against gold under Greenspan was no coincidence. As Fed chairman he became known for incorporating an incredible variety of figures and statistics into his choices, but he still regarded the value of the dollar in terms of gold to be the primary indicator of monetary conditions, and said so in testimony.

After Clinton's failure to do anything that resembled his campaign promises, the Republican Party took a majority in Congress in 1994 for the first time since the Eisenhower administration. Speaker of the House Newt Gingrich led the charge, with a policy platform called the "Contract with America," which proposed a number of fixes to the political system. Its most important economic step was a cut in the capital gains tax, with indexing for inflation. It was a revival of Bush's capital gains tax cut plans from a few years earlier. Gingrich played his political cards badly, however, and was stymied for two years.

In the 1996 presidential election, the Republicans nominated Bob Dole, whose policy platform was nearly a blank slate. As something of an afterthought, Jack Kemp, the leader of the pro-growth wing of the Republican Party since the mid-1970s, was nominated as vice president and a small tax-cut program was added to the platform. The tax-cut plan, a mishmash cooked up by political advisers, had been previously criticized by Kemp as unworkable. Tax technicians concluded that the tax cut would create little tax savings and would lead to higher taxes in some cases.

Voters sided with Clinton in the election, but kept the Republican Congress. Gingrich's influence faded, and his combative, confrontational style gave way to a more bipartisan approach. The capital gains tax-cut plan made its way slowly though Congress, and Clinton finally signed the Taxpayer Relief Act in August 1997. The dollar rose modestly in late 1996, but as passage became more likely it rocketed higher in 1997, breaking above $330 per ounce of gold in July

1997, just before the final passage of the act. In addition to the reduction in the official tax rate, the Taxpayer Relief Act contained a number of important capital gains provisions, including the creation of
the Roth IRA, with tax-free withdrawals, a rise in estate tax exemptions, and exemption of home sales from capital gains taxation.

The 1990s are remembered today as a decade of economic boom,
but in 1996 it didn't seem that way. The first half of the decade, 1990
to 1994, consisted of a recession and a slow recovery. In 1995–1996,
it had become fashionable to argue that the economy was capable of
growth of only about 2.5 percent a year. The boom really began in
late 1996 and 1997 with the passage of the tax cut, which allowed the
U.S. economy to grow at a faster rate. It also drove the dollar to
extraordinary new highs, which touched off economic crises around
the world and pushed monetary conditions in the United States into
deflation.

    The move in the dollar from $395 per ounce at the beginning of
1995 to $330 per ounce in July 1997 was dramatic enough—the dol-
lar had not been this high since 1993—but it remained at least within
the Plaza-Louvre-accords band that the economies of the United
States and other countries around the world had become accustomed
to over the previous 15 years. The deflationary effects of the dollar
rise became more intense as the dollar leapt above $300 per ounce in
November 1997. When Volcker had driven the dollar to $300 per
ounce in 1982, countries around the world suffered debt crises and
currency collapse as their dollar pegs broke. Volcker at least turned
back before causing any more damage. The dollar's rise to $300 per
ounce again in early 1985 set off negotiations to tame the strong dollar, which led to the Plaza Accord. (The rise in 1985 didn't cause a
currency crisis, because countries still floated freely from the dollar
after 1982, many of them still in crisis from that year.)

    But Greenspan didn't turn back. Greenspan had always seen gold
as an inflation indicator, not a benchmark of value that could indicate
either inflation or deflation. For him, a lower gold price just meant

less inflation. Indeed, Greenspan, in his writings as a market commentator, indicated that he had been perfectly happy with the deflationary dollar in 1982 and 1985 as well.

The dollar finished 1997 at $290 per ounce, a level it had not seen, except for brief moments, in 18 years. Developing countries everywhere that had pegged to the dollar in the early 1990s and whose corporations borrowed heavily in dollars were in crisis. Over the 1990s, most foreign investment and development had taken place in the Asian countries, and so the disaster was termed the Asia Crisis.

The recessionary effect of the deflation in the United States was muted at first because of the boost from the tax cuts. However, commodities prices tumbled in 1997–1998, and commodities-related industries in the United States such as steelmaking, oil, and agriculture suffered badly, just as they had in 1982 and 1985.

During the period from 1997 to 2000 the U.S. economy bifurcated. On one side were the manufacturing, materials, and industrial sectors that suffered immediately from monetary deflation and the high foreign exchange value of the dollar. On the other were the entrepreneurial and tech-related sectors that benefited from the capital gains tax cut, and were, at least in the short term, relatively immune from the effects of deflation.

Just as inflation is bad for an economy overall but favors some sectors, notably commodity producers, deflation is also bad for an economy overall but can benefit certain sectors, at least for a limited time. This advantage helped fuel what became a mania centering on tech-related businesses and their stocks.

The stock market, as measured by popular market indexes, headed into the stratosphere from 1997 to 2000, but most stocks actually fell, and most businesses stagnated. At the end of 1999, a year the S&P 500 gained 19.5 percent and the Nasdaq composite index 85.6 percent, a full 70 percent of NYSE-listed stocks were lower than they were a year earlier. Official S&P 500 operating earnings peaked in 2000, but the National Income and Profits Accounts corporate profits data series, which is standardized and based on corporate tax returns, shows that profits for U.S. corporations peaked in 1997 and were flat or declining for several years thereafter. However, instead of admitting their mediocre results, corporations engaged in aggressive use of accounting tricks to maintain an illusion of steadily rising profits.

Many have tried to paint the episode of 1999–2000 as an "inflationary bubble" caused by Fed's "money creation," but there is little evidence of such a thing. The idea that Greenspan goosed the economy with easy money (i.e., devalued the dollar) in late 1998, leading to an inflationary bubble in equity prices, is appealing at first sight, but it does not align with the evidence of the time. (The reduction in Fed policy rates was supportive of asset values, however.)

If anything, the Fed should have solved the deflation problem by supplying more money. Monetary deflation slowly caught up with the U.S. economy and contributed to the economic slowdown that revealed the stock valuations of March 2000 to be frightfully overextended.

Greenspan's record was more than a little spotty, certainly far inferior than what could have been accomplished under a gold standard. Bill Martin's record during the Bretton Woods era was much better. Greenspan owed his exalted reputation to the fact that he made little mistakes instead of big ones—or at least the effects of his big mistakes were felt primarily in foreign countries. Greenspan was certainly the most successful of the four Fed governors since the age of floating currencies began in 1971. The citizenry knows that there is no guarantee that the next Fed governors will be as good—in fact it seems unlikely—and was happy to keep Greenspan at the Fed for as long as possible. Better the devil you know, as the saying goes.

Part Three

Currency Crises around the World

CHAPTER 13

JAPAN'S SUCCESS AND FAILURE

Tax Cuts, a Golden Yen, and the Greatest Monetary Deflation in History

A reduction in the tax burden must be continued, with emphasis on direct taxes, especially the personal income tax. However, we cannot reduce taxes without meeting our revenue needs; therefore [it is necessary to produce] an increase in revenue as the result of increased economic activities which are motivated by the tax reduction.

—**Tax System Examination Commission of the Japanese Government, 1954**

The policy of reducing the ratio between the volume of a country's currency and its requirements of purchasing power in the form of money, so as to increase the exchange value of the currency in terms of gold or of commodities, is conveniently called *deflation*.

—**John Maynard Keynes, *A Tract on Monetary Reform*, 1923**[1]

In 1600, after a long period of constant warfare, the warlord Tokugawa Ieyasu defeated all his rivals and united the island nation of Japan under one government. Thus began the Tokugawa era, a time of relative peace and prosperity that lasted until 1868. More than a few Westerners remain enthralled by the exotic medieval society which persisted, anachronistically, up to the middle of the industrial nineteenth century.

Tokugawa declared himself shogun, or generalissimo. Like elites everywhere, the shogun feared change, which confers little advantage to those who are already in positions of power, but instead raises the risk of future downfall. The new shogun set about creating a clockwork system that could continue, without changing, for centuries. The country was closed off to the outside world, cutting off the subversive influence of Christian ideas and technologies imported from the West. Roles in the feudal economy were fixed. Peasants were tied to the land. Merchants and artisans were part of monopolistic guilds, and entry was primarily by birth. Sons of farmers became farmers; sons of merchants became merchants; sons of nobles became nobles.

What money did exist was a hodgepodge of coins and paper bills, which were occasionally debased and whose value drifted according to the needs of state treasuries. Between 1819 and 1837, there were nineteen debasements, as the increasingly financially strapped central government resorted to printing more money for finance. But much of the economy was not monetary at all, and existed at the level of barter. Peasants grew rice, and governments took a 30 to 80 percent share of their harvests, leaving them only a subsistence portion. Merchants were not officially taxed, but over time they were more and more often "asked" to subscribe to "loans" to the government, which bore no expectation of repayment.

Unlike feudal Europe, however, which tended toward a collection of quasi-independent units, Japan was united under a strong central government manned by a large bureaucracy. It thus bore similarities to imperial China, or the ancient Egyptians, or, for that matter, the Soviet Union.

Change could not be stopped completely, and the growing merchant class introduced an element of disruption into the eternal lord-peasant relationships. The central state's finances also steadily worsened, and it gradually became more oppressive in its taxation. But the rate of change was often imperceptible, and the Tokugawa clockwork system may have continued for many more decades if it had not been interrupted, as Ieyasu feared, by outside pressure.

Passing whalers were peeved at Japan's lack of hospitality, but the Western world was willing to let it be until the mid-nineteenth century. In 1852, the United States had just completed its transcontinental railroad and looked forward to trade with China and the rest of Asia, which would take it through Japanese territorial waters. China had been forcibly opened to trade in the Opium War of 1842. In 1853, Commodore Matthew Perry sailed into Tokyo Bay, and with a mere eight warships threw the country and government into turmoil. At literal gunpoint, Perry extracted a free-trade treaty from the Japanese government.

The historical roots of the Meiji Restoration are complex, but the reformers who overthrew the Tokugawa regime in 1868 intended, among other things, to increase Japan's economic and military strength so that it could no longer be threatened at the passing whim of the Western powers. They saw what had happened to China, which was being parceled out among the Europeans. To prevent further Western intrusion, the Japanese leaders knew that they had to emulate the Westerners, especially their capitalist industrial system. "A wealthy nation, a strong army" became their official motto. But how?

In the 1870s the world's great capitalist power was Britain, and the world's great developing economy was the United States. Like the former communist countries in 1991, the new Meiji government faced the challenge of converting its centrally controlled economy to capitalism. Unlike many of the former communist countries, however, the Meiji leaders were wildly successful.

The United States, that odd country that had declared direct taxation unconstitutional, was the textbook example of how an economy could develop rapidly under low taxation. But the U.S. government's dependency on tariffs for revenue was problematic, and had been one cause of the horrifying Civil War only a decade earlier. Besides, Japan's government was already bound by free-trade treaties that limited tariff rates to no more than 5 percent. The British had hammered home the idea of low tariffs, free trade, and broad, simple taxes to generate revenue.

The Meiji leaders (mostly former bureaucrats of the shogun) incorporated both of these principles as they designed the new economic system. The tax on rice harvests, which bit as high as 80 percent in some situations, was abolished. Merchants were no longer asked to give "loans" to the government. Instead, a minimalist taxation system was designed whose centerpiece was a 3 percent tax on land values, instituted in 1873. This single tax provided nearly all the government's revenue for the rest of the nineteenth century. In 1875, a major reform of the tax system was undertaken, in which 1,600 official taxes, the revenues of most of which did not pay the costs of collection, were reduced to 74. In 1879, the property tax accounted for 80 percent of tax revenue, the remainder brought in by a smattering of excise taxes and tariffs.

To implement the property tax, the government had to end hereditary land rights and legalize ownership, sales, and trading of land. The 3 percent tax was not quite as low as it seems—as a rule-of-thumb, land values were at first assessed at 10 times the harvest value, so the 3 percent was 30 percent of the crop. But it did mean that the marginal rate, the tax rate on additional output, was effectively zero, and commercial endeavors weren't taxed at all. Previously, bountiful harvests often invited the heavily indebted governments to demand more taxes—since the peasants could afford it—so the marginal rate approached 100 percent. The tax system was also standardized and made quite a bit less arbitrary. Payment was made in money, rather than in rice or other commodities.

Land tax rates were reduced in 1877. Also, over the following four years agricultural prices nearly doubled, while the assessed value of the land, and thus the land tax payments, remained the same. It was, in effect, a further tax cut.

As a result of the treaties with foreign powers in 1858 and 1866, enacted under military threat, Japan, which had practiced total isolation, became at one stroke one of the most trade-friendly countries in the world. All manner of internal tariffs and restrictions on trade between regions were also abolished. Trade-related industries exploded in scale. In just five years after the opening of trade in 1858, production of raw silk doubled.

The Meiji reformers also undertook major structural changes. Formal social classes, with their regulations of dress and conduct, were abolished. Guilds were disbanded. People were free to choose their trade or occupation. The samurai class, which had become a class of government bureaucrats in the centuries of peace since 1600 and supported by state disbursements, was eventually dissolved and the samurai were forced to enter the productive economy. Primary education was made compulsory.

Japanese people had little experience with large-scale industrial enterprises, so the Meiji government founded a number of state-funded corporations, whose purpose was in part to provide an example of how such organizations were operated. Whatever the educational benefits of the experiment, the state industries suffered chronic losses, and in the 1880s were privatized en masse.

The U.S. and British examples also included a strict gold standard, of course, and the Meiji reformers moved to implement one immediately. The Tokugawa monetary system had been a grab bag of floating regional currencies. Metal coins of various shapes, weights, finenesses, and degrees of wear circulated alongside a menagerie of paper currencies. By one account, there were 1,694 paper monies in circulation, with subcategories that included gold notes, silver notes, copper notes, rice notes, *Eiraku-sen* notes, umbrella notes, string notes, and potter's wheel notes.

They had often been devalued in the face of chronic government fiscal difficulties. A new nationwide currency, the yen, was introduced in 1871 and a gold/silver standard based on the U.S. National Banking System was instituted in 1876, with one yen worth one U.S. dollar. The gold link was almost immediately abandoned, however, as the central government printed banknotes to pay for military expenses to put down the Satsuma Rebellion of 1877. Even so, it was far better to have one floating currency in use across the country than hundreds of floating currencies.

The government undertook a round of deflation, reducing the supply of currency, and reinstated a de facto silver standard in 1882. In 1897, a gold standard replaced the silver standard, at a parity of about two yen to the U.S. dollar.

By 1904, the economy had developed to such an extent that Japan's government, which had cowered before a handful of U.S. warships in the 1850s, shocked the world by defeating Russia, a major European power, in the Russo-Japanese War. This gained Japan much respect among the Europeans, and broad acceptance. (In recognition of a war well fought, the defeated Russian general made a present of his fabulous horse to the general of the Japanese forces, who proudly displayed it in a stable in Tokyo that was nearly as big as his own house.) In less than 40 years since the Meiji Restoration, Japan had become the only non-European country to join the small club of developed economies, a serious player in the great game of empire, a colonizer rather than a colony. A century later, still no other country has this distinction. By the eve of World War I, Japan's empire included the Korean peninsula, Formosa (now Taiwan), and parts of eastern Russia and Mongolia.

Taxes and tariffs rose gently before World War I, but the Japanese governments always took care to keep taxes on production light, instead focusing on consumption taxes, such as a tax on alcoholic beverages, which provided a large portion of government revenue. These were chosen for their intrinsically low and declining marginal rates, which provide fewer disincentives to economic growth. An income tax was instituted as early as 1887, but at a rate of only 3 percent on incomes over ¥30,000 (equivalent to roughly $300,000 today), and even at that it was often evaded. Taxes on business income, interest income, and inheritances were also instituted, but at similar low-single-digit rates. Tariffs rose to the 10 to 15 percent range, at the time among the lowest in the world.

Japan's economy struggled after World War I compared to its earlier successes, but not as badly as those European countries that labored under punitive wartime taxation systems and monetary deflation. Japan's government imitated the European powers and floated the yen from gold in 1916. (Japan was officially at war since 1915, although few battles were actually fought.) Though it floated, the yen remained close to its prewar value. Throughout the 1920s the yen traded 10 to 20 percent below its previous value of around ¥40 per ounce of gold. In 1920, top income tax rates were raised to 36 percent, and an excess-profits tax was instituted, but generally lower rates were given to investment-related income. The economy groaned under the unnecessary taxes, but it managed to expand slowly. Tariffs also rose through the decade. Duties of 100 percent were imposed on 120 luxury items after the disastrous Tokyo earthquake of 1923. In 1926 punitive tariffs were applied to a wide range of goods. In late 1926, the government also attempted to return to the gold standard, and raised the value of the yen from about $0.40 U.S. dollars to about $0.49. Other taxes were also hiked that year, supposedly to further aid the deflation. The unhealthy combination of mild deflation and tax hikes was followed by a financial crisis in 1927, which in Japanese history looms larger than the overseas events of 1929. Another attempt to deflate to the prewar parity and restore the gold standard, in 1930, ultimately failed in the face of the worldwide abandonment of the gold standard in the autumn of 1931.

The increasing military and centralized control of the economy in the 1930s can easily be associated with higher taxation, but, just as was the case in Germany under Hitler and Italy under Mussolini, actually the opposite was the case. A moratorium on new taxes had already been imposed by finance minister Korekiyo Takahashi. Later, to get industrialists to accept central oversight of their operations, the government offered a bouquet of tax reductions. Beginning with the Oil Industry Law of 1934, a series of measures were passed in which businesses were required to obtain government approval for their yearly plans, and in return they received exemption from land taxes, income taxes, and corporate taxes, extra bounties and subsidies, compulsory amortization of plant and equipment, special privileges for debenture flotations, and government compensation for losses. Despite the worldwide economic contraction of the 1930s, most statistics measure more economic expansion in Japan during that decade than during the 1920s.

In World War II, Japan suffered the most complete destruction of physical capital endured by any country in modern history. At the end of the war, enemy bombers flew over Japanese cities unopposed. The major cities were leveled to rubble, with the nuclear detonations at Hiroshima and Nagasaki merely accomplishing in a few minutes what took a day of saturation bombing by conventional means in Tokyo or Osaka.

Some have claimed that this destruction was for some reason to Japan's economic advantage, or that Japan's explosive growth in the decades that followed was somehow foreordained. Immediately after the war, however, it did not appear that way. From 1946 to 1949, the occupation government led by General Douglas MacArthur, the Supreme Commander of the Allied Powers, had near-complete control over economic policy. Staffed by New Dealers, SCAP's policies were disastrous. In the period from 1946 to 1949, income taxes were raised and made more progressive; corporate taxes were pushed higher and excess-profits taxes were imposed that did not allow depreciation allowances to be adjusted for inflation; a heavy levy on wealth was applied; and excise taxes were increased, including the introduction of a VAT tax.

This was bad by any measure, but at the same time the yen, which traded around ¥2 per dollar before the war, was radically devalued in an effort to reduce unemployment. In 1944, about ¥17.7 billion of currency circulated. In 1948, under SCAP oversight, the amount of currency in circulation had expanded to ¥355.3 billion. Hyperinflation wracked the country, and large swaths of the economy went underground to escape the tax collector. At the end of 1939, the yen traded at ¥4.264 per dollar, and at the end of 1946, as SCAP's rule began, the yen was temporarily pegged at ¥15 per dollar. By 1949, under SCAP, the yen's value had fallen to less than 1/300 of a dollar.

In 1947, a mere two trains a day ran on the Tokaido Line, the primary transport connection between Japan's largest cities. The economy was totally moribund. In the midst of economic collapse, SCAP instituted wage and price controls and put a greater number of industries under government control.

This was not quite an accident of SCAP, which had an official policy of crippling Japan's economy so that it could not again become a military threat in Asia. "Economic demilitarization" was the official U.S. term. Japan's industrial development was to be set back to the level of 1926–1930. Steel production was to be capped at 2.5 million tons annually. Japan was ordered to pay war reparations. This took the form of the dismantling of what few industrial facilities remained after the Allied bombing. Aircraft, light metals, and bearing factories were taken apart and shipped overseas. Half of the equipment of shipyards, along with that of electric generating plants, machine tools workshops, and chemical factories were stripped and removed. At the same time, a generation of leading corporate managers and industrialists were "purged" by SCAP, and large business organizations were fractured into ineffectual smaller units.

All of this changed when, in 1948, it became increasingly clear that Chiang Kai-shek's Kuomintang army in China would be defeated by Mao Tse-tung and the communists. U.S. policy toward Japan quickly reversed itself. Japan would rebuild and become an industrial power in Asia to offset the Chinese communist influence. In May 1948, Washington declared that it would allow Japan to attain a level of development of 1930–1934 (but no more). In October of that year, with the Kuomintang near defeat, the U.S. National Security Council passed Resolution 13-2 that declared that the United States would henceforth expedite Japan's economic recovery. In December of 1948, Washington replaced SCAP's hapless Keynesians with a team including Joseph Dodge, a Chicago banker assigned to straighten out Japan's monetary system. The tax system would be put on a more pro-growth track by a group led by Professor Carl Shoup of Columbia University.

Dodge repegged the collapsing yen to the dollar, and thus to gold through the Bretton Woods system, at ¥360 per dollar, or ¥12,600 per ounce of gold. Dodge, an advocate of classical economic principles, also cleared away SCAP's wage and price controls, liberated industry from government control, demolished subsidies, ended U.S. economic aid, and brought the central government's budget into balance. From 1949 to 1965, Japan's government was required by law to balance its budget each year. The budget restriction was intended to eliminate the temptation to print money to pay the government's bills, but it also outlawed the Keynesian deficit-spending measures that helped bring about Japan's economic stagnation 40 years later.

Shoup devised a plan that immediately brought down tax rates and increased exemptions and basic deductions. In Shoup's plan, the top rate would fall from 85 percent to 55 percent. The excess profits tax would be abolished, and corporate taxes would be reduced. Shoup's reforms were submitted to parliament in 1950.

Japan's conservative politicians immediately understood Shoup's pro-growth strategy, and they set about slashing taxes further than Shoup ever intended. Shoup had set the top 55 percent rate to apply at an income of ¥300,000, but by the time his plan was passed by the brand-new parliament, the threshold had been bumped higher, to ¥500,000. The existing VAT tax, which was included in Shoup's proposal, was eliminated.

In June 1950, the Korean War began, with the North Koreans soon backed by the Chinese army. SCAP reacted by becoming even more aggressive at promoting growth in Japan. Japan's heavy industry was encouraged by the United States to provide munitions for the conflict. Business leaders were depurged. Large conglomerates were allowed to reassemble.

The demand for munitions certainly gave a boost to industry while the war lasted, but it was the tax cuts and gold-linked yen that propelled Japan's economy forward for the next two decades. World War I had also caused a great demand for military goods in Japan, but the brief wartime boom was followed by a decade of chronic recession.

Politicians continued to slash away at taxes, but through the surreptitious method of dramatically raising tax brackets and introducing exemptions and deductions rather than by lowering tax rates.

They still had to please the overlords of SCAP, who might not like what the Japanese were doing to the tax system they had been given. In 1951, interest and dividend income were taxed at a separate, lower rate. By 1952, the threshold of the 55 percent tax bracket had been raised to ¥2 million. In 1957, the 55 percent bracket was raised to ¥10 million. In seven years, that tax bracket had been raised to apply to income 33 times higher than in Shoup's original plan. Other tax brackets were similarly raised.

The San Francisco peace treaty of 1951 formalized the end of the war between Japan and the United States. SCAP was gone in 1952. No longer required to please their masters at SCAP, in 1953 the politicians outdid themselves with a barrage of tax reductions. Shoup's wealth tax was eliminated, and his principle of "taxing all income the same" was completely discarded. Like the Meiji reformers, the conservative politicians of the 1950s understood that to achieve their growth ambitions, they had to minimize taxes on investment and capital. Capital gains on equities were completely exempted from taxation. Interest income was taxed at only 10 percent. A lower rate also applied to dividends. A cornucopia of business deductions, exemptions, and rapid depreciations was allowed. The economy began to roar. In 1955, interest income was made completely tax-free. In 1956, over 50 new tax measures to promote economic growth were enacted.

Between 1950 and 1974, Japan's government cut taxes every single year—even, until 1965, while adhering to Dodge's legal requirement to balance the budget. When asked how the tax cuts would be funded, the conservative politicians merely replied that the tax cuts would allow the economy to grow enough to produce more tax revenue. And they were always right. Every year tax revenues increased beyond expectations, and every year it became necessary to pass a supplementary budget of extra spending proposals to keep the budget in balance.

Economic activity exploded. In 1955, the country had gross domestic product of ¥8.369 trillion. It grew to ¥16.009 trillion in 1960, ¥32.866 trillion in 1965, and ¥73.345 trillion in 1970—all in noninflationary gold-linked yen. In 1955, two conservative parties joined to form the Liberal Democratic Party, which consistently favored growth-friendly policies. The LDP was countered by the minority Japan Socialist Party, which tended to favor social policies (such as measures to combat the industrial pollution, which, by the mid-1960s, had become a terrible problem). The political arrangement of a primary pro-growth party, matched with a subsidiary party focused on welfare, is a near-ideal arrangement for any country, and the country thrived under the dual leadership.

U.S. economists criticized the Japanese accomplishments. In 1958, a member of the Shoup commission called the tax cuts "foolhardy from an economic point of view," arguing that they were creating too much growth! Tax rates and tariffs, they argued, had to be kept high to suppress economic growth, or Japan's persistent trade deficit would supposedly reach "currency crisis" proportions. Instead, in the face of U.S. protests, the Japanese government lowered tariffs dramatically beginning in 1960. By 1965, 90 percent of import value was freely imported. Japan began to register its first current account surpluses as it exported capital overseas.

Until 1985, Japan's monetary course had roughly followed that of the United States. Between 1970 and early 1985, the yen had risen from ¥360 per dollar to about ¥240 per dollar, which is to say that Japan suffered a bit less inflation during the 1970s and early 1980s than the United States. During the 1980s and 1990s, the dollar fluctuated broadly around $350 per ounce of gold.

Beginning in late 1985, the yen soared higher in value. Between the Plaza Accord of 1985 and the yen's peak in 2000, the yen nearly tripled its value against gold, from around ¥75,000 per ounce to ¥28,000 per ounce. A rise in a currency's value is, of course, deflation, and this dramatic and prolonged appreciation in currency value produced a dramatic and prolonged era of deflation in Japan. The recessionary effects of monetary deflation were much worsened by the introduction of a new consumption tax and a series of tax hikes that were specifically designed to suppress asset prices. See Figure 13.1.

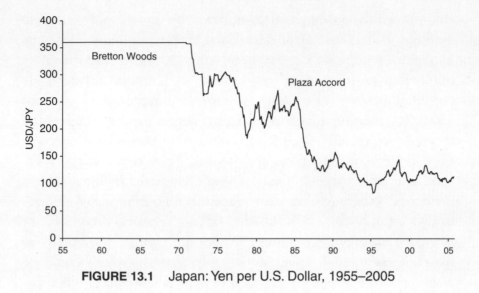

FIGURE 13.1   Japan: Yen per U.S. Dollar, 1955–2005

The first effect of the deflation, oddly enough, was to boost the economy through lower interest rates. In response to the deflation, interest rates dropped dramatically after 1985, which fueled investment, especially in the property sector.

The boom of 1985–1989 was further aided by a series of tax cuts. In 1985, again following Reagan's lead, the Japanese leaders began talking about rolling back their marginal tax rates and reducing land-related taxes. And this time, they promised, there would be no new consumption taxes.

The economy began heating up in 1986 in anticipation of future tax cuts. Like Reagan, the Japanese planned marginal rate cuts phased in over three years, beginning in April 1987. Land prices, which in inflation-adjusted terms had stagnated since the early 1970s, once again began rising as they had throughout the 1950s and 1960s. A generation of young people began to migrate from rural areas to the major cities, driving up rents. Also, the government had instituted new land-use restrictions that prevented the conversion of farmland to residential areas, limiting the supply of new land for development.

The land market remained extremely illiquid, and newcomers

were forced to bid up the prices of the tiny number of properties available. But a handful of deals done at extraordinary prices was enough to revalue land everywhere. After all, higher assessed values resulted in more property tax revenue and greater collateral for corporate lending. The higher value of corporate landholdings was capitalized into the stock market. Corporations had lots of assets and relatively low profits, since Japan's tax system encouraged corporations to accumulate assets rather than declare profits taxable at 50 percent, and double-taxed at rates up to 88 percent if distributed as dividends. Share buybacks were banned. It was far more tax-efficient to reinvest operating profits in assets or new ventures, depreciable or labeled as tax-free "expenditures," with the profits "distributed" to shareholders through rising stock capitalizations, which could be reaped tax-free. Nippon Steel, with its large landholdings, was eventually bought and sold as a real estate investment, the value of its property exceeding the value of its steelmaking operations. As a result, price-earnings ratios reached levels that would be astronomical in other markets.

Commentators in both Japan and the United States began to point out a supposed bubble in asset prices. Real estate–related industries had also acquired a bad reputation, not only because of high rents, but also because, as they chafed against tenancy laws and rent-control restrictions that were extremely favorable to tenants, they employed organized-crime strongmen to encourage long-term renters to evacuate the landlords' properties. The United States didn't like the Japanese real estate industry, either, as a number of high-profile purchases in the United States (typically on extraordinarily good terms for the seller) fueled nationalistic fears about an impending Japanese economic invasion.

Rising land and equity prices had been a fact of life during the high-growth 1950s and 1960s. But as land and equity prices headed higher in the late 1980s, many in government were increasingly convinced that the bubble needed to be suppressed by punitive taxation. These ideas went over especially well at the Ministry of Finance, which had interpreted its role as a tax increaser since 1974.

In 1987, facing U.S. trade restrictions, the Japanese government also began to buckle under pressure from the United States to "increase domestic demand." The U.S. government imagined that if Japanese citizens could be encouraged to save less and spend more, the Japanese would tend to buy more U.S. goods and services rather than U.S. assets, and the trade deficit would shrink.

This translated into a series of new taxes on wealth, capital, and investments, which supposedly made consumption relatively more attractive—the exact opposite of the strategy Japan's leaders had followed since the Meiji era. Japan had become a world economic power by keeping taxes on investment and capital low. But beginning in 1988, it began undoing many of the pro-growth tax measures it took in the early 1950s.

The Ministry of Finance (MoF), still concerned about deficits, had pressured the Liberal Democratic party to raise taxes throughout the 1980s, and in April 1988 finally succeeded in instituting a 20 percent withholding tax on interest income, which had been essentially tax-free since 1955 (70 percent had been tax-free, and the remainder was often evaded). In 1989, a new 26 percent capital gains tax on equities was instituted, the first such tax since 1953, although its bite was reduced by the addition of a lower alternative withholding tax of 1.05 percent of the sale price. A new securities trading tax of 0.3 percent of the sale price was imposed. Also in 1989, Carl Shoup's VAT tax, which had been struck from his original 1950 plan, reappeared in the form of a 3 percent consumption tax. (Few seemed concerned that taxing consumption contradicted the supposed goal of increasing consumption.) Faced with the punitive 1988 U.S. Trade Act, the Japanese government was even persuaded to cripple its own auto industry with a 6 percent tax on new cars. A 2.5 percent surtax on corporate profits followed, plus new taxes on inheritances and money-losing companies.

At the time, the general government was running a budget surplus, which was in no small part due to briskly rising tax revenues and economic expansion fueled by the income tax cuts. Nevertheless, the consumption tax was justified as a way to make up for lost revenue from the income tax cuts.

The public reacted in outright fury. Demonstrations were held against the imposition of the consumption tax. In the month before the new consumption tax was instituted in April 1989, Prime Minister Noboru Takeshita's public approval rating reached 7 percent, the lowest figure ever reported. Soon after, he was removed from office in a scandal. In an Upper House election in 1989, the Liberal Democratic Party lost its majority for the first time in the party's history.

The Bank of Japan (which at the time was overseen by the Ministry of Finance) also became convinced that it had caused the supposed bubble with so-called easy money, although there was no evidence of inflation. The 10-year Japanese government bond yielded less than 5 percent in late 1988. If anything, the economy was showing signs of deflation. The consumer price index went negative in the late 1980s. Indeed, it was negative in 1989, the height of the supposedly inflationary bubble, if the figure is adjusted for the new 3 percent consumption tax. The wholesale price index actually fell between January 1985 and January 1990, from 122.3 to 107.8, which is consistent with the deflationary pressures caused by the rise of the yen after the Plaza Accord. See Figure 13.2.

No matter. The Bank of Japan started tightening anyway. The

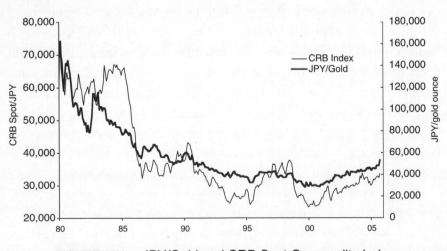

FIGURE 13.2 JPY/Gold and CRB Spot Commodity Index in JPY, 1980–2005

overnight rate went from around 3.45 percent in May 1988 to 8.25 percent in March 1991. The yield curve inverted in July 1989 and stayed that way until April 1992. A policy of yet further rises in the yen's value was a natural corollary, with additional pressure for a higher yen coming from the United States.

Yasushi Mieno replaced Satoshi Sumita as the governor of the Bank of Japan on December 17, 1989, and immediately set about squashing the supposed bubble in asset prices. A week later, on December 25, the "grinch that stole Christmas" shocked the market with an unexpected interest rate hike. Mieno, who thought that rising asset prices had caused social inequalities, publicly declared that he aimed for a 20 percent drop in land prices—and soon upped his goal to a 30 percent drop. He also claimed that the rising yen would help reduce Japan's trade surplus. In 1991 he was voted the Central Banker of the Year by *Euromoney* magazine.

In 1990, as interest rates headed higher, as the yen continued to rise and put more deflationary pressure on the economy, as the government was purposefully blowing up the property sector with huge tax hikes, and as the bite of the new consumption taxes were felt, the Japanese economy finally buckled under the strain.

Beginning January 1, 1990, a week after Mieno's Christmas surprise, the holding period on land required to get favorable capital gains tax treatment was extended from 5 years to 10, and the favorable rates were soon eliminated altogether. The Japanese stock market peaked on the last trading day of 1989, and from the first trading day of 1990 it began a bear market that persisted for more than a decade. Also beginning in January 1990, banks were told that growth in real estate–related lending could not exceed growth in other forms of lending. This choked off funding for land buyers. The effect of the capital gains hike and the lending ban, combined with soaring interest rates and continuing monetary deflation, was to bring land transactions nearly to a halt. Industry insiders knew land values were falling, and the stock market reflected the fact, but because very few land transactions were actually made, official government land price statistics kept their high levels in 1990 and 1991.

The price indexes that apparently refused to fall provided impetus for the government to redouble its efforts to crush the supposed bubble in land prices. Dramatic increases in property taxes and capital gains taxes on land were imposed in 1992.

Property taxes on land had been low in the 1980s. One study found that the effective property tax rate in Tokyo in 1987 was 0.065 percent, compared to rates of 3 to 4 percent in the New York/New Jersey area. Since local governments often gave property owners a break by not revaluing their asset prices for tax purposes, effective tax rates were steadily heading lower. In 1991, plans emerged for a new 0.3 percent national property tax, which was imposed in 1992. That year, the chairman of the government's tax advisory panel said, "The land value tax is very important for dragging down land prices in Tokyo or in other large cities, which are still quite high."

A number of other property-related taxes appear to have been imposed or raised during this period: a city planning tax (property holding tax) of 0.3 percent, a registration and license tax of 5 percent of the sale value of a property, a real estate acquisition tax of 4 percent of the sale value of a property, an office tax of 0.25 percent (holding tax), a special land ownership tax of 1.4 percent (holding tax). The new 3 percent consumption tax also applied to buildings. The effective rate of the basic fixed-assets tax (property holding tax) also increased by leaps and bounds. In 1990, when tax-assessment values were at their peak, the fixed assets tax and city planning tax brought in ¥6.964 trillion of revenue. In 1996, after six years of harrowing declines in property market values, the taxes brought in ¥10.181 trillion. The effective tax hikes continued afterward, and revenues from that tax appear to have peaked in 1999.

Capital gains taxes also soared higher in 1992 as new surtaxes were imposed nationwide, much as they had been levied in central Tokyo beginning in 1988. Capital gains on holdings of less than two years were taxed at a rate of nearly 90 percent, while long-term holdings were taxed at a rate of 60 percent.

U.S. hand-wringing about capital inflows from Japan, which it called the "trade deficit," reached a zenith in 1990 with the signing of the Structural Impediments Initiative by Washington and Tokyo in June of that year. Among the 240 changes that the United States demanded of Japan was a commitment to spend ¥430 trillion yen over the next decade on public works projects. At the time, ¥430 trillion was about equal to the country's annual gross domestic product. In 1995, the agreement was updated to ¥630 trillion of spending in the following 13 years. Despite gargantuan expenditures on public works in the 1990s, which helped drive the government deeply into debt, the total amount spent on public works during the decade never approached these fantastic sums.

The Structural Impediments Initiative was ridiculous by any measure, but bureaucrats, politicians, and construction companies were not exactly opposed, since they, too, saw the opportunity to get a share of the tsunami of spending to which the Japanese government had committed itself. As the economy broke down in 1992 and the Nikkei approached 14,000, the Japanese government began a series of public spending projects to provide stimulus. The public works–centered "machine politics" that had fueled the Japanese political system since the 1960s had already left the country with far more public projects than could be justified by any reasonable standard. Throughout the 1990s, the government embarked on ever-larger public spending schemes, which resulted in increasingly worthless or even outright destructive exercises in hole digging and concrete pouring, a few temporary jobs, and an explosion of government debt.

Another of the 240 items of the Structural Impediments Initiative was the assertion that high land prices constituted a trade barrier, because it was expensive for U.S. companies to buy land to set up businesses in Japan (though no more expensive than for Japanese companies). Japan's government was exhorted to lower its land prices and threatened with horrid Super 301 trade restrictions if it didn't comply with the U.S. government's demands.

The combination of ever-increasing yen deflation and higher asset-related taxes eventually caused even the stout Japanese economy to crumble.

Since 1955, the Liberal Democratic Party had provided the political impetus for growth, while the Japan Socialist Party provided a correction to the LDP's excesses and welfare policies to ensure that all citizens were able to participate in the country's economic advance. That system finally exploded in 1993, as it became all too clear that the LDP had abandoned its pro-growth role. Now, instead of an opposition party of welfare and security, the country needed a new political force for growth.

That took place in 1993, as a pro-growth wing of the LDP, promising dramatic tax cuts, split from the party and allied itself with a coalition of opposition parties increasingly focused on pulling the country out of the deepening recession. In 1993, this coalition took power under the immensely popular Morihiro Hosokawa, the first non-LDP prime minister since 1955.

Hosokawa at first promised tax cuts. However, he was unable to resist the political influence of the Ministry of Finance, which intended to push the consumption tax to double-digit European levels. In a midnight press conference in February 1994, without consulting his political allies, Hosokawa announced that he had changed his policy goals and now favored a rise in the consumption tax to 7 percent from 3 percent. That same month he also unveiled his economic recovery plan, which consisted of another round of public spending. His popularity collapsed, and three months later he was gone from office, ostensibly because of a scandal involving a trucking company.

The Bank of Japan finally backed off its rising-yen policy in 1995, when the yen reached an incredible ¥80 per dollar and ¥32,000 per ounce of gold. The Bank of Japan directly expanded the monetary base through bond-buying operations, and the yen sank to the ¥110 per dollar range and about ¥42,000 per ounce This level was still rather deflationary, as evidenced by price indexes which continued to fall that year, but the economy was reflated enough to allow a weak economic recovery. A small cut in income taxes was also made by means of raising the progressive tax brackets, although rates were not changed. Most of the punitive capital-related taxes that had been passed at the beginning of the decade remained.

The economy recovered just enough, actually, to prompt the Liberal Democratic party to attempt to get the central government's finances in order. The LDP planned to raise the consumption tax to 5 percent, deregulate the financial system and contract government spending. A new opposition party, the Shinshinto, in addition to various reforms, planned to raise the consumption tax to 10 percent. Voters held their noses and pulled the lever for the LDP. In 1997, the consumption tax was raised to 5 percent.

Beginning in 1997, the yen began a new round of deflation. The fundamental cause was a rise in the dollar in the same year, which set off the Asian financial crisis. A falling yen took much of the blame for the crisis, although there was almost zero connection—the yen was actually rising in value at the time, but since the dollar was rising even faster, it appeared that the yen was falling. Nevertheless, the Japanese government was prompted to drive its currency higher, in line with the rising dollar.

Starting in 1998, Japan's government began to hesitantly undo the policy damage it had done in the previous 10 years. Superhigh taxes on capital gains on property were rolled back somewhat, though they remained at high levels. In 1999, there was a reduction in income and corporate tax rates—a fine idea, but not sufficient to pull the economy out of recession while it still struggled with extreme monetary deflation and high asset-related taxes. More attention was gradually paid to monetary problems, and in February 1999, the Bank of Japan finally cut its interest rate target to zero. Even so, the interest rate–targeting system did not adequately supply enough base money to relieve the monetary deflation and drive the yen's value down to more reflationary levels. Indeed, the tax cuts that year may have helped boost the yen higher. The Japanese economy fell into a deep freeze. In 2001, the Bank of Japan was forced to abandon interest rate targeting altogether and adopted a "quantitative easing" framework. Direct adjustment of the monetary base is always the best means to manage a currency. The yen soon began to trend lower, and the system, imperfect as it was, eventually allowed Japan to emerge from its long deflation, with the yen's value in gold terms breaking above its 10- and then 20-year moving averages.

The solution to the problems in Japan during the 1990s was always the correction of the incredibly destructive fiscal and monetary errors committed during the beginning of the decade. Ever since the Meiji era, Japan's economic success had been built on low taxes and stable money. It was crippled in the 1990s by rising taxes (especially on assets), and hideously deflationary monetary conditions. From its nadir of ¥200,000 per ounce in 1980 to ¥28,000 per ounce in 2000, the value of the yen rose by about a factor of 7, probably the most intense and prolonged monetary deflation ever experienced in human history.

Monetary deflation seems to have been solved for now—indeed, there is significant risk of monetary inflation if the reflation is overdone—but there is much that can still be done to restore the Japanese economy to the robust health it enjoyed in the 1960s or 1980s. On the fiscal side, capital gains on equities should be tax-free, just as they had been since 1953. Capital gains tax rates on land should be returned, at a very minimum, to the rates that prevailed in the mid-1980s of around 20 percent for long-term holdings. Better yet, the tax should be eliminated altogether. The revenue from this tax, less than ¥2 trillion a year, is trivial compared to the amount of new wealth that would be created by its elimination. Transaction taxes on property, which can account for over 10 percent of the purchase price, should be eliminated.

Freeing the property market from taxation would have an extraordinary effect in Japan, where property has an exaggerated role in the economy. Roughly 20 percent of the entire economy is directly property-related (real estate and construction), while quite a bit more—such as the steel, concrete, capital goods, retail, services (hotels, golf courses), and building materials sectors—is indirectly related. In the longer run, the economy can only benefit by steps to allow land to be put to its highest productive use and by steps that allow the accumulation and increase of assets and capital rather than their destruction.

Some have estimated that the effective property tax rate has increased by a factor of 10 since the late 1980s. Property taxes should be lowered. Interest income, which was essentially tax-free until 1988, should once again be made tax-free. The double taxation of dividends has always discouraged corporations from declaring taxable profits. Dividends should also be made tax-free on the individual level. Ever since the Meiji era, Japan's economic success has been predicated on low taxation of investment and capital. If it returns to this strategy, it will again thrive.

To return to a semblance of the successful pre-1989 tax system would also require the elimination of the 1989 consumption tax. But this tax, with its low rates and high revenues, is actually a rather efficient tax. It now returns nearly as much revenue as the corporate income tax or the individual income tax on employment income. Instead of eliminating the consumption tax, corporate and individual income tax rates should be reduced dramatically. One simple way to accomplish this would be to eliminate local-level income taxes and give localities a larger share of the revenue from the consumption tax. Doing so would lower Japan's top individual income tax rate to 37 percent from 50 percent and the corporate rate to 30 percent from 40 percent, rates comparable to those in the United Kingdom. As it stands, Japan's corporate tax rates are among the highest in the world.

A more aggressive solution would be to eliminate the corporate income tax altogether, reasoning that the consumption tax is a far better way to raise revenue, and reduce individual income tax rates at both the national and local level with the expectation that a lower income tax will lead to more declared income and stable revenues.

These tax-cutting strategies would no doubt worry those who assume that tax cuts automatically produce a falloff in tax revenues. But tax revenues didn't rise at all during the 1990s, despite the rising tax rates. The central government received ¥49.9 trillion of tax revenue in 2000, less than the ¥50.8 trillion it received in 1988, 12 years earlier, before the consumption and capital gains taxes were introduced. (The consumption tax produced ¥9.9 trillion of revenue in 2000.)

In 2001, as a result of a decade of commitment to an ineffective deficit-spending strategy, Japan's government had debts variously estimated at 120 to 200 percent of gross domestic product. The danger remains that Japan's leaders will try to pay off these debts with higher taxes. Debt-related concerns were behind the rise in the consumption tax in 1997. The result was more recession, exploding deficits, and depressed tax revenues.

The important figure is not the debt itself, but the ratio of debt to gross domestic product. Once again, it is far, far easier to double GDP than it is to try to pay off half the debt with an economy in recession (the result of big tax rate increases), when demands on the government for welfare spending would be higher than ever. Any government that makes growth a priority should have no difficulty doubling nominal GDP within a decade, without inflation. Japan's nominal GDP nearly quintupled during the 1960s, and South Korea's GDP nearly tripled during the 1990s, even with the Asian currency crisis. If Japan's GDP doubled during the decade from 2005 to 2015, and then doubled again in the next decade, the debt/GDP ratio would fall to an easily manageable figure without paying back a single yen. Indeed, this is how the United States solved its own debt problem in the 1950s and 1960s. At the end of World War II, the U.S. government had debts of around 120 percent of GDP. In 1970, after 25 years of moderate growth during which the debt actually increased, the ratio was around 30 percent.

These fiscal steps, combined with monetary steps to relieve the deflation, should return Japan's growth rate to 4 to 6 percent annually. But there's no reason to stop there. Why not go for double-digit expansion? To do so, Japan's leaders should reinvestigate the strategies that produced the explosive growth of the 1960s. One of the most important principles expressed by the leaders of that era was the idea that government tax revenue should be no more than 20 percent of GDP. They stuck to their principles, cutting taxes when necessary (it was necessary every year), and throughout the decade the ratio remained in the high teens. This figure did not include social security–type payments, but even adding those in, during the 1960s, Japan's government accounted for around 22 percent of GDP. Since the private sector is responsible for virtually all growth, one can imagine that 80 percent of the economy that was private was carrying the 20 percent that was public, a ratio of 4:1.

During the three decades since, the ratio has gradually climbed. Today, Japan's government accounts for around 38 percent of GDP. The 60 percent of the economy that is private is carrying the 40 percent that is public, a ratio of 1.5:1. Much of this increase has been due to rapidly expanding payroll taxes. The basic payroll tax rate rose from 6.2 percent in 1970 to 14.3 percent in 2002, and it is already scheduled to march higher yet. These are matched by employers, so the total share of payroll has risen from roughly 11.6 percent in 1970 to 25 percent today. This is much too high a burden. In the United States, payroll taxes account for about 13 percent of the first $65,000 of payroll. Japan's payroll tax applies to the first yen earned, and, unlike in the United States, there are no upper limits—it applies to the last yen earned as well. On top of this tax, the regular income tax applies. Thus the true top income tax rate in Japan is 25 percent (payroll taxes) plus 50 percent (top income tax) of the remaining income, or 62 percent. This is excessive and creates a totally unnecessary impediment to economic and fiscal health—and goes a long way to explain the relatively low revenues from the income tax.

A strategy that aims for double-digit growth in Japan must lower these payroll taxes so that they account for no more than 15 percent of payroll. The 1970 effective payroll tax of 11.6 percent would be a fine goal. Better yet, the payroll tax should be rolled into general income taxes. For maximum growth, top effective income tax rates, including the payroll tax, should be no higher than 25 percent. Corporate income taxes could also be reduced to no more than 20 percent. Better yet, they should be eliminated completely. That would make Japan the most competitive place to do business in the world. After a while, the world's most competitive businesses would be headquartered there.

This may seem radical, but such things are indeed possible. After all, Hong Kong manages to provide all the government services of advanced countries—police, fire protection, parks, a judicial system, primary and secondary education, and a modest welfare system—with a top income tax rate of 17 percent, a corporate tax rate of 16 percent, no payroll taxes (there is a new mandatory private pension account system with a 5 percent rate), and no consumption tax. There are no taxes on capital gains, dividends, interest income, or inheritances. Hong Kong's tax revenue is equivalent to about 15 percent of GDP. Its government has historically run consistent budget surpluses. Bermuda's government gets by with only a tariff. And Japan did rather well, during the Meiji era, with little more than a modest property tax. The flat-tax examples set by Estonia and Russia have been so successful that they have been imitated throughout Eastern Europe, with even Turkey's government, whose debt overhang tops even Japan's, now promising to reduce its corporate tax rate to 20 percent, from 33 percent in 2004. (The Turkish government expects this to create more tax revenue with which to pay off its debt.)

The second part of the solution is monetary stability. While the yen has for now returned to a nondeflationary level of around ¥55,000 per ounce of gold (an estimate of the present "center of gravity"), there is no guarantee that more monetary deflation does not lie ahead—or inflation, if the yen's value continues to decline to ¥70,000 per ounce or beyond—either of which could derail the most worthy tax cut plans just as was the case in the 1970s. The long-term solution, of course, is a gold standard.

Japan's two great periods of economic success, from 1868 to 1914 and from 1950 to 1970, were both eras in which floating currencies were replaced with hard currencies based on gold (or, for a while, silver), and taxation was light to encourage economic activity. If the country wishes to have another great era of wealth creation, it need only repeat this strategy: Peg the yen to gold and reduce taxation barriers to commerce.

CHAPTER 14

THE ASIA CRISIS OF
THE LATE 1990s

Worldwide Currency Turmoil and
Economic Disaster Caused by a
Mismanaged U.S. Dollar

It has been a year since the world was jolted by the September 11 incident [2001 World Trade Center disaster in New York City]. The international community, especially the super powers, has declared an all-out war against terrorism. To them, terrorism is confined merely to physical attacks on countries and their people. In fact their economic onslaught on developing countries which have brought unrest, miseries and the downfall of Governments, is equally violent. In fact, the remedies which they prescribed destroyed these nations. The high interest rates, withdrawal of subsidies and floating the exchange rate further worsened the economy and resulted in instability. Those who benefited were the currency speculators. Indeed, economic terrorists do not differ from other terrorists.

**—Malaysian prime minister Mahathir Mohamad, 2003 budget speech,
September 20, 2002**

The crisis in dollar-pegged economies in 1997 and 1998 was caused by a combination of a rising dollar and flawed pegging mechanisms used by governments of dollar-pegged countries worldwide. The Typhoid Mary in this contagion was the U.S. dollar, which was being mismanaged by the Fed.

The first dollar-pegged currencies to feel the strain were in Asia, particularly Thailand, Indonesia, the Philippines, and Malaysia. Korea

341

was a special case, as we will see, since the Korean won was not directly pegged to the dollar. Brazil and Russia soon suffered the same disaster. Countries whose currencies were pegged to the dollar but who had more stable and secure mechanisms, such as China and the currency board–pegged regions of Hong Kong and Argentina, suffered from dollar deflation, but not the disastrous effects of broken pegs.

The episode was, first and foremost, a currency crisis. This should be rather obvious, and yet even while these economies were still burning down, Western observers immediately tried to place the blame on all manner of nonmonetary factors, whether lack of transparency, crony capitalism, excessive real estate investment, capacity gluts, current-account deficits, computerized trading, misallocation of capital, or a dozen other things. None of these were responsible for the crisis. If currencies had remained sound, the Asian economies would have placidly continued their upward climb, crony capitalism or not. Currency management is the responsibility of the monetary authorities at the Fed and at other central banks.

A rising dollar caused currency and debt crises with dollar-pegged currencies before, notably in 1976 and 1982. The strong-dollar episode of 1985 was less of a problem, since most dollar pegs had been broken three years earlier.

The crisis had its roots, ironically enough, in the period of relative dollar stability between 1991 and 1996, when Greenspan watched gold to keep the dollar's value between $330 and $395 per ounce. The currencies of the developing countries had floated more freely during the turbulent 1980s, when the wild swings in the dollar between $300 and $500 per ounce scared off most attempts at fixed exchange rates. As the dollar stabilized somewhat in the early 1990s, governments of a number of developing countries were emboldened to more closely tie their currencies to the dollar, thus enjoying the benefits of stable exchange rates. The Philippines stabilized the peso in 1992, near 25 pesos per dollar. Indonesia stabilized the rupiah in 1992, near 2,030 per dollar. Malaysia stabilized the ringgit in 1992, at 2.5 per dollar. Brazil, which had suffered from chronic hyperinflation, stabilized the real in 1994 with a crawling peg near 1.0 per dollar. Russia, which also had hyperinflation in the early 1990s, stabilized the ruble near 5 per dollar in 1995. Thailand's peg broke in the strong-dollar event of 1985, and was repegged afterward. Argentina linked to the dollar with a currency board in 1991—like Brazil, ending the hyperinflationary policies of the 1980s. Hong Kong's currency board dates from late 1983, after the previous currency arrangement was blown up in the rising-dollar episode of 1982.

The new regime of currency stability made it possible for capital from the developed countries to flow more easily to the less-developed regions and allowed more stable trade relations and the expansion of export-related industries. A new cycle of wealth creation began. The less-developed regions, with their vast pools of underutilized land, labor, and talent, offered a relatively high return on capital, which was represented by a relatively high rate of interest.

It doesn't matter if a bridge is rickety if nobody travels on it. However, a bridge that nobody travels on is not particularly useful. A bridge that can support the passage of thousands of people is much more useful, but it must be made strong enough to bear the traffic. Thus it is with currency links as well. It is not so difficult to maintain a peg if there are few cross-border interactions. Even the rickety pegs of the developing countries could make do, but only when paired with strict capital controls that choke off cross-border interaction. But high levels of traffic demand a more secure peg, such as a currency board or, ultimately, currency union. In time, many realized that it was the cross-border interaction, in trade but also in capital, that helped create new wealth in the developing countries. More capital holders sought higher returns by investing in the developing countries. Industrialists in the developing countries sought foreign capital to bring their development ideas to fruition. Borrowers and lenders, and buyers and sellers eager to trade, lined up at either end of the bridge. Many leaders and intellectuals called for a reduction in the capital controls that prevented cross-border interaction.

The natural result of these capital flows was expanding current-account deficits in the developing countries as their economies boomed. This was benign in itself, since a current-account deficit is simply the statistical shadow of cross-border investment. Corporations in developing countries were borrowing, directly or indirectly, from lenders in the developed countries, much the same as had the United States throughout the nineteenth century or Japan in the 1950s and 1960s. However, large amounts of cross-border investment means that a greater and greater part of developing countries' economies were exposed to exchange-rate risk. Since most of the loans were denominated in dollars and often of relatively short maturity, the risk was borne by the corporations in the developing countries. Foreign lenders bore the risk indirectly, as default risk.

The problems began in late 1996, as the dollar began to rise in anticipation of a capital gains tax cut in 1997. The effects were immediately felt in Thailand. There were no tax cuts in Thailand, so there was no reason for the baht to appreciate along with the dollar. The Thai central bank began to intervene in currency markets in late 1996, and the Thai stock market sank. The dollar kept rising, however, and by the end of June it had risen all the way back to the upper limit of the Greenspan trading band, at $334 per ounce. Thailand attempted to keep the baht pegged to the rising dollar through sterilized market intervention, but this was ineffectual. As it became more apparent that Thailand's central bank was not managing its currency effectively, the risks of a breaking of the peg increased, which only decreased demand for Thai baht and put more pressure on the peg. On July 2, 1997, running low on foreign reserves, Thailand's central bank ceased its intervention in the market, and the baht began to fall against the dollar. See Figure 14.1.

The dollar made a quick move upward a few days later, jumping from $332.35 per ounce on July 3 to $318.00 per ounce on July 7, two trading days later. This was a definitive break outside the $330 to $400 trading band for the dollar that was maintained through the early 1990s. Indeed, the dollar hadn't climbed to such heights since 1985, 12 years earlier, when it caused the crisis that was resolved by the Plaza Accord. The International Monetary Fund actually congratulated Thailand for abandoning its peg, which probably emboldened other countries that were suffering the same problems to also

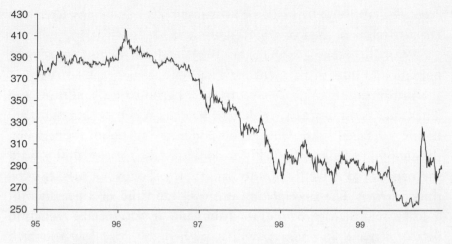

FIGURE 14.1   U.S. Dollar per Gold Ounce, 1995–1999

abandon their pegs (and emboldened speculators to bet on devaluation). The Philippine peso peg broke on July 14. The Malaysian ringgit peg broke the same day, and so did the Indonesian rupiah peg. Not much notice of this was taken at first, and the currencies sank only a little in the days immediately following.

The baht had been pegged at 25 per dollar. At the end of July, a month after the peg broke, the baht was trading around 30 per dollar, a fall of about 20 percent, or roughly equivalent to the amount that the dollar (and baht) had risen over the previous year. If there had been no cross-border trade, the fall in the baht would hardly have been noticeable. If cross-border trade was limited only to exchanges in the spot market such as the buying and selling of goods, excluding long-term contracts such as debt obligations, the fall in the baht would have caused a disruption in market prices, and maybe even a short-term competitive advantage for Thai exporters. The problem was that Thai industries had borrowed a considerable amount of money from overseas lenders, and these debts were denominated in dollars. There is nothing intrinsically wrong with borrowing and lending. The foreign lenders offered lower interest rates than Thai lenders, and the Thai borrowers offered higher interest rates than borrowers in the lenders' own countries. The problem emerges when currency instability alters the effective terms of the loans. See Figure 14.2.

With the breaking of the baht's peg, the dollar-denominated debt burdens and interest payments of Thai borrowers began to rise. On the margin, the weaker Thai borrowers began to go bankrupt, and Thailand's economy as a whole decelerated. When corporations are highly leveraged with debt, as they often are in boom times when they attempt to expand quickly, it does not take a major shift toward the negative to drive them into bankruptcy. The stock market continued lower. The decelerating economy and the disappearance of any apparent management of the baht naturally produced a reduction in the demand for money, which pushed the baht lower, which caused a still-higher debt burden and more bankruptcies. The entire Thai banking system began to creak under the weight of bad loans. Foreign lenders began to see where this was heading and refused to roll over debt obligations, demanding repayment of principal instead. Foreign equity investors dumped Thai stocks.

By the end of August, the same dynamic was taking place in Malaysia, the Philippines, and Indonesia as well. A sinking currency led to increasing debt loads, bankruptcy, capital flight, a collapse of currency demand, and further declines in the currency. By this time it

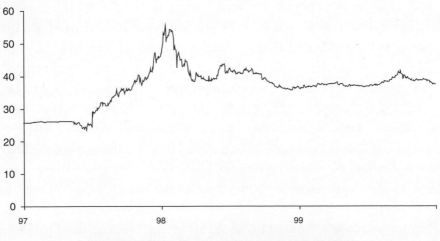

FIGURE 14.2   Thailand: Baht per U.S. Dollar

was becoming apparent that a crisis was brewing. At any time, these countries' central banks could have halted the decline by declaring a policy of currency support and reducing the supply of outstanding currency through central bank open market sales of domestic assets, such as bonds. Unfortunately, they believed the fiction that, with their foreign currency reserves depleted, there was nothing they could do. The supposedly laissez-faire ideology of the time said that countries should abandon their currencies completely and allow their values to be set by the market. The market's opinion, of course, was that a currency that had been thrown to the dogs was not worth very much.

In the 1980s, the Korean won loosely followed the dollar in its ups and downs between $300 and $500 per ounce. In 1990, the currency arrangement was changed, and the won was loosely pegged, apparently, to gold. From January 1990 to May 1993, the won rarely deviated by more than 5 percent on either side of 270,000 won per ounce of gold. In 1993 the apparent peg value moved to around 303,000 won per ounce of gold, and from July 1993 to November 1997, the value of the won again rarely deviated by more than 5 percent on either side of this value. The won/dollar exchange rate varied by a much wider margin during this period. See Figure 14.3.

Yet a band of 5 percent on either side of the peg is an extremely

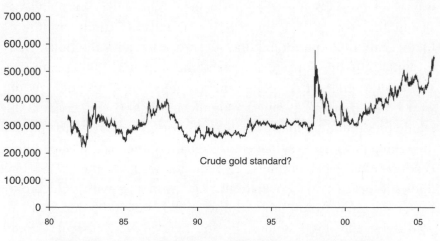

FIGURE 14.3   Korea: Won per Gold Ounce, 1980–2005

messy sort of gold standard. The Korean central bank maintained this peg in the same way that Thailand, the Philippines, and Malaysia maintained their dollar pegs: with a combination of capital controls and crude manipulative techniques. Except for the target of their pegs, Korea followed a course much like the other countries in the early 1990s, with a reduction of capital restrictions and a great expansion in international capital flows, including a large degree of dollar-based borrowing.

As the dollar rose in 1996–1997, the Korean won naturally fell against the dollar. The won began 1996 at 770 per dollar and 298,000 won per ounce. On July 1, 1997, it was trading at 888 per dollar and 297,000 per ounce. This process was drawn out over months, but the effect was the same for Korean corporations that borrowed in dollars as it was for Thai or Indonesian firms. Debt burdens increased, and the heavily debt-leveraged corporations faced cash flow difficulties and bankruptcy. As countries broke their dollar pegs in July 1997, naturally fears of a sinking won/dollar exchange rate intensified, and won-selling pressures increased. The Korean central bank did not have any effective mechanism by which to counteract this selling pressure. The won/gold link was maintained through October and early November, but during this time the dollar made a new surge upward. The dollar ended October at $311 per ounce, and on November 14 was at an eye-popping $301 per ounce. The dollar naturally rose against the won as well, from 910 per dollar at the beginning of October to 1,029 per dollar on November 19, with the dollar trading at $302.70 per ounce that day and the won at 313,000 per ounce, at the outer edge of its long-term trading range with gold. As the won broke the psychologically significant 1,000 won/dollar level, selling pressure intensified. The Korean central bank tried to counter this selling pressure with ineffectual sterilized foreign exchange intervention rather than by aggressively reducing won base money through domestic open-market operations. The won peg with gold broke, and at the end of November, the won was at 343,000 per ounce of gold and steadily losing value. The dollar ended November at $296.80 per ounce of gold, higher than it had been in nearly 20 years. In early

January of 1998, it reached as far as $279 per ounce. From the beginning of 1996 to January 1998, the dollar had risen in value by 50 percent.

There was no easy solution to the rising dollar for those countries pegged to the dollar. To follow the dollar higher meant inducing deflation; to break the peg with the dollar meant risking currency turmoil and bankrupting debtors. To keep the dollar pegs, the solution would have been to undertake open market operations to reduce the supply of currency, and also to offer growth-enhancing tax cuts, mirroring the U.S. capital gains tax cut, which would have increased demand for the currency. The easiest way to push a currency higher is with fiscal, not monetary, steps. Monetary steps alone can prevent a currency from falling, but the amount of supply reduction needed to push a currency quickly higher can put intense pressure on the banking system and in itself is contractionary, which can create a contradictory force. Dollarization was another option.

An alternative solution might have been to repeg the currency (whether baht, rupiah, or peso) around 20 percent lower in value against the dollar and support the new value of the currency with domestic open-market operations—in effect, establishing a currency board. Even better, the currency's peg could have been shifted from the dollar to gold, as Korea may have done in 1990, but unlike in Korea, the gold peg should have been maintained with currency board–like mechanisms. Once again, in either case, positive pro-growth fiscal measures would have helped increase the demand for the currency, thus helping to ensure its stability.

The worst-possible solution would have been to allow the currency to sink with no management whatsoever and in addition to pile on severe contractionary measures such as tax hikes and double-digit short-term interest rate targets. This, in the end, is exactly what the International Monetary Fund (IMF) demanded of these countries, through their humiliating "Letters of Intent," after tempting leaders with big bags of money.

The IMF's first package for Thailand, of $4 billion, was established on August 20, 1997. Its provisions included a reduction in government spending and a series of tax hikes, including a rise in the value-added tax to 10 percent from 7 percent. The purpose of the tax hike and spending restrictions was to turn the government's finances from a deficit of 1.6 percent of GDP in 1996–1997 to a surplus of 1.0 percent. The IMF was, in effect, blaming Thailand's problems on its government deficit. Monetary policy was a hodgepodge of high interest rates and monetarist targets. The "new framework for monetary policy" was intended to be appropriate for the "new managed float of the baht." In November 1997, "additional measures to maintain the public sector surplus at 1 percent of GDP"—tax hikes and spending cuts—were instituted. The baht fell further.

The result was economic disaster. Demonstrations broke out in protest of increased taxes on petroleum products. The Thai leaders soon made a policy U-turn, dragging the reluctant IMF along. On February 24, 1998, a letter of intent was issued that modified the deficit targets to allow a deficit of 2 percent of GDP, larger than the deficit before the crisis. Monetary policy was altered to favor a tight monetary stance aimed at exchange rate stability. On May 26, a letter of intent was issued that focused on a deficit of 3 percent of GDP and lower interest rates. An August 25 letter focused on maintaining deficits of 3 percent of GDP through 1999 and a monetary policy that would continue to aim at stabilizing the exchange rate while keeping interest rates low. On December 1, a letter announced that public-sector deficits would be targeted at 5 percent of GDP. In April 1999, the VAT rate was lowered back to 7 percent from 10 percent. The baht began to recover in February 1998, after Thailand changed its policy toward tax cuts and monetary restraint. At the end of 1998 the baht had been returned with great precision to its 1996 value of around 10,000 baht per ounce of gold. Interest rates plummeted, and in 2001 prevailing baht-denominated interest rates were actually lower than those in the United States.

The idea that Thailand's currency problems were caused by government debts and deficits was absurd. The total debt of the government, $6.8 billion in 1996, was equivalent to about 4.1 percent of GDP. This included about $4.8 billion of foreign debt, while the central bank held $37 billion of foreign reserves. The Thai government could have paid off all its foreign debts with pocket change. So exactly who was being bailed out by the IMF? What, in other words, was all that money for? In the words of Hubert Neiss, the director of the IMF's Asia and Pacific Department at the time:

> The three crisis countries were also caught between a rock and a hard place because of the huge foreign currency debts of their domestic banks and corporations. Full debt service could not be maintained without some debt relief in the shape of loan rollovers and restructuring to allow more time for repayment.
>
> Defaulting on debt service would have forced foreign banks and other creditors to suffer immediate losses. . . .
>
> Each of the three Asian countries receiving billions of dollars in international loans marshaled by the IMF decided to support continued debt servicing while seeking to negotiate debt relief with creditors. The IMF arranged additional official inflows of money to strengthen national reserve positions. It also facilitated debt negotiations with foreign commercial banks to provide the necessary balance of payments relief and some burden sharing by creditors.[1]

In other words, the IMF was bailing out big banks in developed countries on their loans to the Asian private sector. It is a stretch even to say that the IMF covered the losses of the big money-center banks, since, after all, the IMF was making loans, not gifts, to the governments of the developing countries. The loans had to be paid back. The foreign money-center banks were bailed out by the taxpayers of Thailand, Korea, Indonesia, and the Philippines—all while the IMF pressured governments of those countries to bankrupt their own domestic financial institutions and corporations by the dozen. The result is that the large banks of the developed countries saw their competitors vaporized and were able to buy up their assets for a song. In Latin America, this process is nearly complete, after decades of monetary disasters have eliminated virtually all locally owned banking institutions.

The IMF often claimed that it was serving as a lender of last resort, a hideous misappropriation of the term. The IMF is not a central bank. It cannot create base money. Its loans have nothing to do with liquidity-shortage crises.

Much of the money on the line in the Asian currency crisis was Japanese, since the Japanese banks had been aggressive in financing Asian development. In 1997, the Japanese government, which was very critical of the IMF's tax-hike, high interest rate, and devaluation approach to the crisis, proposed to set up an Asian Monetary Fund, with initial financing of $100 billion. (Shouldn't Japanese banks be bailed out, too?) This idea met with intense resistance from the IMF and the U.S. Treasury, and eventually died. For all its claims for open competition, the IMF and the U.S. government tolerate no competition in the realm of international economic advice.

The crisis in Indonesia was almost identical to the one in Thailand. When the Indonesian government gave up trying to keep the rupiah peg at around 2,300 per dollar, the IMF at first cheered the move, saying that a floating exchange rate would "enhance the effectiveness of macroeconomic policies aimed at sustaining high rates of growth with financial stability." The debt-servicing/currency decline combination soon started working on Indonesia just as it had on Thailand, and the IMF was soon pushing loans on Indonesia as well, combined with the usual "conditions." Indonesia had run a budget surplus of 1 percent of GDP over the previous two years, but the economic disaster was causing tax revenues to fall. The IMF, once again, blamed the economic problems on the looming government budget deficit, and recommended tax hikes to maintain the surplus, notably a rise in tobacco, alcohol, and gasoline taxes and an elimination of VAT exemptions. Local subsidies on petroleum products were eliminated, which soon caused rioting in the streets. Short-term interest rate targets were raised to stifling levels in an effort to support the currency. All that it accomplished was to further destroy the capital environment in the country, especially since the Indonesian government was at the same time committed to allowing a floating rupiah. The result of that, of course, was a further decline in the rupiah's value. See Figure 14.4.

After its failure in Thailand, the IMF stuffed its loan–contingency program for Indonesia with every item on the most ardent reformers' wish list. Subsidies on fish meal were to be eliminated. Reforestation funds were to be used exclusively for reforestation programs. The local content program for motor vehicles and dairy products was to be eliminated. Branching restrictions on foreign banks were to be lifted. Export taxes on cork and waste aluminum were to be scrapped. Quotas limiting the sale of livestock were to be abolished. Stumpage fees were to be reviewed and raised. A compulsory 2 percent after–tax contribution to charitable foundations was to be eliminated. And so it went, for page after page.

The point of all this housecleaning was to increase confidence in Indonesia, yet there didn't seem to be any lack of confidence from 1993 to 1996, when Indonesia remained thoroughly "unreformed." Indonesia hadn't had a recession in 20 years. President Suharto had taken over an economy in ruins 32 years earlier and had spent three decades building it into a development success story. Although Suharto and his family and associates also became wealthy in the process, often through their involvement in state-run monopolies,

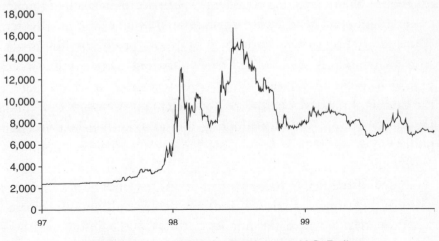

FIGURE 14.4   Indonesia: Rupiah per U.S. Dollar

nevertheless the economic growth directly added to the livelihood of the general populace of Indonesia.

People had confidence, at least, in the stability of the dollar peg. In 1997 and 1998, when Indonesian banks and corporations were going bust in droves and inflation was on the order of 6 to 10 percent per month, when there were riots in the streets in protest of the government's IMF-inspired economic mismanagement, none of these pathetically minor reforms could help the fact that the Indonesian economy was burning to the ground. Rather, it became clear that the IMF's reform program was economic poison. In the week after the announcement of a new IMF program January 15, the rupiah lost another 40 percent of is remaining value.

The IMF had become the avenue by which every do-gooder on the globe could force the Indonesian government to be remade in their vision. Reformers within the Indonesian government itself joined the party, and gleefully added their own pet projects to the IMF's list of loan conditions. Liberals wanted human rights and environmental conditions, and conservatives wanted various free-market reforms, which often amounted to provisions that would make it easier for multinationals to buy up big swaths of the Indonesian economy at fire-sale prices. One of the very first so-called reforms was the elimination of the 49 percent limit on foreign ownership of Indonesian firms. Indeed, it has often been found that countries experience an increase of foreign direct investment after they are impoverished by an economic disaster. The country becomes a source of cheap labor, the cheaper the better. The multinationals are insulated from disastrous monetary and fiscal policies because they take care of their financing and taxpaying in the capitals of the developed world, where the governments would not for a microsecond consider adopting the tax-hike/rate-hike/devalue policies that the IMF recommends for dozens of poorer countries worldwide.

None of the IMF's 100-plus conditions for lending did anything to solve the monetary crisis in Indonesia. Nor did the IMF's loans, which merely provided the financing to allow the Indonesian taxpayer to bail out the foreign lenders. The only thing that did support the rupiah, briefly, was a proposal to institute a Hong Kong–style currency board. The idea came from Steve Hanke, a professor of economics at Johns Hopkins University, who was invited to Jakarta by President Suharto to discuss the plan. When Suharto made promising comments about the plan on February 10, 1998, the rupiah soared to 7,450 per dollar, from 9,500 per dollar the day before. By this time, the Asian leaders understood that currency instability lay at the root of their difficulties and that Hong Kong's currency board had enabled it to maintain its dollar peg throughout the crisis. Once the decision had been made, the peg could have been created in a matter of days, probably around 5,000 or 5,500 rupiah per dollar. Hanke had set up a similar peg for Bulgaria in 1997. The IMF, however, stridently rejected the currency board plan, claiming it would undermine credibility and policymaking. (The IMF was established for the sole purpose of maintaining and strengthening the currency board–like arrangements of the Bretton Woods system.) Suharto came under intense pressure to stick with the IMF's program, to the point of receiving direct phone calls from U.S. president Bill Clinton. Suharto and Hanke eventually proposed to undertake every single item of the IMF's reform plan—plus adding a currency board. It was "IMF-plus." The IMF rejected the offer. Eventually, Suharto buckled under the pressure, gave up his currency board proposal, and sided with the IMF. The rupiah collapsed once again, reaching as low as 15,700 per dollar in June 1998. The result of the currency collapse was skyrocketing prices for basic foodstuffs.

The final unspoken "reform" that was loaded on the IMF's program was the resignation of Suharto himself. Jakarta was rocked by several days of rioting, mostly concerning rises in the prices of basic commodities and petroleum products. All direct results of the IMF's reform program, which demanded an end to subsidies on food and gasoline, stripping away such relief when it was most needed. The day before Suharto's resignation, the International Monetary Fund declared that it would suspend its aid package until "the political situation clarifies." The Indonesian military is reported to have suggested to Suharto at that point that he step down.

It is no coincidence that pro-independence movements in East

Timor escalated soon after the Indonesian economy began to fall to pieces. The East Timorese had been uncomfortable with Indonesian rule since Indonesia forcibly annexed East Timor immediately after the Portuguese withdrew from the colony in 1975. Separatist urges were muted, however, when Jakarta's rule was producing rising living standards across the archipelago. The economic crisis due to currency instability caused these old tensions to flare up anew, and the East Timorese voted for independence from Indonesia in a referendum August 1999. Virtually the first act of the new East Timorese government was to use the U.S. dollar as the regional currency. The remaining rupiah were collected and shipped back to Jakarta. Did the great outpouring of international support for Timor's independence from the Indonesian state have anything to do with the region's enormous natural gas resources? The Indonesian government still faces separatist movements in Acer and Irian Jayah.

A funny thing happened, however, in June 1998. The rupiah stopped falling. Instead, it turned around and rocketed higher. Indonesia's central bank dropped its interest rate targeting, and like Thailand and Korea, began to focus on direct monetary base adjustment. The rupiah hit a low of 16,550 per dollar in June 1998. That month, rupiah base money had grown 74 percent from the year earlier, and the official consumer price index was rising at a 57 percent annual rate. In July of 1999, the rupiah hit a high of 6,685 per dollar, and base money was up only 10 percent on the year. In September 1999, the official CPI had dropped to a 1.25 percent annual rise. In 2002, the Indonesian central bank officially recognized base money adjustment as a primary tool to meet its policy target of currency stability.

The Russian ruble peg with the dollar broke in August 1998 for essentially the same reason as those of the Asian countries—it couldn't keep up with the rising dollar or deal with the worsening sentiment and corresponding decline in ruble demand. The fact that oil prices were also depressed, by both the decline in demand resulting from the Asian collapse and the deflationary effects of the strong dollar, hardly helped. Brazil's and Russia's currency crises were a bit belated in part because

356

both central banks allowed some flexibility in their peg, a crawling peg, which, although such arrangements are typically an excuse for continuous slow-drip devaluation, did manage to remove a bit of the pressure created by the rising dollar.

Unlike the Asian countries, Russia and Brazil had the supposed advantage of getting IMF support well before their currencies collapsed. But, not surprisingly perhaps, it was the IMF's lending conditions themselves that provided the proximate cause for the currency meltdown in both countries. Specifically, in a memorandum issued July 16, 1998, Russia agreed to raise taxes with the goal of "targeting a primary surplus of at least Rub 84 billion, or about 3 percent of GDP." This approach, of attempting to create fiscal surpluses, had already been abandoned by the Asian governments by early 1998 for a combination of direct base money restraint, tax cuts, and fiscal deficits, which produced immediate relief and currency recovery.

The surplus would be created through spending reductions and, of course, tax hikes, specifically making the 20 percent VAT tax applicable to all goods, removing tax exemptions, introducing an additional 5 percent sales tax, increasing land taxes, adding a 3 percent import duty surcharge, increasing gambling taxes, eliminating tax deferrals, and increasing the excise tax on gasoline. Few questioned why a country whose tax revenues amounted to less than 13 percent of GDP needed a 20 percent VAT tax and a 5 percent sales tax, on top of high rates for income, property, and corporate taxes—indeed, whether the high rates themselves were leading to chronic tax evasion and the criminalization of the entire Russian economy, and whether higher tax rates would simply make the situation worse.

To its great credit the Duma, Russia's parliament, rejected the tax hike plans, but the central government pushed through a presidential decree to raise land taxes by a factor of 4. An increase in payroll taxes was also introduced, beginning August 1, 1998. These tax hikes simply added more downward pressure to a currency that was already sagging badly. Russia's central bank attempted to support the currency through high interest rate targets, which choked off commerce and made Russian debt even less attractive.

The investor George Soros again appears in this story. Russia's crude peg with the dollar in 1995 created a semblance of monetary stability, which allowed a bit of economic expansion in Russia. In 1997, Soros made a large investment in Svyazinvest, the Russian state telephone holding company, and faced heavy losses if the Russian economy sank back into monetary chaos. In mid-August 1998, when Russia was at the brink of losing control over its currency Soros made a number of public pleas in Western and Russian media for a one-time currency devaluation of 15 to 25 percent followed by the establishment of a currency board. He also argued for major tax reform.

Soros's long experience with international investing shone through. The prescription was excellent. The devaluation would have readjusted the ruble peg for the rise in the dollar, the currency board would have eliminated future currency risk, and the tax cuts would have both supported the currency and led to future economic expansion. The plan was not adopted, however, in part because of the belief that establishing a currency board would require a large foreign currency reserve, which would likely have to be established by a loan. Such a reserve is not necessary. The central bank need only adjust base money supply in accordance with the currency peg.

As always happens, some insisted that a currency board wouldn't work or that it could not be implemented in Russia, willfully ignoring the fact that Estonia, a former Soviet province, instituted a currency board linked to the deutsche mark (now the euro) in 1993, in the midst of hyperinflation, with great success. A major financial publication argued that a currency board wouldn't work for Russia because currency boards make it impossible for governments to finance budget deficits by printing money. Surely that must be one of the merits of a currency board.

If anything, the idea that Soros wanted a currency devaluation made the situation that much worse (his currency board idea was conveniently forgotten by the Western press). The ruble, which was trading around 6.3 per dollar in early August, began to fall a few days later, and finally stabilized around 29 per dollar, implying an inflation of roughly 400 percent. Soros lost over a billion dollars on his Svyaz-invest position, which he called the worst investment of his professional career.

The disastrous result of the IMF program in Russia set the stage for the rise of Vladimir Putin to the head of the Russian government in August 1999. Citing the example of Germany's Ludwig Erhard, Putin expounded a vision of 7 percent growth rates for decades at a stretch, a radically optimistic view for a country that had spent the previous two decades falling to pieces at an ever-increasing rate. Putin was almost certainly inspired by Estonia's example of a currency board and simplified flat tax. In 2001, the formerly Soviet workers in Estonia were making $500 a month, while Russian workers across the river in Ivangorod were making $50.

Putin zeroed in on the tax code and in 2000 passed a radical 13 percent flat income tax, the lowest in the world. A long list of other taxes were lowered or discarded altogether. The flat tax has the additional advantage of being inflation-proof, since there are no tax brackets to creep up. The tax cutting helped stabilize the ruble at around 29 per dollar. The result: The Russian economy grew 8 percent in 2000, the first year of high growth since the 1960s, and income tax revenues doubled. In 2001, Putin delivered a big cut in corporate taxes as well, with the result that many more corporations came out of the underground economy. The tax cuts helped decriminalize the Russian industrial sector, and as more corporations paid taxes, tax revenues immediately headed higher. A strong ruble policy, replacing what amounted to a de facto crawling (sinking) peg, combined with still more tax cuts, including a big reduction in payroll taxes, put the Russian economy into a boom eerily similar to Germany's in the 1950s. The stock market exploded higher. Perhaps it will be known as the "post–cold war miracle economy."

The contagion of the Asian crisis ended in early 1999, primarily because, after Brazil's peg with the dollar broke in January of that year, there were no more such dollar pegs in the world left to break (China's had survived due to strict capital controls). Brazil's crawling peg, which allowed a depreciation of 7.5 percent per year against the dollar, relieved a bit of the pressure on Brazil's currency, the real, which was caused by the rising dollar. This allowed Brazil to postpone the day of reckoning by a few months.

The Brazilian government's response to the crisis was the same hopeless combination of high interest rate targets and fiscal austerity, including tax hikes. Instead of shrinking the money supply automatically, as a currency board would have done, Brazil's central bank stuck to an interest rate–targeting system, with the target SELIC rate (i.e., the central bank's overnight lending rate) pushed as high as 43 percent in a self-defeating attempt to support the currency. This pushed commercial loans to rates of between 50 and 90 percent, while rates on consumer loans went as high as 150 to 250 percent. Shrinking the base money supply to support the currency, pushing up its fundamental value, would have cost almost nothing; as it was, Brazil lost roughly $40 billion of foreign reserves (which are government assets) in a useless attempt to bully the market into pricing the real at a rate higher than its true value.

In return for a $41.5 billion rescue package, taxes were pushed higher as part of an austerity program imposed by the IMF. The plan was supposed to help the government run a primary fiscal surplus of 2.6 percent of GDP in the face of a deteriorating economy and sagging tax revenues. Nowhere did the question arise: Why did Brazil have to run a surplus so that it could borrow huge amounts of money from the IMF? Borrowing from the IMF is deficit financing, plain and simple. The fact is that Brazil did run a primary fiscal surplus in 1998, of about 1 percent of GDP, but it did nothing to support the currency.

Once again showing the collective wisdom of democratic institutions, the Brazilian Congress resisted many of the tax-hike proposals, particularly an increase in payroll taxes and various financial transaction taxes. Tax rates eventually headed higher, however, stifling the economy and making it difficult for the central bank to support the currency.

A breakthrough came in late 1999, after the central bank president

Francisco Lopes was replaced by Arminio Fraga. (Fraga had worked for Soros as the manager of the Quantum Emerging Markets Growth Fund). In November 1999, Fraga landed on direct liquidity management, not interest rate targeting, as a means to support the deteriorating real. The Asians had supported their currencies through similar means. The real headed higher, so much so that the Brazil's central bank eventually intervened in currency markets to suppress the real's climb. The interest rate target was never abandoned, however. In 2001, as the real began to sink once again, liquidity management was forgotten and the central bank was once again relying on ever-higher interest rate targets, which simply pushed the real lower and lower. Fraga eventually argued that the solution to Brazil's declining currency value was a devaluation.

After the abject failure of the ill-conceived and poorly managed pegs in Asia and the failure of the floating (i.e., sinking) currency regimes that followed, monetary advocates with hard-money leanings tended to favor currency boards (or currency union), which would have indeed enabled these countries to avoid the disasters of 1997–1998. Nevertheless, currency boards do not offer a clear solution, either, when they target another country's floating currency. Hong Kong and Argentina, the largest regions using dollar-pegged currency boards, did not escape the Asian crisis unscathed. Far from it. Nor did China, which did not have a currency board but which managed to keep the renminbi pegged to the dollar because of existence of considerable capital controls and large foreign exchange reserves. When currencies are pegged to other floating currencies, it often deemed necessary to adjust the peg. (In several centuries of experience, however, it has never been necessary to adjust a gold peg.) Of the many haphazard solutions to the problem of the rising dollar, one of the best was from Malaysia, which repegged the ringgit at 3.8 per dollar from 2.5. The end result of this move was to leave the ringgit's value in gold terms almost exactly where it was in 1996.

As the dollar rose, the Hong Kong dollar, Argentine peso, and Chinese renminbi rose alongside it, driving all of these regions into monetary deflation. Official consumer price indexes in both Hong Kong and China underwent outright price declines in 1998 and 1999. This is particularly significant because both regions had previously displayed rises on the order of 5 to 8 percent per year in the official CPI indexes, as a natural consequence of high growth. From 6 percent annual rises to 2 percent annual declines is a swing of a whopping 8 percentage points. Both Hong Kong and China were thrown deep into recession, especially the farmers of China, who faced falling prices for foodstuffs.

Argentina, which also has a commodity-heavy economy, was pitched into recession by the deflation as well, and the government undertook a series of six tax hikes to counter the falling tax revenues resulting from the recession. The combination of monetary deflation and higher taxes caused intense recession, and tax revenues ended up lower after the tax hikes than they were before. The agriculture-dependent Argentine economy was hit particularly hard by falling worldwide prices for soft commodities such as grains, which hit multidecade lows during the deflation. Argentina was perhaps the final victim of the dollar rise that caused the Asian crisis.

As the Argentine government's fiscal situation grew more precarious in 2001, expectations grew that Argentina would abandon the peso's currency board with the dollar. A peso devaluation would amount to a debt default on domestic peso-denominated bonds, and would almost certainly lead to a default on Argentina's external dollar-denominated bonds since the Argentine government tax income, which is paid in pesos, would be insufficient to pay the dollar interest on the debt. For these reasons, the market yield on Argentine debt slowly crept higher, until it was in excess of 14 percent. At those yields it was nearly impossible for the Argentine government to issue new debt. As the yield on government debt reached such levels, the yield on Argentine corporate debt was higher, which put the economy in a deep freeze as financing came to a halt. Unemployment rose to 15 percent and kept climbing. The central government began defaulting on its obligations to state governments, which put state governments in a financial bind. The state governments responded by paying state employees with a secondary currency, the *patacones*, which soon fell in value on the market. Concerns naturally rose that the central government would soon be paying its bills with the printing press as well, implying a radical devaluation of the peso.

The crisis came to a head as depositors in banks demanded their money back in the form of dollars, as was allowed under the mechanism of the currency board. To meet the withdrawals, banks needed to borrow dollars on the money market. Banks, in short, suffered from a liquidity-shortage crisis. The currency board authority is not in the business of making dollar loans or managing money market interest rates. It is not a lender of last resort. This is often cited as a drawback of a currency board, but it is not. Argentine banks would properly borrow on the worldwide dollar money market, which does have a lender of last resort, the Federal Reserve. (Anyone who wanted pesos would bring the dollars to the currency board and get pesos in return.) The problem was that, due to fears that the currency board would soon be abandoned, Argentine banks were considered a bad risk and couldn't borrow dollars. (Perhaps this would have been a good time for the IMF to step in? It didn't.) Many people said the currency board was doomed, although a currency board is inherently foolproof and cannot fail if it is properly followed. The fear, of course, was that it would not be properly followed. Currency boards do have the problem that, when their future is in doubt, conditions can be created that make their abandonment even more likely.

Argentine citizens, who had become very familiar with devaluation during the hyperinflationary 1980s, also saw a devaluation coming and began rampant tax evasion. In a devaluation, it is best to pay taxes as late as possible, since the currency in which the taxes are paid will be worth less in the future. Indeed, paying the late fees on taxes becomes a much better option than paying the taxes themselves. This tax evasion further worsened government finances.

With all of the worries about the future of the currency board, the easiest way to resolve the currency crisis would have been to quickly dollarize the Argentine economy. Throughout the 1990s, dollars had been as much in use in Argentina as pesos, and many large financial transactions and contracts were done entirely in dollars. Indeed the natural operation of the currency board would have led to this result eventually, as sinking confidence in the peso would finally result in the redemption of all pesos for dollars. The problem was not the circulating currency, or base money, but all of the contracts denominated in pesos. The government could have decreed that all peso-denominated contracts would be payable in dollars. The currency board had enough dollar assets to buy up every peso in existence. In the space of a week or two, pesos would simply cease to exist and the currency board would dissolve, having no currency left to manage. Since the peso and the currency board would no longer exist, worries about peso devaluation would quickly dissipate and the interest rate premium charged due to devaluation risk would disappear. The spread on Argentine government bonds would fall to probably around 400 basis points, or a yield of 4 percentage points higher than comparable U.S. Treasury bonds. That would result in enormous savings for the Argentine government, which would find itself in surplus. The government could then go about slashing away at the taxes that had been imposed over the previous five years, firing up the economy, reducing unemployment, and further increasing tax revenue. (This is roughly what happened after the government defaulted, and the economy boomed.)

The fact that the Argentine government did not dollarize—although dollarization had already been successfully adopted at the time by Ecuador and El Salvador—was further proof that the government was thinking about ending the currency board and devaluing the currency, despite its public insistence that it was not.

Because of the widespread use of dollars and dollar-denominated contracts, a transition to a gold standard would have been more problematical, but better in the long run. The first step would have been to declare all dollar contracts to be payable in pesos, thus "pesoizing" the economy. The peso would then have been pegged at some non-deflationary value, probably around 350 pesos per ounce. This would have involved about a 20 percent reduction in peso value from the deflationary conditions that had prevailed in 2001. In time, yields on Argentine government debt would fall, finally arriving in the 3 percent range if the economy and currency were well managed. Given the rather meager abilities of the Argentine leadership at the time, however, dollarization would have been a more foolproof solution and, despite its flaws, probably a better choice.

Instead, the Argentina government declared the pesoization of the economy, imposed a long-term bank holiday, in effect swindling depositors from their claims, and, at the suggestion of the IMF and other such advisers, canceled the currency board. The value of the peso plummeted, and citizens braced themselves for hyperinflation. The government, seeing its tax revenue collapse and unable to issue debt, soon began an official policy of paying its bills with the printing press. Additional excise taxes and restrictions on trade were imposed, yet another drag on the disintegrating economy. With depositors unable to withdraw their deposits, the financial system froze in place, and the economy, what remained of it, moved to an all-cash basis. It was the worst conceivable solution.

The Argentine government finally ceased payment on its debt. Indeed, the government's default was blamed for the entire economic disaster. But a government's relations with its lenders is, in principle at least, independent of the economy and economic policy as a whole. The government could have defaulted and retained the currency board, or defaulted and dollarized. It could have defaulted and cut taxes radically, especially since, when relieved of its interest payments, government accounts were well in surplus. The Argentine government instead decided to take the entire economy down with it, a wholly unnecessary act of spite.

One advantage of disasters is that they clear the way for major policy changes. If Argentina is going to have an independent currency, instead of linking to a major currency like the dollar or euro, it might as well have a great independent currency, such as one linked to gold. If the Argentine government found itself completely without resources, it could do as the fledgling U.S. government did in 1789: Simply declare that gold would be the basis of all monetary transactions and leave the private sector to take care of its monetary affairs, such as the issuance of gold-backed banknotes, on its own.

The second step would be to implement a tax system designed to produce revenue of about 10 to 15 percent of GDP while creating the fewest and lowest barriers to commerce and wealth creation. This could take the form of a 10 percent across-the-board tariff, a 10 percent VAT, and a 2 percent property tax. All income taxes, corporate taxes, payroll taxes, financial transaction taxes, and additional excise taxes would be eliminated. Taxpayers would find these taxes easy to pay and thus not worth avoiding. The tax authorities would find the taxes easy to enforce, since they are simple and few in number. Some years later, a low income tax (such as 15 percent on income over $20,000) could be imposed should it be determined that the citizenry wished to devote a greater share of total production to government services.

Indeed, Argentina's economics minister just before the collapse, Domingo Cavallo, said he wanted a tax system with only two taxes: a VAT and an income tax. What he did, however, was to raise taxes further.

Under such a system, it would not be difficult for the Argentine economy to enjoy double-digit growth rates for several decades. Japan suffered an economic and physical destruction far worse, after the end of World War II, but made a blazing comeback with a tax system that was not nearly as good.

Argentina's collapse threw the economic profession further into doubt. The standard conservative solution (currency boards) was shown to be inherently flawed. Since the Argentine currency board was linked to a floating U.S. dollar, it did not provide a stable currency and instead squeezed the economy with a monetary deflation. The standard liberal solution, the floating currency that followed the currency board's demise, was far worse. Until the proper solution— a gold standard—is rediscovered, governments will tend to oscillate between these two poles, finding in turn that each is worse than the other.

There's little evidence that much was learned by the IMF or the U.S. Treasury from the Asian currency crisis. The same horrible combination of austerity, tax hikes, a monetary policy based on a stratospheric interest rate target, currency neglect, and a raft of pointless reforms continues to be foisted upon those dozens of smaller countries who mistakenly put their faith in the developed world's economic expertise.

Despite all the academic journals published and Ph.D.s issued, a lot of economic policymaking is done by the application of vague and usually fallacious principles whose roots are often centuries old. Certainly one of the oldest and most destructive is the notion that economic problems, and especially monetary problems, are caused by government debts and deficits. This idea, still popular today, was a root cause of the Great Depression of the 1930s and also of much of the pain inflicted during the Asian crisis. The gut reaction of the IMF today is not much different than that of the world's most learned economists in 1931, who were convinced that, in order to support the pound, the British government needed to raise taxes and reduce deficit spending, with the result that the pound was devalued a week later. These experiences led to the conviction of the Keynesians that governments should allow deficit spending in a recession. Governments loved this advice, as it gave them free rein to spend more of taxpayers' money. The proper conclusion of the 1930s should have been not to spend more, but to tax less.

In most cases, there is virtually no relation whatsoever between the central government's debts and currency values or interest rates. If anything, the Asian crisis should serve as a ringing counterexample to this claim, since many of the affected countries had some of the cleanest government accounts in the world, certainly far superior than the developed countries. Thailand and Korea had government debts of less than 10 percent of gross domestic product in 1996.

Malaysia and Indonesia had somewhat larger debts (42 percent and 24 percent, respectively), but their governments ran surpluses in the period from 1993 to 1996. Even the Philippine government, which bore considerable debts, managed to run surpluses from 1994 to 1996. If an economy is growing rapidly and the government is running surpluses, there will be no difficulty in servicing the debt. Even if the principal is not repaid at all and the government continues to run small deficits, the rapidly growing economy will produce a steadily shrinking debt-to-GDP ratio.

The root of the notion that currency values and government debt have some connection is probably the ancient fear of devaluation by governments who wish to pay their bills by using the printing press, or in older times, by debasing the coinage. Even the best governments—the United States in the 1860s, for example—have oppressed their citizens with printing press financing throughout the centuries, but the practice became much rarer during the twentieth century. Sophisticated debt markets allowed governments to finance large spending plans, even full-scale wars, at modest interest rates. Using the printing press to pay the government's bills has been so thoroughly discredited that even the world's sorriest and most corrupt governments shrink from the notion. (Devaluations today are justified by other means.) The Asian governments never for a moment considered the option, nor did they need to since they were in fine financial health.

The second reason for the bizarre and unwholesome fixation on government finances is simply that governments everywhere are rife with waste and corruption. There's nothing wrong with deficits if the money is spent on programs that will produce a return—financial or social—for the country. The problem is that so often governments borrow money simply to waste it again. Complaints about the deficit are really complaints about government waste. There was hardly a peep of protest when the U.S. government ran deficits on the order of 30 percent of GDP to fund the military during World War II, because the military spending was not perceived as waste.

As for the endless reforms foisted on governments such as

Indonesia, despite their good intentions, they often do more harm than good. When an economy is suffering from bad capitalism, the natural reaction is an increase in socialist-type policy, such as an improved welfare system, which is not a bad thing at all in these situations. The effect of further capitalist reforms, such as freeing prices, reducing subsidies, privatizing state-held industries, and so forth, no matter how good they may be in principle, is to make a country even more capitalist at the exact time when capitalism is falling apart. This merely fans the flames of destruction. Certainly it makes no sense at all to sell state assets, such as a privatized industry, at the time when such assets are at their absolute nadir in value. No sense for the seller, anyway, although it is good for the buyer.

The idea of raising interest rates to support a currency is a mangled reflection of the Bank of England's gold pegging system of the nineteenth century. Today the IMF constantly bullies unsuspecting governments into adopting interest rate–targeting systems and rate targets at ridiculous double-digit levels in an attempt to keep currencies from falling. The strategy almost never works, because there is no direct connection between interest rate targets and the base money contraction that would actually help support a currency. The step is usually justified as an attempt to make debt more attractive, although it should be obvious that the most attractive debt in the world, the sovereign debt of the governments of the developed countries, trades at low interest rates. Bond traders will tell you that they look for falling interest rates, not rising. Even if the high interest rates did make some short-term debt more attractive (although buying debt and buying a currency are completely different things), the high rates make virtually every other sort of asset unattractive, from long-term debt to equities to real estate. By choking off financing and investment, the high rates actually tend to reduce the demand for money, causing the currency to fall further. To understand what happens in countries subject to absurdly high interest rate targets, simply imagine what would happen in the United States if the Fed suddenly targeted an overnight Fed funds rate of 25 percent. It's hard to believe that U.S. Treasury bonds would become more attractive. The carnage in the stock market would be spectacular. The dollar would almost certainly fall as a result. See Figure 14.5.

The proper way to support a currency is to first declare the intent to support the currency and then to reduce the supply of currency through open-market operations. This will tend to temporarily push short-term interest rates higher in the immediate term, but the longer-term effect will be lower interest rates as currency risk recedes. In practice, rates tend to fall within about three to five days. In Hong Kong, for example, where the currency board used strict base money adjustment to manage the currency, the Hong Kong Interbank Offered Rate (HIBOR) overnight rate made occasional spikes during the Asian crisis but was generally between 4 and 6 percent—and this was the strongest currency board in the world, while Brazil's real collapsed despite an interest rate target of over 35 percent! As currency risk recedes, the currency becomes more trustworthy and demand for it increases. A currency board such as the one proposed by Steve Hanke in Indonesia would have automatically reduced currency supply to support the rupiah—although in practice, what might have

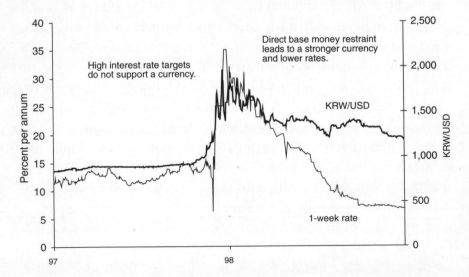

FIGURE 14.5   Korea: Korean Won per U.S. Dollar and One-Week Rate

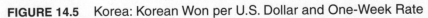

happened (and what indeed happened with just the rumor that a currency board would be instituted) is that the increased confidence created by the currency board would have led to a sharp increase in rupiah demand, so that there would be no need to actually contract the supply of rupiah, and indeed under a currency board the supply might increase! See Figure 14.6.

In the end, Korea, Thailand, and Indonesia supported their currencies in much this way, by first declaring the intent to restore the currency's value and, second, by managing the supply of money directly through a shifting array of monetarist quantity targets. The Bank of Thailand published the baht/gold price daily on its home page, as did the *Bangkok Post*, so it is perhaps no surprise that the baht made a picture-perfect return to the baht/gold levels of 1996. Once again, base money management was a primary tool. Both the Thai baht and the Korean won began to recover their value in January of 1998. Between January 1998 and January 1999, the baht monetary base increased only 1 percent. The won monetary base actually shrank 14 percent during the same time period. Like the Bank of Thailand, the Bank of Korea returned the won with great precision back to its precrisis value of around 305,000 won per ounce, although this level was by that time somewhat deflationary and the won was moved somewhat lower.

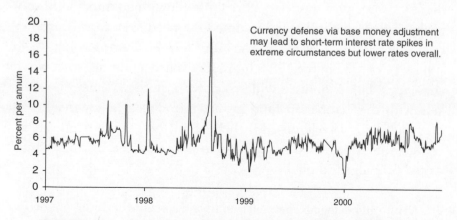

Currency defense via base money adjustment may lead to short-term interest rate spikes in extreme circumstances but lower rates overall.

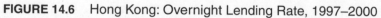

FIGURE 14.6 Hong Kong: Overnight Lending Rate, 1997–2000

One result of the Asian crisis is that the intellectual mainstream has finally begun to grasp the fact that a monetary system can be only hard or soft. It is either subject to explicit rules or subject to discretionary policymaking. Monetary systems that are "fixed but adjustable," that supposedly allow both a fixed exchange rate and discretionary policy twiddling, that attempt to be both hard and soft at the same time, are inherently contradictory and prone to collapse. On one end lies an automatic currency board–like mechanism, pegged to another currency or to gold. On the other end is a floating currency mismanaged by bureaucrats. In between lies a no-man's-land. Unfortunately, the reaction of the intellectual mainstream after the Asian crisis has been to gravitate to the soft-money pole. A floating currency causes a constant, chronic drain on an economy, but at least it is not subject to catastrophic failure. In a sense, it is precollapsed. Floating currencies are not so much a monetary system as they are a lack of a system.

The Asian financial crisis set the stage for an animated public debate between Malaysian prime minister Mahathir Mohamad and the investor George Soros. Mahathir immediately identified currency instability as the root cause of the crisis and blamed the crisis on currency speculators, in particular Soros, who had gained some renown for betting in 1992 that the Bank of England did not know how to properly manage its currency. Soros and Mahathir actually have very much in common. Mahathir was not blaming speculators so much as the environment of monetary chaos that allows speculators like Soros to flourish. Mahathir later proclaimed the need for a world currency to finally eliminate currency instability forever. Soros has long held similar views, and in the 1980s himself unveiled a proposal for a world currency. Mark Mobius, a widely known investor in emerging markets with the Templeton fund group, introduced his own solution in a *Wall Street Journal* op-ed in February 1998, at the depth of the crisis. Mobius proposed a single Asian currency, the "asian," which would be pegged to gold.

A fixed and inalterable monetary standard takes the decisions out of
the hands of political decision-makers—an attractive prospect for

investors concerned about the value of their assets. Gold asian coins would be issued in several denominations; asian paper currency would be exchangeable into gold coins on demand and available at banks throughout the region.

When the U.S. broke the 1944 Bretton Woods pledge to maintain the price of gold at $35 per ounce in 1967, an era of relatively stable exchange rates ended. The results of the "managed floats" and "crawling pegs" have been disastrous.[2]

Perhaps Mahathir and the Malaysian government learned a bit from all of this: In 2004, they were discussing the introduction of a pan-Islamic currency pegged to gold.

CHAPTER 15

RUSSIA, CHINA, MEXICO, AND YUGOSLAVIA

The Communist Gold Standards and Hyperinflationary Collapse

I.

Russia's chronic currency devaluation during the nineteenth century, accompanied by a stunted financial system, was certainly one reason the country did not fully participate in the Industrial Revolution that enriched Western Europe, the United States, and Japan. The State Bank of Russia finally pegged the ruble to gold in 1897, which was followed by a period of substantial economic progress. However, this promising era lasted less than two decades. The peg was abandoned in August 1914, a result of the beginning of World War I. The printing press was soon used to finance the government's war effort, and the ruble was drastically devalued. At the same time, the Russian government instituted fixed prices for many commodities needed for the war effort, in effect raising taxes on citizens as they were paid with a steadily depreciating currency. The combination of fixed prices and a devalued currency proved to be intolerable. Economic output tumbled, and popular resistance steadily increased. When the government fell to the Bolsheviks in November 1917, the ruble's value had fallen by about 7:1 compared to its prewar value.

Monetary policy was in disarray, and more devaluation followed as the Bolsheviks argued among themselves whether to reestablish a sound currency or to move to a moneyless, centrally planned economy. By 1919, a moneyless economy appeared naturally as a result of the collapse of the ruble. The advocates of currency reform eventually prevailed, however. As part of the New Economic Policy of 1921, Vladimir Lenin established the *chevronets*, a gold-linked currency that gradually replaced the devalued currencies then in use. Russia's currency reform mirrored currency reforms taking place elsewhere in Europe—in Germany, for example—and the new currency traded on markets at a fixed value of $0.5146, or about two rubles per dollar. Although quite a bit of economic turmoil lay ahead for Russia, it would nevertheless enjoy another five decades of relatively stable money.

Lenin's New Economic Policy established a system that mixed both capitalist and socialist elements. It was a far more liberal system than what soon followed. As capitalist systems around the world collapsed during the 1930s the Soviet system also lurched sharply toward socialist central planning. Stalin nationalized huge swathes of the Soviet economy. Nevertheless, elements of capitalism, including the use of money, remained. The banking system was combined into a single state bank, which held the savings deposits of citizens and made loans to state-owned enterprises. The system was created and maintained by the use of extremely coercive measures, yet it was still successful enough to give Russia the productive capacity to fight a war against a major industrialized country, Germany, and later to claim superpower status during the cold war standoff with the United States. When Nikita Khrushchev stated that "we will bury you" in 1958, the statement was taken seriously both within and outside of the Soviet Union. Within Russia, support for the Stalinist system remained strong into the 1960s. During the 1950s and 1960s, when much of the capitalist world struggled under extremely high tax rates and an intelligentsia that supported them, especially in the less-developed countries, the Soviet system provided a competitive alternative. Vietnam, after trying the tax-and-devaluation policies suggested by advisers from the Kennedy administration, eventually chose the communist alternative.

Despite the cold war, after World War II Russia managed its monetary system by taking part, unofficially, in the Bretton Woods system. The ruble was loosely pegged to the dollar, which in turn was pegged to gold. During the 1950s the rate was four rubles per dollar. After a monetary reform in 1960, the ruble had an official rate of $1.11 per ruble, or 0.987412 grams of gold. Russia broke its dollar/gold peg in 1971, when the United States went off gold, and instead pegged to a basket of major Western currencies. This proved to be a fatal error, for as the dollar was devalued in 1971, dragging other currencies in tow, the ruble was devalued alongside, with all the attendant inflationary consequences.

The markets of the capitalist countries were able to adjust to the devaluation, but the fixed prices of the Soviet system could not. The Soviet bureaucrats struggled to keep the system working with a floating, devalued currency, but the end result was economic decay even more accelerated than in the West.

The fact that the West enjoyed a relative economic advantage was certainly one reason that the inflation was allowed to persist as long as it did. If Russia had followed Karl Marx's principles and maintained an independently gold-linked ruble while the capitalist countries destroyed themselves with inflation, the outcome of the cold war may have been radically different.

In the 1980s, the economic and military might of the capitalist West managed a recovery, but the Soviet system did not. By the Soviets' own statistics, the economic growth rate fell to the 1 percent range in the 1980s from the 4 percent range in the 1960s. Within the Soviet Union, support for Stalinism crumbled, and in 1985, two years after the Reagan boom began in 1983, Mikhail Gorbachev was made the general secretary of the Communist Party. Gorbachev set about forging friendlier ties with the West and introducing more capitalist elements in the Soviet system, his perestroika reforms—a return, in a sense, to something like Lenin's New Economic Policy.

Although the Soviet pricing system was in tatters, nevertheless the ruble had remained relatively sound throughout the 1980s. The official ruble rate was 0.65 rubles per dollar, and in early 1989 the black market rate was about four rubles per dollar. Unlike Lenin's reforms, which began with a gold-linked currency, the perestroika reforms took place in an environment of currency deterioration. As new markets were slowly liberalized, they sucked talent and productive resources out of the state economy and tended to trade in dollars. The ruble economy shrank, demand for rubles declined, and the ruble's value steadily headed lower. In September 1989, the black market rate was 10 to 15 rubles per dollar. The Soviet system, which had struggled with the inflation of the 1970s, broke down even further as the monetary system deteriorated. There was no central bank per se, but merely a printing press. The government began to finance its enormous deficits with new banknotes, pushing the ruble into hyperinflation. The government's Western advisers said not to worry about the ruble now, but to "liberalize prices"—as if prices had any meaning when the currency was falling to pieces.

The ruble, the Western advisers said, could be fixed sometime in the future, after Russia had made the transition to a market economy. But one reason communism had developed in the first place, in Russia and China, was that market economies break down when they are undermined by unstable currencies and excessive taxes.

As the ruble declined in value, prices in the market economy and the state economy further diverged. In 1989, wages in the state economy averaged 215 rubles per month, a figure still stuck in the 1960s. Wages in the market economy could exceed 4,000 rubles a month. Workers paid at state-level wages could survive because prices of state-produced necessities were also fixed at 1960s levels. The state sold crude oil at three rubles a barrel. The result was that as the ruble's value fell, the stores were stripped bare of goods by workers in the market economy. Coal miners went on strike when there was no soap to be had in their stores. The potential for bribery of government workers, who were paid state wages, was immense.

A group led by Wayne Angell, a governor of the Federal Reserve's policy board, made a trip to Moscow in September 1989 to recommend a gold peg for the ruble. At the time, the Soviets had about $26 billion of gold bullion, more than enough to purchase every ruble in existence at a rate of four rubles per dollar. The Soviet Union was one of the world's foremost gold producers. Angell's group suggested that the ruble should be pegged to gold somewhere between one and three rubles per dollar (350 to 1,050 rubles per ounce of gold), near its official exchange rate, which would minimize the amount of adjustment that would have to take place in prices as they were liberalized. Instead, the currency would be adjusted to match existing prices. Since the Russian people had no debts, but only savings in the state bank, there would be little deflationary pain associated with the move. Instead, Russian citizens would receive a very large windfall, in effect a transfer of wealth from state hands to private hands, which of course was the whole point of the transition from communism to a market economy. Citizens had savings of 350 billion rubles, steadily accumulated through hard work, which would become worthless under hyperinflation. But if the ruble's value were fixed at a generously high rate, the savings would form the seed capital for a new wave of grassroots enterprises. With a gold peg in place, the demand for rubles would skyrocket, and the supply of rubles would not have to be contracted very much, if at all. The Soviet government could then issue long-term debt to its own citizens at 5 to 6 percent annually, the rate at which the fledgling U.S. government issued debt in the early nineteenth century rather than using the printing press to simply print more money. In 1989, the market rate on a one-year gold loan was about 2.0 percent. The presence of ruble-denominated debt would create a political interest group committed to a stable currency to offset the dollar-based exporters who favored devaluation. The Soviet government, which owned virtually everything in 11 time zones, a sixth of the world's land mass, would be able to capitalize its enormous wealth.

It was, needless to say, a proposal of towering ambition and cutting-edge sophistication. In 1920, as European governments discussed reestablishing gold standards broken in World War I, such a proposal would not have been far from the mainstream. In 1989 it was simply bewildering. Many Soviet politicians listened with great interest and inherently understood the argument. It was obvious to them that the economy was on the brink of hyperinflationary collapse. The Soviet economists were baffled that these Westerners—a governor of the Fed, no less—would advocate something they had never read in the Western textbooks. In the end, the Soviets took the advice of the IMF and the Harvard Institute for International Development, preferring the certainty of economic disaster to the unknowns of a gold standard. The idea of a bond payable in gold was too uncomfortable at the time, but as confidence in the ruble imploded, the government was forced down a similar path. By April 1990, only seven months later, the government had issued bonds payable in cars, television sets, and refrigerators.

To their credit, the Western advisers did recommend, intermittently, that the government attempt to slow the hyperinflation by reducing the supply of ruble notes. But the problem was not the supply per se, but the fears that the government was not committed to protecting the ruble's value. This line of thinking led to a decree in January 1991 that ordered all higher-denominated ruble notes to be turned in to the state bank for smaller denominations, but with a maximum of 1,000 rubles per person. Note holdings in excess of 1,000 rubles were rendered worthless. The plan incinerated the value of huge swathes of banknotes (held by people who, quite rightly, had little faith in banks), proof positive that the government was not concerned with maintaining the value of the currency. Why hold rubles when the government was going to declare them worthless? The end result was a lower value of the ruble and more inflation. In August 1991, the ruble traded at 77 per dollar.

If the problem of ruble collapse wasn't enough, the government was also pushed by the Western intelligentsia into attempting to deal with its large deficits through the imposition of new taxes. The Soviet system had no taxes. They were implicit within the centrally planned system. Beginning in 1990, the government essentially imposed a West German tax system upon the already-crumbling economy—failing to observe, apparently, that even West Germany, which had every conceivable advantage, including one of the world's best currencies, had been in effective recession for 20 years. A 50 percent income tax was applied at an income of 1,500 rubles a month— a tax rate that, due to inflationary bracket creep, soon applied to nearly every ruble earned. A VAT of 20 percent, payroll taxes in excess of 40 percent, a corporate tax of 35 percent: The result was simply the criminalization of the market economy, as people found it easier to operate in the black market than to pay taxes. Once companies dropped out of the official economy, there was no need to follow the other rules of the state, and neither was there any protection of contracts and property given by the state. The Russian economy eventually became a vast mafia. Instead of operating on tax revenue, the lower levels of the government operated on bribes.

Hyperinflation was bad enough in Germany in the 1920s and in Latin America in the 1980s, but it was even worse for the Russians. In Latin America, people still owned real property that constituted a store of value in the hyperinflation—real estate, cars, consumer goods, small businesses, equities, foreign bank accounts. The Russians owned nothing but their ruble-denominated bank accounts. Pushed once again by the Western intelligentsia, in December 1991 Boris Yeltsin declared that on January 1, 1992, exchange controls would be lifted and the ruble would float freely on the foreign exchange market. While this seemed to be a step toward liberalization, it was, in effect, an announcement that whatever government apparatuses and policies remained to sustain the value of the ruble and hold together the economy would be wiped away. The government had given up the fight. It would accept the tattered, collapsing ruble and give its blessing. The central bank continued to finance the deficit with the printing press. The tourist ruble rate was floated on December 3, and the ruble's value fell to 100 per dollar from 47. In January 1992 it traded for 180 per dollar. And so it went, down, down, down. At the beginning of 1995 it traded for 4,897 per dollar.

The result of Yeltsin's reforms were that Russia's measured gross domestic product fell 14.5 percent in 1992, compared even with the horribly depressed levels of 1991, and industrial production fell 18 percent. Between 1991 and 1995, GDP fell 35 percent and industrial production fell 46 percent. For comparison, measured U.S. industrial production fell by 46 percent from its peak in 1929 to the nadir in 1932. Russia suffered the equivalent of a Great Depression on top of a Great Depression, on top of the economic weakness it had begun with in the mid-1980s. Yeltsin faced continued opposition to his reforms from politicians inevitably described in Western media as "communist hardliners," who argued that Yeltsin was producing exactly the kind of capitalist disaster that communism had been designed to prevent. In the midst of this maelstrom, the Western advisers prompted Yeltsin to undertake the biggest privatization plan in world history, selling state assets when their market prices were at absolute lows. This enriched a tiny handful of robber barons, who promptly shipped their wealth off to Switzerland.

Prices for many other goods, such as petroleum, were also liberalized, and taxes were raised even further. The ultimate effect was the collapse of the communist economy, which simply fell to pieces. There was no transition to a market economy. No market economy could exist under such conditions of hyperinflation and impossible taxes. What emerged, instead, was a chaos economy. What factories remained in operation began to pay their employees with the products of the factories themselves. In this way, corporate and income taxes were evaded. Workers would receive crates of toilet paper, brake pads, or mattresses, which they would then barter in the informal (and often illegal) marketplace for goods from workers in other factories, thus evading the VAT. Soviet agriculture turned toward its own self-sufficiency. Workers ate what they grew. City dwellers started their own gardens in backyards and on rooftops to ensure a steady supply of calories.

The situation began to improve after a crude dollar peg was established for the ruble in 1995, but that was soon destroyed as a consequence of the dollar rise in 1997–1998.

The result of shock therapy and the disintegration of the Soviet economy was the breakup of the Soviet Union itself. In September of 1991 the three Baltic states were cut loose. In December of 1991, no doubt aware of the disaster that was going to strike in January 1992, the month the ruble had its throat slit, 12 more central Asian states declared themselves independent of Russia. However, their economies had been tightly interlinked with Russia's as part of the Soviet economy, and they continued to share the ruble. Most at first wanted to remain within the general Russian economic sphere, but as Russia's economy and currency imploded, the newly created states began to distance themselves. In 1992, as the ruble became worthless, the newly independent states began issuing their own currencies, with varying degrees of success. Fifteen new currencies appeared. Estonia had the most success, after instituting a deutsche mark–linked currency board in 1993.

Gorbachev long held hope for a kind of Marshall Plan for the Soviet Union, but the Marshall Plan was itself a reaction to the Soviet threat in Europe. The United States had begun to realize, in the summer of 1947, two years after the end of World War II, that a weak Europe would be unable to defend itself against Soviet aggression and indeed might welcome communism as an alternative to the chaos economy—including punishing taxes and hyperinflation—that prevailed in Europe at the time. In 1948–1949, the United States organized a transfer of funds to European governments in an effort to jump-start economic growth. The money itself, as is generally the case with government spending, was actually all but irrelevant; the important thing was the foreign policy decision to encourage high growth in Europe. Around the same time, the same thing happened with regard to U.S. policy toward Japan in response to the communist threat from China.

The United States dispatched the Chicago banker Joseph Dodge to Germany to help reestablish a proper monetary system. (At the time it was apparently clear to U.S. advisers that money served as the foundation of the market economy and therefore took top priority.) Dodge aided the great German finance minister Ludwig Erhard in establishing the deutsche mark in 1948, which was pegged to the dollar and thus, indirectly, to gold. Dodge soon traveled to Japan, where he accomplished a similar trick with the yen.

Erhard also slashed the high tax rates that had driven Germany's economy underground. Beginning in 1948, Erhard discarded price controls and began to tear away tax burdens by the handful, like the Japanese primarily through the increase in tax bracket levels rather than a reduction in nominal tax rates. (Like Japan, Germany was under Allied occupation and Erhard probably wanted his pro-growth reforms to remain rather surreptitious.) Until 1948, the 50 percent income tax bracket was applied to an income equivalent to 2,400 marks, or about $600! In 1948, that bracket was raised to 9,000 marks, and the rate at which the top 95 percent bracket began was raised to 250,000 marks from 60,000. By 1958, the top rate had been reduced to 53 percent and the 50 percent bracket began at an income of 78,420 marks. The fact that the Allied occupation government allowed and encouraged Erhard to undertake these pro-growth steps shows the change that had taken place in U.S. policy toward Germany's economic growth, but it took place before Marshall Plan aid arrived. Germany, whose postwar growth was the most impressive in Europe, received less aid than Great Britain or France.

Before the Marshall Plan, however, the United States had loosely followed the Morgenthau Plan, named after Roosevelt's Treasury secretary during World War II. After defeating Germany, the policy of the United States was to demolish the German economy so that it could never again pose a threat in Europe. This policy had the support of France, which had done the same thing to Germany after World War I through the Treaty of Versailles. The U.S. occupation in Germany followed the same techniques of "economic demilitarization" as the U.S. occupation in Japan immediately after the end of war. Remembering the consequences of the Treaty of Versailles, at the Potsdam Conference the Allies decided that reparations by the Germans would be paid in material rather than financial form. Remaining German productive assets, factories, and capital goods were dismantled and shipped to France and Russia.

Morgenthau and his followers believed that the Versailles treaty had been too lenient. It had, after all, allowed the Germans to rebuild enough to again pose a threat in Europe. That the Germans would want revenge was assumed; the question was only whether the Allies would allow them the economic strength to achieve it. The Joint Chiefs of Staff Directive 1067, drafted April 26, 1945, invested General Dwight D. Eisenhower with the duty "to take no steps toward the economic rehabilitation of Germany [or such] that would tend to support basic living conditions in Germany on a higher ground than that existing in any one of the neighboring states." What this meant, in practice, was to keep the stifling tax rates and hyperinflation that had been left in the wake of the war. The Russians and the Americans, allies in the war, would cooperate to keep Germany thoroughly subdued.[1]

Morgenthau outlined his vision in a secret memo to Roosevelt in 1944, later printed in Morgenthau's book *Germany Is Our Problem*, published in 1945:

Demilitarization of Germany: It should be the aim of the Allied Forces to accomplish the complete demilitarization of Germany in the shortest possible period of time after surrender. This means completely disarm the German Army and people (including the removal or destruction of all war material), the total destruction of the whole German armament industry, and the removal or destruction of other key industries which are basic to military strength. . . .

The Ruhr Area: Here lies the heart of German industrial power. This area should not only be stripped of all presently existing industries but so weakened and controlled that it can not in the foreseeable future become an industrial area. The following steps will accomplish this:

(a) Within a short period, if possible not longer than 6 months after the cessation of hostilities, all industrial plants and equipment not destroyed by military action shall be completely dismantled and transported to Allied Nations as restitution. All equipment shall be removed from the mines and the mines closed.

(b) The area should be made an international zone to be governed by an international security organization to be established by the United Nations. In governing the area the international organization should be guided by policies designed to further the above stated objective.[2]

For reparations, not only did Morgenthau recommend the stripping of industrial assets, he recommended the transfer of German territory to invaded countries and "forced German labor outside Germany."

"The German people are not going to be enslaved," President Roosevelt reassured readers in a preface to the book, "because the United Nations does not traffic in human slavery."

That there was no Marshall Plan for Russia should not have been a surprise to the Russians. With the communist threat gone, there was no need for one. Throughout the twentieth century, the first instinct of the victors had always been to crush the defeated. There was no formal enunciation of this decision, no published Morgenthau Plan, no Directive 1067. But each element in the U.S. and world political system played its part in the unnamed project. When George Soros suggested a Marshall Plan for Russia in an East-West conference in Potsdam in 1989, he was openly laughed at, with the guffaws, Soros reports, led by Margaret Thatcher's deputy minister for foreign affairs William Waldegrave.[3] The economists had no shortage of terrible ideas to sell overseas. The political parties were unanimous in their opinion that the Russian economy would bounce to life if only more reforms were undertaken. The U.S. Treasury and the IMF gave their blessings. The U.S. media parroted the establishment opinion, as it always does.

Indeed, nobody seemed to get hurt in the exercise except for the Russian people. The Soviet Union had splintered. The Russian economy was reduced to rubble. It was proclaimed a great victory for democracy and capitalism, and in a sense it was, for the democratic capitalist states that had fought the Soviet Union in the cold war. Yeltsin, the agent who pushed through this destruction, the man who blew up the Russian parliament with tanks in 1993, is still hailed as a champion of democracy, while Vladimir Putin, who won the 2000 elections with a whopping 21-point lead and has since produced the most economic growth that Russia has seen in several decades, is typically portrayed in Western media as a murky threat. (The Western favorite in the 2000 elections, the Yeltsin-like "liberal reformer" Grigori Yavlinsky, won 6 percent of the vote.)

The Russians placed great faith in the goodness of human nature. They thought they were enjoying the best the West had to offer, as the West insisted was the case. They assumed that Jeffrey Sachs of the Harvard Institute for International Development and the other Western economists stomping around Moscow in those days were the modern-day equivalent of Joseph Dodge. The Russians should have known better, especially after the so-called reforms they undertook always seemed to make the problems worse. Economic warfare has always been an adjunct to physical warfare. When the United States waged war with Iraq in 1990–1991 and Afghanistan in 2001, it attempted to destabilize those countries' economies with hyperinflationary counterfeit currencies.[4]

II.

In the 1930s, China was the only major country remaining on a silver standard. Metallic coinage and raw bullion had served as money since paper currencies were abandoned during the Ming dynasty. This presented a problem after the 1870s, as silver lost its monetary qualities worldwide and fell in value. The 16:1 ratio of silver to gold that prevailed during most of the nineteenth century rose to as high as 76:1 in 1933, a decline in the relative value of silver of about 5:1. However, this process was spread over six decades and did not cause major disruptions for the Chinese economy. In 1935, the U.S. government actively bought silver in a program to support silver prices and help the U.S. silver industry. (The silver industry had been seeking concessions from the Democratic Party since the 1870s.) The silver-to-gold ratio spiked up to 54:1, and as the U.S. government purchased silver at artificial prices, silver flowed out of China, leaving the country in deflation.

In 1935 the Nationalist government in China organized an issuance of banknotes, thus reducing China's reliance on metallic silver. The notes traded at a stable rate of about four yuan per dollar in 1935–1936. In effect, the notes were linked to gold. In 1937, the invasion of China by the Japanese military led the Nationalist Kuomintang government to print unredeemable banknotes to finance defense expenditures. After 500 years of using metallic money, it took only two years after the introduction of paper money for the government to begin devaluing it. The yuan steadily weakened, although the pace of decline was not dramatic at first. In 1944, after seven years of devaluation, the free market rate of the yuan had risen to about 100 yuan per dollar, and by the end of 1947, 10,000 per dollar; in May 1949, the yuan traded at 1 trillion per dollar. At that time, banknotes were being burned in furnaces for heat. The Nationalist government lost all popular support and that month fell to Mao Tsetung and the communists.

It did not particularly help the Nationalists that top corporate tax rates were raised from 10 percent to 25 percent between 1936 and 1946, or that top income tax rates rose from 20 percent to 30 percent while rampant bracket creep pushed lower-income earners into the top brackets. To win the support of the populace, which Mao's guerrilla army needed for military victory, Mao promised to reduce taxes.

The Nationalists fled to Taiwan, which had been insulated from the mainland hyperinflation because it was under Japanese rule during the war and had an independent currency afterward.

In 1950, Mao organized a monetary reform, and the yuan was pegged to gold via a peg to the dollar. The hyperinflation problem was immediately solved. During the 1950s and 1960s, the yuan traded close to 2.4 yuan per dollar. Like the Soviet Union, China followed the rest of the world into inflation in the 1970s, but Chinese leaders decided to switch to a market economy a decade earlier than the Soviets, and on their own terms rather than those of the IMF or other Western intellectuals. In 1978, Deng Xiaoping began the step-by-step market reforms that, over the following two decades, led to the near-complete conversion of the centrally controlled Chinese economy to market capitalism. As the restrictions of the communist economy were lifted, the economy boomed. In 1979 the "Special Economic Zones," offering rock-bottom tax rates, were established in populous coastal areas. Between 1978 and 1990, gross domestic product increased at an average rate of over 9 percent a year—exactly as it should for an economy enjoying the newfound advantages of the capitalist system. The yuan maintained its value relatively well during the decade and was closely linked to the dollar after the liberalization of foreign exchange in 1985. The yuan lost some value against the dollar during the first half of the 1980s, before it was fixed at 3.7 per dollar beginning in July 1986. To move from 2.4 per dollar in 1950 to 3.7 per dollar in 1986 is, by developing economy standards, an excellent record of monetary stability. The British pound did worse over the same period.

By 1988, China had enjoyed a decade of success with its conversion from centrally planned communism to market capitalism, made possible by a currency that was reasonably, if not perfectly, sound. One of the reasons the Chinese had adopted communism in the first place was because the market economy cannot function with a collapsing unit of account. Why didn't the Soviets or other communist countries follow the Chinese example in 1989? It is a measure of the great faith placed in the advice from Western advisers that they instead chose shock therapy, with its galloping tax hikes and hyperinflation, rather than the gradualist approach of China. China's government received the same shock therapy advice from the West, but it was dismissed. In the early 1990s, while what remained of the Soviet economy was crumbling into a collection of fiefdoms controlled by robber barons, the Chinese economy was growing at more than 10 percent a year.

Nevertheless, the Chinese government was not able to completely resist the West's devaluationist rhetoric, and the yuan's value slipped. It was devalued to 4.7 per dollar in December 1989 and then began a slow deterioration beginning in November 1990. Much of this was due to Western pressure to supposedly decentralize and deregulate money and credit creation, which resulted in stepped-up creation of base money by the central bank and a deteriorating foreign exchange value for the yuan. In July 1993, Zhu Rongji took over the central bank and, ignoring criticisms from the West that he was trying to recentralize economic power—as if guaranteeing the reliability of the national currency was akin to a return to Maoism—restabilized the yuan at 8.3 to the dollar. The dollar peg caused China to import U.S. deflation in 1997–1998, only a few years after China had overcome the inflation resulting from the earlier devaluations, but for the most part, the relative monetary stability and predictability of the peg has formed the monetary foundation for China's successful return to market capitalism. From 2003 to 2005, China reduced and then eliminated agricultural taxes on rural farmers, allowing them to operate tax-free for perhaps the first time in 5,000 years.

III.

From 1941 to 1948 the Mexican peso was pegged at five per dollar. It underwent three devaluations from 1948 to 1954, finally ending at a peg of 12.5 per dollar, a dollar parity it kept for over 20 more years. During most of that time, the dollar itself was pegged to gold under the Bretton Woods system, and thus the peso was also indirectly linked to gold. Those years of currency stability were splendid for the Mexican economy. In 1963, for example, the country's annual nominal GDP was 194.8 billion pesos, and in 1968, five years later, it had grown to 340.6 billion—an annual growth rate of nearly 12 percent! Despite cultural prejudices about Latin American laziness, in fact Mexicans are as capable as Asians or Europeans at producing breathtaking economic expansion. (Brazil and Argentina, however, were pursuing devaluationist policies even during the 1960s.)

The peso's peg remained after the dollar was devalued in 1971.

It's not hard for a currency to follow another one lower. The problem, for currencies that have a fragile, informal, soft peg rather than the hard fix of a currency board, is following another currency higher. The same problem that befell dollar-pegged Asian economies in 1997 was also suffered by Mexico in 1976. After bottoming around $180 per ounce of gold in early 1975, the dollar rose steadily until it hit $105 per ounce in August 1976. That upward move in the dollar was too much for the peso peg, which slipped to 24.3 per dollar in November 1976. The peso was repegged in early 1977 at 22.8 per dollar. This was rather bad luck for the Mexican government, because the dollar began to fall rapidly after Carter won the presidential election in November 1976, relieving pressure on the peso/dollar rate. If Mexico had held out for one more month it would have been able to avoid the devaluation.

Despite the inflation of the 1970s—or because of it—the decade was good for commodities producers in Mexico, who enjoyed oil prices that never seemed to stop rising. U.S. banks made large loans to Mexican corporations, especially commodities producers. As the peso and the dollar fell together in the late 1970s, the strategy worked. The problem, once again, came as the dollar started to rise after bottoming at $850 per ounce in January 1980. In July 1980, the peso began to show weakness, trading at 22.9 per dollar. In January 1981, it had slipped to 23.3 per dollar. In January 1982, with the dollar around $390 per ounce, more than double its January 1980 value, the peso was down to 26.4 per dollar. Then the peso blew out completely. In March it traded for an average of 45.5 per dollar, and in August it traded for 69.5 per dollar. The dollar hit $304 per ounce that summer. Similar currency breakdowns were happening throughout Latin America at the time.

Commodities prices were falling and Mexican borrowers were unable to pay their debts to U.S. banks and bondholders. In peso terms, the debts had exploded in size. The one-way rise in oil prices that had lasted throughout the 1970s reversed itself: Oil peaked near $39 per barrel in February 1980 and had slipped to about $33 per barrel in the summer of 1982. This was the crisis that prompted Paul

Volcker to bail out the Mexican borrowers (or rather, the U.S. banks that had loaned the money) by buying Mexican dollar bonds, in the process lowering the value of the dollar and abandoning monetarism.

The U.S. economy recovered from the recession of 1982, but the peso and the Mexican economy never did. Over the next few years, encouraged by the devaluationists of the IMF and the effects of the tax hikes in their punishing austerity plans, the peso sank into hyper-inflation along with other currencies throughout Latin America.

In March 1988 the peso was stabilized at 2,281 pesos per dollar—or 2.281 pesos per dollar after a redenomination that knocked three zeros off the exchange rate. In July 1988, Carlos Salinas won the presidency, ushering in a six-year period of stable money and pro-business fiscal and regulatory reforms. Among other successes, Salinas and his finance minister Pedro Aspe helped create the North American Free Trade Agreement with the U.S. and Canada, which began in 1993. At the end of the Salinas administration, in 1994, the peso was trading at 3.4 pesos per dollar, but the dollar had risen during the same period. In gold terms the peso had done extraordinarily well: In March 1988 it traded for 1,025 per ounce of gold, and in February 1994 it traded for about 1,190 per ounce. During that period, the economy boomed and the stock market rose by approximately 1,200 percent.

Mexican law prevented Salinas from running for another term, and Mexico's currency problems began during the election for the new president. In November of 1993, Salinas picked Luis Donaldo Colosio Murrieta as the next presidential candidate of the ruling Institutional Revolutionary Party (PRI). The nomination virtually assured Colosio the presidency, since the PRI had not lost an election in 65 years. In January of 1994, an uprising in the impoverished state of Chiapas began a year full of political jitters. The revolutionaries argued, among other things, for full suffrage of all Mexicans, which would help bring an end to the domination of the PRI party, its control by the Mexican oligarchs, and the succession-by-presidential-decree represented by the Colosio nomination. In March 1994

Colosio was assassinated, resulting in the closure of the Bolsa stock exchange and jitters as far away as Wall Street.

When the Bolsa reopened it fell dramatically. That month the peso sagged to an average of 3.28 per dollar, after a year and a half of trading very close to 3.11. In April the peso traded at 3.35 per dollar. The assassination had apparently caused a quick reduction in peso demand, which tended to cause the value of the peso to fall. At this point the correct response would have been to extinguish some peso base money supply, thus supporting the peso's value. This did not happen, and the peso remained threateningly weak. The longer the peso was allowed to languish, the greater the doubts about its future reliability became. Another political assassination in September 1994 just added to the general worries and to the weakness of the peso.

With Colosio gone, the field was open for other presidential contenders. Most of the PRI candidates took the advice of their academic economists and, smelling a devaluation ahead, promoted an orderly devaluation. One candidate did not, the relatively untested Ernesto Zedillo, who pledged to keep the peso stable. Zedillo won by a wide margin in the August election, his first foray into politics. Zedillo also replaced the splendid Pedro Aspe with Jaime Serra Puche as finance minister. Despite Zedillo's election promises, both Zedillo and Puche held Ph.D.s in economics from Yale, a center for devaluationist theory in the United States (and the source of a steady supply of IMF economists).

At first, most investors expected Miguel Manacera, the director of Mexico's central bank, to support the peso by selling assets and reducing peso supply. After all, it had been Manacera that had put a halt to peso devaluation and hyperinflation in 1988 with exactly this technique. During other episodes of peso weakness in the following six years as well, Manacera had supported the peso by draining peso liquidity. But Manacera never said a word in support of the peso in the worried months leading up to its official devaluation on December 22.

Indeed the central bank, under Manacera's supposed watch, was throughout 1994 busily making the problem worse. From April 1994 the bank never mopped up excess base money liquidity in the market; instead, it continually bought assets and created even more peso supply. At the beginning of the crisis, Mexico had $30 billion in foreign exchange reserves, enough to buy up every peso in existence twice over. Instead, the central bank undertook its pointless "sterilized" interventions, selling dollars and buying pesos, and then turning around and selling pesos and buying peso debt. The monetary base steadily grew, from about $14 billion in April to $16 billion at the time of the devaluation. Mexico's foreign reserves inevitably trickled away, and not a thing was done about the weak peso and excess peso supply.

The official reason for the devaluation—that Mexico had "run out of reserves"—was nonsense. Even without dollar reserves, the central bank could have sold peso debt from its balance sheet, extinguishing pesos in the process and supporting the peso's value. Even on the day of the devaluation, instead of reducing peso supply the central bank was actually increasing peso supply by buying peso debt with fresh pesos. The peso quickly slid to 5.5 per dollar, and when the peso threatened to rise a bit above that in January, the central bank actually intervened to weaken the peso.

Even after the devaluation, all was not lost. Mexico still had the option of quickly boosting the peso back to 3.5 per dollar by declaring a commitment to reduce peso supply until that value was reached and repegging it there. The Mexican economy was still accustomed to a peso value of 3.3 per dollar or so, and the quick revaluation would have eliminated the need for future inflationary price adjustments. Mexico's leaders and its central bank cannot claim ignorance, for David Malpass, an economist with the brokerage Bear Stearns, published an op-ed piece in the *Wall Street Journal* outlining the specifics of this plan on January 11, 1995, only three weeks after the devaluation. As Malpass explained:

> From a technical standpoint, this experiment in public choice economics is simple. The goal is to get President Zedillo to say the

following words: "The Mexican central bank will cease creating pesos until the peso returns to 3.5. The pesos earned through Mexico's fiscal surplus will be removed from circulation, making pesos scarce. The government undertakes to borrow through dollar-indexed instruments, at any interest rate, the sum of $5 billion per week until the goal is reached. To speed this process, Mexico will use half of its $18 billion international line of credit to buy pesos in the first week."[5]

This plan was not only sufficient, it was massive overkill. After the devaluation, Mexico's monetary base had a value of only about $10 billion. If the central bank did not sterilize the operation by creating new pesos, as Malpass explicitly demanded, the $9 billion from the "half of its $18 billion line of international credit" alone would have nearly eliminated every peso in existence. Malpass's recommended peso buying of "$5 billion a week" would have cut the monetary base in half in five working days. If Zedillo had actually done what Malpass had suggested, Mexico probably would not have had to purchase even $1 billion of excess pesos. As Malpass explained in the same op-ed:

The Mexican government can credibly buy every peso in existence in a matter of weeks. Once the Mexican government announces a full presidential commitment to a thorough peso buyback, world financial markets will complete the process in about two nanoseconds. The profit potential for the Mexican government and the first peso buyers is immense. This public choice experiment is worthwhile if only to find out exactly how many hours it will take from start to finish once President Zedillo makes the commitment.

In other words, speculators would have bought the pesos once it became clear the government was ready to back them up. Indeed, with such a ringing statement of support for the peso, and the obvious technical wherewithal to accomplish the goal, it would have been perfectly possible for peso demand to expand rapidly over the following weeks. The central bank might have had to create more pesos to keep their value from rising above 3.5 per dollar!

Zedillo, needless to say, did not take Malpass's ideas to heart, but they were quickly adopted by leaders of the U.S. Republican Party, who had swept into majority power in Congress in November 1994 elections. Many Republicans had opposed NAFTA and were anxious to put their mark on the Clinton administration's handling of Mexico. (The Congressional battles in 1993 over NAFTA and the Clinton tax hikes illustrated the policy stance of the two parties dating back to the late nineteenth century, with Republicans in favor of higher tariffs and lower domestic tax rates and Democrats in favor of lower tariffs and higher domestic tax rates.) Malpass had served as the Republican staff director of the Joint Economic Committee. The Clinton Treasury was overseen by Larry Summers, a Harvard academic to whom the official Treasury secretary, Robert Rubin, deferred on complex policy issues.

The U.S. Treasury under Clinton had actually encouraged the devaluation, just as the Treasury under Bush had encouraged a devaluation of the peso in 1989, an idea that was rejected outright by Salinas and Aspe. Soon after the devaluation, Summers and the Treasury came up with a $40 billion package to bail out Mexico's creditors—namely, the U.S. banks that had lent money to Mexico's government and corporations and that now faced a default. Under this plan the $40 billion would go directly to New York, and the Mexican government would be obliged to pay the money back to the United States and the IMF, leaving the Mexican taxpayer to pick up the tab. Not a dollar was earmarked for the only thing that would have done any good for Mexico: namely, buying pesos in unsterilized foreign exchange intervention.

The plan died in Congress. Republicans demanded that the plan include an explicit goal of repegging the peso at 3.5 per dollar, along with the monetary mechanisms to attain that goal. Anti-NAFTA forces argued that cheapening Mexican labor through a currency devaluation would unfairly hurt U.S. competitors. (On the other side of the border, Mexican exporters made the same arguments in support of devaluation.) A new plan emerged using $20 billion from the Treasury's Exchange Stabilization Fund, which existed for exactly this purpose. Republican Senate Majority Leader Bob Dole, advised by Senator Robert Bennett of Utah, considered insisting that the White House have Alan Greenspan sign an official promise to use the ESF funds in the way Malpass described, shrinking the peso base and supporting the peso's value. Senator Al D'Amato, chairman of the Senate Banking Committee, demanded that the ESF be used to buy pesos.

Republicans eventually agreed to the use of the ESF, believing that it would be used as they described with Greenspan at the center of the operation. Instead, in February 1995, the Treasury bypassed Greenspan, claiming that he was uncooperative, and bundled the $20 billion from the ESF into a package of further tens of billions of loans from the IMF and the Bank for International Settlements, all of which was used in a pointless bailout of U.S. banks. No stabilization of any currencies took place. The Bank of Mexico was actually busy creating even more pesos, claiming a liquidity crisis. Treasury Secretary Rubin encouraged them to print still more, arguing that if the official inflation rate was running 60 percent a year, then the Bank of Mexico could expand the monetary base at a rate of 40 percent a year and it would constitute tight money. It looked like a return to 1980s-style hyperinflation. Interest rates skyrocketed. To pay off the IMF loans that the Mexican government had taken upon itself to bail out the New York banks, the IMF demanded a rise in the VAT tax to 15 percent from 10 percent, pushing the economy further down its spiral of decline and causing more peso weakness. The peso eventually fell to 10 per dollar before being supported by the introduction of a new monetary mechanism, the *corto*, which directly reduced the supply of peso base money. In the seven years following the devaluation, the Mexican stock market never regained its heights of early 1994, in dollar terms, even while Wall Street and markets worldwide boomed in the late 1990s.

Certainly there were some advisers to Bob Dole who suggested that it would not necessarily be such a bad thing if the Clinton Treasury was responsible for a major financial disaster. Wasn't it obvious that Dole and the rest of the Republican leadership had supported the correct solution for the peso?

Jack Kemp, the senior Republican whose economic insights had been so influential since the mid-1970s, testified before the Senate Banking Committee in March 1995.[6] Mexico's problems, Kemp argued before the senators, were caused by Mexico's government, specifically its failure to properly manage the supply of pesos and instead to embark on ineffective, sterilized foreign exchange intervention while printing even more pesos. The Mexican government, Kemp noted, was following the advice of the International Monetary Fund and the World Bank.

Kemp's solution was simple: to have Mexico's central bank sell assets out of its portfolio, in turn shrinking the supply of peso base money and supporting the peso's value. This technique, Kemp argued, could keep the peso pegged to the dollar for the next hundred years, if necessary. He suggested that a rate of 3.5 pesos per dollar would be an appropriate target. The IMF-approved technique of raising interest rate targets, Kemp argued, would not work, because this technique has no direct link with either the peso base money supply or the peso's value. Indeed, such a policy could well make the problem worse as markets reacted to the central bank's high interest rate target.

Kemp asked that the Exchange Stabilization Fund be used explicitly to purchase pesos in the open market and hold them in custody, effectively reducing their supply. Combined with a policy by the Mexican central bank to stop printing new pesos, the strategy would have the effect of raising the peso's value to the target of 3.5 per dollar.

It was a flawless plan, delivered right into the senators' ears.

But could they even understand what Kemp was talking about? Probably not, and the Clinton crew had their own ideas. Kemp, who had been a gold standard advocate since the 1970s, is one of the few people in the world today who fully understands monetary mechanics and the proper operation of a gold standard. In 2001, with the U.S. dollar worth more than its Plaza Accord value of ⅓₀₀ of an ounce of gold and thus inducing deflationary effects on the economy, Kemp argued that Greenspan should drop his interest-rate-targeting policy and begin buying bonds directly, expanding the dollar monetary base until the dollar's value fell below ⅓₀₀ of an ounce of gold. The Fed took these arguments to heart, and, although it did not go so far as to abandon its interest-rate-targeting policy and adopt a gold standard, it did cut its target rate to an unheard-of 1.0 percent in 2003 while publicly fretting about Japan-style deflation. Just as they had missed the debates of 1995, most financial market observers were completely unaware of the Fed's quick adoption of the ideas from Kemp and others, just as they were unaware of the deflation itself. The Fed's decision to ignore Kemp's advice to target gold had consequences, alas, as its interest-rate-targeting policy then led not only to a correction of the 1997 to 2002 deflation (the reflation of 2003) but to a dramatic overshoot into inflation. The world has a funny way of making central bankers pay for their ignorance and obstinacy, and there may be another debate about the Fed's proper operating policy in which Jack Kemp will be a featured speaker.

Dole became the Republican presidential candidate in 1996, and Kemp was his running mate. Though the pair made many political errors during the race, they never got credit for trying to stop the disaster in Mexico, nor did Clinton and his administration ever get the blame. The academic economic establishment rallied around their chieftain, Larry Summers, who represented all that they wanted to become. The academics somehow convinced themselves that the U.S. had done all that it possibly could have, and that, in fact, the U.S. Treasury's total botch of the situation—not-quite by accident, either—was a ringing success! The U.S. media accepted this assessment at face value, and never did understand or even notice the economic debates that were taking place in Congress beneath their noses. The Treasury and the IMF's solution for Mexico—namely, to throw a lot of money at Mexico's foreign creditors while encouraging more devaluation and tax hikes—later served as a blueprint for the Asian financial crisis as well. All the Asian currencies could have been supported in exactly the same manner that the peso could have been supported, with minimal cost or effort.

In the end, the Republican Party itself forgot about the debates of early 1995. After George Bush won the White House in 2000, the new Bush Treasury and the IMF promptly blew up yet another promising developing economy in a display of incompetence that rivaled any act of the Clinton crew. As the Turkish lira began to feel pressure on its dollar peg in late 2000, the IMF forced the government to undertake more tax hikes, and after the peg blew up in early 2001, the IMF, with Treasury approval, suggested that the solution to the problem was to privatize Turk Telecom. (There are always foreign investors eager to buy a nice telephone monopoly at the right price, and some of them have influential friends.) For some reason, as the lira spiraled down in value, neither the Treasury nor the IMF nor the former World Bank executive named as Turkey's economics minister managed to figure out that Turkey was undergoing a currency disaster. Turkish citizens, however, knew only all too well. One disgruntled Turkish voter was inspired to hurl a cash register at the head of Turkey's prime minister, Bülent Ecevit.

IV.

In 1984, Yugoslavia announced itself to the world by hosting the traditional debutante ball of proud emerging countries, a Winter Olympics. The event went off without a hitch, and few thought of Yugoslavia as anything but happy and prosperous. By late 1993, the country was torn apart by civil war and the dinar had become a confetti currency, having been devalued by a factor of 100 *septillion* (26 zeros) just since 1991. What happened?

Yugoslavia's problems began in 1980, as a result of the sharp rise in the dollar that year. Indeed, Yugoslavia's experience mirrors Mexico's, with the main difference, perhaps, that while Mexico stopped its IMF-led hyperinflation in 1988, Yugoslavia, following an IMF package in 1987 and especially after the implementation of shock therapy in 1990, instead stepped up its currency devaluation to astounding rates. Civil war was the natural outcome, as the formerly distinct republics that made up the post–World War II Yugoslav federation decided, one by one, that they might be better off on their own.

The dinar had some problems since Josip Broz, also known as Marshal Tito, unified the region in 1945, but for the most part it was a reasonably sound currency. From 1965 to 1970 it was pegged at a stable 12.5 dinars per dollar, the same rate as the Mexican peso at that time. During the currency turmoil of the early 1970s the dinar slipped to about 17 to 18 per dollar, but it held that parity until 1980. Tito's brand of market socialism had its flaws, but it had been reasonably successful: Between 1960 and 1980, Yugoslavia's official GDP grew at an average annual rate of 6.1 percent. Although this high headline figure masked a number of economic problems, nevertheless in 1980 the country boasted a 91 percent literacy rate and a life expectancy of 72 years. Yugoslav workers made an average of about $3,000 a year. Tito's socialism relied on central state planning but was considerably more liberal than Soviet Stalinism. A number of capitalistic elements were allowed, including borrowing from overseas banks. Though ostensibly communist, Yugoslavia remained independent of the Soviet bloc. Tito rejected any alliance with the Soviets, and he jailed the pro-Soviet opposition. Stalin had ejected Yugoslavia from the Warsaw Pact in 1948. The state was peaceful, and ethnic tensions were never a major problem. Tito died in May 1980.

Yugoslavia's success with communism was something of an embarrassment to the West, which was struggling badly with capitalism in the period from 1971 to 1982. The United States had long tried to pull Yugoslavia into the sphere of capitalist Western Europe, while the Soviet Union attempted to pull Yugoslavia into the sphere of Eastern Europe. As long as communism was successful in Yugoslavia (or the Soviet Union), neither would quickly change to capitalism. During the first Reagan administration, the United States developed a strategy to undercut the Soviet economy and ultimately bring around the collapse of communism. This was known as the "Reagan Doctrine." In September 1982, the United States developed National Security Decision Directive (NSDD) 54, which called for stepped-up efforts to promote a "quiet revolution" to overthrow Communist governments and parties. In March 1984, the "secret sensitive" NSDD 133, declassified in 1990 with heavy censorship, set a goal of the "eventual re-integration" of Yugoslavia "into the European community of nations," implying that Yugoslavian socialism could not be allowed to continue.[7]

Western banks lent considerable sums in Yugoslavia in the 1970s, as they had to borrowers in emerging countries around the globe during that decade. The dinar's history of trading at a fixed rate to the dollar, combined with relatively low interest rates on dollar-denominated debt, made this an attractive proposition for both lenders and borrowers. But as the dollar shot higher beginning in 1980, the dinar/dollar peg came under intense pressure, just as had Mexico's currency link. At the same time, dollar interest rates had shot up to double-digit levels, presenting a new burden for Yugoslav borrowers. In the political vacuum surrounding Tito's death, the IMF and Western banks swept in with a debt restructuring plan that included numerous macroeconomic reforms. One such reform was a focus on exports, supposedly to run a "trade surplus" and acquire "hard currency," which, according to the twisted logic of the IMF, required a devaluation of the dinar.

The dinar dropped from an average of 19 per dollar in 1979 to 29 per dollar in 1980 and 63 per dollar in 1982. Much of this move was due to the rise in the dollar between 1980 and 1982, so the dinar itself did not undergo a radical drop in value. However, the effect on dollar-denominated borrowers in Yugoslavia was catastrophic. Between 1979 and 1982, the dinar value of their debts more than tripled. At the same time, dollar interest rates remained in double-digit territory. More IMF "reforms," including more devaluation, tax hikes, and trade restrictions, were steadily laid upon Yugoslavia, just as was being done at the same time throughout Latin America.

In 1983, the dinar had fallen to 126 per dollar. In 1986, it fell to to 460 per dollar. This was bad indeed, mirroring what was going on in many Latin American countries. Beginning with the IMF program in 1987, however, the dinar's collapse accelerated. In 1987, it took 1,240 dinars to buy a dollar. In 1989 it took 11,816, a tenfold devaluation in only two years. And then, beginning in 1991, the dinar went into freefall.

In 1989, the IMF recommended an utterly insane solution to the economic problem: more devaluation, of course, but also freezing the wages of workers. If there had been one advantage of Yugoslavia's market socialism over the Soviet model, it was that the market elements could compensate for the devaluation by altering prices, including wages. By freezing wages, the IMF forced Yugoslavia into the same impossible corner that caused the Soviet economy to collapse soon after. At the same time, the IMF recommended that state industries deemed "unprofitable under structural adjustment" (i.e., those that were struggling in the environment of economic meltdown) should be closed, which immediately led to an explosion of unemployment. And if that weren't enough, the IMF demanded that the regular transfer of payments from the federal Treasury to the republics and autonomous regions should be stopped, and instead the revenue should go toward servicing foreign debt. On top of the currency disaster and the economic disaster it produced (measured GDP was falling at about a 10 percent annual rate in the late 1980s), the republics faced higher taxes to be paid to the federal government while receiving less in return. It was an invitation to declare independence.

At this time, Prime Minister Ante Marković reported, in a visit to Washington to see President George Bush, that ethnic tensions were rising in the provinces. Bush suggested that Marković stick to the IMF program. Marković did, with the result that over a thousand more enterprises were forced into bankruptcy. Soon after, 650,000 Yugoslav workers went on strike, united in solidarity despite their diverse ethnic backgrounds.

In this environment, the Communist Party leader Slobodan Milošević won the 1989 elections, committed both to resolve the economic problems and also to keep Yugoslavia in one piece rather than let it break up into independent states. One of Milošević's first steps was to reject any more reform ideas from the IMF and the United States and to cease the structural reform plans that were already in use. This infuriated the Western powers. The United States retaliated a month later, in November 1989, with Foreign Operations Appropriations Law 101–513, which, on top of cutting off all aid to Yugoslavia's federal government, also demanded, in Section 599a, that immediate, separate elections be held in each of Yugoslavia's six republics, with the clear implication that the United States supported the dismantling of Yugoslavia and the re-Balkanization of the Balkans. The validity of these free elections was to be decided by the United States. If the victors of the elections were deemed sufficiently democratic, they would get buckets of cash in the form of resumed aid payments. Secessionist parties in the regions were soon getting checks in the mail from the U.S. government.

In June 1991, Croatia and Slovenia, two of Yugoslavia's six republics, declared independence from the Yugoslavian federation (now increasingly identified as the republic of Serbia). One of the new Croatian government's first acts was to deny citizenship, jobs, pensions, landownership, and passports to a large ethnic Serb minority. Milošević, arguing that Croatia and Slovenia's declaration violated the Yugoslav constitution's specific procedures for republics seeking separation, sent troops into Slovenia. The European Union declared a trade embargo on Yugoslavia in response, a terrible blow in light of Yugoslavia's extensive trade with the rest of Europe. Milošević backed off and allowed Croatia and Slovenia to secede. Macedonia also departed, under friendly terms and without conflict, in the autumn of 1991. The ethnic Serbs in Croatia, who found themselves in a new country with no political relation to the republic of Serbia or the remains of the Yugoslav federation, fought a four-year civil war for their own independence from what they saw as a neofascist Croatia. In the end, the Croatian Serbs were ousted from Croatia, this bit of ethnic cleansing accomplished with U.S. military assistance.

Croatia and Slovenia had been independent republics before the creation of the Yugoslav federation, but Kosovo had always been merely a regional designation, along with Vojvodina, contained within the republic of Serbia. Milošević refused to allow Kosovo to secede as well and suppressed the violent Kosovo Liberation Army (KLA), a group that the U.S. State Department classified as a terrorist organization and that was likely financed with drug money. By this time, however, the United States had decided to side with the secessionists in Serbia's civil war and openly supported the KLA. Milošević was universally demonized in the U.S. press, labeled in straight news stories as a "tyrant" or a "dictator," although he continued to win fair elections. *Newsweek* (January 4, 1993) typified media coverage of Yugoslavia when it reported that up to 50,000 Muslim women had been raped by Serb militias. The charge came from a European Commission report that perhaps 20,000 women had been raped. Simone Veil, a member of the investigative team and president of the European Parliament, protested that this estimate was based on interviews with two women.

Bosnia-Herzegovina, another of the six original Yugoslav republics, declared its independence from Yugoslavia in 1992, and Milošević withdrew Yugoslav federal forces from the region soon after, in effect accepting Bosnia's independence. That year a peace accord, mediated by the European Community, was struck between warring Bosnian groups and Yugoslavia. In March 1992, the accord was signed by all parties, which would have allowed Bosnia to remain a union of autonomous provinces. However, the United States promised one of the signatories, Alija Izetbegović, supreme presidential power in Bosnia if he withdrew his signature from the accord, rendering it worthless. He did, rose to power as promised, and a three-year civil war ensued within Bosnia. Ethnic Serbs in Bosnia, with arms from the now-retreated federal Yugoslav army, were horrified with the installation of Izetbegović as president, a Muslim fundamentalist who had been imprisoned three times for "inciting racial hatred" and "advocating an ethnically pure Bosnia."

During the Bosnian civil war, the ethnic Serbs in Bosnia (who, like ethnic Serbs in Croatia, no longer had a political connection to Serbia) attempted to connect two historic Serb sectors by clearing a 300-kilometer corridor through the mountains, driving out Muslim villagers and leading to charges of ethnic cleansing. At the same time, moderate Muslims in Bosnia were also agitating violently against the new fundamentalist regime.

Milošević had nothing to do with the Bosnian civil war, having cut the republic loose and washed his hands of the affair, but he took the blame in any case. In 1992, the U.N. Security Council imposed Resolution 757 on what was left of Yugoslavia, which had been reduced to the republics of Serbia and Montenegro. The resolution banned all imports and exports, including oil; froze all assets; banned all financial contact and international travel; and suspended all scientific and cultural exchanges. The resolution was rushed through by the U.S. delegation two days before a U.N. report certified that Milošević was in full compliance with demands that federal Yugoslavian troops withdraw from Bosnia. Yugoslavia, which had allowed Croatia, Slovenia, Macedonia, and Bosnia to secede with little more than some fist shaking, became the first country to be expelled from the United Nations. The World Court had already ruled that Yugoslavia was not an aggressor in the Bosnian conflict. In a 1995 conference in (strangely enough) Dayton, Ohio, Milošević was asked to broker a peace agreement between combatants in Bosnia, although Bosnia had separated from Yugoslavia three years earlier. He did, and Bosnia was in turn separated into two smaller pieces. However, despite his peacemaking efforts, the embargo on Yugoslavia remained.

In early 1999, with fighting against the KLA continuing in Kosovo, Milošević met with representatives from the United States at Rambouillet, France, to create a peace plan. Milošević agreed to withdraw troops from Kosovo and return Kosovo to the level of political autonomy that it had enjoyed during the 1980s. Indeed,

Milošević acquiesced to all the U.S. demands, except for one. Washington's proposal allowed NATO military occupation of all of Yugoslavia. Appendix B, paragraph 8, reads: "NATO personnel shall enjoy, together with their vehicles, vessels, aircraft and equipment, free and unrestricted passage and access throughout the Federal Republic of Yugoslavia, including associated airspace and territorial waters." No sovereign nation could accept such demands, as the U.S. representatives well knew and, reportedly, admitted to journalists at Rambouillet under embargo.[8] Milošević could not accept, even if he wanted to, as he was bound by the Yugoslav constitution, which explicitly stated: "No person possesses the right to accept the occupation of Yugoslavia."

On March 23, 1999, the Yugoslav National Assembly approved a 10-page resolution filled with concessions "to facilitate a peaceful diplomatic settlement." The resolution was reported by Western media, but it was ignored by the U.S. government. On March 24, the United States began a 78-day bombing campaign of Yugoslavia (including Kosovo), which destroyed health care facilities, schools, petrochemical plants, refineries, and power-generation stations. And, in an "accident" thought by many to be anything but, the Chinese embassy in Belgrade was hit by a U.S. cluster bomb, an explosive device that had been declared illegal under international law. The assault was carried out under the auspices of NATO, which, unlike the U.N.'s own peacekeeping force, could be mobilized without getting the agreement of Russia or China on the U.N. Security Council or, for that matter, the U.S. Congress, whose agreement was supposedly necessary for declarations of war. It was the first offensive act in NATO's history, and it was soon condemned by NATO members Greece and Italy. Voters in Germany, a core NATO member, passed a referendum calling for a halt to the bombing.

Yugoslavia held one last election. On September 24, 2000, Vojislav Koštunica beat Milošević by 10 points, but fell a half point short of the 50 percent majority needed to win the presidency in the first round of voting. As per the Yugoslav constitution, a runoff election was to be held on October 8. (Milošević was widely accused in

Western media of fixing the election, raising the question of why, if that were true, he lost.) The day after the preliminary election, in preparation for the runoff, the United States passed a bill that authorized $105 million in financial aid for opposition groups in Serbia, namely, Koštunica.[9] The money was on top of financial assistance provided for the first election. How much is $105 million? In the U.S. presidential election of 2000, U.S. citizens provided about $150 million to the Republican and Democratic parties combined. Milošević lost the runoff. The United States later paid Koštunica's government $1 billion, a lot of money in a country where wages had fallen to $50 a month, for the extradition of Milošević to stand trial for war crimes in the Netherlands.

The West's demonization of Milošević never fooled the citizens of Serbia, who knew him best. In late 2003, while he was still in captivity and on trial for war crimes, they reelected him to parliament.

CHAPTER 16

THE RETURN TO HARD CURRENCIES

Good Money Is a Cornerstone of Good Government

The most important thing about money is to maintain its stability. . . . You have to choose between trusting the natural stability of gold and the honesty and intelligence of members of the government. With due respect for these gentlemen, I advise you, as long as the capitalist system lasts, to vote for gold.

—George Bernard Shaw, 1928

Could it be better? The answer is yes.

Proof begins with the people who manage money. If anything is evident from this history, it is that the task attracts a very low level of talent, one that is protected in its highly imperfect profession by the mystery that is thought to enfold the subject of economics in general and of money in particular. . . .

There is reluctance in our time to attribute great consequences to human inadequacy—to what, in a semantically less cautious era, was called stupidity. We wish to believe that deeper social forces control all human action. There is always something to be said for tolerance. But we had better be aware that inadequacy—obtuseness combined with inertness—is a problem. Nor is it inevitable. In the past, economic policy has been successful. We must assume that it was successful not by happy accident but because informed and energetic people made it so.

It will be no easier in the future than in the past for the layman or the lay politician to distinguish between the adequate individual and the others. But there is no difficulty whatever in distinguishing between success and failure. Henceforth it should be the simple rule in all economic and monetary matters that anyone who has to explain failure has failed. We should be kind to those whose performance has been poor. But we must never be so gracious as to keep them in office.

—John Kenneth Galbraith,
Money: Whence It Came, Where It Went, 1975[1]

No nation in history has ever survived fiat money, money that did not have precious metal backing.

—Ronald Reagan, 1980

Greenspan recommended to a Senate committee [in September 1997] that economic regulations all should be sunsetted. Senator Paul Sarbanes accused him of "playing with fire," and asked him whether he favored a sunset provision in the authorization of the Fed. Greenspan coolly answered that he did. Do you actually mean, demanded the Senator, that the Fed "should cease to function unless affirmatively continued?" "That is correct, sir," Greenspan responded. "All right," the Senator came back. "The Defense Department?" "Yes." The Senator could scarcely believe his ears. "Now my next question is, is it your intention that the report of this hearing should be that Greenspan recommends a return to the gold standard?" Greenspan responded, "I've been recommending that for years, there's nothing new about that. . . . It would probably mean there is only one vote in the FOMC for that, but it is mine."

—R. W. Bradford, "Greenspan: Deep Cover Radical for Capitalism?"
Liberty Magazine, **November 1997**

It may take many more years, even decades, but the era of soft money is slowly coming to a close. The world really has no choice but to move back toward a framework of hard money. The never-ending and completely unnecessary difficulties of floating currencies can be solved in no other way. The potential benefits of a return to hard currencies are enormous, not only for the billion or so people of the developed world, but especially for the 5 billion people of the developing countries.

Once a country, or the world as a whole, has decided to return to some form of hard currency, it must then decide what sort of system it will adopt. The best system, as always, is the one that maintains the greatest stability of currency value, over a week, month, year, decade, or century. It should also be easy to implement and cause no disruption on its introduction. As for accomplishing this task, even today there are no serious challengers to a gold standard, not even in the form of a proposal, and certainly none that have weathered the test of history. There is no reason to discard the hard-won knowledge of generations of human experience. The hard-money system of the future will be based on gold, just as were the hard-money systems of the past. Gold has not been a flawless foundation for monetary systems. Perfection does not exist in human affairs. It has, however, been the most flawless.

The sole remaining academic argument against returning to hard currencies is the idea that macroeconomic management (currency devaluation) is necessary in the event of a 1930s-style breakdown. We are still living in the shadow of the 1930s. Currency devaluation has been tried literally hundreds of times since the 1940s as a remedy for all manner of economic ills, and it has failed every single time. And if, every century or two, a situation did develop in which currency devaluation was the best prescription, governments would still be able to adjust the gold parity appropriately. The U.S. government devalued in 1934, even outlawing possession of gold, but it did not leave the gold standard.

A gold standard links the value of paper currencies to the value of gold. This is accomplished by some system to adjust the supply of base money such that the currency maintains a fixed value relative to gold, in much the same manner as quarters and dimes maintain a fixed relationship with dollar bills.

A new gold standard should include a provision for convertibility. The history of nonconvertible gold standards is not very good. Britain, during the suspension of convertibility during the Napoleonic Wars and World War I, did not have an official policy of deviating from the gold standard. Yet it nonetheless drifted away. When dollar/gold convertibility was unofficially suspended in 1968, an official end to the era of hard money followed only three years later. Convertibility makes governments legally liable for keeping their monetary promises. It is a political necessity, if not strictly a technical one. While the government should maintain a modest reserve of gold to meet possible redemptions, there should be no reserve requirement.

A trading band should be included. A band of 2 percent on either side of the parity price would suffice. If the parity price is set at $350 per ounce of gold, with a 2 percent band, the government would sell dollars (buy gold) at $343 per ounce and buy dollars (sell gold) at $357 per ounce. Both would be unsterilized transactions, with a direct effect on the supply of base money. However, before the currency reached these points, the government would adjust the supply of base money through purchases and sales of government bonds. When the currency is higher than its parity, the government would buy bonds and expand the base money supply, depressing the currency's value back to its parity. When the currency is slightly below its parity, the government would sell bonds, shrinking the base money supply and supporting the currency. Through the process of base money adjustment, the value of the currency should never reach the point at which the government would be obligated to buy or sell gold.

The Federal Reserve and institutions like it around the world would be returned to their original intended purpose: the prevention of liquidity-shortage crises. The lender-of-last-resort function could be accomplished in two ways: through a discount rate or a threshold open-market rate. Either rate should be set well above normal market rates. A rate of 10 percent would be appropriate. When normal market short-term interest rates reach 10 percent, a sign of a liquidity-shortage problem, the Fed would either provide loans through its discount window or buy securities on the open market (probably through repurchase agreements). Either act would create more base money, alleviating the crisis. When the market rate falls again back below 10 percent, Fed creation of base money would cease. (Base money would continue to be managed on a longer-term basis by the mechanism of the gold peg.) Whether through open-market operations or the discount rate, the Fed would be active only a few times a year at most, and could go several years without lender-of-last-resort activity.

If, in the rare case, the overnight interest rate rose dramatically as the result of efforts to protect the gold peg, the Fed should remain inactive to avoid "sterilizing" the gold peg's operation. Such a scenario would be likely only under extraordinary speculative pressure, which itself would appear only during extreme situations, such as existed in 1931, for example.

The Fed would not be responsible for bailing out insolvent institutions with long-term financial difficulties. Bank bailouts, as are occasionally warranted, would be accomplished through specific legislative acts of Congress, as they have been in the past and in other countries.

In the broader scope, it would be good to ask whether a privately owned institution such as the Fed should even manage the currency. Perhaps it would be best for the government to issue currency directly (as John F. Kennedy attempted in the 1960s), or, perhaps, for a multitude of private banks to issue currency under government oversight, all linked to gold, as was the case with the national bank notes system prior to the Fed's creation. Governments of less geographically expansive areas may find that their countries can get along fine with issuance of currency by private commercial banks, as is the case in Hong Kong, or with currency created by some external body, as is the case in dollarized countries today, and arguably in the eurozone as well.

This framework is almost identical to the system in use worldwide in the late nineteenth and early twentieth centuries, the finest monetary system that has yet existed on this planet. This is a fully modernized version of the classical gold standard, not the various imposters that try to claim that title. It has been thoroughly tested in dozens of countries worldwide, developed and developing. It works. Very well, in fact.

Today's interest rate–targeting systems have also led banks to reduce their amount of reserves, potentially exposing them to day-to-day volatility if central banks did not offset these flows on a daily basis. Banks may need to increase their reserve holdings to accommodate day-to-day changes in the availability of funds in the short-term money market. (Under the pre–World War II gold standards, banks held much larger reserves for this reason.) Also, the central bank should, as is done today, offset the inflows of base money into government accounts held at the central bank (which effectively reduces base money) with equivalent liquidity provisions. These are small technicalities, which need to be addressed but are easily solved.

The most controversial element would be the transition from the existing system of floating rates. The choice of dollar/gold parity is very important. Obviously, the old Bretton Woods rate of $35 per ounce is no longer possible, for that would imply a deflation that would certainly wreck the U.S. economy. Likewise, a parity of $1,000 per ounce would imply a radical dollar devaluation. The correct parity is the economy's "center of gravity," the point that balances the forces of inflation and deflation and the interests of creditors and debtors. A long-term average, such as a 10-year dollar/gold price average, is a good first approximation of this center of gravity. At the end of 2005, an appropriate dollar/gold parity was around $350 to $380 per ounce. Whatever parity is chosen, it does not matter if it is up to 10 percent away from the theoretically ideal value in either direction. Such a small difference will not cause any noticeable economic turmoil. The economy will adjust to the new parity over time, and after a few years the economy's center of gravity will be exactly on the parity point. Missing the center of gravity by more than 10 percent would certainly raise the risk of causing noticeable inflation or deflation, however, which could be blamed on the gold standard itself although it would be a result of human error.

A transition to a gold standard of this design would be seamless. No new currency would be issued. Gold coins would not be necessary, although it would be possible to legalize the use of private-issue gold coins as currency. Existing currency would become redeemable for gold on demand. Trade and commerce of all forms would proceed uninterrupted.

On a certain day, the newspapers would simply announce that

the change had been made. And the world would quietly enter a new golden age.

In the early 1980s, only a decade after the end of Bretton Woods, it was conceivable that the United States and the world could return to a gold standard in a single step. Ronald Reagan nearly did it. Many people had a memory and understanding of how the system worked. Today, after more than three decades of soft money, perhaps such a scenario would be more difficult. People who were 30 in 1971, when the gold standard ended, are at retirement age today. Legislators, policy specialists, journalists, economists, and bureaucrats responsible for monetary policy today have lived their entire adult lives in a regime of soft money, and the majority have little inkling that any alternative exists.

This is unfortunate, but it holds a hidden advantage. It will be necessary to learn the basics of hard money again from square one, which offers a chance to clear away the encrustations of misunderstanding and misconception that have plagued monetary issues since World War I, and earlier as well. Square one is where all learning should begin. The bad habit of beginning at square 26 is behind the endless nonsense that passes for monetary discussion today. Complex issues are untangled with simple principles.

The first step toward a gold standard today would probably be the rediscovery by central banks that they can manage their currencies through the supply of base money. Countries such as Korea, Indonesia, Mexico, China, Estonia, and Hong Kong have been experimenting with this already. It has become familiar to many in the financial markets, who have pushed it upon errant central banks such as the European Central Bank and the Bank of Japan. The European Central Bank and the Bank of Japan have to a large degree refused this pressure. Though it would seem that central bankers would be excited by such a discovery and at least undertake some small-scale experiments, in fact central banks are highly reluctant to adopt such a change. It would imply that central banks have been grossly negligent in their prior currency management. This is, of course, true, but it is not something that central bankers, who have egos proportionate to their awesome powers, would like to admit, not even to themselves.

At some point, however, central bankers' bumbling will become too obvious to ignore. They will have to recognize that they actually have control over their currencies. The question will then be how to use this newfound power to manage currencies wisely. That discussion inevitably ends at the gold standard.

If the U.S. government instituted a gold standard of this sort, Japan and Europe would probably follow within five years. Japan and Europe have long been in favor of currency stability and fixed exchange rates, more so than the United States. Developing countries, many of which are already on some sort of currency peg system with a major currency, would also be linked into the world gold standard within a few years, if not months. Floating currencies would simply disappear, as suddenly and spontaneously as they appeared in the spring of 1973.

The transition would be somewhat more difficult if the euro were the first to return to a gold standard. Such a move would naturally make the euro a superior currency to the dollar for use worldwide, and a period of transition would ensue whereby the world would adopt the euro as its primary international currency and drop the dollar. Eurozone economic growth would accelerate, as long as it isn't choked off by heavy taxes or regulation. The U.S government would not like this usurpation of its economic supremacy, but after complaining somewhat, it would probably also go onto the gold standard to remain competitive.

If a country besides the United States pegged to gold, it would be exposed to the dangers of fluctuations in the world's major currency, as the dollar would remain for at least a few years. As was the case during the 1930s and 1970s, when a major currency is devalued, countries that are on a gold standard face the prospect of being "beggared" by the devaluing country. Indeed, it is quite possible that the United States would engage in a devaluation precisely to undermine such gold standard attempts, although the act would no doubt be obscured by rhetoric about the current account deficit or other such nonsense.

Japan would have an even more difficult time than Europe. Japan has long been in a subordinate position in relation to Europe and the United States, particularly as it has only a token military, but such currency leadership would propel it to front-runner status. Britain was not the world's financial center when the pound was anchored to silver and then gold beginning in the late seventeenth century. Europe and the United States could put pressure on Japan to drop its gold standard plans. Japan would probably have to stitch together a gold-based currency bloc in Asia to give the yen a clear advantage in international trade over the dollar. Should this be accomplished, the accelerated growth of the region would probably lead Europe and the United States to adopt a hard-money system as well. Alas, such leadership has not existed in Japan for several decades.

Somewhat more peripheral countries, such as Argentina, China, or Russia, can also adopt gold standards, but they may experience intense criticism from the developed world. Major countries' currencies would continue to float, so the smaller countries would not be able to enjoy the advantages of fixed exchange rates. Since many smaller countries are highly dependent on trade, this would present a problem for the gold standard as opposed to, for example, a currency board with a major currency. However, a gold standard remains preferable to an independently floating currency for a small country, and is certainly better than endless devaluation, whether in leaping bounds or by the slow poison of the crawling peg. If a dozen smaller countries were able to establish gold standards, a slow spread to major countries could develop. For a small country to lead the world onto the gold standard would take a degree of vision and leadership that comes along only once a century, if that often. Nevertheless, Japan was a small country once—and still is in a physical sense, though it now has the world's second-largest economy. The Islamic countries, in particular, seem interested in establishing a currency based on their tradition of the gold dinar. In Vietnam, it is common today to purchase a home with a mortgage denominated in taels of gold, amortized over 10 years or more. There is a low murmur of interest in a "golden ruble" in Russia.

China and Russia, historical great powers now returning to prominence, could easily propel themselves to the forefront if they adopted a gold standard. China and Russia have some of the most sophisticated and forward-thinking leaders in the world today, and it is possible that they could team up and switch to hard-money systems together. The spectacle of such a broad swath of the globe and 1.5 billion people, brushing off the conventional wisdom of Washington and Brussels and taking an independent course would no doubt cause great consternation in Europe and the United States. But if China and Russia held the course through a decade or so of criticism, and avoided crippling their economies through tax hikes, Europe, Japan, and the United States would be forced to join the hard-money system or face being left behind by the resurgent Eastern Hemisphere.

A return to hard money would eliminate, as much as is possible, the monetary distortion of the price information that guides the actions of the citizenry. Success and failure would once again be determined by relative merit in the market economy, not by erratic changes in the value of the currency. Capital would be deployed more accurately, and productivity would increase. Manufacturers who are now forced to build several factories worldwide to diversify their foreign exchange risk could instead concentrate simply on the location that offers the greatest productivity. After a number of years, interest rates would likely fall to below 4 percent for long-term government bonds and stay there. Price indexes would lose relevance and may again become an academic curiosity, as they were before 1930.

Trade frictions and accusations of "dumping" would die out, and pressure to raise tariffs would abate. Efforts to create large "free trade zones" would find less political resistance. International investing would become much less risky and interest rates would tend to converge at low levels worldwide. There would still be economic disasters, probably caused by sharp rises in taxes, but currency disasters, the trademark policy error of the twentieth century just as the liquidity-shortage crisis was the trademark crisis of the nineteenth, would at last become a thing of the past. Governments, no longer able to manipulate their currencies to achieve policy goals, no longer able to blame their central banks for economic stagnation, would be forced to compete on the relative merits of their tax and regulatory structures. This dynamic is already happening in Europe since the advent of the euro.

Since the early 1970s, a whole set of industries has developed to deal with the environment of floating exchange rates. These industries are counted in GDP as "production," although they represent the waste created by the regime of soft money. The establishment of a gold standard would render them obsolete. Lawyers, accountants, bond dealers, foreign exchange and derivatives specialists, and many others would be free to find new ways to contribute to the economy, just as agricultural efficiencies long ago freed the citizenry from farming. These industries consume many of the most talented young people from each generation, including the graduates of top universities. Bonds would once again become boring and safe. A move of 1 percentage point in yields would take a decade.

The chaos industries stretch throughout the economy, from police officers to social workers to prison guards. Chaotic monetary relationships are reflected in chaotic social relationships, because, in the end, monetary relationships are social relationships. Money is a sort of promise. While hard money is not a cure for all social ills, it is at least a cure for the social erosion caused by soft money.

Like any change, a switch from soft money to hard money would create winners and losers. The potential losers include a broad swath of the elites of society. The chaos industries may not take kindly to being made obsolete. Foreign exchange and fixed-income (bonds) and derivatives dealing have become major sources of banks' income. These businesses would continue to exist under a gold standard, of course, but foreign exchange trading could be accomplished by a competent high-school graduate instead of a steel-nerved supertrader. As currency risk disappeared, all manner of risk-management industries would dwindle away.

The Federal Reserve and other central banks have the most to lose. Today they wield enormous powers, unchecked by any democratic accountability. They are large bureaucracies, and no bureaucracies encourage their own demise.

The International Monetary Fund's towering influence world-wide has monetary instability at its root. The IMF has been able to commandeer the economic policy of dozens of countries through the mechanism of currency disasters. That is likely why IMF policy so often favors creating yet more currency disasters in the form of repeated devaluations, or tax hikes that lead to devaluations, creating an endless cycle of IMF dependency for much of the world. The IMF gives expression to a dark side of humanity, in which the powerful maintain their superiority through the impoverishment of entire continents of fellow humans. Economic disaster guarantees an endless supply of maids, janitors, prostitutes, and low-paid widget makers. This dark side senses a threat to the status quo from the economic empowerment of the people of Asia, Africa, and Latin America. Currency devaluation, along with tax hikes, is the mechanism by which this primal desire is satisfied. In the world as a whole, the developed countries are the established elites, ever afraid of a challenge from below and a threat to their dominance. No matter how bad the situation may be, for the elites it is nevertheless a situation in which they have been able to rise to and stay at the top.

Today's dominant countries could still maintain a leadership role, not because no one else is powerful enough to depose them, but because their leadership is so beneficial that no one has any interest in deposing them. The developing world is desperate for good leadership, and the dream of being guided along the path to prosperity is one reason they invite the IMF to their countries again and again.

Under a world gold standard, the IMF would be returned to its intended role of furthering monetary stability. Like the Fed, this implies a dramatic reduction of its influence.

It took a philosopher, John Locke, and a preacher, Adam Smith, to provide the intellectual leadership to bring the Western world onto a hard currency. Academics didn't fully accept today's soft-money rationalizations until after 1936, years after it had become commonplace in world governments. Even so, it took John Maynard

Keynes, the self-taught writer with a bachelor's degree in mathematics, to lead the change. When ambitious academics sense that supporting hard money will advance their careers, rather than retard them, they will support it en masse. As the political tide flows away from soft money and toward hard money, when the wheel has turned once again as it has so many times in the past, the economic intelligentsia will sense the change and produce a flood of rationalizations about why the world needs a gold standard, just as they now produce a flood of rationalizations about why the world does not.

Good money will once again be recognized as a cornerstone of good government. After a few years, nobody will remember that it had ever been any other way.

NOTES

CHAPTER 1 Good Money Is Stable Money

1. Nicholas Copernicus, "Treatise on Debasement," in *Minor Works*, translated by Edward Rosen, Johns Hopkins University Press, Baltimore, 1985, p. 177.
2. John Maynard Keynes, in *Essays in Persuasion*, W.W. Norton & Company, 1991, p. 103.

CHAPTER 2 Hard Money and Soft Money

1. John Stuart Mill, *Principles of Political Economy*, A. M. Kelley, 1999, p. 74.
2. See Robert Mundell, "Uses and Abuses of Gresham's Law in the History of Money," *Zagreb Journal of Economics*, vol. 2, no. 2, 1998.
3. See Bruce Bartlett, "Economic Policy in Ancient Rome," *Cato Journal*, vol. 14, no. 2, pp. 287–303.
4. Glyn Davies, *A History of Money: From Ancient Times to the Present Day*, University of Wales Press, 1996, p. 183.
5. Davies, *History of Money*, pp. 181–182.
6. Richard Von Glahn, *Fountain of Fortune: Money and Monetary Policy in China, 1000–1700*, University of California Press, Berkeley, 1996, p. 63.
7. William S. Atwell, "International bullion flows and the Chinese economy circa 1530–1650," *Past and Present*, no. 95, 1981.
8. See Richard Jastram, *The Golden Constant*, John Wiley & Sons, New York, 1977, p. 15.
9. See Niall Ferguson, *The Pity of War*, Basic Books, New York, 1990.

CHAPTER 3   Supply, Demand, and the Value of Currency

1. Mill, *Principles of Political Economy*, p. 455.
2. Ludwig von Mises, *Human Action: A Treatise on Economics*, Fox & Wilkes, San Francisco, 1996, p. 411.
3. Ken Landon, "Deutschebank Forex Daily: Tokyo Morning Comment," Deutschebank, August 8, 2000.
4. Robert A Mundell, "The International Monetary System in the 21st Century: Could Gold Make a Comeback?" Lecture delivered at St. Vincent College, Latrobe, PA, March 12, 1997.
5. Mill, *Principles of Political Economy*, p. 457.
6. David Ricardo, *Principles of Political Economy and Taxation*, Prometheus Books, New York, 1996, p. 101.
7. Von Mises, *Human Action*, pp. 418–419.
8. Von Mises, *Human Action*, p. 424.

CHAPTER 4   Inflation, Deflation, and Floating Currencies

1. Robert Mundell, "Inflation from an International Viewpoint," in *The Phenomenon of Worldwide Inflation*, American Enterprise Institute for Public Policy Research, Washington, DC, 1975.
2. Nicholas Oresme, *The De Moneta of Nicholas Oresme, and English Mint Documents*, translated from the Latin with introduction and notes, Thomas Nelson and Sons, London, 1956, p. 30.
3. Von Mises's definition from his 1912 book *The Theory of Money and Credit* differs slightly from the one used in this book, where inflation may occur even when the supply of money is contracting, if the demand for money is contracting even faster. In *Human Action* of 1949, von Mises says: "Changes in the money relation [balance of supply and demand for money] are not only caused by governments issuing additional paper money. . . . Prices also rise the same way if, without a corresponding reduction in the quantity of money available, the demand for money falls because of a general tendency toward the diminution of cash holdings" (XVII:4). This is wholly consistent with the theoretical outline of this book. In 1912, floating currencies had been rare for a century. In 1949, von Mises had the advantage of the floating currency experience of the 1930s and 1940s; von Mises's focus on the "money relation" and the

"objective exchange value" of money signals his commitment to the value-oriented classical school of monetary theory.

4. Keynes, "Inflation and Deflation," in *Essays in Persuasion*, p. 78.

5. Adam Smith, *Inquiry Into the Nature and Causes of the Wealth of Nations*, Prometheus Books, New York, 1991, pp. 589–590.

6. Henry Hazlitt, *Economics in One Lesson*. Harper & Brothers Publishers, New York, 1946, p. 189.

7. Copernicus, "Treatise on Debasement," in *Minor Works*, p. 176.

8. Nicholas Oresme, *De Moneta,* p. 47.

9. Keynes, "Social Consequences of a Change in the Value of Money," in *Essays in Persuasion*, p. 80.

10. Ricardo, *Principles of Political Economy and Taxation*, p. 103.

11. Andrew Carnegie, "The A B C of Money," *North American Review*, vol. 152, 1891, p. 723.

12. Source: www.usagold.com/gildedopinion/greenspan-gold.html.

13. George Soros, *The Alchemy of Finance: Reading the Mind of the Market*, John Wiley & Sons, New York, 1987, p. 69.

14. Ragnar Nurkse, *International Currency Experience*, Geneva: League of Nations, 1944, quoted in Barry Eichengren, *Globalizing Capital: A History of the International Monetary System*, Princeton University Press, Princeton, NJ, 1996, p. 51.

CHAPTER 5 The Gold Standard

1. Charles Issawi, *An Arab Philosophy of History: Selections from the Prolegomena of Ibn Khauldun of Tunis (1332–1406)*, Darwin Press, Princeton, NJ, 1987, p. 77.

2. Karl Marx, *Capital*, chapter 3. (Note: References without publisher or page numbers are from Internet-available sources in the public domain.)

3. Carnegie, "The A B C of Money."

4. Smith, *The Wealth of Nations*, p. 250.

5. Ricardo, *Principles of Political Economy and Taxation*, p. 245.

6. Smith, *The Wealth of Nations*, pp. 251–252.

7. Ricardo, *Principles of Political Economy and Taxation*, p. 247.

8. Alexander Hamilton's report to the House of Representatives, 13 December 1790, in *American State Papers, Finance*, 1st Congress, 3rd session, no.

18, I, 67–76, quoted in Jude Wanniski, *The Way the World Works*, Regnery Publishing, Washington, DC, 1998, p. 216.

9. David Hume, "On the Balance of Trade."

10. For another discussion on this topic, see Friedrich Hayek, "Genesis of the Gold Standard in Response to English Coinage Policy in the 17th and 18th Centuries," in *The Trend of Economic Thinking: Essays on Political Economists and Economic History*, University of Chicago Press, 1991, p. 151 (127–154). Hayek says: "Hume prefaces his inquiry with the observation that 'money is not, properly speaking, one of the subjects of commerce; but only the instrument which men have agreed upon to facilitate the exchange of one commodity for another.' The significance of this remark lies in its repudiation of the mercantilists' excessive preoccupation with money. From Hume's perspective, it is therefore a matter of indifference how great a stock of money a country has."

11. Earle Amey, "Gold," United States Geological Survey, 1998.

12. See Mark Skousen, *Economics of a Pure Gold Standard*, Foundation for Economic Education, Irvington-on-Hudson, NY, 1996, p. 86.

CHAPTER 6   Taxes

1. John Stuart Mill, "Essays on Some Unsettled Questions of Political Economy."

2. Jean-Baptiste Say, *A Treatise on Political Economy, or the Production, Distribution and Consumption of Wealth*, book 1, chapter 15.

3. Lao Tzu, *Tao te Ching*, translated by Ursula K. LeGuin, Shambhala Publications, 1998, p. 154.

4. Khaldun, *Al Muqquadimah*, pp. 87–88.

5. Say, *A Treatise on Political Economy*, book 3, chapter 8.

6. Ricardo, *Principles of Political Economy and Taxation*, p. 106.

7. John Maynard Keynes, *The Collected Works of John Maynard Keynes,* vol. 9, *Essays in Persuasion*, Macmillan, London, 1972, p. 338. In Bruce Bartlett, "The Futility of Raising Tax Rates," *Policy Analysis*, no. 192, April 8, 1993, Cato Institute, Washington, DC.

8. Hazlitt, *Economics in One Lesson*, pp. 28–29.

9. Andrew Mellon, *Taxation: The People's Business*, Macmillan, New York, 1924, app. E, pp. 216–227. Quoted in Wanniski, *The Way the World Works*, p. 131.

10. Henry George, *Progress and Poverty*. Macmillan, New York, 1952, pp. 832–33. Quoted in Bruce Bartlett, *Reaganomics: Supply Side Economics in Action*, Arlington House Publishers, Westport, CT, 1981, p. 15.

11. Smith, *The Wealth of Nations*, pp. 508–509.

CHAPTER 7   Money in America

1. In the debates leading to the tariff of 1842, Senator John Calhoun made a fascinating speech, elucidating a concept that, if he had lived in a more mathematically inclined age, might have been christened the "Calhoun curve":

> [D]uring the eight years of high duties [tariffs], the increase of our foreign commerce, and of our tonnage, both coastwise and foreign, was almost entirely arrested; and that the exports of domestic manufactures actually fell off, although it was a period exempt from any general convulsion in trade or derangement of the currency. . . . the eight years of the reduction of duties, which followed, were marked by an extraordinary impulse given to every branch of industry—agricultural, commercial, navigating, and manufacturing. Our exports of domestic productions, and our tonnage, increased fully a third, and our manufactures still more. . . .
>
> But is this a revenue bill? I deny it. . . . No two things, Senators, are more different than duties for revenue and protection. they are as opposite as light and darkness. the one is friendly, and the other hostile, to the importation of the article on which they may be imposed. revenue seeks not to exclude or diminish the amount imported; on the contrary, if that should be the result, it neither designed nor desired it. While it takes, it patronizes; and patronizes, that it may take more. It is the reverse, in every respect, with protection. It seeks, directly, exclusion or diminution. . . .
>
> On all articles on which duties can be imposed, there is a point in the rate of duties which may be called the maximum point of revenue—that is, a point at which the greatest amount of revenue would be raised. If it be elevated above that, the importation of the article would fall off more rapidly than the duty would be raised; and if depressed below it, the reverse effect would follow: that is, the duty would decrease more rapidly than

the importations would increase. If the duty be raised above that point, it is manifest that all the intermediate space between the maximum point and that to which it may be raised, would be purely protective, and not at all for revenue. . . . It results from the facts stated, that any given amount of duty, other than the maximum, may be collected on any article, by two distinct rates of duty—the one above the maximum point, and the other below it. The lower is the revenue rate, and the higher the protective. (5 August 1842)

Clyde N. Wilson, ed., *The Papers of John C. Calhoun, vol. 16, 1841–1843*, University of South Carolina Press, 1984, pp. 354–357.

2. Congressional Record, 66th Congress, 2nd session, December 2, 1919, vol. 59, part 1, p. 53. In Bartlett, "The Futility of Raising Tax Rates."
3. Andrew Mellon, *Taxation, the People's Business*, Macmillan, New York, 1924, pp. 9–13.

CHAPTER 8   A History of Central Banking

1. Clifford Moore and John Jackson (translators), *Tacitus: Histories, Annals*, Cambridge, MA, Harvard University Press, 1937 (reprinted 1956), pp. 179–183. (*Annals*, book VI, pp. xvi–xvii.)
2. Tiberius's own bullion-hoarding efforts, like those of the Chinese, may have created a persistent shortage of circulating coinage throughout his reign. Though the natural imports of bullion, and mining, would have offset this hoarding as per David Hume, such mechanisms are longer term in nature and would likely have left the Roman economy particularly exposed to shorter-term fluctuations in the demand for money. In AD 14, Tiberius inherited from Augustus a private cash hoard of 100 million sesterces, kept as bullion coins in the imperial treasury. Tiberius, in turn, left a treasury of 2.7 billion sesterces to Caligula, an increase of 27 times.
3. Edwin Lefevre, *Reminiscences of a Stock Operator*, John Wiley & Sons, New York, 1994, pp. 111–115.
4. Richard Timberlake, *Monetary Policy in the United States: an Intellectual and Institutional History*, University of Chicago Press, Chicago, 1993, pp. 232, 258.
5. Congressional Record, 63rd Congress, 1st session, p. 4691. In Timberlake, *Monetary Policy in the United States*, p. 223.
6. Timberlake, *Monetary Policy in the United States*, p. 256.

7. David Ricardo, "The High Price of Bullion, a Proof of the Depreciation of Bank Notes."
8. Friedrich Hayek, *Contra Keynes and Cambridge: Essays, Correspondence*, Bruce Caldwell, ed., University of Chicago Press, Chicago, 1995, p. 232.

CHAPTER 9   The 1930s

1. Quoted in William Greider, *Secrets of the Temple: How the Federal Reserve Runs the Country*. Simon and Schuster, New York, 1987, p. 317.
2. John Stuart Mill, "Essays on Some Unsettled Questions of Political Economy."
3. Kung-chuian Hsaio, *A History of Chinese Political Thought,* vol. 1, translated by F. W. Mote. Princeton University Press, Princeton, NJ, 1979, p. 359.
4. James Denham Steuart, *An Inquiry into the Principles of Political Economy*, book 2, chapter 27.
5. Steuart, *An Inquiry into the Principles of Political Economy*, book 4, chapter 3.
6. Kung-chuan Hsiao, *A History of Chinese Political Thought*, vol. 1, p. 455.
7. *The Public Papers and Addresses of Franklin D. Roosevelt,* vol. 1, *The Genesis of the New Deal, 1928–1932*. Random House, New York, 1938, p. 798. In Bartlett, "The Futility of Raising Tax Rates."
8. Roger Middleton, *Towards the Managed Economy: Keynes, the Treasury, and the Fiscal Policy Debate of the 1930s*, Routledge, Kegan and Paul, 1985, pp. 73–74.

CHAPTER 10   The Bretton Woods Gold Standard

1. Von Mises, *Human Action*, p. 478.
2. Richard Nixon, *Six Crises*, Doubleday, Garden City, NY, 1962. Quoted in J. Bradford Delong, "America's Only Peacetime Inflation: the 1970's," 1995 (unpublished).
3. Public Papers and Addresses of the Presidents of the United States: John F. Kennedy, 1963 (Washington: U.S. Government printing office, 1964), pp. 73–92. In Bartlett, "The Futility of Raising Tax Rates."
4. Bruce Bartlett, *Reaganomics: Supply Side Economics in Action*, p. 151.
5. F. A. Hayek, "Can We Still Avoid an Inflation?" In Richard M. Ebeling, ed., *The Austrian Theory of the Trade Cycle and Other Essays*, Ludwig von Mises Institute, Auburn, Alabama, 1996, p. 93.

6. Herbert Stein, *The Fiscal Revolution in America*, University of Chicago Press, Chicago, 1969, p. 3.
7. Conference Resolution XXV.140, Organization of Petroleum Exporting Countries. Quoted in Bartley, *The Seven Fat Years*, p. 31.
8. Wyatt Wells, *Arthur Burns: Economist in an Uncertain World*, Columbia University Press, 1994, p. 144.

CHAPTER 11   Reagan and Volcker

1. Bartley, *The Seven Fat Years*, pp. 164–165.
2. Greider, *Secrets of the Temple*, p. 688.
3. Robert Mundell, "The Dollar and the Policy Mix," *Essays in International Finance*, no. 85, May 1971, International Finance Section, Department of Economics, Princeton University, Princeton, NJ, p. 24.
4. Jude Wanniski, "A Gold Polaris, Part II," Polyconomics Inc., Morristown, NJ, 1995.
5. Charles Kadlec and Arthur Laffer, "The Monetary Crisis: A Classical Perspective." In Canto, Kadlec, Laffer, eds., *The Financial Analyst's Guide to Monetary Policy*, Praeger Scientific, New York, 1986, p. 5.
6. Michael K. Evans, *The Truth About Supply Side Economics*, Basic Books, New York, 1983, p. 7.
7. Wanniski, *The Way the World Works*, p. 351.
8. Bartley, *The Seven Fat Years*, p. 109.
9. Greider, *Secrets of the Temple*, p. 645.
10. Bartley, *The Seven Fat Years*, p. 212.
11. "Fed Keeps Rates Steady to Pressure Tokyo, Aides Say," *Wall Street Journal*, April 22, 1987.
12. Jane Hughes, "Latin America," in Scott MacDonald, Margie Lindsay, and David Crum, eds., *The Global Debt Crisis: Forecasting for the Future*. Pinter Publishers, New York, 1990, p. 23.
13. William Niskanen, *Reaganomics: An Insider's Account of the Policies and the People*, Oxford University Press, Oxford, 1989, p. 274.

CHAPTER 12   The Greenspan Years

1. Alan Greenspan, "Gold and Economic Freedom," in Ayn Rand, *Capitalism, the Unknown Ideal*, Signet, 1985.

2. Alan Greenspan, "Can the U.S. Return to a Gold Standard?" *Wall Street Journal*, September 1, 1981.
3. Remarks by Chairman Alan Greenspan at the 15th Anniversary Conference of the Center for Economic Policy Research at Stanford University, Stanford, California, September 5, 1997.
4. Remarks by Chairman Alan Greenspan before the House Financial Affairs Committee, July 20, 2005.
5. Steven K. Beckner, *Back from the Brink: The Greenspan Years*. John Wiley & Sons, New York, 1996, p. 41.
6. "U.S. Said to Allow Decline of Dollar Against the Mark," *New York Times*, October 18, 1987.
7. "Why Greenspan Is Bullish," *Fortune*, October 26, 1987, p. 28.
8. Beckner, *Back from the Brink*, p. 117.

CHAPTER 13   Japan's Success and Failure

1. John Maynard Keynes, *A Tract on Monetary Reform*. Prometheus Books, Amherst, NY, 2000, p. 142.

CHAPTER 14   The Asia Crisis of the Late 1990s

1. Hubert Neiss, "In Defense of the IMF's Emergency Role in East Asia," *International Herald Tribune*, October 9, 1998.
2. Mark Mobius, "Asia Needs a Single Currency," *Wall Street Journal*, February 19, 1998.

CHAPTER 15   Russia, China, Mexico, and Yugoslavia

1. There is evidence that General Eisenhower caused the deaths of 1.7 million German POWs after the end of the war by purposefully denying them food, water, shelter, or latrines in their POW camps. See, for example, *Other Losses* by James Bacque (Little Brown & Co. Canada, 1999). Bacque also argues that the United States carried out an overt policy of "depopulation" of Germany after World War II, causing another 6 to 8 million German deaths by starvation and disease (*Crimes and Mercies: The Fate of German Civilians Under Allied Occupation, 1944–1950*. Little Brown & Co. UK, 2003).

2. Henry Morgenthau, *Germany Is Our Problem*, Harper and Brothers, New York, 1945, pp. v–vi.
3. George Soros, *The Crisis of Global Capitalism*, PublicAffairs, New York, 1998, p. 218.
4. "Crisp and Even," *Economist*, December 20, 2001.
5. David Malpass, "The Mexican Peso: 3.5 or Bust," *Wall Street Journal*, January 11, 1995.
6. See David Gitlitz, "The Mexican Maelstrom," Polyconomics, Inc., March 10, 1995.
7. Sean Gervasi, "Germany, U.S. and the Yugoslav Crisis," *Covert Action Quarterly*, Winter 1992–1993, no. 43.
8. Kathryn Albrecht, "Whatever Happened to Yugoslavia?" *Horsefly* (Taos, NM), vol. 1, no. 3, December 15, 1999. This excellent and valuable article must be credited with much of the information about Yugoslavia in this chapter.
9. "U.S. Calls on Milosevic to Concede Election Loss," *Los Angeles Times*, September 26, 2000.

CHAPTER 16   The Return to Hard Currencies

1. John Kenneth Galbraith, *Money: Whence It Came, Where It Went*, Houghton Mifflin Co., Boston, 1975, pp. 302–303.

INDEX

Wage(s), 74, 78, 85–86, 139, 207, 378, 382, 403
Waldegrave, William, 386
Wallich, Henry, 285
Walras, Léon, 17
Wampum, as currency, 9, 153
War, economic impact of, 30–33, 38–39, 42, 85, 111, 125, 154, 158–160, 163, 167–168, 188–189, 198–199, 202–204, 218, 221, 222, 226, 229–230, 235–237, 242, 245–247, 303, 317, 320, 322–324, 338, 366, 376–377, 379, 384, 383–384, 400, 411, 414–415
Washington, George, 16
Watergate, 259
Wealth creation, 137, 297, 302, 343
Weather conditions, economic impact of, 7
Welfare spending, 134, 212, 218
Whip Inflation Now (WIN) program, 259
White, Harry Dexter, 240

Wilson, Woodrow, 167–170, 197
Windfalls, 74, 80
Won, 347–348, 371
World Bank, 42, 239–240, 400
World Economic Conference, 229
World gold standard, 41
World monetary system, 15, 38, 41–43, 107, 200, 211–212, 229, 253–255, 257, 265, 267, 372–373, 416

Yavlinsky, Grigori, 387
Yeltsin, Boris, 381, 386–387
Yen, 16–17, 43, 45, 56–57, 59, 90–91, 231, 233, 261, 263–264, 296, 298, 319, 322–331, 333, 335–336, 338, 340, 384, 417
Yield, 53, 177, 216, 241, 246, 293–294, 297, 300–301, 304, 307, 330, 418
Yuan, 388–340
Yugoslavia, 81–82, 400–408. *See also* Dinar

Zedillo, Ernesto, 393, 395–396

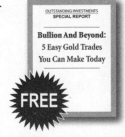